Incarnational Ministry

Incarnational Ministry

*Planting Churches in Band,
Tribal, Peasant,
and Urban Societies*

Paul G. Hiebert and Eloise Hiebert Meneses

Baker Books

A Division of Baker Book House Co
Grand Rapids, Michigan 49516

Published by Baker Books,
a division of Baker Book House Company
P.O. Box 6287
Grand Rapids, MI 49516-6287

Second printing, July 1999

Printed in the United States of America

Library of Congress Cataloging-in-Publication Data

Hiebert, Paul G., 1932–
  Incarnational ministry : planting churches in band, tribal, peasant, and urban
  societies / Paul G. Hiebert and Eloise Hiebert Meneses.
      p.   cm.
  Includes bibliographical references and index.
  ISBN 0-8010-2009-3 (pbk.)
  1. Missions—Theory. 2. Religion and sociology. 3. Sociology, Christian. I.
Meneses, Eloise Hiebert. II. Title.
  BV2063.H463   1995
  266'.001—dc20   95-452

For information about academic books, resources for Christian leaders, and all new releases available from Baker Book House, visit our web site:
                                   http://www.bakerbooks.com

To

Bria
Holly
Andy
Mary

The joys of our lives

Contents

Introduction

In recent years Christian leaders have discovered the value of the social sciences for their work. Bible translators find modern descriptive linguistics essential to their work and cross-cultural workers learn much from anthropology and communication theory. Church planters now see the importance of understanding social dynamics and theologians see the need to understand cultures and worldviews in developing contextually sensitive theologies.

This incorporation of social science insights into the life of the church is not without its dangers. An uncritical acceptance of them can undermine, in the long run, the biblical foundations of Christian faith. Not all scientific theories are compatible with the basic premises of Christianity.

Theology and the Social Sciences

How can we learn from the sciences without destroying our Christian understanding of reality? A number of answers have been given to this question in the past centuries.

Reductionism

The simplest solution to integrating theological and scientific thought is reductionism. Here all phenomena are ultimately reduced to a single explanatory system. For example, in the past many western medical practitioners explained all illnesses in biophysical terms. Patients might have psychological symptoms, but these were seen as side effects, not the root causes of their illnesses. Consequently the remedy lay in the use of proper drugs, surgery, and other physical treatments. Nowadays, some psychologists reduce all human behavior to the effects of early childhood and some economists think people act only out of premeditated self-interest.

Figure 1
Reductionism

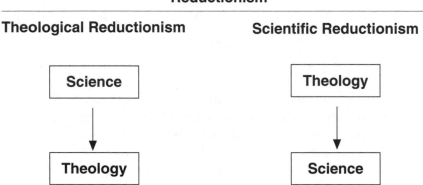

Theological Reductionism   **Scientific Reductionism**

Theological Reductionism

One form of reduction, common among evangelicals, is theological reductionism (fig. 1). We take theology seriously, but are afraid of the social sciences.

Some Christians reject scientific knowledge altogether. They attribute all human problems, such as illnesses, to spiritual causes and refuse to go to science for answers, for fear that science will lead them astray. Others are willing to make use of scientific knowledge because it is useful, but do not seriously examine the conceptual foundations on which it is built.

There is a real danger in this approach. First, there is a measure of mental dishonesty in it. On the one hand, most of us are willing to use what the sciences have to offer—modern medicine, radio, television, airplanes, computers, communication theories, counseling insights, and knowledge of human societies. On the other hand, we are unwilling to give credit where it is due for these advances in human knowledge and technology.

Second, and more seriously, in using the ideas and the products of science for practical purposes, we bring its fundamental assumptions into our thinking unawares. It is not uncommon, for example, to find Christians who express faith in Scripture, but who live their lives on the basis of pragmatism and materialism.

Scientific Reductionism

Another form of reductionism is scientific reductionism (see fig. 1). This is common among non-Christian scientists who reject the claims of Christianity. Some see it as a useful fiction that holds societies together. Others see it as a harmful opiate that justifies oppressive social systems. Most see it as a human creation having little to do with statements of truth.

Few Christians would consciously admit to such reductionism. It is, however, one of the fundamental assumptions on which many scientific theories are built, and an uncritical use of these theories undermines our faith in God.

Compartmentalization

A second way to integrate theological and scientific thought is compartmentalization—what Clifford Geertz calls the "stratigraphic method." The validity of each system of thought is accepted, but the two are assigned to different compartments (fig. 2).

Many people, including theologians such as Friedrich Schleiermacher, argue that science is a matter of facts and truth. Religion, they say, is a matter of feelings—It provides people with meaningful experiences. Others, such as Immanuel Kant, argue that religion is a matter of morality—it provides people with values that

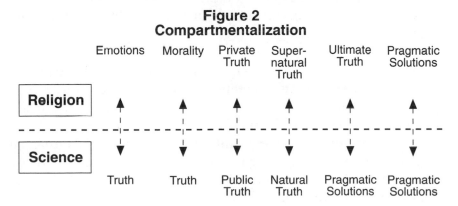

Figure 2
Compartmentalization

	Emotions	Morality	Private Truth	Super-natural Truth	Ultimate Truth	Pragmatic Solutions
Religion	↑	↑	↑	↑	↑	↑
Science	↓	↓	↓	↓	↓	↓
	Truth	Truth	Public Truth	Natural Truth	Pragmatic Solutions	Pragmatic Solutions

regulate their behavior and make corporate life possible. Most Christians reject this view. Christianity, they hold, is about facts and truth.

Modernity imposes another dualism on us. As Lesslie Newbigin points out (1989), in the west science is seen as public truth. All students, including those in Christian schools, must study mathematics, physics, chemistry, and social sciences. Religion, however, is seen as a matter of private opinion. No classes on Christianity, or Islam, or Hinduism are required. In fact, they cannot be taught as truth in public schools.

While this compartmentalization enables people of different religions to live peacefully together, it undermines their convictions that religious beliefs are foundational to all truth. Christian "beliefs" are left to govern Christians at home, but scientific "truth" rules their public lives (Bellah et al. 1985).

Compartmentalization in a more subtle form finds wide acceptance in Christian circles. Many Christians affirm Christian truth with regard to the gospel and supernatural matters such as sin, salvation, miracles, and prophecies, but they use scientific theories to explain immediate "natural" events. This leads to an otherworldly Christianity and to the secularization of everyday life. It also produces a sharp distinction between evangelism, which is seen as a spiritual matter, and "social" ministries such as healing and education, which are left to science.

A recent variation of this dualism is to use theology to define the gospel, but to use the methods of social and business sciences to grow churches. This approach fits the western worldview with its emphasis on human control, pragmatism, problem solving, and doing something.

Reducing Christianity to emotions, values, private opinions, or supernatural truth secularizes large areas of our lives. If we preach Christ, but turn to secular science for answers to our everyday problems, we lose sight of him. We are busy planning and working, but there will be little of God in what we do.

We cannot divorce theology and science without weakening our Christian faith or trivializing science. Scripture is clear: God created both the heavens and the earth, and he continues to be constantly involved in both.

Integration

A third approach to theology and science is to seek to integrate the two. Ideally we would like a grand unifying theory that incorporates all theological and scientific knowledge in one system of explanation. In reality this is impossible because we are finite humans and cannot comprehend at one time the infinite complexity and full story of God and this universe. At best our theological and scientific theories are partial pictures of reality.

The analogy of maps helps us understand the nature of human knowledge. To understand a city we need a number of maps, each of which tells us some truth about it. We need maps of roads, political jurisdictions, sewage and electrical systems, building zones, and so on. It is impossible to chart all the facts about a city on one map. Similarly, to describe human realities we need different maps including theology, anthropology, sociology, psychology, biology, chemistry, and physics. Each contributes to our understanding of the whole. None is complete by itself.

Another useful analogy is blueprints. To construct a house we need different blueprints diagramming different parts of the building: structure, wiring, plumbing, and landscaping. The analogy of blueprints is an apt one because there is one master blueprint that presents the basic structure of the house. As Christians we hold that this encompassing blueprint is a biblical worldview that helps us see the big picture of reality present in Scripture and in nature. This begins with the God of the Bible and includes the reality of an orderly creation, humans shaped in the image of God, the fall, redemption through the death and resurrection of Christ, and eternal life in him. The fullest expression of this worldview is found in the New Testament and in the teachings of Jesus. Theological and scientific theories chart the details and applications of this worldview. When they conflict, we must reexamine both our anthropological and theological understandings as well as our worldview to seek a resolution.

The blueprints of the same house must also be complementary; that is, the information they provide must fit together without contradiction. For example, the electrical blueprint should not show wires running where the structural blueprint shows no wall. In complementarity we take the theories of each discipline seriously in its own context, but we also check to see that they are congruent with our other theories (fig. 3).

Figure 3
Integration Through Complimentarity

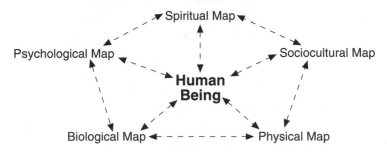

Ministry

In this book we will use both theological and scientific insights to examine how we can best plant living churches in different types of societies. We will draw on the social sciences to help us understand human societies and cultures in both Bible times and today. We will draw on theological insights to motivate and guide us in church planting in these societies.

We will follow three steps in the process.

Phenomenology

The first step in ministry is to analyze different types of societies and cultures from a phenomenological or descriptive point of view. Our purpose is to understand them as those living in them do. We refer to this as an *emic* approach to the study of cultures.

In an emic analysis we must report accurately what people say. If people say that they speak with their ancestors, that women become pregnant by wading in a lagoon, and that shamans see spirits, we report these as facts that they believe to be true. This does not mean we agree with the ultimate truthfulness of what they say. Rather, it means this is what people believe and act on. This is also the basis on which they respond to the gospel.

It is important in this step to avoid passing judgment on people's beliefs until we understand them, at least in part. If we judge them prematurely, we often jump to wrong conclusions. Moreover, if we pass critical judgments, people will not tell us their deeper beliefs for fear of our ridicule.

The second approach to the study of cultures is an *etic* one. Here we examine them using the categories and the methods of anthropology, which is both the science and the art of studying and comparing cultures. We need both emic and etic analyses to understand a culture.

Ontology

As Christians we cannot stop with phenomenology, with simply reporting what people and we believe to be true. We must move on to ontology and test these beliefs to determine which are true. If we stop with phenomenology, as many social scientists do, we are left with a philosophical relativism in which every belief is treated as true and every cultural practice as good. This does not fit our human experience, nor does it square with Scripture.

What are our tests for truth? How can we avoid ethnocentric judgments that use our own cultural norms to judge the beliefs and practices of others?

Reality Testing

In many matters we can use reality testing. All cultures use this to test ordinary experiences. One man reports he has twenty cows and another says he has only nineteen. They count the cows to see who is right. A woman sees an apparition in a glass, and we show her that this is her reflection in a mirror.

Most reality testing is not so simple. In science, reality testing has been systematically developed using instruments and measurements that help us gain accurate knowledge about the world around us. For example, many scientists using different instruments and running independent studies work together to test the effectiveness of a new medicine. If they do not reach a general agreement, they run more tests. Similarly, in cross-cultural settings, independent verification by observers from other cultures helps us test what we believe to be true.

The problems of reality testing become more difficult when we deal with human beings. We must study not only their external bodies, but also their inner beliefs and feelings. This is not easy to do because people often are not willing to share their inner thoughts, or cannot express them in words. The social sciences have developed methods to help us find out what does go on in people's heads.

In reality testing, we must examine not only people's beliefs, but also our own. Our initial temptation is to assume that we and our sciences are true, and that other systems of explanation are wrong. But modern knowledge, too, is rooted in a worldview and that worldview, like all human worldviews, is flawed.

How can we judge between different beliefs embedded in different worldviews? One method is that of comparison. When we study other cultures and worldviews, we become more aware of our own deep assumptions. Moreover, the process of comparison forces us to detach ourselves from our own culture and to develop a semidetached or metacultural perspective outside any one culture that enables a part of ourselves to step outside of our own culture and to compare it with other cultures (fig. 4; see Headland, Pike, and Harris 1990). To the extent that we live in only one culture, our judgments are culture-bound. To the extent we involve ourselves deeply in other cultures as missionaries and anthropologists, we are able in a measure to stand outside our own culture and to compare all cultures from a position outside them.

Metacultural grids themselves are not totally free from cultural biases, but many of these biases have been tempered by the fact that missionaries and anthropologists who formulate them live

Figure 4
Stages in Studying Cultural Differences

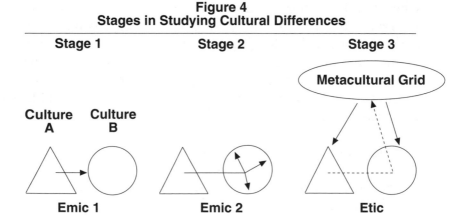

deeply in more than one culture and thereby learn to see reality as others see it.

The comparative method of anthropology gives us another means to test reality. An illustration can help us understand this etic approach to the study of cultural differences. Each culture has its own list of diseases and beliefs regarding the causes of those diseases. Villagers in parts of South India believed that *mashishkum* (roughly equivalent to smallpox) is caused by an angry goddess, Maisamma. To placate her they offer her sacrifices of water buffaloes and food. Modern science explains smallpox in terms of a virus and has used vaccinations to eliminate it from earth. Today the shrines for Maisamma lie largely abandoned. Knowing the villagers' ideas of disease helps us understand their behavior, but in this case, science did more to eliminate the disease. The reality of the spirit world revealed in Scriptures, however, causes us to reject the modern scientific denial of the reality of all spirits.

We need to be humble in our judgments, but we must judge after we have tried to understand deeply other peoples and their cultures. Our anthropological insights are not always right, but they are based on a constant questioning and testing of our own assumptions and conclusions.

Theological Testing

A second criterion for testing reality is Scripture. Because this is divine revelation, it provides us an objective understanding of ultimate reality. It is truth as God knows it to be.

God revealed himself, however, in the context of specific human cultures and histories in ways the people understood. Moreover, our understandings of Scripture today are shaped in part by our own culture and worldview. We must, therefore, test our understandings of Scripture with those of Christians from other cultures to correct our cultural biases, because others often see our biases more clearly than we do ourselves.

Our theological framework as authors is evangelical and Anabaptist. We believe that God revealed himself in history to his people, that his supreme self-revelation is in the person of Jesus Christ who was God incarnate, and that this revelation is accurately recorded in Scripture. We see the church as the body of

Christ, in the world but not of it—a countercultural community of those for whom Christ is the Lord of their everyday lives. It is the hermeneutical community in which we exercise our theological and reality tests for truth.

Ministry

The third step in our approach to planting and nurturing churches is ministry. Phenomenological analysis and ontological critique help us understand reality. We cannot stop there, however; we must invite people to faith in Jesus Christ and fellowship with his people.

Some accuse us of being colonial if we share our views with others. However, we are equally colonial if we withhold knowledge from them that might improve and save their lives. We have the moral obligation to share with people knowledge we have that may save them from danger, evil, and hell. They must choose how to respond to this truth.

In communicating the gospel to non-Christians and in discipling young believers, it is important to begin where they are in their cultural and social settings. Too often we know the gospel well, but are insensitive to the fact that all people, including ourselves, live in specific contexts. Unwittingly we equate the gospel with our own culture and judge other cultures to be pagan. Consequently, people reject Christianity because they see it as foreign, or they adopt it and become outsiders in their own lands. We need to understand the sociocultural contexts of the people we serve.

Conversely, we may know human cultures well, but lose sight of the gospel. We are in danger then of making the gospel anything we want it to be. We no longer hear the transforming Word of God, only the placating words of humans.

We argue here for an incarnational approach to cross-cultural ministry. In this we make a distinction between human cultures and divine revelation given to us in Scripture. We realize, though, that revelation must be expressed in specific cultural forms for us to understand it. This means that the Bible must be translated into different languages, and the gospel expressed in thought forms and practices meaningful to people. It means also that the messenger must identify as closely as possible with the people she or he serves.

When we understand God's message in our own cultures, it both affirms and judges us. It affirms that we are created in the image of God and that he loves us. It also declares that we as individuals are sinners and need salvation. It affirms that much in the cultures we create is good, because it expresses God's image within us. It also declares that much in our cultures and societies is evil, because we have made ourselves the gods of our own creations. There is both personal and corporate good and evil.

Our response to human cultures must be an ongoing process of critical contextualization (Hiebert 1987). In this we critically examine different areas of culture in the light of God's Word to test what is good and can be kept, and what is evil and should be changed. We seek to transform cultures into what God wants them to be. Our standard is not western culture, which itself needs to be judged. Rather it is the kingdom of God—what God originally intended when he created human beings and societies.

Transforming a society is a process. We must begin where people are. We cannot expect new Christians to leave their old ways and adopt new ones instantaneously. Too often this is what we have tried to do in missions. But then we must lead people step by step to Christian faith and maturity in their own settings. We must help them also to study their own societies and cultures in the light of Scripture, and to change their lives through the power of the Holy Spirit.

In this book we look at different types of societies and cultures and how their differences affect Christian ministry. Frequently we try to plant churches using methods appropriate to one kind of society in societies where they do not fit. The hindrance to the growth and spiritual maturation of churches is often not the offense of the gospel, but our ignorance of the ways their cultures and societies operate. It is our hope that a better understanding of humans and their contexts will enable Christians to be more culturally sensitive and more effective in their ministry.

1 | Theoretical Foundations

There is no simple formula for planting churches. They are the work of God and of humans. On the one hand, God acts in the lives of people, calling them from sin, giving them the power to respond to his call, and gathering them together in communities of faith. On the other, humans invite others into the church and disciple them in Christian maturity. In one sense, churches are like no other human groups because of the work of God's Spirit within them. In another sense, they are very much like other social groups, burdened by the normal problems of human life and relationships. The church is a reflection of the incarnation: it is both divine and human.

It is our purpose in this book to look at the human side of the church. In doing so we are not ignoring its spiritual nature or taking this for granted. The planting and nurturing of churches is first and foremost a spiritual ministry. The evangelist and church planter must begin with a solid theology and ecclesiology and a living faith. He or she calls people to encounter God and to share a spiritual life with one another in a particular church.

It is our intent to add insights on the human nature of the church—insights gained from the social sciences that have studied deeply the dynamics of human organization. God plants his church among people who are fallen, yet created in his image. These people bring their humanness, transformed and yet to be transformed, into the church. For effective church planting we need to know both how God works and how humans work.

Each of the social sciences has developed key concepts that it uses like tools to examine human beings. We will use two of these concepts, society and culture, that have been developed in sociology and anthropology. We must leave for another book the study of other key terms such as personality and mind, which are used in psychology, and their significance for church ministries.

Society

All people live in societies, or communities of humans who relate to one another in orderly ways. Without some social order, human life is impossible. Even the ascetics living alone in the desert were given life and nurtured by other humans.

Order in human relations is created by each community for itself. It is the result of human interactions that, over time, lead to socially acceptable ways of doing things. Patterns emerge as people relate, imitate one another, learn from their parents, or are forced to behave in certain ways by those with power over them. Patterns help people to understand what is going on and how to behave in different situations. Social order makes community life possible and meaningful.

Social systems are not static. They are reinforced or changed every time humans interact. When, as church members, we let Pastor John preach on Sunday morning, we are acknowledging the fact that he is our pastor and we are his parishioners. If we decide someday that he is no longer our pastor, we will prevent him from leading church services. We may even decide we want another kind of pastor and so change the social order of the church.

Order varies greatly from one society to another. In small bands it is based largely on ties of kinship and personal acquaintance. In modern cities social organization has many layers and is based more on institutions, voluntary associations, and networks. Relationships are less personal and are based on contract and law.

In evangelism and church planting we need to understand the ways people organize their relationships, because these affect profoundly how they make decisions, gather resources, organize activities, marry, rear children, worship, and respond to the gospel. Too often we assume that other societies are like our own—for instance, that mothers around the world treat their children in the same ways and that husbands everywhere are expected to show affection for their wives and to provide for their children. This is not the case. Our ignorance of the social patterns of other communities is a major barrier to planting churches in them.

In examining social systems, we will look first at different levels of organization and then at the dimensions of social relationships.

Levels of Social Organization

Human societies are often complex. We need only to look at a modern city to see this. How do fifteen million people and more live together to form an urban society such as Mexico City, Beijing, or Calcutta?

To understand how these societies function, we need to examine their organization on several different levels. On the lowest level, all human societies are based on countless transactions between individuals. On an intermediate level, people form groups to accomplish certain tasks. On the highest level, complex social systems emerge that enable people and groups to live in large societies such as cities, nations, and the world. Here we will look at the major categories of social organization that we will use later in examining different types of societies.

Status and Role

The basis of society is interactions between individuals in everyday life. A mother scolds her child, two friends play golf, and a shopper pays a clerk for merchandise. In each of these relationships much is unique to that situation. Each mother, child, friend, shopper, and clerk is unique and each transaction has its own historical context. The behavior in each of these settings must also fit socially defined patterns understood by both parties if the relationship is to continue. If the mother scolds her child in a socially unacceptable way, others will intervene. If the shopper walks out of a store without paying for the goods, the community will enforce its rules with socially defined sanctions.

Two concepts help us understand these basic social transactions: *status* and *role*. Status is a socially defined position in a society. In American society, for example, statuses include mother, son, doctor, plumber, teacher, pastor, pilot, and so on. In South India they include *brahmin* (high-caste Hindu), *vaidudu* (a type of doctor), and *mantrakar* (magician). Each society has its own sets of statuses.

It is important to separate in our mind social statuses from real people. Real people occupy statuses, but the statuses exist apart from these people. For example, a church may have a position called pastor. There may be no one in that status at the moment, but the church may be looking for someone to fill it.

People must occupy one or more statuses in society to be a part of it. In our society, a person may be a child, lawyer, teacher, or any other status recognized by the society. He or she cannot function without a status. If a stranger appears, we do not know who she is or how to relate to her until we can place her in one of the statuses we recognize.

Each status is associated with a role: the patterns of behavior that we expect of those who occupy that status. In our society the pastor must preach, the shopper must pay the clerk, and the driver must drive on the right side of a two-way highway. If people do not behave properly, they are disciplined or removed from their statuses.

Statuses in a society are linked to each other to form paired relationships. For example, the position of teacher is linked to that of student, husband to wife, and employer to employee. Most statuses, in fact, are linked to more than one other status. As teachers we relate to students, principals, parents, other teachers, and the public. Together these form the *role set* of the status of teacher. There are different role expectations for each of the roles in a role set. The teacher acts differently toward a student than he does toward the principal, and that relationship is different from his relationship to the parents of the students.

To illustrate the usefulness of status and role in examining social organizations, let us look at the American family. It is made up of eight statuses (husband, wife, mother, father, daughter, son, brother, sister), and eight pairs of relationships (table 1). A family with only one child does not have a full set of family relationships. By contrast, a large family may have several instances of mother-daughter or mother-son relationships.

In everyday life the relationship between a particular father, such as Tom Smith, and his sons, John and Henry, will vary according to their individual personalities and the specific settings in which they interact. From a social point of view, however, we look for the common patterns underlying all father-son relationships

Table 1
Primary Role Pairs in an American Family

Husband - Wife

Mother - Daughter

Mother - Son

Father - Daughter

Father - Son

Sister - Sister

Brother - Brother

Brother - Sister

in a given society. For example, many North Americans believe a father should treat older and younger sons alike. The oldest should not be favored or get all of the inheritance. In other societies, fathers are expected to favor their oldest sons, as was true of the Old Testament Israelites.

Using status and role analysis, we can examine the social organization of a family system. We can also trace historical changes in that system. For example, the relationship between husband and wife is currently being redefined by our society. This affects the other relationships in the family, such as mother-child and father-child.

It is important to remember that each society has its own sets of statuses and roles. Even such basic relationships as husband-wife, father-son, and mother-daughter are not the same in different societies. For instance, a Trobriand Island "father" gives the yams he raises to his sister to support her and her children. He, his wife, and his children live on the yams brought to him by his wife's brothers. To him, this arrangement seems as natural as parents working to earn money to support their own family seems to us.

Networks

Interpersonal relationships are the basis for all social activity. Linked together, they give rise to the simplest form of social organization, namely, social networks. A social network is a web of relationships that links people to each other. For example, John knows Maria, George, and Macee (see fig. 5). Maria knows Julius and Margaret. Margaret knows Sarah. A network is not a social group because those in a network do not all know and interact with one another. Sarah, for instance, knows only Margaret, and George and Macee know John but not Maria, Julius, Margaret, and Sarah.

Figure 5
A Network

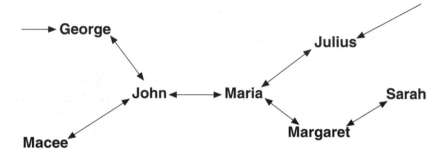

Social networks are important as channels of communication. In all societies people get important information through gossip and word of mouth. Moreover, networks are important means of social control. John may not like what Julius is doing and may say this to Maria, knowing that Maria is Julius's friend. This second-hand communication allows messages to be sent without the volatility latent in direct confrontation.

Networks also play an important part in the formation of social groups. If John organizes a party, he invites George, Macee, and Maria. Maria asks if she can bring her friend Julius. At the party these people all learn to know each other and plan to meet weekly for lunch. Sarah is part of the larger network, but she is not a part of the group because she does not interact directly with the others.

Groups

On another level, we can analyze social organization in terms of the kinds of social groups that people form. A group is a set of people who relate to each other face to face for specific purposes. For example, people in a local church form a group because they belong to the same congregation. In their church they may have smaller groups such as classes, committees, and cliques.

In all societies, groups enable people to join together to accomplish common goals. People may gather together to organize a factory, a school, or a recreational club. In each of these, they must create statuses and roles and link these together to form a single social system.

Kinship groups

Groups fall into three basic types depending on the nature of the relationships on which they are built: kinship, association, and geography. Kinship groups are based on the ties of marriage and descent. The primary kinship group is the nuclear family made up of husbands, wives, and their children. In many societies families include several husbands (polyandry) or several wives (polygyny).

Extended families are made up of several nuclear families linked together by blood and marriage. In India, for example, extended families include aged parents, their married sons and grandsons and their families, and their unmarried daughters and granddaughters. These all live and work together and often share a common kitchen and house.

With a few notable exceptions,[1] families are the basic building blocks of all societies. We will see later, however, that their nature and functions vary greatly among tribal, peasant, and urban societies.

On a larger scale, kinship ties are used to organize lineages and clans. A lineage is a group of people known to be linked to each other by blood ties through either male or female descent. A patrilineage is made up of men linked through male descent to a common known forefather. Usually their wives and unmarried daughters are also members of their lineage. A matrilineage is made up of women traceable through female lines to a common ancestress, plus their husbands and children.

Patriclans and matriclans are the same, except that the lines of descent fade into myth as one goes back to the founding ancestors. In other words, these are groups of people who believe they are linked to one another through their common ties to some distant progenitor, but who cannot actually trace the links. Often there is a myth of common origin and the founder of the clan may be thought to have been a god or an animal. We will see that lineages and clans are powerful ways to organize societies. They enable people to organize large groups to carry out community tasks such as crop production, defense, government, and social welfare.

The highest level of kinship organization is a tribe or an ethnic community. The former exists more or less by itself, the latter with other ethnic communities in a larger society. Both tribes and ethnic communities include all people who believe they are the same kind of people because they share the same kind of blood and marry one another. Marriage to someone of another blood is seen as threatening to the ethnic group. Because tribes and ethnic communities can be large, numbering in the tens and hundreds of millions, we will examine them under societal categories.

People believe ethnicity is based on genetic ties, but it is important to remember that their beliefs do not always match genetic realities. What matters is how people socially interpret biological ties. A great many social mechanisms, such as adoption, surrogate marriages, and fictive descent override biological realities. Ultimately, all cultures choose to define some genetic ties as kin, and to deny or to ignore other such ties.

Geographic groups

A second kind of group is based on ties of geography: people who are grouped together because they live in a common place. The smallest stable geographic group is the community. The members of a community live out their daily lives and deal with the common problems of everyday life together. Examples of this are a nomadic camp, a village, and a neighborhood in a city. The largest stable geographic groups are nation states that are held together by political ties. We will discuss these in detail later.

Associations

A third type of group is made up of people who gather or organize on the basis of a common interest (such as clubs), common tasks (such as schools and work crews), or common identity (ethnic and alumni associations). Groups may be organized on more than one of these principles. For instance, the German Baptist Church uses both ethnicity and association as the bases for its organization. The German Baptist Church of Mount City also uses geography to define its identity.

Some groups, like crowds, audiences, and mobs, are temporary gatherings that are loosely organized. Others, such as clubs, professional associations, and churches, are more formally organized and endure over time. Membership may be voluntary, as in a sandlot baseball team, or coerced, as in a drafted army. Admission may be open to all or restricted to a few.

Associations are extremely flexible. They are readily organized for any common purpose, and members can be added or dropped quite easily. This makes it possible for people to move from one place to another and change their social ties rapidly. Moreover, simple gatherings can be organized into more enduring associations that may grow into complex institutions such as business corporations and political parties. Because of their flexibility, associations have emerged as the dominant form of social group in modern, complex societies.

Institutions and Social Systems

As societies grow larger, institutions and complex social systems emerge that enable people to organize increasingly complex systems of relationships. An association, such as a local flying club, can grow into a major airline with a vast array of personnel, ground workers, planes, and technical services. Similarly, a local factory may grow into a multinational business conglomerate. In the process of this growth, what starts as a social group ends up as a complex organization that links many groups of people together. An airline, for example, develops relationships with other institutions that manufacture planes, supply fuel, maintain airports, sell tickets, provide insurance coverage, produce meals, and deliver late luggage, to name a few.

Large institutions, such as banks, industrial corporations, governments, armies, universities, denominations, and medical systems, are the backbone of modern social organization above the level of families, communities, and clubs. As we will see, institutions develop their own internal social organizations and subcultures and provide people in urban settings with much of their social identity.

Societal Categories

Societal categories are part of the mental maps people have of their society. For example, in the U.S. we mentally group Americans as Democrats, Republicans, and Independents. And we categorize them as Christians, Jews, Muslims, Hindus, and so on. These categories help us think about the way the society is ordered.

Societal categories regulate social relationships. In North America, being middle class rather than lower class, and urban rather than rural, affects how we behave. It also influences the way we are treated and the way we treat others. Societal categories also give rise to social groups. People who are Democrats organize local caucuses (social groups) and try to influence the Democratic Party (the institution).

There are two types of societal categories that we should note here: *ethnicity* and *class.* As we have seen, an ethnic group consists of people who share a consciousness that they are the same kind of people because they share the same blood. In other words, they believe they have common ancestors, share a history, and are linked by ties of descent and marriage.

Ethnicity, as a societal category, divides a society into different types of people. People of the same ethnicity turn to one another for mutual support and base their identity on the larger category of which they are a part. They usually look at people in other ethnic communities as outsiders.

Classes are sets of people who have in common a certain range of income. They also share a set of occupations and a lifestyle. In North America people of the same class live in similar homes, drive similar cars, go to similar clubs, have similar interests, and share similar values. They feel comfortable with others in their class. They are part of what Robert Bellah (1985) calls "life-style enclaves"—groups of people held together primarily by similar occupations, incomes, and values.

Societies

The largest units in social organization are whole societies. These are composed of the people who belong to one social system and one territory. The boundaries of a society are often fuzzy, and it is sometimes easier to define its core than to delimit its boundaries. One way to determine where the boundaries are is to take note of how people greet one another. People from other societies are greeted as strangers and outsiders. Armies from the outside will be fought as enemies.

In small societies one ethnic group constitutes a whole society, speaks one language, shares one culture, and occupies the same territory. We will refer to these societies as *tribes*. Unfortunately, like many words in our day, such as "native" and "indigenous," the word *tribe* is seen in some parts of the world as demeaning. This is true in parts of Africa where the word is sometimes associated with notions such as primitive, backward, and uncivilized, or where tribalism is a great threat to national unity. Because we found no other good word in English to refer to this type of society and because "tribe" is used in anthropology as a term with strong affirmative connotations, we will use it here. We do so not in the popular or negative sense of the term, but in a positive technical sense.

In anthropology, a tribe is a monoethnic society occupying a given territory and having one language and culture. Tribal peoples live by hunting and gathering food, by horticulture, or by pastoralism. Their technology may be simple, but that does not mean that they are backward. They often have rich, complex social systems, philosophies, and religions, as well as beautiful music and art. Down through history, tribes have been the dominant way that humans have organized their societies. There is much that we can learn from them for our lives today.

Large peasant societies are made up of multiple ethnic groups and classes. For example, Indian villages organize many castes and classes into relatively autonomous agricultural communities. Such villages often have clear geographical boundaries, but these are porous. Traders, government officials, religious leaders, pilgrims, and many others constantly pass through the village.

Cities, by contrast, have no clear boundaries and are made up of many ethnic groups and lifestyle enclaves. They may be politically and territorially defined, but they shape and are shaped by their sociocultural contexts and by the world.

Dimensions of Social Relationships

All human relationships and social organizations have five dimensions (fig. 6, following page). One or another of these may

Figure 6
Dimensions of Social Relationships

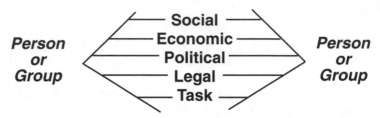

be the focus of the activity in a given relationship or organization, but the others are always present in the background.

Social Relationships

By social we mean the nature, allocation, and use of relationships. This includes the statuses and roles of those involved in the relationship. It also includes the types of social and societal groups people form, their institutions, and their larger societal systems.

Some relationships are egalitarian—they take place between people who see themselves as equals. Others are hierarchical. Some are informal. Others are formal—they are carefully regulated by rules of etiquette and order. Some are temporary and others are lasting. All these factors have to do with the social dimension of relationships and structures.

Economics

Economics has to do with the nature, allocation, and use of resources. All societies use material resources. People plow fields, catch fish, build houses, ride horses, and make music. They heat their houses, fly, and communicate by electromagnetic waves. To do so they create tools that enable them to shape the material world around them. These natural assets, tools, and products are among people's economic resources.

Economic resources also include intangible assets such as people's labor, time, specialized knowledge, the right to sing a song, and magical powers. Each society defines what it sees as economic resources.

Each society also decides who owns the resources and who can use them. For instance, in our society fish in most lakes are a resource and they are owned by people who catch them. In many migrant band societies, land and trees are resources anyone can use, but no one can own. In agricultural villages land is one of the most valued commodities and usually can be owned by individuals. Among the Eskimo, only the writer of a song is free to sing it. Others must ask permission to do so.

Politics

Politics involves the nature, allocation, and use of power. Power is an essential part of all human relationships. It is the ability to persuade or to influence through prestige or moral authority. It is economic power, or religious power such as the ability to curse or condemn to hell. It includes the power of the weak to ignore, disobey, boycott, and badger. Ultimately, it is physical coercion and the ability to destroy another or protection and the ability to care for the vulnerable.

In ordinary relationships power is hidden because everyone plays by the social rules. If the social order itself is challenged, however, power is often exercised to reestablish it. For example, the pastor and the laity relate cordially on Sunday mornings in church, but when a lay person tries to preach without authorization, the others will prevent him or her from doing so.

Law

The fourth dimension of human relationships and organization is law. This has to do with the nature, allocation, and use of legitimacy. Legitimacy is the people's consent to let certain persons have and use power.[2] A person may use power to take control of a situation, but if she or he does not have the publicly recognized authority to do so, the act will be seen as a revolution. If she or he acts as a recognized leader, the actions will be seen as part of normal government.

The allocation of legitimacy varies greatly from society to society. In ancient Egypt it was thought to be given by the gods and allocated to the Pharaoh by birth. In dictatorships it is based on conquest followed by rituals of legitimization. In democratic societies it is given to the rulers directly by the vote of the people.

The nature of legitimacy, too, varies greatly. In some monarchies the ruler has absolute power. In many democracies the leader is subject to the constitution and a body of law. As we will see, there are stateless societies that have no formal governing bodies. In these societies, governmental functions are allocated to other social agencies such as clans, villages, and age-based associations.

Politics and law are closely related to each other. We will, therefore, often speak of them as one. A careful analysis of the situations, however, will show that both are present.

Task

A final dimension of every social activity focuses on a task—the purpose of the activity. People work together to build a road, celebrate a wedding, choose a leader, or worship God. In the process they relate to one another using resources, power, and legitimacy.

Tasks also require communication. All human interaction involves the exchange of ideas, feelings, and judgments that are communicated by the symbol systems of the society, such as language, gestures, facial expressions, writing, and drawings. Such exchanges are essential to organize social activities.

Interaction between Social Dimensions

It is wrong to assume that these social dimensions act independently from one another. All are present in every human relationship and social organization and each affects the others. At times it is hard to differentiate between them. For instance, high social status often enables a person to gain wealth or political power. Conversely, political leaders may be able to convert their power into social prestige and wealth.

An example of the interaction between the dimensions of social organization can be seen in the relationship between a mother and her daughter. Socially, their statuses are mother and daughter. They are, therefore, expected to act in certain ways toward each other. These patterns of behavior are their roles. Because of her status, however, the mother controls many resources the child wants: the mother's attention, candy in the jar, and staying up late.

Politically the mother can pressure her daughter to obey by giving orders, by offering rewards or, if necessary, by using force. Legally the society recognizes the mother's right to use this power and will not intervene except when the mother goes beyond the socially recognized use of force. In the evening the child wants to watch television, but the mother wants to read her a Bible story. The disagreement is over which task to do. The child exercises her power by crying. The mother negotiates a compromise by communication, such as allowing some of each.

Power, authority, resources, tasks, and interpersonal contact are all intertwined in this relationship. Still, at any instance, one or another of the dimensions may be the focus of the relationship. When the mother and daughter read the Bible together they are engaged in communication. When the daughter refuses to participate, the task of Bible study cannot continue until the issue of the power to make decisions is resolved.

Similar analyses can be made of human groups. People organize a church to worship God and to communicate the gospel to the world. The church also has a social side to it. Members seek statuses in the congregation and gather in fellowship. The church must deal with the economic dimension of life: buildings, salaries, volunteer time, and copyrights on songs. It must also deal with political issues such as leadership selection and use of power. It is regulated internally by legal matters such as its constitution, by-laws, and rules of order; and externally by government zoning rules, lawsuits, and noise regulations. It is impossible to organize a church that focuses only on worship and witness and is free from economic, political, social, and legal concerns.

Institutions are organized for specific purposes. Political groups focus their attention directly on the control of power. Banks, factories, and businesses are concerned primarily with economic matters. Government bodies deal mainly with legal matters. All these, however, must deal with all of the dimensions of organization we have examined. This multidimensional nature of human social organization can be seen in table 2 (following page).

Culture

A second key concept we will use in analyzing humans and their activities is *culture*. In ordinary English, we use this term to refer to the beliefs and the behavior of the elite. For example, a cultured person is one who listens to Bach, Beethoven, and Brahms, not the

Table 2
The Multidimensional Nature of Social Organization
(An Example of American Society)

Level of Analysis	Dimensions					
	Social	Economic	Political	Legal	Task
Relationships (mother–daughter)	love	providing	protecting	authority	child rearing
Networks	conformity	allocating jobs	getting elected	contracts	knowing people
Groups * family	a unit of society	common household	parents vs. minors	common property	mutual survival
* social club	friendship	mutual assistance	lobbying	restricted membership	entertainment
* local church	fellowship	charity	leaders vs. congregation	corporation	worship God
Institutions * multinational company	business ties	buying, exchanging	power over	local country's laws	making money
* denomination	association by class	redistribution of money	hierarchy of leaders	nonprofit organization	relating churches by theology

Beatles and Bombs. We will use the term here in an anthropological sense.

There has been much debate in anthropology regarding the best way to define culture. By culture we mean "the more or less integrated systems of beliefs, feelings, values and worldview shared by a group of people and communicated by means of their systems of symbols." Obviously we need to examine this definition for it to make sense.

Communication by Systems of Symbols

Human beings are unique among earthly creatures because we have the ability to create mental images or maps of the external world that we use to think about the world and to choose a course of action. We can also manipulate these maps to think of other possibilities and to work to achieve them. We imagine a house and build it. We think of distant friends and phone them. In short, we use our mental images to understand the past, to live in the present, and to plan for the future.

This ability to construct mental maps of the outside world is based on our ability to create symbols. A symbol is anything that stands for something else in the minds of a person or a group of people (fig. 7, following page).[3] For example, we see real trees and have a mental image of them. We create the spoken word *tree* to represent them. Thereafter, when we hear the word *tree* we retrieve mental images of the real trees we have seen.

By using symbols we can think about the world outside. We can also think of things we have not experienced. For example, we see white cows, but not blue ones. We can, however, combine the ideas of "blue" and "cow," and paint a blue cow. We imagine flying, and eventually build airplanes to do so. Symbols enable us to manipulate the world in our mind and then to reshape the world outside.

Symbols also enable us to communicate with others. Because symbols link thoughts with external forms, such as words and pictures, that can be experienced by other human beings, we are able to communicate our thoughts to them. We say "trees" and other people think of trees, even though there are no trees in sight. We write letters and communicate with people far from us, and read

Figure 7
The Nature of Symbols

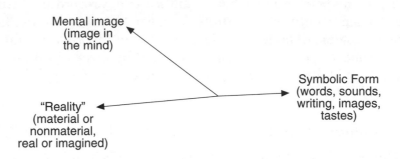

Mental image
(image in
the mind)

Symbolic Form
(words, sounds,
writing, images,
tastes)

"Reality"
(material or
nonmaterial,
real or imagined)

in books the ideas of people who died centuries ago. All culture is based on this human ability to develop symbols shared by a community of people that enable them to think about, communicate about, and manipulate the world in which they live.

The problem we face is that symbol systems differ markedly from culture to culture. Not only do people in different cultures speak different languages, but also those languages use different categories to order the world. In English, we speak of six colors in the rainbow. Telugu speakers in South India speak of two. We use bells to warn us of danger. Other cultures use them in worship.

Systems of Beliefs, Feelings, and Values

On another level, culture consists of systems of ideas, feelings, and values (fig. 8).[4]

Figure 8
Dimensions of Culture

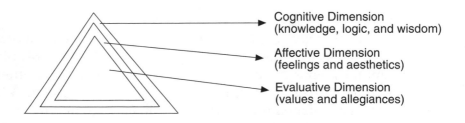

Cognitive Dimension
(knowledge, logic, and wisdom)

Affective Dimension
(feelings and aesthetics)

Evaluative Dimension
(values and allegiances)

The Cognitive Dimension

Culture includes the beliefs and knowledge shared by the members of a group or a society. Without shared beliefs, communication and community life are impossible.

Beliefs link categories into theories of explanation. For example, Americans speak of malaria, smallpox, diphtheria, and cancer and believe these are produced by natural causes. South Indians speak of "hot diseases" that produce fevers and "cold diseases" that produce chills and attribute them to the anger of female spirits such as Maisamma and Poshamma. The Tiv of Nigeria attribute many of their diseases to angry ancestors.

Our cultural knowledge tells us how to repair and drive cars, how to bake cakes, how to rear a child, how to make an atomic bomb, and how to worship God. A Bushman's knowledge enables him to find giraffe and to kill them with poisonous arrows.

Cultural information is stored in many ways. Many of us store it in writing. We turn to books, newspapers, billboards, and even sky writing to retrieve it. Other cultures store most of their information in stories, songs, riddles, and other forms of oral tradition that are easily remembered. As we will see, this distinction between oral and literate societies is of vital importance in planting churches in different types of societies.

The Affective Dimension

Culture also has to do with the feelings people have—with their attitudes, notions of beauty, tastes in food and dress, likes and dislikes, and ways of expressing joy and sorrow. People in one culture like their food hot, in another sweet or bland. Members of some societies like to express their emotions and are aggressive; in others they learn to be self-controlled and calm. Some religions encourage the use of meditation, mysticism, and drugs in order to achieve inner peace and tranquility. Others stress ecstasy through dance, drums, and self-torture. Still others evoke feelings of awe and fear. In short, cultures vary greatly in how they deal with the emotional sides of human life.

Aesthetics plays an important role in most areas of life. We want clothes that are not only functional, but also beautiful. We want food that tastes good. We decorate our homes, paint our bodies, and create art, literature, dance, drama, entertainment, and other forms of expressive culture.

Emotions also play an important part in human relationships. We communicate love, hate, scorn, and a dozen other attitudes by our facial expressions, tones of voice, and gestures.

As western Christian leaders, we often overlook the importance of the affective dimension of life. We stress the preaching of cognitive truth in church services and downplay the importance of feelings of worship. We rationally push to get work done and don't see the emotional distress caused by our actions.

The Evaluative Dimension

Each culture also has values by which it judges acts and people. It ranks some occupations high and others low, some ways of eating proper and other ways unacceptable, some actions moral and others immoral.

Value judgments can be broken down into three types. First, each culture evaluates cognitive beliefs to determine whether they are true or false. For instance, Europeans in the Middle Ages believed that malaria was caused by a noxious substance in the air. Today they attribute it to sporozoan parasites. In other cultures people believe it is caused by spirits that live around the village. In each of these cases the culture determines what people believe to be true.

Each culture also judges the emotional expressions of human life. It teaches people what is beauty and what is ugliness, what to love and what to hate. In some cultures people are encouraged to sing in sharp, piercing voices, in others to sing in deep, mellow tones. Even in the same culture what is appropriate depends on sociocultural settings and subcultures. Tuxedos and formal gowns are out of place at skating parties, and business people normally do not wear shorts and tee shirts to work.

Finally, each culture has its own moral code and judges what is right and wrong behavior. For instance, in North American culture it is worse to tell a lie than to hurt people's feelings. In other cultures, however, it is more important to encourage other people, even if it means bending the truth somewhat.

These three dimensions—ideas, feelings, and values—are important in understanding the nature of human cultures, and we will refer to them frequently.

The Gospel in All Three Dimensions

In planting churches we need to keep the three dimensions of culture in our minds, for the gospel has to do with all of them. On the cognitive level it has to do with knowledge and truth—with an understanding and trust in biblical and theological information and knowledge of God. On the affective dimension it includes feelings of worship, love, and joy. On the evaluative dimension it has to do with our allegiance to Christ and our obedience to God's moral standards. To value ourselves or anything else above God is idolatry.

All three cultural dimensions are essential in conversion. We need to know that Jesus is the Son of God, but that knowledge alone is not enough: Satan knows well that Jesus is God incarnate. We need feelings of affection and loyalty to Jesus. But knowledge and feelings must lead us to a decision to turn to Christ as our Savior and to obey him as the lord of our lives. Faith is our response to what we know and feel. It prompts us to action.

All three dimensions are also important in building the church. In our services we need sound doctrine, deep feelings, and responses. We do not proclaim the gospel simply to inform people or to make them feel good. We are calling them to become followers of Jesus Christ.

Worldview

People in a society share symbols, beliefs, feelings, and values. Beneath these are the basic categories and assumptions people make about the nature of things and the logic that relates these to form a coherent understanding of reality. These basic assumptions about the nature of reality form what we call the people's *worldview.* Martin Marty calls a worldview "the mental furnished apartment in which one lives" (1991).

Like glasses, worldviews shape how we see the world around us. They are what we look with, not what we look at. And because people in other cultures have different worldviews, they see reality differently at even the most fundamental levels. Worldviews are largely implicit. Like the glasses we wear, it is hard for us to see our own worldview. Others see it better than we do ourselves.

Our worldview assures us that what we see is the way things really are. Those who disagree with us are not only wrong; they are crazy and out of touch with reality. If our worldview is shaken, we are deeply disturbed because the world no longer makes sense to us. As Clifford Geertz points out (1979, 83), there is no fear greater than meaninglessness—of not understanding the world in which we live. Even death itself can be endured if it has meaning.

Worldviews serve several important functions. On the cognitive level our worldview gives us a rational justification for our beliefs and integrates them into a more or less unified view of reality. On the level of feelings, it provides us with emotional security. On the level of values, it validates our deepest cultural norms. In short, our worldview is our basic map *of* reality, and the map we use *for* living our lives.[5]

Finally, as Charles Kraft (1979, 56) points out, our worldview monitors culture change. We are constantly confronted with new ideas, behavior, and products that come from within our society or from without. Our worldview helps us select those that fit our culture and reject those that do not. It also helps us reinterpret those we adopt so that they fit into our overall cultural pattern.

Worldviews change over time. New ideas may challenge our fundamental assumptions, and internal inconsistencies in our beliefs create tensions. To reduce the stress we modify or drop some of our assumptions. The result is a gradual worldview transformation of which we ourselves may not even be aware.

At times our worldview no longer makes sense of our world. If another and more adequate one is presented to us, we may reject the old and adopt the new. For example, Muslims and Hindus may decide that Christianity offers better answers to their questions than do their old religions. Such worldview shifts are at the heart of what we call conversion.

Integration

Cultures are more or less integrated (fig. 9, following page). By this we mean that they provide us with a more or less coherent way of looking at things. If our belief systems contradict one another too much, we are torn by cognitive dissonance and the fear of meaninglessness.

Cultural integration, however, is never complete. In part, this is true because cultures constantly change. New ideas are introduced that run counter to some old ideas and tensions emerge.

Figure 9
Integration in Cultures

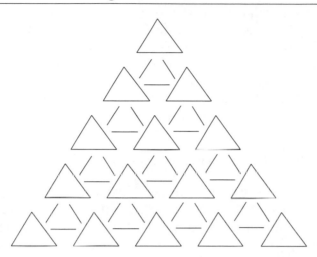

For instance, the development of new methods of birth control led to an increase in premarital sex in North America and to rising immorality.

Another reason cultures are not fully integrated is that groups and individuals in a single culture often hold different beliefs. The rich, for example, see things differently than the poor and one ethnic group than another. There are differences between the folk beliefs of the common people and the theories of the specialists in such fields as medicine and religion.

If a culture loses its ability to provide a way of life that makes sense to its people and no longer meets their basic needs, it disintegrates. We see this when societies are overrun by other, more powerful ones.

Consensus and Commonality

Finally, a culture is "shared by a community of people." It is created by people to enable them to live together. Humans are social creatures and depend on one another for survival and meaningful existence. They need care during their childhood and in their old age. They find their greatest joy and fulfillment in the company of others. Social isolation is among the greatest punishments they inflict on one another.

All human relationships require a large measure of shared understandings between people. They need a common language and some consensus on beliefs and worldview for communication and coordinated action to take place. In other words, they must share a common culture.

This relationship between culture and society is very important and we must examine it in greater detail.

The Relationship between Society and Culture

Social and cultural systems are symbiotically related. Neither can exist without the other (fig. 10). In general, social systems are patterns of social behavior. Cultural systems interpret that behavior.

On the one hand, societies shape cultures. We talk to one another and in so doing reinforce and change our language. We organize activities and create rules to do so. We make computers and soon think of the mind as a supercomputer. In everyday life we create and recreate our culture (Filbeck 1985).

On the other hand, culture shapes society. Culture is the map we use to live our lives. Without this map, the world is meaning-

Figure 10
The Symbiotic Relationship Between
Social and Cultural Systems

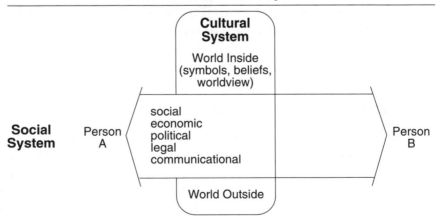

less and chaotic. We try to act as good fathers and mothers by doing what our culture tells us "good fathers and mothers" do. We kneel, bow, or hold up our hands in prayer because our culture tells us that is how to worship God. Our cultural knowledge enables us to produce food, make tools, heal the sick, build cars, and fly airplanes. These, in turn, alter radically the way we live and relate to one another. In short, culture makes social life possible.

Because of this constant interaction between how we live and how our culture tells us to live, it is not always easy to distinguish between what is social and what is cultural. Nevertheless, it is helpful for analytical purposes to do so. For example, each culture prescribes how good fathers and mothers should rear their children, but a particular couple may act differently from the norm. If their social behavior differs too much from the cultural norm, other people in the society will act to stop it.

Types of Societies

In this book we will examine the social and cultural systems of different types of societies to learn how to better plant churches in them. To reduce the thousands of human societies to a few basic types is simplistic. Each society and each culture is different, and we must study each one carefully before we begin work in it.

Nevertheless, there is some value in developing a broad theory that enables us to examine and compare different types of societies and cultures. Such a theory can help us to look at our work in new ways. Most church workers are not social scientists and have not learned to see the social and cultural dynamics at work in their ministries. For them, this book is a general introduction to the ways in which the social sciences think about human realities. We hope they are stimulated to study more carefully the people among whom they work. Learning to know a people is the first step in an incarnational ministry. It is an exciting, lifelong adventure that has great benefits for those who undertake it. For those already versed in anthropological thought, this book seeks to apply what they know to church planting. Most anthropology texts examine the nature of societies and cultures. They do not apply this knowledge to missions and the church.

A comparative study such as this also forces us to think of our own sociocultural settings and how these affect us and our ministries. It is hard for us to see the glasses through which we view the world. One way to do so is to compare ourselves with other cultures and see how they look at us. If we are unaware of our own cultural assumptions, we tend to equate the gospel with what we believe and do and try to make others like ourselves.

Finally, a general theory has heuristic value. It forces us to think in broad terms and to see the big picture. What we present here is not a final answer, but a preliminary analysis that we hope will stimulate further research and theoretical reflection.

Over the past century, anthropologists have studied societies around the world. In the process they developed a general taxonomy of societies: bands, tribes, peasants, and cities. These are generalized categories or *ideal types.* An ideal type is an abstract category based on a cluster of characteristics. In reality, societies of that type have many but not necessarily all of these characteristics. For example, we speak of bands as small, mobile societies that live by hunting and gathering food. In fact, some bands are stationary for relatively long periods of time and may cultivate a few plants. Nevertheless, we refer to them as bands because they share most of the characteristics common to band societies.

Ideal types help us classify societies. They also help us understand how societies change. Some nomadic bands settle down and become tribes or peasants. Others are overrun by modern societies and their survivors eke out a living as unskilled laborers on the fringes of cities.

Over the broad sweep of human history there has been a movement from small, simple societies to large, complex ones. In the process new forms of organization have emerged. Hunting and gathering for food has been replaced in most societies by agriculture. Social systems built on kinship ties are being replaced by ones based on geography and association. Small rural communities are giving way to sprawling cities.

This process is not evolution. It is human history, superintended by God, that began when God created humans and placed them in a garden (Gen. 1–2) and will end in a city (Rev. 21–22) when God establishes his perfect kingdom.

Bands

As far as we know, small bands of people living by hunting and gathering food were common in early human history. These bands moved when food was no longer available in the vicinity. They consisted of a few related families with an outsider or two. Their organization was flexible and new bands were readily formed as populations increased or fights broke out between members.

Some bands developed specialized ways of living. For example, the peoples of inner Asia domesticated horses and adopted a nomadic life. They developed extensive empires based on raiding the agricultural societies around them.

Today bands have been pushed largely onto lands that farmers and city folk don't want. Among them are the Eskimo, the Bushmen who have retreated into the semidesert wastelands of the Kalahari Desert in South Africa, and the Aborigines of Australia. Others, such as the Pygmies of central Africa, are found in forests and mountains.

Tribal Societies

Another form of human society is the tribe. As we noted earlier, the word *tribe* has positive connotations in some parts of the world and negative ones in other areas (see p. 31).[6]

Small tribes, like bands, depend on hunting and gathering for food, but they also use horticulture and animal husbandry. People ring trees and burn the dead wood in a technique known as slash-and-burn. They then plant crops around the stumps. Because the land loses its fertility in a few years, the people must move to clear a new piece of forest and begin the cycle anew. Horticulture enables the people to live in the same place for five years or more and this fact shapes the cultures they create.

As tribes grow in size, the nature of their organization changes. They settle in villages, develop more sophisticated technological knowledge, and organize complex forms of government. Tribes may have as many as twenty million members or more. Some, like the Ashanti and Ghana of West Africa, have given birth to extended empires.

Today tribes are found around the world. Like bands, however, many have been pushed off their lands by peasants and many are being absorbed into modern nation states. The changes are often traumatic. Tribal identities do not easily yield first place to other identities such as nationalism, in part because nations and other forms of social organization do not provide the sense of community and security that ethnicity does.

Peasant Societies

Horticulture often has led to full-scale agriculture. Animals are used for plowing; copper, bronze, and iron are shaped into tools; and fertilizers and irrigation are used to enable people to use the same fields for centuries. The result is larger, more permanent villages in which people of different ethnicities may live. What holds them together is farming, markets, festivals, and the economic interdependence created by technical specialization such as carpentry, smithery, pottery, weaving, and masonry.

New levels of social organization emerge in peasant societies. They are not autonomous societies. They are agricultural communities that are part of larger states. Families and kinship ties remain, but over them appear feudal lords, kings, and modern state governments. These rulers tax the peasant farmers in the countryside to maintain their cities, courts, and armies. In turn, they promise protection and public services.

Peasant societies are also associated with institutionalized religions. Religious leaders in bands and small tribes are part-time shamans, witchdoctors, magicians, and sorcerers. In large societies, with their growing specializations, full-time priests, prophets, and religious scholars emerge. Temples, schools, and written texts also appear.

The transition from tribal to peasant societies is often slow and difficult. In history it occurred first in China, India, the Near East, and North Africa. From there it was exported to Korea, Japan, Europe, North and South America, and Australia.

In the Bible, Israel made this transition during their stay in Egypt. The sons of Jacob went down as heads of tribal lineages. Their descendants learned agriculture, built permanent settlements, made copper and iron tools, and organized a central government when they conquered Canaan. The transition was complete only with the rule of David and Solomon.

Urban Societies

The fourth type of society we will examine is the city. This is based on complex systems of government, religion, business, transportation, and information exchange.

Cities have a long history. They began in the Middle East, China, India, Central and South America, and West Africa. Most were walled forts enclosing royal courts and temple complexes built by taxing the surpluses of the surrounding agricultural communities.

In the past four centuries cities of a new type have emerged: cities based on business, commerce, and services. These cities without walls now dominate the world. Their growth in the past century has been phenomenal. Never in human history has there been so massive and rapid a change as the current migration of people into cities and their assimilation into urban ways of life.

Anthropologists have a fairly clear understanding of bands, tribes, and peasant villages, but their knowledge of cities is fragmented and limited. This is due to their interest in simple societies and to the complex nature of urban societies, which are hard to study.

Ideal types help us see general similarities and differences between societies. But they overlook the characteristics that make each society unique. It is important, therefore, that we study the specific societies and cultures in which we work in greater depth.

With this theoretical framework in mind, we will examine bands, tribes, peasant villages, and cities to see how we can best plant churches in them.

2 | Band Societies

Around the world small bands of people live on the edges of larger, more powerful societies. A few of these peoples, such as the Bushmen of the Kalahari Desert, the Aborigines of the Australian outback, and the Pygmies of Central Africa, are well known. Most, like the Dorobo of East Africa, the Chenchu and Boyas of central India, the Kirghiz of Afghanistan, and the Maxakali of Brazil, are forgotten peoples—ignored by a world of increasingly complex societies and by the church that has largely failed to reach them in meaningful ways. The gospel, when it comes, often comes through powerful outsiders from dominant societies that have driven them off their lands. God has not forgotten these people, however, and today there are Christians bringing them the gospel as the good news of salvation and life, and not the bad news of oppression and cultural extinction.

In the past, bands occupied much of the earth. They lived by hunting and gathering food. As agriculture and industry spread, however, they have been forced onto lands useless to pastoralists, farmers, and urban dwellers.

Today band life is largely shaped by the ecological environments on which the people depend for their livelihoods and the geopolitical forces of the world. Some, like the Bushmen and the Australian Aborigines, live in semiarid lands, gathering desert roots, berries, and fruit, and hunting rodents, wild boar, kangaroo, and giraffe. Others, like the Dorobo and Twa, live in forests on terrain too steep to farm. They live on honey, game, and other forest produce. Still others, such as the native American societies on the Northwest Coast and the Eskimo, live largely on fish, seal, wild berries, seed, and fruit.

Bands are effective food foragers, able to survive where few others can. Wild food is generally seasonal and limited, so the groups are small and nomadic, but when food and water are plentiful, people join together in larger groups for celebrations, religious rites, visiting, and gossip.

Few if any bands today are autonomous. Most live in symbiotic relationships to neighboring agricultural, pastoral, or even urban societies. For instance, in East Africa the Dorobo and Twa trade honey and other forest produce with neighboring villagers for grain and manufactured items and with pastoral peoples for milk and leather goods. The Pygmies of central Africa trade forest products, labor, and even wives with the neighboring Bantu horticulturalists for outside products. Even the Bushmen and the Aborigines now depend on the outside world for iron tools, clothing, and staples. Despite such dependencies and strong government efforts to settle them, most band societies have resisted assimilation into sedentary agricultural communities. They prize their freedom and community life.

Social Order

The social organization of bands is shaped by their small size and their dependence on game, fruit, seeds, and other wild food. These two factors affect all dimensions of people's lives.

Social Organization

The social organization of bands is simple. It consists of an association of kin-related people numbering between twenty and five hundred, depending upon the availability of food. Thus it is based primarily on interpersonal relationships and on small groups. There is no need for the complex institutions and societal structures characteristic of large societies. People have a simple technology and depend on wild food for their livelihood. Consequently, they live close to nature and its cycles of day and night and the seasons of the year.

Interpersonal Relationships

Bands are sometimes called face-to-face communities because they are so small that everyone knows everyone else intimately.

People are known primarily as individuals with their own idiosyncracies, rather than by socially defined positions.

Life is lived in the open, and there are few secrets. The only privacy is found in the small shelters that protect people from the weather and wild animals—and these shelters hide little. Consequently, each person's business is everyone's business. In marital quarrels anyone can shout comments or take sides. In making a decision about hunting or moving, everyone has a say.

There are few formal statuses other than those of sex, age, and kinship. All able-bodied men are involved in hunting, warring with other bands, and defending their camps. Adult women bear the young, forage for food, gather wood, prepare meals, and carry goods when the camp moves. All care for the children and help in camp chores. The very young and the very old stay around camp, cared for by those around.

Formal kinship roles are limited primarily to the nuclear family made up of husband and wife and their children. Ties to other relatives are loose and easily broken.

There are no full-time specialists—no chiefs, doctors, or teachers who live on food given them by others. Even band leaders and religious practitioners generally have no formal office. One person may be recognized as a headman, but he cannot force people to do what he wants. Another is known as a shaman or a healer, but just as everyone else does, he or she must gather food to live.

Most bands are highly individualistic. People are free to come and go as they wish. There are few social means other than gossip and ostracism to make people do what they do not want to do. Consequently, even marriages are dissolved if either partner wants to leave.

Bands are also egalitarian. There is little social hierarchy, even between the sexes. Men and women do different things, but neither has much power over the other because the other is free to leave at will. Men's and women's roles are more flexible than they are in more structured societies. Women assist in the hunt by driving animals ahead of them, and men gather food as they go through the forests or take care of the children without being scorned by their friends. For example, Pygmy women are supposed to adjust the leaves on the roofs of huts when it rains, but when told to do so by her husband one woman replied, "Fix it yourself! It's on your side!"

Individuals and families can join a band if the others accept them, but they leave when they choose to do so. Social ties are based less on coercion and more on choice and the need for one another.

Groups

Family ties and voluntary association are the glue that holds a band together. Families are made up of a couple, their younger children, and an aged parent or two. Even in societies that allow polygamy, the majority of couples are monogamous.

Marriage is usually based on love and negotiation. The Eskimo choose their partners, while Pygmy men often exchange sisters, if the women are willing. Child-rearing practices are often quite permissive. Individual assertiveness is encouraged because this is essential to survival. Where food is very scarce, families may practice infanticide when a second child is born too soon after the first. Old people may also commit voluntary suicide so that they do not take food needed by productive adults and children.

Temporary small groups form around specific tasks. A group of old men hunt together because they are more likely to bag game than if they go alone. Some beat the forest while others wait at the mouth of the circle to kill the game. Women often gather food in small groups.

The band itself is a voluntary association (fig. 11). People gather together for fellowship, mutual assistance, and protection. To live

Figure 11
The Structure of Band Societies

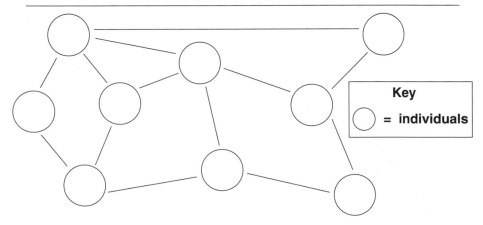

Key

◯ = individuals

alone is to die. However, if the band gets too big and there are not enough resources in the nearby lands to sustain it, it must break up. The result is a seasonal variation in the size of bands. When food is plentiful, several bands join for weeks of celebration, ritual enactments, and social exchange. When food is scarce, the people separate into small bands to follow game and move to distant food sources. In arid regions, water is the determining factor. When rains come, animals and humans spread out over the land. When the rivers dry up, they are drawn to the few permanent water holes in the land.

Economic Resources

Band societies live close to nature and draw largely on human and natural resources. Other than drying, they have few ways to preserve food for long periods of time. Consequently, they are deeply affected by the seasons of the year and natural disasters such as droughts, floods, and fires. Some months they have more than enough food; the following months they eat less.

Bands have no complex technology. They use digging sticks, spears, bows and arrows, spoons, and other simple artifacts made of wood, stone, or bone; bags and cloth made of bark, animal skins, and woven fibers; clay pots; body decorations made of feathers, seeds, and bones; and simple shelters made of branches, leaves, stones, or ice. Few use beasts of burden to carry loads or plow fields. The most common domesticated animal is the dog. People make clothing appropriate to their environments. Some in the desert wear little, while others cover themselves to protect themselves from the sun and dehydration. Those in cold climates use furs and heavy cloth. Most add aesthetic decorations: borders on cloth, bracelets and anklets, and body paint.

The primary sources of energy are humans and fire. The latter is used to cook and warm people when it is cold. On an average people spend less than four hours a day working. Although societies vary somewhat on this point, men generally bring in about a third of the calories in the form of meat, which is high in protein. Women provide two-thirds of the food in the form of roots, berries, nuts, seeds, leaves, and other starches (Pfeiffer 1977, 58).

Hard as it is for us to understand it, hunters and gatherers enjoy what Lorna Marshall (1961, 243) calls "a kind of material plenty." They draw on readily available raw materials and make and discard simple tools as they need them. People's wants are limited to the basics of life, and the accumulation of goods and wealth is a liability rather than an asset because when they move they must carry everything. It is truly said that a hunter's wealth is a burden, at least for his wife.

Economic goods are important in social relationships. They are shared or given as gifts to cement relationships. Their ownership may help maintain social differences. For example, among the Yiri Yoronto of west Australia, only adult males made and owned the stone axes used by all. Women and children had to borrow these for their work. When traders introduced steel axes and gave them to women as well as men, the control men had over women collapsed, and the society experienced a painful transformation (Sharp 1952).

For the most part, however, there is little private ownership in band societies. In fact, there is little that is owned at all. Wild game, food, trees, and land simply exist and are free for the using. A band may claim a certain territory so long as it is there, but when it moves on, others can make use of it. Where water is scarce, bands lay claim to certain water holes during dry seasons, but they share these when others pass by.

People are expected to share what they own. For example, when an Australian Aborigine kills a kangaroo, he should give the left hind leg to his brother, the tail to his father's brother's son, the loins and fat to his father-in-law, the forelegs to his father's younger sister and the head to his wife. He keeps the blood and entrails. These people, in turn, share their food with other relatives nearby. This distribution assures everyone of at least a small portion when someone makes a kill.

Other goods, too, are shared continually in elaborate networks, which the Bushmen call "paths for things." Wiesner (Pfeiffer 1977, 64) has documented the movement of more than two thousand articles—blankets, beadwork, knives, eyeglasses, safety pins, arrows, and bags—from relative to relative along paths extending more than three hundred miles. A Bushman may keep a gift for a few weeks or months, but sooner or later he or she passes it on. These networks of sharing are well known and people know what they can expect to get and from whom, and what they must share and with whom.

The networks of giving renew ties of good will and constitute a form of insurance against hard times. When a person is sick, old, short of food, or wants to move on, she or he is sure of being cared for or welcomed somewhere else.

In recent years most band societies have developed barter relationships with neighboring tribes and agricultural societies. They provide those societies with meat, honey, leaves, grasses, and other forest and desert products. In turn they get milk, grain, cloth, iron tools and, in more recent years, manufactured products like bottles, dark glasses, matches, and safety pins.

Today there are no truly isolated band societies. Beads, cloth, axes, guns, bottles, plastic containers, and other products of the world have found their way into the lives of band people. To obtain these goods, band people are forced increasingly to find wild products for trade and to work in stock camps and villages for low wages. The appeal of these outside commodities is great, yet it runs counter to people's desire to remain independent and free.

Politics and Law

In band societies there are no councils, courts, police, armies, or jails, and no written laws or constitutions. No adult can legally force another adult in the band to do something. Such power as exists is persuasion, gossip, loud accusations, boycotts, and crying. On a few occasions coercive power is exercised by the group against an individual. The members may join to break a selfish man's house and tools, beat him, or drive him from the camp. Usually, though, less coercive means are used. A man who fails to do his job in a hunt is jeered, and a woman who is a bad mother is publicly ridiculed. Other punishments are invented after a crime has been committed and the whole community participates in deciding what to do. Given the strong interpersonal nature of band life, however, such discipline is very effective.

There are no officially chosen leaders, only those who gain the respect of the others because of their knowledge, charisma, and ability to lead. The leader is first among equals. If he does not do a good job, people quit listening to him and turn to someone else for leadership.

Bands have no formal laws. They draw on tradition, on stories remembered about what they did in the past in similar situations, but they invent a new solution for the present crisis because it is always a little different. The character of the persons involved, the specific facts of the situation, and the outcome of possible sanctions are all discussed in great detail before a decision is made.

Decisions are based on consensus, for without consensus they cannot be enforced. Discussions continue until an action is chosen to which all give at least nominal consent. Consequently there is usually no alienated minority. Each person feels that she or he has been heard.

For the most part, social pressure is used to get band members to fit into the group and its values. For example, accumulating wealth in any form is condemned. As one Bushman put it, "When a young man kills much meat he comes to think of the rest of us as his servants and inferiors. We can't accept this. We refuse one who boasts, for some day his pride will make him kill somebody. So we always speak of his meat as worthless. This way we cool his heart and make him gentle" (Pfeiffer 1977, 62–63). Such social pressure is so intense that individuals with valuable objects feel guilty for having something others want. He or she soon gives it away with a sigh of relief and without a sense of superiority.

There is no social organization higher than the band. Consequently there is no one who can make peace or enforce a settlement between them when disputes arise (reading 1). Conflicts over water or land are solved by raids and battles. Today modern governments have begun to intervene to keep peace.

Reading 1

The Avenging Party

Baldwin Spencer and F. J. Gillen

The men living in the country around Alice Springs in the Macdonnell Range [central Australia] were summoned by **Inwurra**, that is, properly accredited messengers carrying

Reprinted with permission from Baldwin Spencer and F. J. Gillen, *The Native Tribes of Central Australia* (London: Macmillan, 1899).

Churinga, who had been sent out by the Alatunja of the group, to assemble for the purpose of making war upon the Iliaura tribe, which occupies the country between eighty and a hundred miles to the north of the Ranges.

For a long time the northern groups of the Arunta tribe had been in fear of the Iliaura, who had been continually sending in threatening messages. . . . Several deaths, also, which had taken place amongst the Arunta, had been attributed by the medicine men to the evil magic of certain of the Iliaura men. When the messengers and the men summoned had assembled at Alice Springs, a council of the elder men was held, at which it was determined to make a raid on the Iliaura, and accordingly a party was organized for the purpose. Such an avenging party is called an Atninga.

When all was prepared the Atninga started away from the north, and after travelling for several days, came upon a group of Iliaura men, consisting of about a dozen families, near to whom they camped for two days.

As usual on such occasions, the Iliaura sent some of their women over to the strangers' camp, but the fact that the use of the women was declined by the visitors at once indicated that the mission of the latter was not a friendly one. . . .

In the Iliaura community were two old men, and with them matters were discussed by the elder men amongst the Arunta at a spot some distance from the camp of the latter. After a long talk extending over two days, during which the strangers set forth their grievances and gave the Iliaura men very clearly to understand that they were determined to exact vengeance, the two old men said, in effect, "Go no further. Our people do not wish to quarrel with your people; there are three bad men in our camp whom we Iliaura do not like, they must be killed. Two are **Iturka** (that is men who have married within the forbidden degrees of relationship); the other is very quarrelsome and strong in magic and has boasted of killing your people by means of Kurdaitcha and other magic. Kill these men, but do not injure any others in our camp, and we will help you."

These terms were accepted by the Arunta, and it was agreed between the old men of the two parties that an attempt should be made to kill the three men on the next day. . . . Shortly after daylight a number of Arunta, led by an old man, went over to the **Thara** [fire] of the Iliaura, all of them being

unarmed, and here they took special care to engage the condemned men in conversation. The remainder of the Atninga
party in full war-paint, with whittled spears in their hair, their
bodies painted with red ocher, carrying spears, boomerangs
and shields, and each wearing the magic **Kirra-urkna** or girdle
made of a dead man's hair, crept up unseen and, suddenly
springing up, speared two of the condemned men from
behind. The third man . . . had grown suspicious during the
night and had accordingly decamped. . . .

When this had been done, the Arunta went to the main
camp of the Iliaura and took the **Unawa** of one of the dead
men, and she became and now is the property of the old man
who seized her, she being a woman of the class into which
he could lawfully marry. . . .

[When the Arunta returned home, they] halted some distance away from the main camp and decorated their bodies,
painting them all over with powdered charcoal and placing
on their foreheads and through the septum of the nose small
twigs of a species of Eremophila. As soon as they came in sight
of the main camp they began to perform an excited war-dance,
approaching in the form of a square and holding and moving
their shields as if to ward off something which was being
thrown at them. This action is called **Irulchiukiwuma** and is
intended to beat off the **Ulthana** or spirit of the dead man.

Tasks

Most social activities in bands relate to subsistence and community life. People spend a great deal of time talking, resting, caring for children, mending clothes, brewing beer, and cooking food.
Most enjoy doing these in company with others. Food gathering
is sporadic and even this is generally done in small groups.
Because there are no specializations, all share the same knowledge, so there is much to talk about.

Social Ideals and Reality

So far we have looked at band societies as they operate in ideal
situations. Everyday life, however, is anything but ideal. Droughts,
floods, and fires make life hard, and disease and death can be vis-

itors in the camp. People argue and quarrel and even kill one another. Raids by other bands lead to cycles of revenge and deaths. Life in bands is not always easy, but band organization nonetheless has made it possible for humans to live in stable communities for many generations.

Cultural Order

The small, unspecialized nature of band societies profoundly affects their symbols, cultures, and worldviews. All share a common knowledge of the world around them and this is rarely questioned or tested. Traditions are handed down from generation to generation and preserved over long periods of time with minimal change.

Symbol Systems

Bands have developed cultural systems appropriate for face-to-face societies. The primary means of communication is the spoken word, with the accompanying and enriching use of tones of voice, gestures, and standing distances to communicate a full range of messages and paramessages. People spend much of their time talking with one another about things they have in common, which is most of what they think and do.

Their lack of writing does not mean that people lack large bodies of information. Rather, they store knowledge in their memories using techniques that facilitate their recall. Stories, proverbs, riddles, and songs are told and retold around the evening fires, and children soon learn them by heart.

Myths are also important, for they describe the origins, history, and present conditions of the band. They speak of gods, ancestors, and culture heroes who brought the people fire and taught them how to live as humans. They give the people an understanding of their relationship to nature, to other people, and to the world around them, and so a sense of their own identity.

Rituals and dances are of fundamental importance in band life. In these, people reaffirm their deepest beliefs and values and express their deepest feelings. Dances speak of their oneness as a band and give expression to the joys of living and its sorrows. They also enable people to join with their ancestors and gods in states of ecstasy and trance and to express their dependence upon and harmony with nature.

Individual rituals highlight the importance of events in life and speak of their meaning. Birth, adulthood, marriage, and death are universal human stages in the cycle of life. The ceremonies surrounding these events give meaning to the individual by marking the stages of life and recalling the story of his or her life. They explain where humans come from, why we are here, what are the important things for us to do, and where we go after death.

Group rituals celebrate communal life: the beginning of a new year, the change in seasons, the first kill in the hunt, and success in battle. These rituals give meaning to the joint experiences of the band.

Other rituals are not so regular. These are performed when special crises arise, in hopes that disaster can be averted. Disease, drought, child deaths, barrenness, storms, and fires make band life tenuous at best. When their ordinary ways of coping with these fail, the people turn, as most humans do, to religious solutions.

Missionaries and others in cross-cultural ministries often misunderstand the importance of rituals in these primal societies. Modern societies are basically secular and antiritual. They generally treat religion as a segment of life divorced from other areas of life. In band societies there is no compartmentalization of life into economic, social, political, and religious spheres. All of these are part of one seamless whole in which religion plays a central role.

Modern people also tend to distinguish between forms and meanings in their symbols. For example, they use names simply to label their children. They see marriage as a way to make public a relationship privately agreed upon. They go to church in order to worship. In other words, the going to church, the singing, and the sermon are not themselves the worship. Worship is an inner experience. Modern people see rituals not as powerful transforming events, but as useful reminders of the way things should be.

For the most part, people in bands do not separate form and meaning in symbols. They give a name to a child, such as Strong or Fleet-Footed, in order to make the child so. They perform a rain dance, not to express their desire for rain, but to make rain come. Marriage rites not only speak of the love between a man and woman, but also make them one and assure them of children. Dances not only remind people of the gods and ancestors. These join the people in the dance. Christians in band societies say, "In going to church we are worshiping." The getting up, the dressing, the walk to church, the singing, and the listening constitute worship.

Cultural Knowledge

Band technologies are simple. It is easy, therefore, to conclude that people's knowledge is very limited. It is true that they are not informed in the many domains of modern knowledge, but they do have a sophisticated knowledge of matters relevant to their lives.

Science

One example of this is the knowledge band people have of their environment and its sources of food. Pfeiffer notes (1977, 59),

> Hunting-gatherers know their land in incredible detail. They know in their mind's eye, without conscious thought, the appearance of several hundred square miles of territory, often flat semi-desert spaces with no markers detectable to strangers. They know their territory so well, so precisely, that they can meet one another at a specific place as reliably as two New Yorkers meeting on the southeast corner of Fifth Avenue and Fifty-seventh Street.

Along with this knowledge of terrain goes a knowledge of plants, game, and other sources of food. Elizabeth Marshall Thomas (1959) tells how one Bushman walked unerringly to a spot in a wide plain with no bush or tree to mark the place and pointed out a barely visible dried vine. He had seen it months before during the rainy season. Now it was the dry season and he was thirsty, so he dug out the succulent root two feet down and drank its milky juice. The average Australian Aborigine knows the location of an estimated four hundred water places, some permanent ones, others that can be used only part of the year.

Equally amazing is the hunters' knowledge of tracking game. Using local plant poisons, bows, and arrows, the Bushmen shoot and kill full-grown giraffe. The poison often takes several days to work, but the hunters know how to track the wounded game by the spoor and broken grasses it leaves behind. Eskimos know from the patterns in the snow what sort of animal has passed, how long ago, and whether it is male or female, juvenile or adult. All this information is critical to their survival.

Band members also have an intimate knowledge of people as well as of nature. With no central authority to maintain order, violence is a constant threat. For the most part, people have learned informal ways to guard against it. Contentious individuals are pressured to move from band to band to diffuse the tensions. Those who boast and claim to be better than others are ridiculed, because violence and arrogance are closely related. Despite such measures, violence does occur. Richard Lee (1969) recorded eighteen killings among the Bushmen, most in groups that numbered more than forty individuals.

Religion

Religion in bands is not separated from other areas of life. There may be a philosopher in the band who reflects on the greater issues of life (Radin 1957), but the religion of the people focuses primarily on immediate human concerns such as rain, game, children, diseases, defense, and death.

There is no sharp distinction between natural and supernatural worlds. People commonly speak of the Sky as a world above the Earth, but it is not far removed. The Sky People are beyond human research, but not detached from human affairs. They decide on rain. When they stoke their house fires, the smoke becomes clouds and the fire lightning. They call out in the loud voices of thunder.

Belief in a High God is widespread. He is seen as good, and as the creator of all things. Moreover, after creating humans, he lived among them, teaching them his ways.

For the most part, the High God is believed to be responsible for mighty, celestial phenomena. He causes famines and other natural disasters, but he also maintains the moral order of the universe. People are awed by his greatness and offer him prayers, but because he is gone, he cannot be persuaded by rituals and offerings to do what people want.

More important in everyday life are the many lesser spirits of the Sky and Earth who live close to humans. These control different spheres of nature: one may be the god of hunting, another of rain, a third of war, and others of different diseases. Others inhabit certain places such as a river, tree, mountain, or mountain pass. Most of these are not good or bad. Like humans, they are seen as both. They help humans who offer them food and respect. They plague those who do not. In many bands, people believe that the ghosts of those who have died unusual deaths, such as a mother in childbirth, a good swimmer by drowning, and a man by murder, become malevolent spirits that harm people who do not protect themselves with amulets and other magic.

People try to maintain good relations with the spirits by placating them with offerings of food and water. Part of an animal killed in the hunt may be burned and water from the first rains poured on the ground. On special occasions or when things go wrong, blood sacrifices may be offered: to produce rain, to make peace between fighting bands, to give thanks for a healing, and to atone for a murder that brings the anger of the gods on the people.

People also turn to magic for power and protection. They believe that invisible forces around them can be manipulated by means of magic and rituals. They use divination to determine the causes of misfortunes or to discern the future. They make amulets from unusually shaped pebbles or strange objects to guard themselves against accidents and diseases, and lie special grass over the doors to protect themselves from the spirits. They place curses on their enemies to destroy them and bless their friends to prosper them.

Religious and magical rites are performed by part-time religious practitioners called shamans. These are masters of ecstatic experiences, healing, and dealing with the spirit world. They are believed to enter the spirit world in trances, to placate the spirits with offerings, and to control magical forces by chants and rituals. For the most part, they act for the benefit of the band and its members, but they also are believed to have the power to bring misfortune on people.

For the most part, shamans acquire their power by surviving some traumatic experience that demonstrates their spiritual propensities. Some recover from near-death sicknesses, some are possessed by ancestral spirits, and some go on extended journeys of deprivation and self-torture until they experience visions. Through these experiences they are believed to encounter and master the spirit world: learning to undergo possession at will, to leave their bodies to fight opposing spirits that have stolen a victim's soul, and to communicate with the ancestors and benevolent spirits.

Worldviews of Band Societies

Hidden beneath the more explicit dimensions of band cultures are their worldviews, their basic views of reality.

Part of Nature

Most bands see humans as part of nature, not separate from it. Humans, animals, insects, plants, birds, rocks, rivers, earth, ghosts, sun, and clouds coexist in the same world, linked together and influencing one another. Humans must seek to fit into nature, not to control it.

Life is lived in dependence on nature, which is controlled by a series of cycles: day and night, new and full moon, dry and wet seasons, feasting and famine, blessing and misfortune. Even birth and death are part of the cycle of nature. An aged person dies in one hut and a baby is born in the next. From the viewpoint of the group, birth and death happen together and the life of the group goes on.

Life is more rhythmic than progressive. Things may change, but because people do not have written records of the distant past, they are less aware of it. The cycles of life go on much as they have in the past.

Orientation to the Present

Life in a band focuses on the present. When food is available, all eat exuberantly. When it is gone, people bear the pangs of hunger with fortitude, just as other creatures do. They offer sacrifices to the spirits and use magic to influence nature. In the end, however, they are aware that they are dependent on the spirits and forces of nature for their lives.

The past is not sharply distinguished from the present. People do not think of having a history that stretches out behind them. Rather the past is the timeless storehouse of ancestors and traditions—the stories told today of those still remembered.

Likewise the future is seen as an extension of the present. People do not think much of the distant future. While they do concern themselves with decisions for the immediate future, these decisions are made based on present circumstances and on their supposedly timeless set of traditions. The view of time held by bands might be described as consisting of the present, the recent past, and the present with its anticipation of the near future. There is little point in doing planning for the long-term future.

Wholism

In such a world there is little segmentation between social, economic, political, and religious matters. Culture is one whole in which religious beliefs pervade all of life. Eating, hunting, dreaming, gathering food, and dying—all have religious, economic, and political significance.

There is little specialization in band life and little storing of goods. Skills such as tracking, hunting, and food gathering are taught by parents to their children. There are no formal schools. Children learn about life as a whole by seeing and doing, as well as by hearing and speaking.

Individualism and Equality

Finally, bands are characterized by a strong emphasis on the freedom of the individual and on equality. In the former emphasis they are like modern industrial societies. Unlike them, however, bands are not stratified (that is, they do not divide themselves into ranked groups). They maintain a high degree of equality between individuals by living in small groups and by depending on personal interactions rather than on large institutions to organize their lives.

Given this individualism, violence is sometimes a reality, and always a threat. Consequently, the accumulation of wealth, arrogance, boasting, competition, the desire for status, the tendency to lord it over others, and all behaviors that cause strife are condemned. There is a strong ethic of humility. A successful hunter must take care to avoid giving the impression that he wants or expects special honor or privileges. Among the Algonquin of Canada, for instance, a successful hunter gives most of the kill to others. When two men hunt, each tries to jockey the other into killing a moose, while making sure the moose does not get away.

This ethic of humility is closely tied to a value on sharing. Greatness lies not in accumulating wealth, but in the ability to share with others and to do so without taking credit for it. A leader is not one who demands honor, but one who leads while making others feel great.

Modern Problems

Though hunting and gathering has been a very successful lifestyle for thousands of years, it is possible that this generation of bands may be the last one! Since food production began about ten thousand years ago, food producers have steadily pushed bands to more and more marginal ecological zones. Even those zones, such as the central rain forests and the deserts, are now being encroached upon by outsiders—not to bring the gospel or enhance the lives of local people, but to seize their nature resources. Logging companies want the trees of the rain forest; miners want the minerals of various kinds, including gold; cattle ranchers want water holes and wells in the desert;[1] and desperately poor and displaced peasants want land to grow crops to feed their families. The result, especially in the case of rain-forest areas, may be the loss not only of the band lifestyle, but also of an ecosystem vital to our global survival.

This destruction is not inevitable or necessary. Some bands have lived in successful symbiosis with outsiders for thousands of years. We have mentioned the Pygmies and their cooperative exchange with neighboring Bantu horticultural communities. Cashdan (1989, 44) notes that, according to archaeological evidence, this relationship has existed in a mutually beneficial manner for over two thousand years. That has been possible because the two cultural groups occupied different geographical and economic niches, neither group tried to dominate the other, and there was little population growth among the food producers, so encroachment on band lands was not necessary.

In another example, the archaeological evidence indicates that band and early food-producing societies in North America traded durable goods from Central America to Newfoundland, again for thousands of years, without the domination of one culture by another. Apparently, it is not contact with outsiders per se that is so damaging to band societies.

This does not mean, however, that bands have not changed. Cultures have always changed and always will. New technologies can make life easier. The Eskimo (or Inuit, as they prefer to be called) have been successful in adapting things of the outside world to their own culture. For instance, many Inuit now use snowmobiles, rather than dog sleds, to travel on the ice and snow. They also use rifles in the hunt. As long as their population does not rise, they will be able to sustain themselves by hunting without damaging the environment and with a great deal more ease than their previous harsh life afforded them.

In fact, it is important that a culture be able to adapt to changing environmental circumstances. If it cannot do this, it will go extinct. The Inuit have also been successful in learning the ways of outsiders in order to defend themselves. They have organized to defend land rights, elected their own leaders to political office, and lobbied to enact legislation that would protect them. As a result, powerful and wealthy oil corporations have been restricted in their ability to exploit Inuit lands. The Navaho (who were a band society in former times) have also organized their nation into an effective political unit and have achieved a high degree of political autonomy as well as control of lands in Arizona and New Mexico. Finally, there is, among the Australian Aborigines, a "back to the land" movement that is repatriating urban slum dwellers to better living conditions in the bush, and raising cultural and personal morale (Cashdan 1989, 48). These are all cases of bands successfully learning to manipulate the outside forces that might destroy them.

In most places, though, the story for band societies is sadly different from this. Three kinds of destruction, each interrelated with the others, are taking place: encroachment upon ecological niches, market expansion, and culture loss.

As we mentioned, most encroachment on band territories is due to the desire of outsiders for natural resources. Ironically, though, some ecologists have also contributed to band societies' loss of a viable niche for subsistence. Western ecologists, when picturing the world in their minds, sharply divide human beings from nature (something foragers do not do so easily). Thus, these ecologists are often inclined to try to protect nature at the expense of local humans, the bands. They fail to remember that humans are also a part of the ecosystem.

In a particularly devastating case (Turnbull 1972), the Ik of Kenya were removed by the Kenyan government from their homelands in order to create an animal preserve. They were given a neighboring area with very poor soil and told to farm. Armed rangers were posted in the reserve to prevent the Ik from "poaching" animals from their former home. By the time Colin Turnbull, an anthropologist, visited them, they had experienced an almost complete cultural and moral breakdown. Since they could not produce adequate food for themselves, they had developed a severe survival ethic: each person defended food for himself or herself at all costs and none shared food with any other. This ethic applied even within the nuclear family. Men and women would take the last bit of food for themselves from the mouth of a dying spouse, and then laugh at having gotten away with the robbery. Mothers would systematically kick their children out of the home to fend for themselves at three years old. Children formed gangs for protection against adults. And old people were left to die alone.

Without doubt, there had previously been a strong ethic of food sharing among the Ik, as there is in all band societies. Furthermore, there is no evidence that their presence in the forest was in any way harming the ecosystem. Quite the contrary, people in bands are concerned ecologists, and the Ik no doubt were careful not to overforage. Removing them from the forest may well have caused an overpopulation in the animals that they hunted.

As a general rule, human beings, like all other creatures that God makes, can live without destroying their environment as long as their population is stable. While there is some evidence that band societies of the past may have failed to maintain their populations, modern band societies control their populations very carefully, using birth control methods.[2] Where band population densities are too high now, such as in the Yanomamo homeland in Brazil, it is because loss of territory and outside food supplies make migration unnecessary. For the most part, band societies in recent times have experienced severe population loss, not gain, due to disease and disruption of their subsistence by outsiders.

Ecologists can be assured that allowing indigenous bands to continue to forage is unlikely to cause the kind of ecological damage that poor peasants and industries are causing.

Encroachment upon ecological niches is one kind of destruction that band societies are experiencing. A second is the socioeconomic destruction that has accompanied the intrusion of the market into band life. Market expansion is a global phenomenon. It is helpful to distinguish market places from market principles. Market places have been set aside for market-style exchange. But market exchange can take place anywhere, and is defined by principles such as the anonymity of the buyer and seller and the law of supply and demand. Ultimately, a market exchange has taken place if both parties are free to pursue their own material interests ("drive a hard bargain") apart from any relationship there may be between them and apart from any traditional ideas about what the proper rate of exchange ought to be.

We have seen that band society not only condones sharing and gift giving, but rests its entire social structure upon them. Gift giving is the polar opposite of market exchange. A gift has been given if one party gives up her or his material interests in favor of another, relationships are the reason for the exchange, and traditional ideas about appropriateness inform what is given and to whom. Given the radical difference between these two types of exchange, the effect on social structure can be dramatic when markets expand from neighboring societies into band societies.

For example, the Miskito Native Americans of the Nicaraguan east coast have long hunted green sea turtles. Traditionally, the turtles, which could weigh as much as 250 pounds, were harpooned by a crew of men in a boat under dangerous circumstances, so the meat was considered very valuable. The turtles were divided up on the beach immediately after the kill and distributed according to the laws of gift giving and social interdependence. The difficulty of obtaining turtles insured that the turtle population could be maintained and the food sharing insured that community solidarity was marked and no meat was wasted.

Beginning in the eighteenth and nineteenth centuries, a global market for green sea turtles developed. Companies from England, France, and elsewhere began to purchase the turtles from the Miskito. By this century they were setting up local offices, providing nets (rather than harpoons) to make hunting easier, and encouraging the Miskito to increase "production" of the turtles for export. The result for the Miskito was not only the breakdown of normal social exchanges and the isolation of nuclear families (who quit sharing with one another), but also, ironically, poverty! The Miskito began depending on outside food sources, bought with cash from sold turtles, instead of working to feed themselves. When turtle supplies ran low, due to overhunting, the companies packed up and left, leaving the Miskito with no turtles and no source of cash. Bernard Neitschmann (1994, 183), describing the situation, concludes,

> The Miskito now depend on outside systems to supply them with money and materials that are subject to world market fluctuations. They have lost their autonomy and their adaptive relationship with their environment. Life is no longer socially rewarding, nor is their diet satisfying. The coastal Miskito have become a specialized and highly vulnerable sector of the global market economy.

The case of the Miskito is similar to that of others. The Mbuti Pygmies have begun to overhunt their meat supply due to the influence of meat traders who travel into their forests to meet them (Cashdan 1989, 45). They now spend twice as much time hunting as they used to. The result is the same: a shift from depending on the wealth of human relationships to support the family in times of need to depending on a stockpile of material wealth for security. Obligations in human relationships are restricted, then, lest the stockpile be reduced by "too much" gift giving to others. When the outside market demand falls off or the resource supply fails due to overuse, people are left poor, both in material and in social terms.

Ultimately, niche destruction and market expansion produce culture loss for many band societies. Traditional ways of doing things, the values placed on relationships, and the worldviews associated with these are so altered by the massive and rapid changes that have come from the outside that the culture as a whole loses its integrity. Life becomes meaningless because the past ways no longer work and the new larger society is hard to understand, much less manipulate.

People from band societies that have been destroyed end up as poor laborers on peasant farms or in urban slums. Formerly foraging Indians (of India) are likely to join the Indian peasant social structure at the bottom as "untouchables." The Aka Pygmies have become agricultural laborers for their neighbors and the San of the Kalahari Desert now work for wealthy cattle owners (Cashdan 1989, 47). Particularly in cities, ex-band members have difficulty adjusting to notions such as regulating daily activities by a clock, negotiating bureaucracies and other forms of impersonal authority, and the exclusivity of private ownership. (We will examine these problems more extensively in chapter 8.)

What is a Christian response to this situation? We have argued that, realistically, change is not only inevitable, but also necessary in order for us to adapt to the changing environment. Furthermore, human beings are integrally a part of the nature that God has created and have always been interconnected with one another around the globe. We cannot try to preserve this group or that one by isolating them from the world any more than we can preserve nature by isolating it from human beings. What *can* we do?

The Bible's answer is clear. We are the caretakers of God's garden and we are to love one another. This means that the type of change must be carefully evaluated. The changes that have affected band societies recently are due to the domination of those groups by technologically and militarily powerful outsiders. Christians can have no part in this kind of domination. Nor can we throw up our hands and declare the situation inevitable. For Christians, there is always another way. That way, in the case of band societies, will surely include the protection of rights to land, the forbidding of economic exploitation, and a willingness to learn from bands about the protection of the environment. Our gospel of Jesus Christ will be welcomed if our actions show this kind of love and concern.

How can we as Christians minister in band societies? How do these people understand the gospel? How do churches grow in such settings? We need to turn our attention to these questions.

The Church in Band Societies

The history of the church's ministry to band societies has been uneven. The early church was born largely in the cities. During the Middle Ages missionaries went to the tribes of Europe and inner Asia, and the church remained primarily a tribal and a peasant phenomenon. For the most part, bands have remained on the margins of the spread of Christianity.

In the modern era, the record of Christian ministry to bands has not been good. In South America, North America, and Australia, missionaries to bands came with people of their own kind who were driving the bands off their land. Consequently, band people equated the gospel with oppression. The few who converted were encouraged to settle down and join the dominant society. There was little encouragement, until recent times, for them to remain nomadic hunters and gatherers.

Planting Churches in Band Societies

Given this checkered history and the nomadic life of bands, how can we minister to them? We need new and creative ways to do so.

Incarnational Ministries

One principle is clear: bands are built on close personal relationships, and those who minister in bands must be willing to take the time to build such relationships and to earn the trust of band people. In bands the basis of life is not programs, institutions, money, and organization. It is relationships.

Intimate face-to-face relationships can be built, however, only when we identify closely with people. We need to love people for who they are, and respect their culture. We need to live with people—to sit where they sit, walk where they walk, and weep when they weep. We need to listen before we judge, and seek to empower people, not control them (see Loewen 1975; Smalley; 1978).

This incarnational approach to ministry means that we must meet people where they are, not where we are. We must learn to see the world as they see it if we are to help them know the gospel in terms they understand. We cannot reject their culture and try to replace it with our own. To do so is to destroy their identity and dignity.

An incarnational identification with band people in lifestyle is hard for westerners. We are addicted to material goods and physical comfort. We cannot imagine living in a lean-to with almost no material possessions, or moving every few weeks. We immediately try to make things better. We have a tinkering mentality that constantly seeks to improve our material well-being. This is not necessarily all bad, but it does not fit with the attitudes of band people, who value relationships over comfort.

As we have seen, cultures have three dimensions—knowledge, feelings, and values. Each of these can be a point of hindrance in our identification with band people. A lack of knowledge leads us to misunderstand people. We need, therefore, to study their culture carefully to see the world as they see it. We must learn the categories they use to order their world, the beliefs they use to explain it, and their worldview. Without such understandings we cannot communicate the gospel to them.

A lack of empathy leaves us trapped in our ethnocentrism. At a deep level we feel that our culture is better than theirs. To counter this we must develop a strong appreciation for what is good in their lives.

Finally, we all tend to make premature judgments based on misunderstandings and ethnocentrism. We need to reserve our evaluations until we in some measure understand and appreciate the people we serve. When we judge, we need to do so using biblical standards, not our own cultural norms. We must also let the Scriptures judge us and our culture.

Identification with people takes time and effort. We begin by living with and like the people and by building relationships of trust. We then come to see ourselves as one with the people and on their side in their confrontations with the outside world.

We must identify with people as far as we are able, but we all have psychological limits to adjustment to new cultures. Moreover, to deny our own cultural identity is to commit psychological suicide. We are insiders-outsiders, much as Jesus was, and part of our value to people is our outside ties. Incarnational ministry is a balance of giving up many things and politely explaining that other things are "the way of my people." At the deepest level, it is to truly love people and to commit ourselves to their good and their salvation.

Separating the Gospel from Our Culture

A second important principle in ministering to bands is to distinguish between the gospel and our own culture. We naturally assume that Christianity is what we believe and practice; consequently, we expect converts in other cultures to do the same. We translate our songs into their language, expect them to listen to sermons based on logic, and teach them how to elect a pastor democratically. We are surprised and confused when they say that to become Christian, they must leave their own culture.

Our beliefs and practices are shaped by the gospel, but they are also shaped by our culture and history. In our theology we use Greek categories of thought and seek to know the ultimate nature of things. Band people use other categories and ask other questions having to do with such things as healing, drought, interpersonal conflicts, and guidance in making everyday decisions. We need to help them to find answers to their questions in the Bible.

We must recognize that forms of worship vary from culture to culture. We like to sing hymns and choruses. Others like monotonic chants and dancing. Each of us identifies most with songs in our own languages and music styles. One sign of a healthy church is that it writes songs and creates its own worship forms.

We must recognize, too, that people organize themselves in different ways. We are accustomed to committees, constitutions, and rules. Band people form loose fellowships with no formal organization. The church needs to adapt its modes of organization to the social practices of people as far as biblical teaching allows. In many ways the loose, egalitarian nature of band organization is more compatible with Christian teaching than the western Christian bureaucratic, pragmatic, and management-by-objective type of leadership that we have borrowed from the world.

The Gospel of Reconciliation and Relationships

Good relationships are the dominant value in band societies, and maintaining harmony, peace, sharing, and humility is stressed. Much of people's time is spent in social interaction. It is important, therefore, that we put relationships ahead of programs in our ministry.

This emphasis on relationships also shapes people's understanding of sin. Societies that emphasize the importance of the group over the individual see sin as broken relationships and forgiveness as reconciliation and restoration of fellowship. We in the west emphasize law and order. We see sin as the breaking of God's rules and restitution as the result of punishment and pardon.

It is difficult for us to communicate to band people the concept of sin as a violation of God's law. They understand, however, if we say that God is angry at us. Most of them are aware that the High God has left them because of their misdeeds. To them it is good news, indeed, that God now is ready to forgive them and take them back into the fellowship of his family. It is also good news that God can break down the hostilities among them and give them peace with their neighbors.

Law, guilt, and judgment are certainly important themes in Scripture, but so are reconciliation, fellowship, and *shalom*.[1] These are images band people understand.

Presenting a Whole Gospel

There is little specialization in band societies apart from the division of labor between men and women, and young and old. People do not segment their lives into religion, economics, politics, and entertainment. Life is seen as one whole, with religion at the center. People hunt and gather for food, but they know that without the blessing of God, their efforts are futile. They hold councils and are sure that their ancestors are present.

In such societies it is important to present the gospel as a whole gospel. It must deal with salvation from sin, with illness, hunger, hostilities in the group, and with other problems of life. The most effective ministries in band societies have been those that combine preaching with praying for the sick and ministering to people in their needs.

Theological Challenges

The church faces new theological challenges in planting churches among band people because new questions emerge that we in the western church have not faced. In the early church theology was the daughter of missions. When new problems arose in the outreach of the church, the leaders formulated a theological response. The first great missionary conference (Acts 15) was called to answer questions raised by the missionary outreach of the church. Today, many of the central issues in theology are being raised on the frontiers of the church's expansion.

Cultural Arrogance

Most Christians approach bands with a sense of cultural superiority. We come from large, complex societies and take pride in our technological superiority. We look on bands as primitive and backward, even though we do not admit so publicly. We assume that band people want a better life, and we define this in material terms. We have no doubt that literacy is better than oral culture, that guns are better than stone axes, and that permanent homes are better than nomadic life. Consequently, we immediately set about to improve the material life of people.

One consequence of this attitude is that we equate Christianity with western culture. Wilbert Shenk writes (1980, 35),

> The seventeenth-century New England Puritan missionaries largely set the course for modern missions. They defined their task as preaching the gospel so that Native Americans would be converted and receive personal salvation. But early in their missionary experience these New Englanders concluded that Indian

converts could only be Christians if they were "civilized." . . .
They gathered these new Christians into churches for nurture and
discipline, and set up programs to transform Christian Indians
into English Puritans.

This view of missions is very much alive today. Unfortunately,
the good news of the gospel has often become for band people the
bad news of uncomfortable clothing, hard labor with little reward,
obedience to the commands of outsiders, and loss of their culture
and identity as they are absorbed into large societies.

Cultural arrogance produces in us a condescending attitude
toward band people. In the past, it was not uncommon for Christians to treat band people as children needing to be protected
from outsiders and taught how to live properly. Missionaries
have not been the only or even the worst examples of western
ethnocentrism. Traders, businessmen, scientists, and tourists
are just as colonial and often more so in their attitudes toward
band people.

Attitudes of superiority are major barriers to evangelism. People
are proud of their freedom and their cultures and are hardly over-
joyed when outsiders tell them their way of life is "primitive." We
must remember that salvation does not mean adopting western
materialistic ways of life.

It is important in working in bands to avoid feelings of cultural
arrogance, or of believing that technological superiority proves
the superiority of Christianity. We rarely question the value of
material prosperity and often equate it with God's blessing. We
overlook the fact that in other areas of life such as building community and caring for the aged, band societies are often much better than our modern ones, and that there is much that we can learn
from them about living.

Exploitation

Today the world is being overrun by modernity, and missionaries are not the only or even the primary agents of change.
Explorers map the territories, logging and mining companies
invade the jungles, businessmen import guns, axes, matches, and
cigarettes, and tourists bring roads, buses, hotels, and prostitution, all in their own interest. Unscrupulous people take advan-

tage of bands because bands do not understand how the outside world works. Governments and multinational corporations control their lives. There are few places band people can hide from the onslaught of the outside world, and few people to help them survive in a global world.

The absorption of bands into the modern world is often forced on band people. In such situations, what is the church's responsibility? We no longer minister to people who live in isolation. Often we are caught between a band society seeking to maintain its own identity and the outside forces seeking to exploit it. We find ourselves not only bringing people the good news of salvation, but also helping them face the world oppressing them from without. We help people register their lands so that mining companies, logging firms, and farmers do not take it. We teach them how to earn money, pay taxes, and protect themselves from the diseases of the outside world. We assist them to preserve a sense of self-respect and pride in their social and cultural identity in the midst of a world that does not respect them.

The church also faces the problems of shattered bands. When band life disintegrates in the face of modernity, families and communities break down and people lose their sense of identity and self-worth. It is not surprising that many of them turn to alcohol for escape and drift on the edges of towns and cities. The church must minister to these broken people who are lost in the cracks of modern societies. It must restore their sense of dignity in Christ and help them build strong families and churches.

To deal with such situations we need a theology of identity and justice. The gospel gives people a new identity in Christ, not in western culture. It calls all cultures, both band and modern, to change in the direction of God's kingdom (see fig. 12, following page). Our task is not to modernize people but to call them to hear God's Word in their lives and cultures. They must decide whether or not they want to adopt modern ways.

When people choose to maintain their cultural distinctiveness, the missionary often must become their defender against the encroachment of the outside world because he or she knows how it works. Christianity has often been the best bridge traditional peoples have to enter the modern world while keeping their own ways of life.

Figure 12
The Missionary Task

Not

But

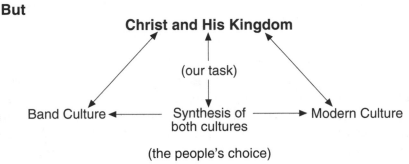

Nomadic Churches

Not all barriers to planting churches in bands have to do with the missionaries. There are difficulties inherent in the lifestyle of the people that require us to think of the church in new ways.

The church has grown mainly among people who are more or less settled. Church worship styles and organization are based on the assumption that members live in one place for relatively long periods of time. Consequently, we who come from such churches have little idea of how to plant churches among band people who are here today and gone tomorrow. How do we plant churches that have no permanent members, no leaders who can direct others, no official rules, no buildings, no constitutions, and no budgets? How do we evangelize new bands without programs? Interestingly enough, we are beginning to face these questions anew in modern cities where people are highly mobile.

The church's response in the past has generally been to settle band people in villages and to introduce them to farming. Most governments are also trying to do the same in order to tax and govern people. Consequently, band people often associate Christianity with oppressive governments.

Some missionaries, such as Christian and Missionary Alliance workers in Tibet, joined band societies and moved with them. This approach demands high commitment. Missionaries must give up their dependence on possessions and live in temporary shelters. They must rear their children in camps without the "benefits of modern educational resources."

Other missionaries, such as some among the Masai of Kenya, have built permanent shelters where bands congregate for longer periods of time. Here they start churches, open health clinics, and teach people basic skills needed to live in a modern world.

With our focus on large cities with their millions of people, we must not overlook the bands on the edges of modern societies. Our response to them is, in part, a measure of our obedience to bring the Good News of God's salvation to all people, particularly those who are forgotten by the world.

4 | Tribal Societies

Band societies were common in early human history, but over time many became tribes. They produced more sophisticated tools, raised herds of animals for food or planted crops, and developed more complex social systems. These changes enabled communities to grow in size and to establish more permanent settlements.

For our purposes we will use John Friedl's definition of a tribe (1981, 362), namely, "a confederation of groups who recognize a relationship with one another, usually in the form of common ethnic origin, common language, or strong pattern of interaction based on intermarriage or presumed kinship." To this we might add that most tribes share a common territory and a common culture. As we will see, this equation of an ethnic group with a language, a culture, and a land breaks down as societies become more complex.

Tribal societies are a particularly successful form of human organization. They have been the basis of stable, enduring communities that have made human life possible on most parts of earth and throughout much of history. Pastoral tribes from Inner Asia invaded and settled Europe, India, and China and established vast empires. Horticultural tribes covered large areas of Africa, Europe, North and South America, Asia, and the Pacific Islands. Fishing tribes occupied seacoasts around the world.

In recent centuries, many tribes have been absorbed by peasant societies or driven to mountains, forests, and grasslands unusable by farmers. Today tribes are being assimilated into nation states around the world and their people are caught between loyalty to their tribe and loyalty to their nation. Modern nation builders consider tribalism a constant threat to their efforts. A great many tribes survive, however, in varying degrees of independence from the world around them. Despite their diversity, these societies have important social and cultural characteristics in common.

The Social Order

Social relations are the heart of tribal life. A person exists only as he or she is part of a group. Boganjolo Goba writes,

> Whatever happens to the individual happens to the whole community to which he belongs, and whatever happens to the community happens to him as well. His life and that of the community is one and cannot be separated for it transcends life and death. Hence he can say, "I am because we are, and since we are, therefore, I am." (1974, 65)

The group, not the individual, is the primary building block of tribal societies.

Tribes have more complex social organizations than bands. This is true in all the dimensions of life—social, economic, political, legal, and functional. This complexity is reflected in the emergence of some full-time specialized roles such as chiefs. It does not, however, lead to specialized institutions such as schools, hospitals, shops, banks, or restaurants. Kinship ties remain the center of life and are used to perform the major functions of social life.

Social Structure

Life in tribes, like that in bands, is based on families and local communities. However, families and communities are linked together in higher-level social systems that can include millions of people and cover large territories. Tribes exploit the power of kinship ties to the maximum. A tribe can be seen as a family of families, or even a family of families of families (fig. 13, following page).

Kinship Ties

Tribes are made up of a series of larger and larger kinship groups. The details vary from tribe to tribe, but social organization always

Figure 13
The Social Structure of a Tribe

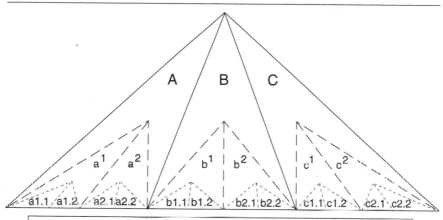

Key		
	A	= Major kinship groupings such as clans
	a1	= Secondary kinship groupings such as primary, secondary, and tertiary lineages
	a1.1	= Family groupings such as extended, nuclear families and mother-children households

begins with closely-knit households. These are joined into extended family groups, which are combined into lineages and clans, which are joined together to form a tribe or a people. The social glue that holds all these together is ethnicity: the ties of blood believed to be shared by all members of the tribe.

Two factors influence the passing of blood from generation to generation: marriage and descent. It should not surprise us, therefore, that both of these play very important roles in tribal life. Families, kinship ties, ancestors, and offspring are topics that we will encounter again and again in our analysis of tribal societies.

Marriage

With few exceptions, the basic group in all human societies is the family. This is built on two relationships: the marriage of a man and a woman and the bond between parent, especially the mother, and child.

In the loose organization of band societies, a high value is placed on compatibility and companionship in marriage. In the

more structured tribal societies, marriage serves other important social functions. It provides the offspring that perpetuate
the extended family, lineage, and tribe. It divides labor between
men and women, builds long-distance kinship and trade ties,
and provides people with an avenue to gain prestige and power.
Sexual pleasure and affection are often of secondary importance
in tribal marriages.

Sex roles in most tribes are highly differentiated. Men hunt and
war; women tend gardens, gather wild food and wood, rear children,
and keep the village clean. This differentiation leads to hierarchy.
Most tribes are strongly patriarchal, that is, men are dominant. In a
few, women have a good deal of power because they are the owners
of property and the family name. Even in these, however, men associated with powerful women exercise most public authority.

Marriage is also used to resolve difficult social crises. The death
of men and women is common in their prime years, when they
bear major responsibilities for having children and maintaining
life. Diseases, accidents, and raids take heavy tolls, in part because
medical care is often ineffectual. Such deaths tear apart the social
fabric. Who cares for a widow and her children? Who helps a wid-
ower nurse an infant child?

In the west we are concerned primarily with meeting the economic needs of a widow. A husband should have a home, savings, insurance, and Social Security to provide for his wife if he
dies. But a widow needs more than money. She needs companionship and a male role model for her sons. She has sexual drives and wants to bear more children to care for her in her old age
and to make sure her family will survive. How does she satisfy
these needs?

In most tribes, such social crises are solved by substitution. Just
as Americans put another person into the presidency when a president dies, or appoint another pastor when one leaves, so tribal
people find another husband to replace one who expires. Generally this is the brother of the deceased or his closest male kinsman
of the same generation.

We see an example of this practice in the Old Testament (see
Deut. 25:5–10). When Ruth was widowed her husband's family
was responsible to provide her with another man. When she lay
down at Boaz's feet to remind him of his duty as the nearest male

kinsman of her husband, he said that there was another more closely related to her than he. Only when that man declined to do his duty did Boaz marry Ruth (Ruth 3:1–4:12). In Jesus' time the Sadducees referred to the same practice (Matt. 22:23–28).

Social substitution is a good solution, for it not only provides economic security, but also satisfies the other needs a widow and her children have. But what if the man already has a wife? In most tribes this is not a problem—he simply inherits the widow as a second wife. The primary concern here is not sexual, but caring for needy people.

Most tribes are *polygamous*, that is, they allow a person to marry several spouses. Many are *polygynous*—they allow a man to take several wives. A few, notably in the Himalayas and the hills of south India, are *polyandrous*—a woman may marry several husbands.

Table 3
Reasons for Polygyny

1. To solve the social crisis created by a husband's death by providing the widow and her children with a substitute husband and father.

2. To provide a family with children when the first wife is barren. There is a strong desire to have children, in part to care for the parents in their old age.

3. To provide security in one's old age by having many children.

4. To make alliances with good families for purposes of social prestige, financial gain, and/or political power.

5. To acquire more workers to work the fields and so make the husband wealthy and powerful.

6. To provide husbands for all women. This is particularly true in societies where many men are killed in raids and wars.

7. To enable an important man to be more hospitable by providing women who can care for the guests and the destitute who come to his home.

8. To provide sexual gratification for a husband in societies where he is forbidden to sleep with his wife for two or three years after she gives birth to a child. This postpartum tabu prevents the birth of another child who might threaten the life of the first because the mother does not have enough milk for both.

9. To provide a man with status and a sense of social well-being because his culture places high value on having many kinfolk around.

10. To provide help to senior wives who are tired of doing the household chores.

There are many reasons other than social crisis for practicing polygyny (table 3, preceding page). Even in societies where it is allowed, however, it is common only among the more powerful and wealthy men. Most families are monogamous.

Family

Marriages create families. In many tribes, however, men do not spend much time at home. They may live and even sleep in the men's house, away from the huts where the women and children live.

Family life centers on the mother-child bond. Each wife has her own hut or corner of a hut and raises and cooks food for herself and her children. The children's primary ties are to their mother. The husband is the link between these maternal groups. He moves from wife to wife as he wishes and as the occasion demands (fig. 14).

Jealousy and quarreling among co-wives is common and many societies encourage sororal polygyny (the marriage of a man to several sisters) in the belief that this will help prevent discord in the household. Others encourage wives to live in separate huts to

Figure 14
Polygynous Family Structure

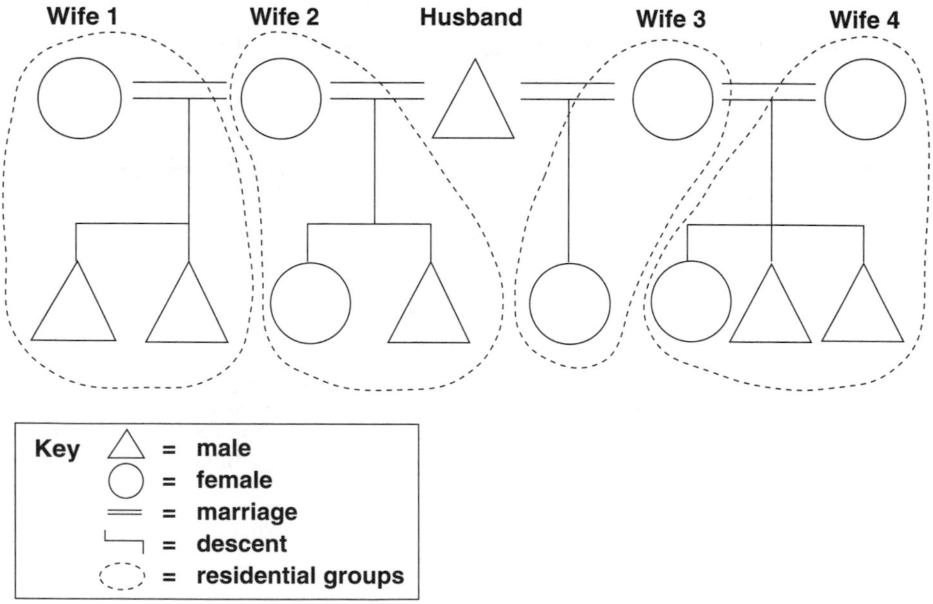

Key △ = male
     ○ = female
     = = marriage
     ⌐ = descent
     ⊂⊃ = residential groups

reduce tensions. Many assign authority to the first wife to make duties clear. It is not uncommon for a first wife to ask her husband to take another wife to help with the household or gardening work, to produce offspring, or to add to her own prestige as the dominant wife in a polygynous family.

Extended families

In contrast to bands, most tribes place great emphasis on larger kinship groups. Individuals who do not belong to families have no one to support them in times of crisis, no one to defend them when others attack them, no one to care for them in their old age, and no one to visit them when they are lonely. Such people are nonpeople in a village.

Extended families made up of several generations are common. In patrilineal societies descent is reckoned through the male line. The family often includes a patriarch, his sons, grandsons, and great-grandsons, and their spouses and unmarried daughters. In a matrilineal society, it includes a matriarch, her daughters, granddaughters, and great-granddaughters, and their spouses and unmarried sons.

In tribes, marriage is not merely a wedding of two individuals. It is a socioeconomic alliance between two kinship groups that has implications for the whole community. Consequently, marriages, particularly a person's first marriage, are generally arranged by the heads of families.

In patrilineal societies a man's first loyalty is to his father. When he marries, he often continues to live with his father and brothers. In matrilineal societies the dominant ties are between mothers and daughters, and men are often expected to join their wives and live in the households of their mothers-in-law.

The extended family provides more security than does the nuclear family of the west. Children grow up with many fathers and mothers, because all men and women in the extended family act as parents to them. In the event of a sudden illness or the death of a parent, others are ready to rear the children. The extended family also provides a check against neglect and maltreatment of children by incompetent parents, which is a real danger in nuclear families. Finally, the extended family provides a strong base for the care of the aged. The burden of this does not fall on only one son or daughter.

Lineages and clans

In tribes, kinship ties provide a person with ever larger circles of relatives: uncles and aunts, nieces and nephews, first cousins, second, third, fourth, and fifth cousins, and so on. Tribes use these extended kinship ties to create large social groups that perform the essential tasks of a society.

Kinship systems can be divided into those in which people believe both parents contribute equally to the life of the child and those that believe that one parent contributes more or something different than the other. The former are referred to as bilateral kinship systems. An example of these is the white, middle-class, American system in which a person sees himself or herself equally related biologically to relatives of both mother and father. This is seen in our use of terms such as "uncle," "aunt," and "cousin" for relatives on both the mother's and the father's side of the family. Both band and urban societies tend to use bilateral kinship systems.

Tribal societies, however, use unilineal kinship systems. These systems trace descent through only the male or the female line. Patrilineal groups are made up of men linked by male descent to a common ancestor (fig. 15). This does not mean that a man has no interactions with his mother's relatives. In fact, they often play a specific and important role as informal associates. His formal relationships and loyalties, however, are to his patrilineal kinsmen. Unmarried women belong to their father's kinship group,

Figure 15
Patrilineal Kinship System

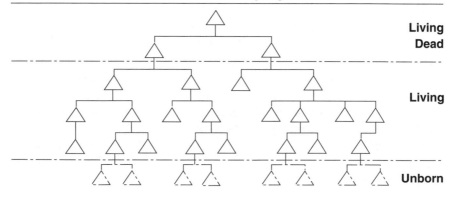

but the status of married women varies from tribe to tribe. Sometimes they retain membership in their father's kinship group; sometimes they join their husband's group.

Matrilineal systems reckon kinship through the female line. Consequently, the core of these groups is a line of women descended from a common ancestress. Males usually belong to the kinship group of their mothers and retain membership in this group after marriage. Matrilineal systems are found where women's work is essential for subsistence and men engage primarily in rituals and warfare.

The basic social unit larger than the extended family in unilineal societies is the lineage. This is the set of kin who can trace their genealogical relationship to one another through a common *known* ancestor. Patrilineages do so through the male line and matrilineages through the female line. Over generations, as parents have children, lineages divide into sub- or secondary and tertiary lineages. In time, ancestors are forgotten and lineages divide.

A clan is a group of lineages that claim descent from one mythical ancestor, often thought to be a superhuman being. Members of the same clan believe they are related, but they cannot always trace the actual genealogical links between them. Clans often symbolize their identity using animals like the bear, leopard, or elk as their totems. As we will see, some societies are totemic. That is, their clans extend kinship bonds to different species of animals and plants.

Unilineal systems are an efficient way of organizing a society. They overcome many of the difficulties inherent in bilateral systems. They divide the society into clearly defined, nonoverlapping kinship groups. Each person belongs to only one clan or lineage and therefore does not face the conflict of loyalties common in bilateral systems. It is easier, therefore, to build large, stable groups that endure over time. The lineage or the clan takes on a corporate nature of its own and the individual is subordinate to the decisions and actions of the group.

The stable, corporate nature of unilineal groups enables them to perform most of the important tasks of a society. Members exchange economic aid and support each other in their quarrels and legal disputes with outsiders. The lineage or clan often owns the land

and assigns it to members for use. It also regulates the behavior of its members and represents them in the tribal government.

A person's identity and significance in most tribes depends on his or her membership in a particular lineage or clan, rather than on his or her personal uniqueness and skills. People are not encouraged to assert their individuality. They are taught to fit into the group and to obey its wishes, because it is the group, not the individual, that is the basis of tribal social realities. Few westerners understand the importance of this fact and its ramifications for all of tribal life.

The fundamental weakness of unilineal systems is their vulnerability to splits and feuds. The division of the society into clans, lineages, and sublineages leads to conflicts between groups. Brothers are generally expected to support one another in quarrels with other men of their sublineage;[1] members of the sublineage help their men in fights with those from other sublineages, and men of lineages or clans join their members in battles with other lineages or clans. These disputes can lead to bloodshed and feuds. Ironically, the principle of descent, which bonds some together so strongly, can cause others to fight, as we in our culture know from the infamous case of the Hatfields and the McCoys.[2]

This tendency to split and feud is countered in several ways. A strong leader can hold the tribe together. So, too, can ties of marriage. In most tribes, members of a clan or a lineage are thought to be members of the same family, so they cannot marry one another. A man or woman must take a spouse from another lineage or clan. Consequently, clans are intermarried and seek to avoid feuds because the men do not want to fight their wives' relatives.

It is common, over time, for extended families in two lineages to continue arranging marriages between them. A man is often expected to marry his son to his wife's brother's daughter, because they belong to different but friendly lineages. For the son's family, this is good because it gets a woman from the same family as his mother, and his mother can mediate tensions between the family and the new bride. For the young woman's family it is also good, because this family is giving a daughter to a family it already knows and because the bride's aunt is there to help her. In addition, in some societies the groom's family will now "owe" a bride to them.

A third way to counter feuds is to reckon kinship on both the father's and the mother's side, but to keep the two separate. For example, the Ashanti of West Africa believe that people are both biological and spiritual beings. They get their bodies from their mothers and their spirits from their fathers. People belong to their mother's biological clan, which determines their residence, use of land, and inheritance of material goods. They belong to their father's spiritual clan and venerate its gods and ancestors.

A person in a double-descent system such as this cannot marry anyone in his or her biological or spiritual clans (fig. 16). Consequently, a person's father, mother, wife, son, and daughter belong to other biological and spiritual clans. To fight those clans means to fight those within his or her own family.

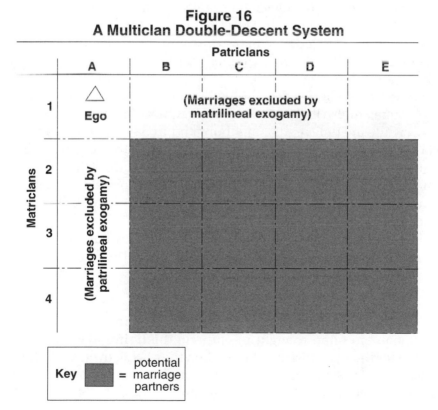

Figure 16
A Multiclan Double-Descent System

Tribe and other tribes

On the highest level of social organization, the tribe itself is a kinship group—the largest group of humans who believe they are the same kind of people because they share the same blood. They cannot marry outsiders, because outsiders have a different blood, and therefore are enemies or half-humans.

Tribes are surrounded by other tribal and peasant societies with whom they interact. During times of peaceful coexistence, people barter with their neighbors and traders pass through the countryside on the way to the seacoast for salt or to the hills for stone. Sometimes these trade relationships are ritualized. For example, the coastal Eskimo formerly held an annual gathering with the inland Eskimo to trade seal lard, walrus bone, and fish for deerskin and wood. To guarantee peace in such potentially dangerous settings, men from the coast formed partnerships with men from inland and sealed their pacts by exchanging wives.

There are no enduring social organizations encompassing different tribes; consequently, there is the constant threat of war. A tribesman is offended by a man from another tribe and raids that man's home, killing him. The dead man's tribesmen must carry out a raid in revenge to preserve tribal and family honor. The process may go on for decades before a peace is negotiated.

At times intertribal wars lead to conquest and assimilation. A powerful tribe defeats its neighbors and makes them servants or slaves. However, the conquerors intermarry with the vanquished and their children are born free members of the tribe. Consequently, in a generation or two there are no more slaves. This is what happened when Israel conquered Palestine. Many of the local peoples became Israelites through marriage.

People fleeing from their own tribes when they commit serious crimes may also seek refuge in another tribe. If they are accepted, they are allowed to join it.

Ancestors and the cosmos

Kinship ties extend beyond the living. They include the ancestors, who are often thought to encircle the living like a cloud—caring for them, punishing them when they bring disgrace to their lineage, and negotiating with the gods and spirits for them. In turn these ancestors must be fed and revered.

Kinship ties also extend to the unborn. Without them the tribe dies, so their well-being must be taken into account in tribal decisions. For example, the Hopi Indians of Arizona recently refused to sell tribal lands to urban developers for a shopping center, even though the developers offered them much money. When the developers asked the Hopi why, they said they had asked the ancestors and the ancestors had given them permission to sell because their descendants would benefit. They had asked the living and the living agreed to sell, because they would get rich. But when they asked the unborn, the unborn said no, because if the land were sold, they would have nothing when they came to earth.

Beyond humans lie the totemic spirits and gods of the tribe. These protect it in a world full of spirits, half-humans, supernatural forces, and witchcraft.

Marshall D. Sahlins points out (1968, 15) that when you live in a tribe, the tribe looks like a series of concentric circles (see fig. 17, following page). Around you are your immediate and extended families. Beyond that are the circles of your lineage and clan. Finally there is the circle of your tribe (those who are fully human), and then the ancestors and the gods.

Geographical Organization

Kinship is not the only principle by which tribal life is organized. A second one is geography.

The household is the basic social and geographic unit. In it people spend much of their time, rear their children, have their deepest relationships, and, ironically, experience some of their most intense hostilities. Politically, the household acts like a little chiefdom within a larger chiefdom. It is mainly self-regulating, with the father having a great deal of power to keep his house in order. The household is also the basic economic unit. For the most part, with its domestic division of labor by sex and age, it raises the food consumed by its members. It is also the basic religious unit, organizing family rituals and placating its ancestors and gods. It is here that social structures are reinforced or changed in the dynamics of day-to-day living.

The center of tribal life is the homestead, the hamlet, or the village, which usually consists of several families. Here food is pro-

Figure 17
Organization of a Tribe
(as seen from within)

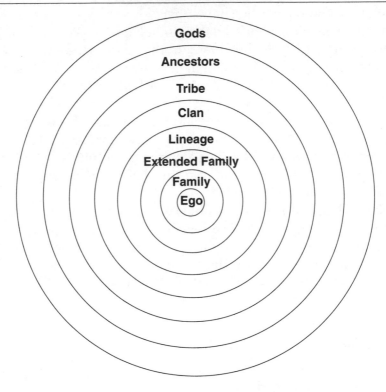

duced, artifacts manufactured, local spirits and gods placated, and raids organized. Land is disbursed by local heads to families living in the community. Game, honey, and other wild resources are shared with neighbors, who are often relatives. In large measure, these communities are self-sustaining and quasi-autonomous.

Villages are linked to neighboring villages by ties of kinship, trade, and ritual. Regional organizations emerge largely as the result of special problems. When neighboring tribes attack, a number of villages may join together for defense. When local feuds threaten everyday life, meetings are held between villages to make peace. When drought strikes, people from several communities conduct rites to appease the tribal gods. Such regional organizations generally center around one task and are created only as special needs arise.

The tribe itself is often the weakest unit of organization. Its peripheral communities may develop close relationships and cultural similarities with people of neighboring tribes (Sahlins 1968, 16). A large tribe often has fuzzy boundaries and may exist primarily as a societal category—a group of people who believe that they share the same kind of blood and can therefore marry one another.

Associations

Kin and geographic groups dominate the social organization in most tribes, but associations also play an important role in everyday life. Women join to form work teams and women's societies. Men organize hunting and military associations and male societies. Specialists such as ironsmiths and potters form simple trade guilds. Such associations vary from informal, short-lived gatherings to formal associations with limited membership, explicit rules and functions, property, and specialized or secret knowledge.

Sex-based associations

Three types of association deserve special mention. The first is associations based on sex. Men's clubs are common. They provide a place for male entertainment and solidarity and a refuge from females, who are often considered spiritually dangerous.

In New Guinea, for example, boys move into the bachelors' house when they approach manhood. They are admonished to avoid their mothers and sisters and to join in male activities. When boys reach puberty, they are formally initiated into the fraternity of men by means of rituals that mark their death as children and their resurrection as men. They are given new names and new male privileges and are told the secrets that set men apart from women and make them superior. Women are rigidly excluded from the club house and from many rituals connected with the men's association.

Initiation rites keep the social order clear, reinforcing sex roles and minimizing the ambiguities of the transition from childhood to adulthood. Young males are boys and associate with women and girls. After the initiation rites, they are men and join other men in male activities.

Many men choose to live permanently in the men's longhouse. They occasionally visit their wives and small children living in nearby huts, but they find the company of men more exciting. In their younger years they plan sexual escapades and courtships; in their older years they plan raids on neighboring tribes and hunts. Men's associations make certain that men act as good fathers and husbands and discipline members who give men a bad name.

Women's associations are not as common. Initiation into womanhood often includes seclusion and special training in female knowledge. Sometimes it includes female circumcision. In some cultures, these associations discipline women who are not good wives or who discredit women in the community.

Age grades

A second important basis for forming associations is age. In many societies in North and South America and in sub-Saharan Africa we find age grades and age sets. Young men of similar ages are initiated into manhood together and form an age set. Throughout life they are "brothers."

Every few years all the sets move up to the grade above. As the initiates grow older they become warriors and a new set of initiates is formed. The warriors defend the society and police the people. During these years they are often allowed to have sexual liaisons that may lead later to marriage. At the next transition, warriors become family heads. They marry, settle down, and have children. As they grow older, the men become junior leaders, then senior leaders responsible for administering the tribe, and finally retired elders who advise the leaders. The number and nature of age grades varies from society to society.

Age grades help resolve the inherent tensions between people of different ages by formalizing the relationship between them. People must treat men in sets above them as fathers and grandfathers and those below them as sons and grandsons. Throughout life, every man has many fathers who discipline him and many sons whom he must rear. Age is also a factor in marriage. Among the Masai of East Africa, for instance, a man may marry the sister but not the daughter of a fellow age mate.

Secret societies

A third type of association is secret societies. These are widespread, especially in tribes in West Africa and North America. The distinguishing aspect of these societies lies in their secret membership and esoteric knowledge. Secret societies commonly practice powerful magic and sorcery by which they inspire fear in the public and gain power for their members. Occasionally, as in West Africa, women have their own secret societies.

Economic Systems

Tribal economies are more complex than band economies. This is seen in two important areas: the domestication of plants and animals, and the development of more complex technologies. These enable people to settle down in semipermanent and permanent settlements and to have large numbers of people living together.

Horticultural Tribes

The domestication of plants has a profound effect on human societies. People are less dependent on the whims of nature for wild food. A few can produce enough to feed many and this eventually enables others to be chiefs, priests, potters, ironworkers, and traders. This specialization of roles has multiplied so that today in North America and Europe, less than 5 percent of the people produce food for everyone. The rest are free to perform a myriad of other tasks.

Simple horticultural societies use what is called swidden, or slash-and-burn, cultivation. People clear the undergrowth in the forest, ring the trees to kill them, burn the fields to clear them, and use simple digging sticks to plant crops between the stumps. The work is seasonal. Preparation of the fields is undertaken in the dry season and cultivation is timed to catch the rains.

The main crops include manioc (originally from South America), maize (American, now worldwide), sweet potatoes and yams (Oceania, now Africa and elsewhere), and taro and banana (Oceania and Southeast Africa, now widespread). Normally one is the principal crop, but others are usually interspersed on the same plot of land.

Horticultural farming depends heavily on human effort. There are no plows or draft animals. Adults spend on an average from five hundred to a thousand hours a year in agricultural tasks or an average of ten to twenty hours a week (Sahlins 1968, 30). The people use simple tools such as digging sticks and iron axes, hoes, and machetes. Fields are small—cleared plots are often less than an acre. In many tropical regions, two and a half acres supply a family of five to eight people for a year.

Swidden societies are seminomadic. Every few years the fertility of the soil is depleted, so people must move on and clear new fields. The old fields are abandoned for a few years to allow fertility to be restored through reforestation. Then the area may be cleared again for another cycle of cultivation and fallow. Because of this periodic migration, social structures remain relatively small and flexible and material accumulations are limited to what can be transported every few years. An estimated two hundred million people, many of them in Amazonia, Oceania, and the Congo basin, still farm by these time-tested methods (Conklin 1961, 27).

The family is the unit of production and consumption. Sex and age determine an individual's tasks. Women rear the children and do most of the agricultural labor, domestic chores, and food preparation. Men do heavy agricultural labor, hunt and fish, and conduct village affairs.

The residence pattern in swidden societies is small hamlets or villages of up to two hundred people, surrounded by scattered agricultural plots and separated from each other by several miles. These small communities are autonomous. They control certain lands, produce the food needed by the people, and govern themselves.

Many tribes have richer soils that enable them to farm the land continuously. Some have developed simple irrigation systems in arid lands, using rivers and streams to raise crops. Others live near oases with their permanent supplies of water and plants. All these tribes are sedentary and develop rich material cultures. Because a great deal of effort is invested in terraced fields and irrigation systems, land is valuable and ownership is carefully defined. Larger political systems often emerge to maintain the cooperation needed to maintain irrigation systems and to keep peace among the people.

Land is the primary resource in horticultural tribes. It is often seen as a gift of God to their ancestors and is closely tied to their identity. People are often known by where they live. There is where their ancestors and gods reside. There is the soil that produced the food that formed their bodies. The equation of a people with their land and the gods of that land is foundational to their view of the world.

Land is generally owned by local lineages, not by individuals. A young man wanting to farm must ask his lineage elders. They allocate lineage land to him. So long as he farms it, he may use it. When he stops, the land reverts to the lineage. It cannot be sold.

Occasionally, when a lineage has extra land, it lends plots to members of another lineage or to strangers who join the hamlet. These people, in return, offer gifts of thanks for the right to use the land. On demand, however, they must return the land to the lineage, for it belongs not only to the living, but to the living dead and the unborn as well.

This understanding of group ownership leads to a great deal of confusion when the modern world, with its individual ownership of property, encroaches on tribal lands. For example, the Native Americans invited the early colonists to settle on unused lands. The colonists thought they were buying the land with the small gifts they gave, but the Native Americans believed that one cannot sell land. It belongs to the gods, ancestors, and people forever. Later, when the Native Americans wanted their lands back, the colonists accused them of being "Indian givers."

Many horticultural tribes have domesticated animals, usually dogs, pigs, and chickens. Some keep goats and cows for milk and meat, not for pulling plows and carts. Animals play a secondary role in these societies.

Large tribes have markets. With the rise of technology and craftsmen who specialize in manufacturing goods, a rich material culture emerges. Baskets, pottery, bronze and iron tools, clothing, body decorations, weapons, and religious objects are made and traded for food and other goods at markets that meet every four or five days. Women are often the chief traders, vending agricultural produce and other wares.

While economics is the immediate reason for these regional gatherings, an important purpose is social. People from surrounding villages gather to trade, gossip, and visit with relatives and friends from other neighborhoods.

Pastoral Tribes

A second type of tribal society centers around the domestication of animals. Pastoral nomads have adapted their lives to open, semi-arid grasslands, rather than tropical forests. They depend on cattle, sheep, horses, and other animals for their livelihood and make little use of plant cultivation.

Pastoral nomads number in the tens of millions. They make up one-fifth of the population of Arabia and one-tenth of the people of the Southwest Asian mountains and plateaus. Classic examples are found in the transcontinental dry belt of Asia (Mongols, nomadic Turks, Tibetans, Lapps) and in sub-Saharan Africa (Bedouins, Fulani of West Africa, Turkana and Masai of East Africa). In the New World they include the Navaho of the southwest U.S. and some of the Quechua in the Andes.

Pastoralists are nomadic because they must move their large herds of animals from pasture to pasture and waterhole to waterhole. Treks are often long and tedious. These frequently follow an annual cycle from specific lands in the wet or cold season to other ones in the dry or hot season. Some nomads cover a thousand miles a year. An old Chinese adage says, "Their country is the back of a horse."

Nomadic camps are generally small, usually no more than one hundred to two hundred people. For short periods, several camps may join for summer festivities, trade, and exchange of brides.

Because pastoralists use animals as beasts of burden to carry their goods, they can have more sophisticated shelters, tools, and other material culture than bands. Nevertheless, too many goods restrict the pastoralists' freedom to move and their ability to care for their stock.

Livestock are people's primary resource. Animals provide people with food (milk, meat, blood), dung for fuel, hides for leather utensils, and wool and hides for clothing and housing. Wood and other natural resources are available on their travels. In extreme climates people may depend on a single species—the camel in North Africa, cattle in Southwest Asia, and reindeer in Siberia. Most pastoralists raise different kinds of animals. For example, pastoralists on the Central Asian steppes raise horses, cattle, sheep, and goats.

The lives of nomads center around the care of their animals. Among the Masai, a man's status is measured by the number of cattle he has. He knows each by name and can distinguish it by color, size, shape of horns, sex, age, personality, and its special characteristics. He needs about 30 cows to insure the survival of a family of eight, but normally has about 100 to 140. Milk makes up about three-quarters of the Masai diet, meat and blood about a quarter. Women and children own their own cattle, but all are cared for by the men.

Animals not only are economic assets, but also are important as gifts. Trade focuses on the exchange of resources for economic purposes. Gift giving, however, is used to reinforce social relationships and not for material gain. Cattle, horses, and other animals are frequently given as marriage gifts to the relatives of the bride in exchange for the children she will bear the groom's family. The exchange is not buying a bride, any more than exchanging Christmas gifts in the west is buying good will.

Animals are also slaughtered for feasts or given to others as signs of hospitality. They are sacrificed as offerings to the gods and ancestors.

Finally, animals are used to pay debts and make restitution. A murderer may be expected to give a sizable gift to the victim's kin to restore relationships between the two groups.

Sheep and other small animals reproduce rapidly, but herds of large animals take a decade or two to double. Consequently, when droughts and disease decimate a herd of cattle, it is easier to replenish the herd by raiding other camps than to raise new animals. Cattle raiding is divisive, however, and ways are needed to keep violence in check and to make certain that all groups have access to scarce resources such as grass and water. As we will see, such decisions are usually made by the leading men of neighboring camps or are imposed on the camps by a paramount chief.

Most pastoralists live in symbiotic relationships to agricultural communities on the margins of their societies. From these communities they acquire metal tools and utensils, weapons, salt, grains, vegetables, cloth for clothing and tents, and other essentials. In return they trade milk, cheese, meat, and skins.

The relationship between camp and village is profitable for both, but often fraught with tensions. Herdsmen have a contempt for settled life and often raid the villages, particularly when droughts force them off the grasslands. Their envy of the riches of the towns, however, often draws them near for trade. Farming people often fear the herdsmen and curse them as uncivilized marauders.

Political and Legal Systems

Power and authority at the level of the household and the hamlet are vested in the heads of the families and local communities. There are no police, no jails, and no army. Leadership in families is generally held by senior males and is inherited. In a hamlet it is often in the hands of the leader of the dominant lineage. Social control is also exercised by the group through gossip, shaming, fining, beating, cursing, and, if necessary, ostracism.

Tribes differ from bands because they have higher levels of political organization with regional power and authority. Broadly speaking, these fall into two types: segmentary stateless societies and chiefdoms.

Segmentary Stateless Societies

Segmentary tribes, for the most part, are agricultural and are found in Amazonia, Melanesia, North America, and several parts of Africa. Unlike chiefdoms, where power and authority are concentrated in centralized superstructures, in stateless societies they are decentralized to the point that small, local communities carry the main burden of government. These communities rarely include more than a few hundred people.

The organizing principle in local communities and in the tribe is segmentation, with opposition and cooperation between the segments (fig. 18, following page). In the local community there are a number of households from one or more lineages. In the tribe there are a number of lineages and/or clans. The structure is the same: several primary segments are structurally equivalent. None is by right superior and none structurally inferior. All are jealous of their own sovereignty and none recognizes a greater political organization standing over and against their separate interests. Moreover, no segment is economically or socially dependent on the others. In other words, they are functionally equivalent.

Figure 18
Segmentary Stateless Societies

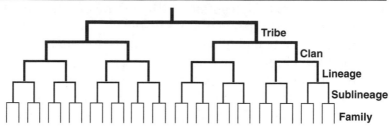

Integration between segmentary units is based in part on common ventures. Sahlins notes, "Certain groups may ally for a time and a purpose, as for a military venture, but the collective spirit is episodic. When the objective for which it was called into being is accomplished, the alliance lapses and the tribe returns to its normal state of disunity" (1968, 11).

Integration is also based on the fact that segments on one level join together on a higher level. Several households stand in opposition to one another, but may belong to the same secondary lineage. This local lineage stands in opposition to other secondary lineages, but unites with some of them to form a primary lineage. A number of these unite to form a clan and clans unite to form a tribe. Consequently, when two men quarrel, the matter goes to the leaders of the sublineage, lineage, clan, or tribe, whoever has immediate authority over them.

Despite these forces for integration, segmentary tribes tend to be loosely organized. Segmentation leads to rivalries, feuds, and raids in which many are captured, maimed, and killed.

On the highest level, as we have seen, there is no government to maintain peace between tribes. The result is often intertribal raids and wars. The conquered are either assimilated into the victors' tribe or move on to another piece of land.

This tension between cooperation and competition makes for fluid relationships. At one moment you are fighting with the next household; the next moment you join it to oppose another lineage. Then you join with members of that lineage to raid another clan or tribe. In other words, you take sides in a fight on the basis of your closest loyalty, not on the issues involved. Relationships take priority over tasks and beliefs.

Leadership in stateless societies is divided among the leaders of the segments. Lineage and clan leaders deal with affairs in their lineage and clan and negotiate with leaders of other lineages and clans. Rarely is there one official leader.

"Big-men" may emerge, however, who dominate a village or a region, not by holding an office, but by strength of their personality, by persuasiveness, by prowess as a warrior, gardener, or magician, or by distributing wealth so that people are under obligation to them. In certain Melanesian tribes, big-men may gain renown in a number of local groups and so unite them for rituals, trade, and war.

Segmentary tribes are essentially egalitarian. Heads of families and lineage leaders exercise considerable authority. Clans and tribes have less solidarity and their leaders exercise less coercive authority. The leaders must depend on their charisma and the support of their kinsmen to persuade others in the clan and tribe to follow them.

Tribes have little social hierarchy for another reason. The poor and weak are members of lineages with powerful leaders who must defend them. The reputation of a lineage and clan depends, in part, on how it cares for all its members, not on the power and wealth of the leaders, just as the success of a baseball team depends on its team's wins and losses, not on the number of home runs its leader hits. There is little evidence of class distinction, and the poor have a voice that is heard by those in power.

So far we have looked at tribes in which segmentation is based on kinship alone. Here the father is the head of the family. Lineage, clan, and tribal leaders are seen as fathers of their respective groups. They are expected to take care of their people. They can demand certain goods and people give them gifts. In turn, they are expected to give generously to those in need.

Some tribes develop more complex systems combining two or more cross-cutting sets of segments (fig. 19, following page). For example, the Jie of Uganda have lineages based on kinship ties. They also have age grades that unite people into groups on the basis of age. Finally, they have strong local groups based on territory. Consequently, most people are related to one another in one or more ways. When two people quarrel, the case is mediated by the lineage head, if they belong to the same lineage; by the leader

Figure 19
Intersecting Segments Found in Some Stateless Societies

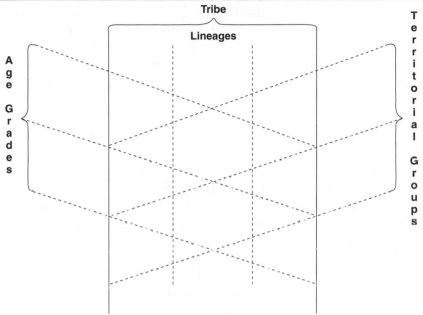

of the age grade, if they belong to the same age grade; and by the village headman, if they live in the same village.

Multiple segmentation facilitates tribal integration and works against feuds. People join their lineage mates to hoe and plant crops and to placate the ancestors. They join members of an age set to build houses, maintain order in the village, and care for cattle. They work with others in the village to organize hunts and to care for one another. People divided by one type of segmentation are united by another.

Chiefdoms

In many tribes, notably of Polynesia and Micronesia, Caribbean America, Central Asia, and Southwest Africa, power is concentrated in the hands of chiefs and councils of elders who hold a socially recognized status or office. Unlike segmentary tribes, where power and authority are diffuse, in chiefdoms those qualities are concentrated in a central legal structure.

Chiefdoms are hierarchical societies. There may be lineages and clans but these are not equal. That of the chief ranks higher than the others. Most chiefdoms have no sharply defined social classes. Rarely are there permanent underclasses set apart from a noble class. At times there are slaves, but, as we have seen, these are generally absorbed into the tribe over time.

In chiefdoms, members of the dominant lineage often must get their wives from the other lineages. Consequently, "noblemen" are relatives of "commoners." Moreover, all lineages own land and raise their own food. They are not dependent on the dominant lineage for their livelihood.

The rise of chiefdoms is more than the appearance of big-men. It is the emergence of a legal system of chieftainship in which a hierarchy of authorities has power over the tribe and its subdivisions. It is a chain of command linking the paramount chief to lesser chiefs and ultimately to local village chiefs. The authority and power of the chiefs lie in the socially recognized offices they hold rather than their own skills and abilities (Sahlins 1968, 260). They acquire these offices either by heredity from their father or by appointment by the paramount chief.

This centralization of power and authority counters the divisive tendencies found in segmented societies. The chief has the right to impose his decisions on his people if they do not agree. Moreover, it enables the chief to mobilize large masses of people to build temples, palaces, and irrigation systems and to command resources to maintain armies and courts. The result is a greater specialization of labor. Farmers, cattle raisers, craftsmen, traders, government officials, and soldiers may eventually be integrated into a single political system.

Centralization also has its costs. Levies and taxes are generally a heavy burden on the people, and leaders often misuse their authority for personal gain and prestige.

The Cultural Order

Tribal cultures vary greatly, in part because they are particularistic. Each tribe has its own gods, its own customs, and often its own language. Consequently, any generalizations about tribal cultures must be taken with a great deal of caution. We must study carefully the tribe to which we minister. Nevertheless, certain cultural patterns are common to many tribes and examining them can serve as a starting point for our study of specific tribal cultures.

Symbols, Myths, and Rituals

Fundamental to a tribal culture are the symbols it uses and the ways in which it looks at and uses these symbols.

Symbols

For the most part, tribes are oral societies. People store their information in their memories and recall and transmit it with the aid of stories, songs, poetry, riddles, proverbs, aphorisms, and dramas. They make extensive use of carvings, masks, paintings, narrative dances, and other aesthetic forms in the performance of rituals and these, too, preserve information for future generations.

Myths and Rituals

Two forms of communication play a particularly important role in tribal societies, namely, myths and rituals. Most tribal societies have extensive myths about creation and about the origins of the tribe and its culture. Other myths explain why things are as they are: how evil and death entered the world, why animals are different from humans, and what causes lightning and thunder.

Myths are not histories or rational explanations of the natural world, nor are they meant to be. To western minds they often appear to be superstitious mixtures of fantasies and contradictions, with little story or plot. These are not, however, the product of a primitive mentality. They are allegorical commentaries on what people think is the underlying hidden reality of the world and life. Myths are based on intuitive insight into the mysteries of the universe and must be understood as philosophies clothed in symbolic and poetic language.

Bronislaw Malinowski points out that myths are the "charters for belief." They help people understand their place in the universe and what they think about things. In contrast, creeds, which organize beliefs in rational systems, are found chiefly in the great religions that developed with the rise of writing and complex civilizations. They are absent, and perhaps unnecessary, in tribal societies.

Myths speak of cosmic processes using words. Rituals do so using actions. In the broadest sense, rituals include all formally defined patterns of behavior, from greeting one another to worship at a shrine.

Like myths, rituals speak of deeper meanings. For example, following is a typical greeting between two Americans who know each other:

Tom	Mary
"Hi."	"Hi."
"How are you?"	"Just fine, and you?"
"Doing O.K. Nice day, isn't it?"	"Sure is. Wish we had more like it."
"Ya, got to go now, see you later."	"Ya, see you later."

On the surface, this looks like a simple exchange of information about health and weather. Further analysis shows that this is not the case. Mary says "fine!" even if she is feeling sick and just had an argument with her boss. Mary is not lying when she says "fine." The whole exchange is not about the weather or how she feels, but about the state of the relationship between Tom and her. She is affirming that their relationship is still good. If she says nothing, Tom's reaction is, "Doesn't she like me?" Rituals speak more about the underlying relationships between people, or between people and other beings such as God, than about what they say to each other.

Another example of how rituals function is an American church wedding. The bride is dressed in white and the groom in formal attire. They treat each other with the greatest love and respect and pledge to live only for the other. They are courteous to their new in-laws. A few months later at home alone, things are often quite different. The new husband and wife argue, ignore each other, and want their own way.

Why then the poetic talk of love and self-sacrifice in the marriage rite? Here the ritual not only publicly establishes a new relationship between them—that of a married couple; it also states the society's ideals for marriage—what a marriage should look like. The fact that no one lives up to the ideal all the time does not make it irrelevant. Without ideals no truly human society is possible.

Rituals use ordinary words and actions and give them special, transcendent meanings. For example, in Christianity we use water in baptism and it becomes a symbol of death and new life; we use bread in the Lord's Supper and it speaks of fellowship and shared life.

However, people in tribal societies use rituals not only to speak of deeper things, but also to cause things to happen. The elders performing the Rain Dance are not merely asking the gods for rain; they believe they are actually causing rain to come. The shaman brushing the patient with a wisp of grass believes he is thereby driving off the evil spirits. The tribesman pouring out water on the ground to assuage its thirst is making sure the earth will be pleased and will bring forth crops that feed him.

Tribal people do not separate symbols from reality in their rituals. This is hard for western Protestants to understand, because they have grown up in societies that divorce symbols from realities and thus have few powerful rituals.

Rituals in tribal societies maintain relationships between the living, the ancestors, spirits, and gods. They also mark the important transformations in people's lives: from nonhuman to child (birth rites), from child to adult (initiation rites), from adult to married person (marriage rites), and from person to living ancestor (funerals). Psychologically, rituals help people to adjust to their new states. Sociologically, they restructure the relationships of the person in the society. Religiously, they change the ontological state of the person.

Cultural Knowledge

Cultural knowledge in tribal societies deals mainly with people, nature, spirits, and magic. In segmented societies, most knowledge is shared by all members of a community. There are few bodies of specialized knowledge except those of the shaman and the craftsmen who work with wood and iron. In chiefdoms, with their greater specialization of roles and knowledge, there emerge communities of people who share different types of technical knowledge.

Tribal knowledge is wholistic. The people make no sharp distinction between supernatural and natural events. They may distinguish between seen and unseen realities, but both are part of this world. Religion is not a segment of life. It is central to the culture as a whole.

For purposes of analysis, we will distinguish between science and religion as different domains of cultural knowledge. We must remember, however, that tribal people do not differentiate between them. When people plant a crop, they know how to prepare the seed and soil, how to plant and weed, and how to harvest the crop. At the same time they know that other forces also affect the harvest. Consequently, they seek to control the rains and pests by using magic and by praying to God to make their seed fertile and their crops abundant.

Science and Technology

All people have basic scientific knowledge of natural causes. Over the centuries, farmers learned how to clear the land, plant the seed, tend the crops, grind the grain, and cook different foods. Hunters learned how to track game in the forest and how to make traps, weapons, and poisons to kill them. Gatherers are experts at distinguishing edible from inedible plants—their, and their children's, lives depend on it. Coastal people know from experience what kind of trees to cut, how to hollow them and make outriggers to stabilize them, and ways to paddle or sail them in rough waters. Seafarers know how to navigate hundreds of miles across an open ocean and reach islands they cannot see when they set out. Potters discovered how to fire clay and smiths how to extract metals from ore and shape them into tools and decorations. Herbal doctors make medicines from trees and bushes. Every tribe has a great deal of such scientific knowledge about nature and the world around it. Without such knowledge, people would die.

Every tribe also has a great deal of knowledge about people and how they function. People have ideas about childrearing, settling disputes between wives, making recalcitrant husbands more responsible, and leading people in corporate activities. In other words, they have their own social sciences.

Magic and Witchcraft

Science, however, has its limits. Where it fails, people often turn to magic, witchcraft, and religion for explanations and control. The tribal's experience has taught him, Malinowski writes (1954, 28–29),

. . . that in spite of all his forethought and beyond all his efforts there are agencies and forces which one year bestow unwanted and unearned benefits of fertility, making everything run smooth and well, rain and sun appear at the right moment, noxious insects remain in abeyance, the harvest yields a superabundant crop; and another year again the same agencies bring ill luck and bad chance, pursue him from beginning till end and thwart all his most strenuous efforts and his best-found knowledge. To control these influences and these only he employs magic.

Even when scientific explanations can give answers to the question "how," there remain the questions of "why" and "why now and why me." A boy dies because a ladder breaks and he falls. A scientific answer to the cause of death is that the ladder was rotting and the boy was too heavy for it. But this does not answer the questions his parents are asking: "Why did it happen to our son; why not the boy who climbed the ladder before him; and why do we have to suffer the pain of losing him?" It is to answer these questions that people often turn to magic and witchcraft for answers.

Magic

Magic is based on the belief that there are invisible forces, like electricity but supernatural in character, that influence events in this world. These forces follow certain laws and those who know them can control these forces for their own benefit. Robert H. Codrington, a missionary in Melanesia, wrote (1969, 118–20),

The Melanesian mind is entirely possessed by the belief in a supernatural power or influence, called almost universally *mana*. This is what works to affect everything which is beyond the ordinary power of men, outside the common processes of nature; it is present in the atmosphere of life, attaches itself to persons and things, and is manifested by results which can only be ascribed to its operation.

Beliefs in supernatural power are widespread. Indonesians speak of *toh*, the people of the West Solomons of *magit* or "soul stuff," the Sioux of *wakanda*, the Crow of *maxpe*, and the Zairians of *elima*.

In many tribes this energy or vital force is seen as the basis of all reality. Gods, humans living and departed, animals, plants, and minerals—all things have energy and exist only as they have vital force. Families, lineages, and tribes, too, have corporate vital force and their happiness and prosperity depend on conserving and strengthening this force.

The vital force exercised by individuals must be kept in balance and steps taken to guard against other forces that are dangerous to one's own life forces. Regarding sub-Saharan Africa Stephen Neill writes (1961, 133),

> The European thinks in terms of 'being' or 'existence.' The African thinks in terms of 'vital force' or 'energy.' Anything that exists is a 'force.' This vital force can be increased or it can be threatened or diminished. When a man's vital force is on the increase, he is well. If an African is tired, he says 'I am dying,' a phrase which sounds ridiculously exaggerated in European ears, but which to the African is perfectly sensible, as implying the sense of a diminution of vital powers which, unless repaired or checked, will lead in the long run to his decease.

Mana, or supernatural power, is found in certain culturally defined places such as in the body of a great warrior, in certain wild animals, and in strange objects that bring success to their owners. It can be acquired by eating part of such animals or warriors, by fasting and abstaining from sexual relations and, above all, by proper rituals. It can be stored and concentrated by people who know how to handle it. It can be lost, making a warrior weak and easy to defeat.

Magic, the control of these forces using the proper chants, amulets, and rituals, is amoral. It can be used for good or for evil. In fact, what is good in the eyes of the one performing the magic may be destructive to the person on the receiving end (Shorter 1985, 100).

Most magic is used to benefit the people, particularly when it is practiced by a community. The shaman or medicine man performs rituals for the family, lineage, or tribe to control the weather, prevent diseases, assure victories in battle over enemies, punish deviants, and bring prosperity.

Used individually and secretly, however, magic often advances selfish and evil ends. A man seeks to gain advantage over a neighbor using "waste away" magic. He curses a rival to kill him or casts a love spell on a woman to compel her into an illicit relationship.

Like electricity, magical power can be dangerous to those who do not know how to handle it. A rock or a tree full of *mana* can kill those who touch it. Consequently, where magic is practiced, there are taboos to protect ordinary people from danger. Magicians, witches, witchdoctors, and other religious specialists, however, know how to control powerful forces without destroying themselves.

Witchcraft

The power of magic is believed to be particularly dangerous in the hands of witches. These are people who are thought to have great power that they can use against others. Some witches publicly acknowledge their practices and are widely feared. Others are falsely accused of being witches: old or mentally deranged people, those with no kin to defend them, and those who are antisocial.

Witchcraft is common in societies in which people explain everything in terms of human actions. They do not believe in accidents, chance, or natural causes. They know that the man cut his leg because his ax bounced off the wood and hit it, but their question is why this happened to this man on this occasion, when he has been chopping wood for years without an accident. In these societies, every misfortune and death is blamed on some person and that person is believed to cause it by means of magic or witchcraft.

Some witches are thought to inherit their powers, others to learn it from other witches. Most are seen as antisocial and as living lives opposite that of normal humans. They stay up at night, have their feet on backward, and fly in the air. They are often thought to transform themselves into wolves, rabbits, cats, and other animals, to travel great distances in a moment of time, and to have special ties to owls, snakes, hyenas, and baboons. They are accused of acting in vile self-interest and of refusing to share what they have with others. In short, the witch epitomizes the opposite of what a given culture considers normal and normative.

Belief in witchcraft serves a number of social and religious purposes. E. E. Evans-Pritchard (1937, 50) notes that in small, strongly group-oriented societies it forces people to conform to the social norms and deters deviance from the group. People fear that if they are different, contentious, or conspicuously successful they will excite the envy of others and will be accused of being witches.

Witchcraft is also a socially structured way to handle interpersonal hostilities. It may provide a channel by which people can deal with hatred, frustration, jealousy, and guilt as well as a socially acceptable opportunity for aggression, vengeance, and gaining prestige and attention. It relieves people's anxieties by allowing them to express fear of another person's malicious intent, and to break off relationships that have become intolerable, something that is common in small, tight-knit societies.[3]

Although witchcraft serves these functions in a society, it is socially pathological. Where it is found, people live in fear of being accused of being a witch and of antagonizing someone else who might secretly be a witch. At times these fears lead to antagonism and hatred that undermine the harmony of the community. In either case, the gospel of reconciliation in Christ is good news indeed.

Religion

The world of tribal societies is full not only of impersonal powers, but also of vital life forces and living beings. Gods, spirits of the air, trees, mountains and rivers, ancestors, ghosts, animals, and plants all inhabit the same land.

Gods and High God

The highest of the beings are the gods who live in the sky. They are powerful and play an important role in giving rain, children, and success in life. Humans make offerings to the gods to make certain that these remain favorably disposed to them and to placate those who are angry.

There is a widespread belief, found in about two-thirds of tribal societies, that there is one supreme creator or High God. The Masai call him Engai. The Yoruba call him Olodumare.

Most tribes believe that this High God is now angry with them. For example, the Ashanti say that a woman pounding grain raised her pounding stick too high and hit him as he sat in the clouds, so he became angry and left people to their own devices (Rubingh 1974, 3). The Ibo of Nigeria say that God became tired of being bothered by every little complaint the people made (Metuh 1981, 13). People still remember him and pray to him in large group ceremonies, but in everyday life they must deal with the spirits, ancestors, ghosts, and witches around them through the use of rituals.

Spirits

Spirits play a very important role in most tribal religions. For the most part these are thought to live on earth, not in some heaven or hell. Many spirits are associated with particular animals, trees, rivers, rocks, or mountain passes. They may be ghosts of those who died tragic deaths. They may be the spirits of lightning or sickness. In most cases, their power is local, extending little further than their abode. In some cases the spirits are seen as good or evil. Most are thought to be like humans, combining both good and evil. They help those who placate them and plague those who neglect them.

Most western people find it hard to think in terms of this-worldly spirits. Given the modern dualism that separates supernatural realities from natural ones, westerners tend to think of gods as living in the heavens and demons in hell. They no longer believe in spirits that live in the forest, river, or mountain pass. To tribals, however, earthly spirits are as much a part of the neighborhood as are trees, animals, and humans. Westerners also find it hard to think of these spirits as neither all good nor all bad, neither angels nor demons.

Ancestors and the unborn

People in most tribes do not see themselves as separate, autonomous beings. They are important because they are linked to others in families, clans, and tribes with whom they share the same life force. To be an autonomous individual is to be as good as dead. As John Mbiti notes, an African says, "I belong, therefore I am."

Central to this corporate view of life is the concept of linkage or connectedness. Life is not seen as divided into discrete units. It is an unending stream that flows from parent to child, from generation to generation (fig. 20, following page). The tie between parent and child is much more than biological. It is social and spiri-

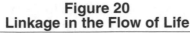

Figure 20
Linkage in the Flow of Life

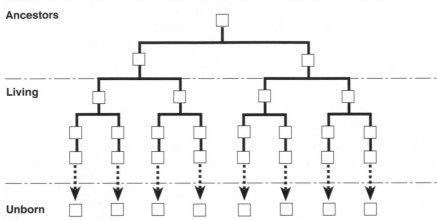

tual. Consequently, the righteousness of the parents brings blessings to their children, and the sins of the parents bring punishment on their children and children's children. In western, individualistic thought, each person and generation begins anew and each person should be judged by her or his own actions. Not so in tribal societies, where good and evil are attributed to whole families and clans.

The concept of linkage provides people with a sense of their identity and security. They are not individuals who happen to live in families. They exist only as they exist in families, clans, and tribes first. These give people birth, rear them, marry them, give them land, help rear their children, feed them when they have no food, transform them into ancestors, and immortalize them by remembering them when they are gone.

Belief in connectedness also provides people with a sense of social control. The good of the family and tribe is more important than personal gain. Therefore parents of the same lineage or clan readily care for and discipline one another's children. Similarly, the group condemns those who seek their own gain at the expense of others. There is no need for jails, because the offender is ostracized.

Linkage continues after death. Parents do not depart; they become ancestors vitally interested in the well-being of the family to which they gave life. People often believe that the ancestors continue to live in the village and must be fed and housed. Mbiti refers to them as the living dead because they continue to exist among the living.

Ancestors are seen as important for a number of reasons. First, they are the progenitors of the family and therefore have a natural interest in caring for it. They have ancient knowledge not known by the living and can advise the living regarding family decisions. They also discipline the unruly.

Second, ancestors exist beyond death and so have knowledge of the spirit world hidden from the living. They see the witches and ghosts that plague humans and protect the living from them.

Third, great ancestors are remembered for their power and achievements. The accomplishments of the living never equal those of the founder of the tribe, the great warrior who delivered them from destruction and the hero who brought culture to the people. For instance, in Israel the people remembered Abraham, Isaac, and Jacob for their accomplishments, especially in responding to God's call.

Not all the dead become ancestors. Some leave no descendants to keep alive their memory, some are so insignificant in life that no account needs to be taken of them, and some suffer untimely or tragic deaths and become malevolent spirits that take out their discontentment on the living. Their bodies may be cremated and the ashes scattered to prevent them from returning to plague the living.

The living must maintain good relationships with the ancestors, those great ones who are no longer visible but who watch over the tribe and care for its interests. They are given food and drink, assigned places of honor at important events, and formally addressed at rituals. Their injunctions must be obeyed to maintain the balance of forces so that the tribe prospers. Angry ancestors cause a great deal of trouble for everyone.

The tribe is dependent on the ancestors and the ancestors on the living who keep their memories alive and care for them. It is important, therefore, to have many children, particularly sons, who will remember you after you are gone.

Ancestor veneration serves several important functions. First, it provides people with a theory of misfortune and how to deal with it. Many disasters occur because people have neglected or

disobeyed the living dead. The living must then appease the ancestors to gain their blessing.

A second function is to reinforce social traditions. Ancestors
become the foundation for law. Tribal customs are not easily
changed when they are given and reinforced by the voice of the
ancestors as interpreted by the tribal leaders and the diviners.
Ancestors naturally prefer old ways and dislike new ones. Consequently, changes normally take place slowly because they must
have the approval of the ancestors.

A third function is to provide people with a cosmic view of reality and their place in it. They are not alone in a harsh, impersonal
world. They belong to large families and are surrounded by powerful ancestors. In this they find security and a sense of history.
What they do is not for themselves but for the group, which is
much larger than themselves.

Finally, belief in ancestors comforts the living, for those who
die remain among them as the living dead.

Totemism

In many tribes, the concept of linkage extends to animals and
sometimes to plants. Just as humans are divided into different
streams of life (lineages, clans, and tribes), so too animals and
plants are separated into different species (tigers, deer, eagles). In
totemic societies, each human lineage is thought to be related to
a particular species of animal and sometimes of plant.

Some tribes see this linkage as purely symbolic. Animal names
are used to portray the identity and spirit of different lineages and
clans, much as American football teams choose names such as
Eagles, Rams, and Colts to represent themselves.

Others believe that there are biospiritual linkages between
human clans and their totemic animals and plants. The people
often have myths showing the connection. For example, they may
tell of Old First Tiger who had three sons—the first a human who
was the father of the Tiger Clan, the second an animal and the
father of Tigers, and the third a plant and the father of all Tiger
Lilies. Humans of the Tiger Clan are, therefore, biologically and
spiritually related to tigers and tiger lilies.

People of a clan do not normally eat their own totemic animals and plants. Rather, they must ensure that these multiply so
that people of other clans have food. They eat their totemic ani-

mal or plant only in special rituals to show their special relationship to it.

In a sense, totemism is a religious ecology. Underlying it is the belief that human, animal, and plant life is linked together in one interdependent world. All nature, therefore, takes on religious significance and religion encourages the careful treatment of nature.

This view that humans are a part of nature and must live in harmony with it is found even in nontotemic tribes. It stands in sharp contrast to our modern view that humans must conquer nature and bring it under their control.

Meaning and Fear

Tribal religions make the world meaningful for people and assign them a place in it. Humans, spirits, ancestors, animals, plants, mountains, rivers, sun, moon, earth, and stars are part of one interconnected world.

Life in such a world, however, is rarely carefree and secure. S. D. Porteus notes (Neill 1961, 137),

Devils haunt to seize the unwary; their malevolent magic shadows [a person's] waking moments. [The tribesman] believes that medicine men know how to make themselves invisible so that they may cut out his kidney fat, and then sew him up and rub his tongue with a magic stone to induce forgetfulness, and thereafter he is a living corpse devoted to death.

In addition there is the fear of witchcraft, sorcery, black magic, curses, bad omens, evil spirits, broken taboos, angry ancestors, human enemies, and false accusations. Crops fail, game vanishes, plagues decimate the village, sudden death takes the young and strong, enemies attack at night, and rivals seek one's life. Life in most tribal societies is precarious and fear is a common thread running through it. In such situations the gospel is indeed good news, for it brings deliverance from the fear of the spirits and powers that plague people's lives.

Life, however, is not all fear. People find security in their kinship groups and joy in their community gatherings. They turn to ancestors and tribal gods for help and to magic and divination to protect them from the dangers that surround them.

Worldview

Behind the cultural knowledge of tribal societies are fundamental assumptions about the nature of reality that shape how the
people view their world. There is a great deal of variation in tribal
worldviews. Nevertheless, some generalizations can be made that
apply to most tribes. Studying them can help us not only to make
sense of tribal cultures, but also to see the worldview we bring
with us when we go abroad (table 4, following page).

Wholistic

As we have seen, tribals see the world as one dynamic whole,
inhabited by people, ancestors, spirits, animals, mountains, and
rivers that are constantly interacting with one another. People
make no distinction between religious, economic, social, or political activities. There are few role specializations other than those
based on age and sex and no specialized institutions such as temples, governments, hospitals, and businesses.

Religion is not simply a segment of a life as it is in western cultures. It is at the heart of all life and affects everything one does:
how one eats, whom one marries, how one plants seeds, and
where one is buried. To convert to a new religion affects everything one does. Western societies, by contrast, slice life into semi-
autonomous segments: economic, social, political, legal, and religious. They see religious conversion as only changing one's religious beliefs and practices.

Organic-Relational

The world of tribal peoples is alive and dynamic. D. Zahan
writes,

> . . . the cosmos does not constitute a world which is fixed, cold and
> silent; on the contrary, it is a world full of meanings, the bearer of
> messages, a world which 'speaks'. Thus man finds in his sur-
> roundings a partner with whom he can enter into communication,
> with whom he must maintain a more or less constant dialogue if
> he wishes to learn about himself. (Buakasa 1986, 35–36)

In such a world, no distinction is made between supernatural and
natural beings. The village, forest, and plains are full of gods, spir-

Table 4
A Comparison of Tribal and Modern Worldviews

Wholistic
do not differentiate between
supernatural and natural
realities
do not slice life into
specialized segments

Segmented
differentiate between
supernatural and natural
realities
have specialized institutions
and areas of life

Organic
value relationships
less predictable world
negotiate activities
adapt to events, accept many
things as out of human control

Mechanistic
value technology and possessions
highly predictable world
plan activities
seek to control events, hold people
responsible for most failures

Human-Centered
group-oriented
stress sharing and mutual help
sense of corporate, relational self
failure leads to shame
strong sense of identity in
group
group ownership of property

Self-Centered
individualistic
stress self-reliance
the self-made person
failure leads to guilt
search for self-identity
through achievements
private ownership of property

Particularist View of Reality
each tribe lives in its own
world
each tribe has its own truth,
gods, and religion

Universalist View of Reality
all humans live in a
single, uniform world
truth, morality, and law
are the same for all

Space- and Land-Oriented
a sacred tie between gods,
ancestors, people, and land
time is cyclical
looks to the past

Time- and Future-Oriented
high value placed on time
and efficiency
time is linear, uniform,
and secular
looks to the future

Sound-Oriented
believe in what has been told
you by reliable people (elders)

Visual-Oriented
believe basically in what you
have seen yourself (eyewitness)

Concrete-Functional Thought
think in terms of concrete,
life-related activities
tell stories, parables

Abstract-Analytical Thought
build analytical thought
systems based on abstract
reasoning
have rational debates

Rituals and Myths Are Important
sense of mystery in life
equate meanings and forms
symbols are things
rituals create and transform reality

Rituals and Myths Are Unimportant
seek to understand all things
separate forms and meanings
symbols merely represent things
rituals are "remembrances"

its, ancestors, humans, animals, and plants living together and experiencing anger, jealousy, concern, and love. They are surrounded by life force, mana, and other powers.

Relationships

In a world full of life, maintaining harmonious relationships with other living beings is essential to life. The Eskimo pours fresh water in the mouth of the seal he has caught because it was tired of salt water and so let itself be caught. The farmer makes an offering to the earth, asking its forgiveness for the pain he inflicts in planting seed. The pastoralist blesses his cattle so that they will bear young.

Relationships must constantly be negotiated. It is impossible, therefore, for humans to fully plan their lives. A man may agree to meet a friend the next morning, but at the last moment relatives stop by, the ancestors demand food, his cow has a calf, or the spirits harass him. It may be afternoon before he can come. People learn to live in an ever-changing flux of relationships—to "go with the flow" of everyday events.

Those of us with modern worldviews see the world as highly predictable. We believe the material world operates according to the impersonal laws of nature and try to control it by our sciences. We order our lives in great detail by means of clocks, calendars, timetables, and pocket schedules. We are upset when things are late or our plans go awry. We are frustrated, therefore, when we live in tribal societies where building relationships is more important than completing tasks and visiting more important than getting somewhere on time.

Morality

A world of relationships is a moral world. Impersonal forces like gravity and fire do not sin. Sin has to do with a break in relationships between humans, gods, spirits, ancestors, animals, and earth. The consequence is a loss of peace and the breakdown of the community. Reconciliation is the restoration of relationships and harmony.

In a relational world, a high value is placed on sharing and taking responsibility for those in one's group. Great people are not those who keep what they have for themselves but those who share freely with those in need.

Ancestors play an important role in maintaining moral standards in the tribe. They punish faults and reward good with peace, health, and fertility. Witchcraft, too, shapes people's sense of morality. It provides them an avenue to blame others for their misfortunes and to absolve themselves.

Fertility

Fertility is important in an organic worldview. The reproduction of life is essential for everything to continue. The fertility cycle shapes people's view of time. Crops are planted, harvested, and replanted. Animals and humans have their rounds of birth, marriage or mating, and death. Rituals are performed at these points to ensure fertility in nature and the tribe.

Many rituals are associated with fertility. This is not surprising given people's direct dependence on nature for food. Prayers are offered to game that is killed so that its relatives are not offended and will allow themselves to be taken in a hunt. Water is poured on the ground to slacken its thirst and to encourage it to provide a bounteous harvest. Dances are performed to ensure good rains. Seed and fields are blessed, and the first fruits of harvest offered to the ancestors, spirits, and gods in thanks. In pastoral societies, rites are performed to ensure and safeguard the reproduction of the animals.

Equally important are rites that guarantee fertility among humans. There are few evils so great as barrenness, which is often seen as a sign of the anger of gods or ancestors or the curse of a witch. Consequently, there are a great many rituals associated with marriage, pregnancy, and birth—to make mothers fertile and to safeguard them and infants during the dangerous months surrounding birth. Equally important are lifecycle rites that mark the other major transitions in life, namely, initiation into adulthood and transformation into an ancestor.

Human-Centeredness

Tribal worldviews, for the most part, are human centered. The universe itself is alive and is inhabited by high and lesser gods, spirits of many types and animals, all of whom share in the same vital force. But it is the ancestors, the living, and the unborn who are center stage (fig. 21, following page). It is the common life they share—as a family, as a lineage or a clan, and as a tribe—that must

Figure 21
Tribal Worldview

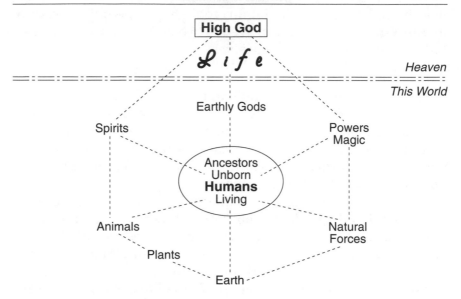

be preserved by supplicating, coercing, or bribing the surrounding gods and powerful but capricious spirits.

Group orientation

Human life finds its ultimate expression in the community, not the individual. Few themes in tribal worldviews are more difficult for western people to understand than this group-centeredness. Most of us take it for granted that all people see themselves as autonomous, individual humans. Self-reliance, personal achievement, and individual choice are unquestioningly good in our minds.

The fact is, in many tribal societies, people see *groups* as the important units of society—families, lineages, and clans. Individuals exist only in and for groups. So long as their group exists, they cannot die, for they will be remembered as ancestors. Their existence is tied to the unity and the continuity of their group.

In tribal societies, personal wants are subordinate to the needs of the lineage and the tribe. Group loyalty, self-effacement, self-sacrifice, sharing, and hospitality are cardinal virtues. Self-centeredness, hoarding, stinginess, and bringing shame on one's group by one's own behavior are sin.

An example of this group-oriented thought is the experience of a white teacher among the Hopi. In class she assigned a task and told students to raise their hands when they completed the work to see who could be first. When no student did so, even though they had completed the work, she became angry. She did not realize that the first one to raise a hand would put the others to shame and would be treated by them as arrogant. Similarly, tribes that adopt competitive games such as soccer often make sure that each game ends in a tie so that no one is shamed. Cooperation is valued more than competition in a group.

Harmony

Harmony is essential to group life, but it is precarious and threatened by the conflicts and uncertainties of everyday life. Change, therefore, is often viewed as a threat.

Social controls and religious rituals play an important part in creating and enhancing harmony. They provide every person a place within the group and prescribe their behavior. They affirm the importance of community in the life of the people.

Humans may preserve harmony, but they do not create it. William Dyrness points out, "[Harmony] is given by God and the ancestors. And it is enshrined in the normal orders of life and death, rainy season and dry, planting and harvest" (1990, 43). But, he adds, "[T]he darker side of life, its vulnerability, is equally important for theology. If life ordinarily goes well, it can also be threatened; indeed, at times life in Africa seems to be a constant struggle to fend off evil influences" (1990, 44). The same can be said for most tribal societies.

Shame

Shame plays a more important role in social relationships than does guilt. When they fail, people feel ashamed that they have let down their group, their ancestors, and their gods. They do not feel much of a sense of guilt at having personally broken some universal law. In fact, there may be little awareness of such laws. All important norms are group norms.

Shame is also tied to success and honor. A group-oriented student is ashamed when the teacher asks her to stand up because she has the best grade in the class. This makes her stand out from the group. Shame is a dynamic that pressures people to conform to their group and so maintains harmony and peace.

Closely tied to shame is the value placed on saving face. Wrongdoers are punished, but in the end they must be allowed to live with face in the group. If they are not allowed to retain some sense of human dignity, they carry resentments that destroy relationships and keep matters from being settled.

Orientation to Land and Space

For westerners the earth is a raw, passive fact, the object of exploitation and economic and industrial profitability. For tribals the earth is the place where the living, the ancestors, and God meet.

Land

At the heart of tribal life is land. It is the basis of life. It provides the food that keeps people alive. It provides the world in which they live.

Land, too, is where the ancestors are buried. Its important features tell the stories of their lives. "Here is where Great Chief Big Hawk defeated the enemy in battle." "That tree was planted over the grave of our great-grandfather who saved the people from drought." "Over there is where our ancestors now live."

Time separates people of one generation from the next but space brings them together. A certain ancestor lived a hundred years ago, but he built this very house. In a sense, Christians understand this religious view of space when they walk the roads of Palestine. We remember that Jacob dug this well, and Christ prayed in this garden. Space brings the past into the present.

Above all, land is important because it is sacred. It belongs to the gods who gave it to their people and who protect it against enemies. We see this in the Old Testament when the Hittites, Philistines, Moabites, and other tribes equated their gods with their people and their land.

Land in tribal societies is not a commodity that people can buy and sell. It belongs to lineages and clans, which allocate its use to their members. If there is extra land, strangers may be given permission to use it until the people need it. In return, the strangers are expected to give a gift in appreciation and return the land on request (see p. 103).

Time

In tribal societies, time is oriented to the present and to the relationships between people and events. It is not a commodity to be bought and sold or something that can be measured or that runs out.

Most tribal peoples see time as the repetition of different events. For example, imagine it is now "Work in the Field Time." We have worked for a while and we will continue to work some more. The present event, therefore, has past, present, and future in it. When we finish working in the field, it will be "Feed the Animals Time." Now "Work Time" is totally in the past. Later it will be "Eat the Evening Meal Time," "Sleep Time," and then "Work in the Field Time" again.

Everyday events are loosely correlated with the cycle of day and night, but no clocks mark precise hours, minutes, and seconds that control human actions. Similarly, the year is divided into seasons such as "Planting Crops," "Weeding the Fields," and "Harvesting the Crops."

Life, too, is marked by cycles of birth, initiations into adulthood, marriage, and death. Individuals come and go but from the point of view of the group, life continues on, constantly renewing itself through offspring.

Because time endlessly repeats itself, there is often little sense of history as a progression of events leading to some future culmination. The important stories are those of the High God and of the origins of the tribe, which are past. Present events have little lasting importance and few tribal societies keep track of histories and biographies. For most, land and space are more important than time and history.

One important exception to this ahistorical view of time is the Israelites in the Old Testament. For them human history was tied closely to the cosmic history of God's acts and therefore took on great significance. If history has meaning, so do human biographies.

Sound-Oriented

As W. J. Ong points out (1969), tribes are oral societies and their worlds are built more on sound than on sight. Such worlds are highly immediate, personal, and relational. Words are spoken in the context of specific relationships and they die as soon as they have been said. Communication is a flux of immediate encounters between humans full of emotions and personal interests. It is only with the advent of recording machines that sounds can be preserved.

Sounds point to the invisible and speak of mystery. In the jungle, the hunter hears the tiger before he sees it. The mother hears a noise at night and is warned of an enemy attack. It should not surprise us, therefore, that sounds lead people to believe in spirits, ancestors, gods, and other beings that they cannot see. Sight, conversely, carries little sense of mystery and leaves little room for what is not seen.

Sounds are widely thought to be powerful and sacred. To say them is to cause things to happen. Ong notes (1969, 637), "Sound signals the present use of power, since sound must be in active production in order to exist at all." The right sounds can cause rain to fall. Other sounds, such as drumming and shouting, protect people from the evil spirits.

In oral societies, knowledge is stored in the forms of stories, songs, riddles, proverbs, and poems that can be easily remembered. These also lead people to think in concrete terms.

Concrete-Functional Thought

All human societies depend on human reason, but different cultures use different types of logic to order their thought. For example, the educated elite in the west value highly abstract thought based on formal analysis. They believe that the principles of logic they discover are universal or true for all people everywhere. Most tribal people use concrete-functional reasoning to deal with the problems they face in everyday life.

Existentialism

For the most part, tribal people are concerned about life here and now. They seek meaning in this existence and want a good life on earth. They are faced with the problems of daily life such as diseases, droughts, floods, and sudden deaths.

This focus on the present and belief in an interconnected world make witchcraft and magic understandable. Tribal religions attempt to give people a measure of control over the uncertainties of their lives by telling them that misfortunes occur in an interconnected world, and that the proper manipulation of these inter-connections can protect people from harm.

This does not mean tribal people have no interest in ultimate realities beyond death. As Paul Radin points out (1957), there are philosophers in all societies who struggle with the greater issues of life and seek the High God that lies beyond the immediate world of local gods, spirits, and ancestors.

Particularism

Tribal worldviews have a particularist view of reality. In con-trast to modern people, who look for universal laws that apply equally to all humans (whether these laws be scientific, legal, or religious), tribal people focus on the particularity of each event.

Each tribe has its own gods and ancestors who live on its soil. Each also recognizes that other tribes have other gods and ances-tors and does not try to convert them to its own beliefs. In fact, it is impossible for others to adopt their gods without becoming a part of their tribe.

When wars arise, each tribe calls upon its gods and ancestors for help, and victories and defeats are attributed to their power. For instance, the Philistines and other tribes thought Israel's God was the God of the hills, because that is where the Israelites lived (Judg. 2:3; 1 Kings 20:23–28). In contrast, Jehovah declared him-self to be not a territorial god, but the God of the universe.

This focus on particularity can be seen in everyday events. When the chief shows up at a modern hospital, the western doc-tor expects him to stand in line like everyone else. His people expect him to go to the head of the line because he is more impor-tant than they. The missionary doctor charges everyone the same for medicines. The tribal expects the rich to pay more for the same treatment. The particulars of each case must be taken into account to determine how a person should act.

Particularism extends to tribal identities. People of one's own tribe are humans. Those of other tribes are not fully humans. The word for foreigners is often "subhumans" and they can be treated as such.

Concrete-functional logic

People in oral societies generally think in functional terms rather than in universal, abstract categories. A. R. Luria illustrates this in his investigation of the Kirghiz of Central Asia.

Luria showed people a picture with a hammer, a saw, a log, and a hatchet. He asked them which of the four did not belong with the others. Western students are taught to eliminate the log because it is not a "tool." The Kirghiz, however, argued that the hammer did not belong. The hatchet and saw can be used to cut the log, they said, and besides, the hammer was of no use because there was no nail. One young man said (1976, 60), "The saw will saw the log and the hatchet will chop it into small pieces. If one of these things has to go, I'd throw out the hatchet. It doesn't do as good a job as a saw." When Luria suggested that the hammer, saw, and hatchet were tools and so belonged together, one Kirghiz said, "Yes, but even if we have tools, we still need wood—otherwise, we can't build anything."

Luria showed people a picture of three adults and a child and asked them which did not belong. Most refused to exclude anyone because they saw two of the adults as a mother and father, the child as their baby, and the other person as an uncle or an aunt. When Luria suggested that the child did not belong because it was a "child," one man said (1976, 55), "Oh, but the boy must stay with the others! All three of them are working, you see, and if they have to keep running out to fetch things, they'll never get the job done, but the boy can do the running for them. . . . The boy will learn; that'll be better, then they'll all be able to work well together."

Luria showed the Kirghiz a picture of three wheels and a pair of pliers and suggested that the pliers should be excluded because it is not a wheel. They said no, if anything has to go it should be one wheel because with a pliers and two wheels they could make a cart, but they couldn't with three wheels and no pliers. In short, people looked at these objects not in terms of forms or abstract categories but in terms of their functions in real-life situations.

Luria also found an unwillingness to depend only on propositional logic. He said to a man, "Cotton grows only in warm, dry places. Now, in England it is cold and it rains all the time. Can cotton grow there?" The man replied, "I don't know. I've heard of England, but I don't know if cotton grows there." When Luria repeated the syllogism, another man replied (1976, 111), "I don't know . . . if it's cold, it won't grow, while if it's hot, it will. From your words, I would have to say that cotton shouldn't grow there.

But I would have to know what spring is like there, what kinds of nights they have."

This does not mean people in oral societies are incapable of abstract, propositional thought. Placed in schools where this form of thinking is taught, they soon learn to think this way. In everyday life, however, they learn to think of things in their concrete contexts, not in terms of abstract categories. Because of this, they are often accused by those from the west of having only a primitive mentality. The unfairness of this judgment becomes more clear when we realize that even we do not use abstract logic of this type in our everyday lives. If we have too many people to fit in the car, do we leave the child behind because she or he "does not belong" with the adults?

Focus on Rituals and Myths

Rituals play a central role in tribal life. For the individual, these include the rites of passage that mark the cycle of life—birth, initiation, marriage and death, crisis rites to treat illness, and prosperity rites to guarantee fertility and success. Community rites include cyclical rites, such as the annual fertility ceremonies and protection rites to guard the village against the spirits. There are also rituals to ensure victory in raids and to end droughts and plagues.

There is little separation of forms from meanings in tribal thought. For instance, personal names not only refer to a person—they shape that person's personality. To name a child Brave Eagle is to give that child the characteristics of the eagle. When a person takes on a new identity, as is the case in initiation rites and conversion to another religion, he or she is given a new name. For example, people in the Old Testament were given new names when they entered new relationships to God (Gen. 17:5; 32:28; Num. 13:16). Similarly, to say a person's name is to invoke his or her presence. It is often taboo for commoners to say the name of the chief, wives to use the names of their husbands, and the living to utter the names of the dead.

It is difficult to understand tribal myths because they often seem to be mixes of fantasies and contradiction. We must recognize, however, that unlike Israel's accounts, such as the exodus, which

are rooted in historical fact, the myths of most tribes are allegorical or poetic commentaries on their views of reality.

Modern Problems

So far we have looked at tribes as if they exist outside the modern world. But this is not the case. Explorers, armies, colonial
rulers, traders, miners, and tourists have come, profoundly changing tribal life. Modern schools and hospitals have introduced the
sciences. Modern governments have introduced money, taxes,
nationalism, and modern concepts of law and order. Missionaries have brought the gospel and planted churches. Businesses
have brought in manufactured goods and created a desire for new
ways of life. Some of these changes have been for the better, some
for the worse, but no tribe today remains unaffected by the outside world.

As recently as two hundred years ago, bands and tribes, taken
together, occupied half of the earth's inhabitable area (Kottack
1994, 362). They constituted 20 percent of the earth's population,
or fifty million people. As is the case with band societies, since
industrialization tribal societies have faced a severe threat to their
physical and cultural survival. But the nature of that threat has
been somewhat different for tribes than for bands.

Tribes are bigger than bands and, at present, tribal societies
occupy much more territory than band societies do. Bands, as we
have seen, are currently found in remote places such as the Kalahari Desert, the Australian bush, the Central African rain forest,
and certain isolated mountainous regions of Asia. Tribes, however, are currently found all across the Central Asian and North
African steppes, throughout the Pacific islands, and in the rain
forests of South America, Melanesia, and Central Africa. They do
not constitute a large percentage of the world's population any
more, but they still occupy a significant portion of the world's territory. That territory is valued by others, though, and so tribal societies, like band societies, have experienced severe problems with
encroachment by outsiders.

A significant difference between tribes and bands is that the former are far more warlike than the latter. During the initial stages
of the colonial era, the concerns of outsiders were mainly politi-

cal. Colonial governments wanted to "pacify" the regions that they had taken by force. Tribal peoples' tendency to raiding and warfare made them natural targets for these pacification attempts. This tendency also made them difficult to pacify, however, and so the violence used to dominate tribal areas was in excess of that used to dominate band areas. In fact, some early classic works in anthropology were the result of failed attempts to pacify tribal peoples. England, in particular, took to sending social scientists to discover how best to control these groups.[4] In the end, of course, the superior weapons of the Europeans allowed them to dominate the globe. But even today, the fierce resistance of tribals continues to disrupt the plans of nations, such as in Afghanistan.

A somewhat different picture emerged under colonialism with those tribals whose political structures were headed by chiefs, rather than big-men. Chiefs, due to their formal authority, are able to provide more political stability than are the charismatic and highly insecure big-men. Hence, there is less inclination to warfare in chiefdoms and a greater willingness to accept authority. The rulers of chiefdoms, when defeated by colonial powers, would try to negotiate with them.

For instance, when the British first encountered the Kpa Mende of what is now Sierra Leone the Mende were a confederacy of small but expanding chiefdoms led by warriors. In 1896, the British declared the entire Mende territory to be under *pax Britannica* and sent in their own military to "stabilize" the area. A widow of one of the chiefs, Madam Yoko, became a chief herself, and was subsequently able to consolidate all of the previous Mende chiefdoms into a single political unit, the largest in that protectorate. Madam Yoko dealt skillfully with the British. She received their officials with warm hospitality and respect, but also defended the interests of her people. When necessary, she conceded to British demands, such as for house taxes, and forced her subordinate chiefs to comply. But when possible, she shrewdly cajoled the British into not interfering with ordinary Mende life (Hoffer 1974).

Madam Yoko's story is typical. Many rulers of chiefdoms under colonialism carefully walked the tightrope of cooperation with the colonial government and consolidation of their own internal power.

Ironically, many of these leaders were deposed by their own people near the end of the colonial era. In the late nineteenth and early twentieth centuries the colonial powers, due to changes in their own political ideologies at home, began to encourage democracy in the territories. The British, especially, educated "native" populations and allowed representation in local parliamentary bodies by the size of the group. Thus, in India, Africa, and elsewhere, people who had traditionally been commoners recognized the possibility of throwing off the yoke of their own traditional aristocracy (the chiefs and their families).

For instance, in Rwanda, the pastoral Tutsi were the traditional kings and the agricultural Hutu were ruled by them. That area was under colonial rule for only a short period, about forty-five years, but when the Belgians granted independence they set up a democracy. The Hutu outnumbered the Tutsi and so could outvote them, but the Tutsi were used to being the rulers. Rwanda has experienced one outbreak of civil war after another since that time. (We will examine this situation further in chapter 6.)

Obviously, modern political problems with tribals must be understood in the light of colonial history. While tribals have never been particularly stable, the upset in their usual political structures that colonialism fostered (over a period of up to four hundred years in some places) has contributed to the modern tragedy of interethnic violence. Even the tribal warring that was a tradition in many places has been intensified by the introduction of modern guns. Christians cannot condone this kind of violence whether it is traditional or not. But assisting tribals to put down their guns will require, as with band societies, that we demonstrate a genuine concern for their welfare, rather than for the welfare of outside governments.

Most tribals have always had significant contact with outsiders. It is true that some horticultural tribes, such as those along the Amazon River in Brazil and Venezuela, have been relatively cut off from other ethnic groups. Those groups are somewhat intermediate between bands and tribes. But other tribes, particularly pastoral groups, have always lived in symbiosis with neighboring populations of agriculturalists. That symbiosis has not always been without conflict. Genghis Khan was a pastoralist who amassed a huge Central Asian empire in the fourteenth century by conquering one neighbor after another. In fact, their ability to move about and their skill and willingness to use weapons allowed pastoralists to dominate much of Central Asia and North Africa until modern times.

Now, however, pastoral and horticultural tribes all live in nation states and are outgunned by the military forces of those states. This has had at least two implications: the restriction of tribals to certain shrinking territories, and the advent of development projects aimed at converting tribals into peasants.

Nation states, as we will see in chapter 6, are very concerned with carefully drawn and maintained borders. Tribals, who often do not consider themselves members of the nation, do not understand or care about these borders. Pastoralists, particularly, are used to moving wherever they must to find pasture, although they know that they may have to fight with the neighboring group to get it. It does not make much sense to them to painstakingly avoid crossing an imaginary line in the mountains because the resident official from the central government says that it is "illegal." Their own lives depend on the health of their herds, and the latter depends on moving to new pasture. In more than one case, the local nations have drawn and redrawn these imaginary lines without respect to the tribals' traditional homelands.

The Kirghiz of Afghanistan, for instance, live high in the mountains and traditionally have herded their animals to lowlands during the winter. Their home, however, is at the tip of the Wakkan Corridor, a small finger of Afghanistan that is surrounded on three sides by borders with Pakistan, China, and the former Soviet Union. When all three of these nations closed their borders with Afghanistan, the Kirghiz were forced to remain in the highlands, suffering intensely from the cold, and unable to give adequate care to their herds.

These same borders also cut the Afghan Kirghiz off from other members of their own ethnic group, the Kirghiz of Russia and China. While Afghan Kirghiz suffered from restriction to shrinking territories, the Russian Kirghiz suffered from the advent of development projects. In the later half of the nineteenth century, under the Soviet government, Russian peasants were sent to Kirgiziya to colonize and were given much of the best land. In 1916, the Kirghiz revolted and were severely crushed. Refugees fled to

China, and those who remained turned eventually to agriculture themselves.[5]

Modern economic development efforts, though sometimes with good intent, often harm tribal groups. This is in part because development efforts are undertaken by governments concerned with their own welfare, rather than the welfare of indigenous peoples, and in part because specialists involved in these projects have an overly narrow model for successful development.

For many Third-World national governments, the purpose of development is to enhance exports to the global market, bring in badly needed foreign exchange to pay off debts to the First World, and, in general, to industrialize and to modernize their countries to be able to compete with others. Sometimes international agencies such as the World Bank or the International Monetary Fund are forcing local governments to push development efforts.[6] In any case, these governments want to bring all areas of their countries into "production." We saw, with the Miskito of Nicaragua (chap. 2), that the competition to produce with a constantly increasing intensity causes the depletion of natural resources and the exploitation of local peoples. Traditional lifestyles are destroyed and people are left poorer, not richer.

But, even development projects designed to help tribal peoples sometimes cause much harm. The Turkana of Kenya have been successful pastoralists for centuries. The Kenyan government, however, thought it best for them to settle down and take up agriculture. Nearly two-thirds of them were convinced to do this and were given land with poor soil in need of irrigation (at an expense greater than the expected income from the farms). In 1972, a severe drought occurred. While television pictures of starving agricultural Turkana in famine camps flashed around the world, the southern Turkana who had not given up pastoralism survived the drought without outside assistance.

The model for development that has been used by many specialists has included a number of unwarranted assumptions. One such assumption is that agriculture is better than foraging, horticulture, or pastoralism because it produces a product for the market. Another assumption is that production processes should use expensive modern technology and should be labor-saving (even in countries that have plenty of labor available and little money).

Another is that higher and higher levels of production are desirable, rather than the maintenance of an adequate subsistence lifestyle with population control. And a final assumption is that the same development model can be used in any environment and with any group of people, regardless of their culture.

These assumptions are the result of imagining that all nations must develop by following the example of the west in the last two hundred years. But development projects that break free from these assumptions and listen carefully to local people about their own needs can be quite effective.

In a very successful development effort in East Africa, cattle ranching was introduced into an area that had not previously had it due to tsetse-fly infestation. First the tsetse flies were eradicated. Then cattle adapted to the local ecology were brought in from a neighboring country. And finally, a mixture of government owned, cooperatively owned, and privately owned ranches were established (Kottack 1994, 355). Numerous Christian NGOs, or non-governmental organizations, such as World Vision and Mennonite Central Committee, are also doing good work, not only in providing the means of subsistence for tribal peoples, but also in linking them to the larger world in ways that are beneficial.

The responses of tribals to encroachment by the modern world have been varied. Some have chosen to fight. The Nuer and the Dinka of the Sudan recently picked up arms to stop the construction of an irrigation canal along the Nile that would have benefited peasants downstream at their expense (Kottack 1994, 372). Some have chosen to learn outside ways and fight with words rather than guns. The Kayapo horticulturalists of Brazil use camcorders to record their interactions with outside authorities and thus hold them to their promises. They have also gotten publicity for their case by engaging the help of the rock star Sting (Kottack 1994, 373). Some have been culturally or physically extinguished. Many North American Native American groups have no survivors. And some have found ways to create new syncretized cultures from pieces of their own past and the modern world. The Melanesians, who initially responded to the extreme impact of World War II on their culture by developing religious cults based on fantastic notions of future wealth[7] have now transformed some of these cults into political parties that participate in local government.

Christian missionaries since the apostle Paul have been concerned with giving material assistance along with the gospel to those who need it. All over the world, they have built hospitals and schools, taught languages needed to understand outside groups, and assisted in the defense of local peoples from unjust authorities.[8] Many modern missionaries are combining their evangelistic work with effective economic development. With tribal societies facing dire economic and political adjustment difficulties, it is appropriate to remember Jesus' words about the importance of a cup of cold water given in his name.

Tribal people are caught between two worlds. One part of them belongs to the tribal world with its traditions, group identity, and meaningful worldview. Another part belongs to the modern world with its rapid, uncontrolled change, glamorous technology, lonely individualism, and secularization. Christians working in tribal societies must understand not only the old traditions of people but also the new forces affecting their lives. We will further examine some of the changes taking place in tribal societies when we look at modern urban societies.

5

The Church in Tribal Societies

Tribal societies, particularly sedentary ones, have been open to the gospel. Much of the church today was born in tribal communities. The early church was an urban church, but when the gospel reached the frontiers of Europe it spread through tribes by means of mass movements. In the past century it has swept through the tribes of the Pacific Islands, Northeast India, and sub-Saharan Africa. Now it is spreading along tribal lines in Papua New Guinea, Latin America, central India, and the Philippines.

What methods have been effective in planting churches in tribal societies and what problems do these churches face in developing mature congregations? These are the questions we want to examine in this chapter.

Planting Churches in Tribal Societies

The methods for planting churches we examined for band societies are equally important in tribal societies. Both bands and tribes are based on strong face-to-face relationships. Consequently, trust in the message is based on trust in the messenger. This has great significance for the methods we use in planting churches in tribal societies.

Resident Witness

Some people hear the Good News from itinerant evangelists or colporteurs selling Bibles and then believe. These cases are God's serendipities. Most tribal churches are planted when missionaries settle among people, learn their language and culture, and present the gospel in ways that people understand. Good examples of this are Christian Keysser's description of church planting in New Guinea (1980) and Don Richardson's work among the Sawi (1978).

Not all missionaries identify themselves with tribal people. Some never learn the language of the people well enough to communicate effectively. Many live on mission compounds, which are islands of western culture. For the most part, these missionaries are less fruitful in ministering to people.

Identifying with the Culture

Identification with people of other cultures takes place on several levels. We need first to learn the language well. Nowhere is our foreignness more obvious than when we speak with strange accents and broken sentences. We need also to adopt people's lifestyle as far as our conscience and psychological make-up allows us. We need to learn to eat their food, dress as they do, and live in their kinds of houses.

There are several areas in which it is particularly hard for western missionaries to adjust to other cultures. One is privacy. In the west a person's home is a sanctuary in which she or he takes refuge from people. In tribal societies a home is part of the hamlet. People come and go freely. When strangers arrive, people stop by to see how these strangers live, bathe, dress, eat, and sleep. There is little privacy.

Another difficult adjustment is hospitality. In tribes this is a key sign of identification with people. Homes are always open to friends and relatives who drop by unannounced and stay uninvited for a meal or two. Food, clothing, cooking pots, and other possessions (including typewriters and cars) belong to the community and must be lent when others in the family or clan need them. To withhold these is to be branded a miser. There is nothing worse in group-oriented societies than inhospitality.

A third area of adjustment for westerners has to do with their culturally shaped need for order. They want to plan their activities and have things to take place "on time." They want things to be "clean" and define clean more in terms of order than sanitation. It is hard for them to get rid of clocks and schedules, to go with the flow of events, or to leave things lying around unsorted.

This compulsion for order is tied to our western emphasis on accomplishing tasks rather than on building relationships. We come to do jobs, so we make plans and act. We want to see success, and success can best be measured by tangible results such as buildings, meetings, and activities. We find it hard to simply sit with people, talk, and earn their trust.

The most difficult adjustments have to do with our children. We choose to make sacrifices for ourselves but can we impose these on our daughters and sons? With whom should they play, where should they go to school, with which culture should they identify, whom should they marry—these are difficult questions all cross-cultural workers face.

There are limits to our abilities to identify with the customs of another culture. These limits are determined by the differences between cultures and by people's acceptance of us. It is easier to identify closely with another culture that is similar to our own, although surface similarities may be deceiving. Moreover, some tribes are more willing to accept strangers than others.

Identification is also subject to our own personalities and attitudes. Our greatest barrier is often our feeling that our culture is superior to that of other people. We need constantly to work to overcome our own ethnocentrism.

Some missionaries adjust to other cultures more readily than others. We all can adapt for short periods of time, but long stays are more difficult. People who are flexible and can change their plans on a moment's notice adapt better than those who need rigid schedules and a great deal of structure in their lives.

It is impossible for any of us to go completely "native." To do so we would have to kill an important part of our identity. The fact is, we are outsiders and people know it. Part of our usefulness to them is the fact that we have contacts with the outside world that can help them. In the end, we must identify as closely as we can with the lifestyle of people but not at the expense of our sanity and ministry.

Adopting Social Roles

On a deeper level we need to find legitimate roles in the society. People need to know who we are and how to relate to us. The role of missionary is a western one and does not exist in other cultures. We need, therefore, to find a role in the culture in which we minister that enables us best to share the gospel.

As we have seen, in tribes the foundational roles are those based on kinship ties. Consequently, people often adopt a missionary as a clan mate. This does not necessarily mean that they love the missionary, only that they are giving her or him a legitimate status in the community. They no longer want to treat the missionary as an outsider whom they must watch with suspicion or kill.

At first we may rejoice when we are adopted as kin, because this means we are now insiders. We discover later that this is not an unmixed blessing. We are now expected to fulfill all the tasks associated with our new status. People expect us to give big gifts at all family functions and participate in clan rituals. They send poor family members to us for food and housing. If we refuse them hospitality, we are seen as bad brothers, sisters, uncles, and aunts.

We may find other legitimate roles in the tribe that enable us to work effectively. Some of these are "friendly outsiders" or "culture brokers" who serve as liaisons between people and the outside world encroaching on them.[1] In these roles we serve as catalysts, helping people to gain ownership of their land and to train their children to live in a modern world while maintaining a sense of their cultural identity.

It is also important that we find legitimate roles in the church. At first we may need to be one of the leaders, but if we remain leaders for any length of time, we create a dependency on ourselves. As soon as possible we must turn the leadership over to the natural leaders in the church and work alongside them. Our temptation is to keep control of the church much too long because we fear that other people cannot do the job as well as we. We need to realize that it is more important in the long run for people to learn how to do the work than to have it done well. We need to give young leaders the greatest right we give ourselves, namely, the right to make mistakes.

Learning to Love

Ultimately, identification requires a deep love for the people themselves. We may live like the people but not really love them. People soon know this. They also know if we genuinely love them, even though we live in foreign houses and eat foreign food. If we must choose, it is more important to love people than to live as they do.

But genuine incarnational love for people gives us a deep desire to learn about their ways and to share with them both ourselves and the gospel. It leads us to treat them as equals with dignity and respect. It enables us to trust them not only with material goods, but also with power and positions of leadership. It prevents us from treating them with condescension as "children" or with disdain as "uncivilized." Love is the basis for all identification. When we love people and see them as humans like ourselves, we are able to identify more fully with them in lifestyles and roles than when we act out of duty alone.

As we have noted, those of us from the west have a difficult time in focusing on people rather than programs, on relationships rather than results. Our society stresses planning, performance, and production. Our churches look for action and measurable results. It is hard for us, therefore, to take time to listen to people and to wait for them to take the lead. But relationships are at the heart of the gospel and the church. Our goal is to help people carry on the work rather than to do it ourselves.

Bridges of Understanding

Communicating the gospel in a new culture is difficult at best. Not only is the message itself new, but also the cognitive categories of the new culture are inadequate to fully express gospel truths. People's concepts of God, sin, salvation, forgiveness, and eternal life may bear little resemblance to those in the Bible. Where do we begin?

Several principles of cross-cultural communication apply. First, we must begin with the people's own worldview and beliefs and reshape these over time in the light of Scripture. We cannot erase their old worldview and replace it with a new one. The process of planting the gospel in a new society, of nurturing converts to Christian maturity, and of planting living churches is a long one. This does not mean the missionary should remain in charge until the task is done. It does mean that leading people to Christ and leaving them often leads to still-born Christians and weak churches.

Second, there are often bridges of understanding that we can use to communicate the gospel to people in other cultures. Don Richardson (1981) points out one such bridge, namely, the concept of a High God. As we have seen, many tribes believe in a powerful and good creator God, who left humans when they offended him. Charles Taber writes (1978, 60),

> When missionaries first arrived in the area of the Baoule of Ivory Coast and started talking about the Creator, they found immediate recognition: "Of course, we know him; his name is Nyamien." And when the missionaries proceeded to describe the attributes of the God they knew, they again found almost impatient agreement: "Of course, Nyamien is all-powerful, of course he's benevolent, of course he's eternal, etc. When you've said Nyamien, you've said it all. Only children don't know that."

Richardson points out that Christians can use this category, which often has little content other than Supreme Being, and fill it with Christian meaning. For example, the missionaries used Katonda among the Baganda, Panthianm among the Mizos of Northeast India, Nyamien among the Baoule of Ivory Coast, and Iywa among the Karen of Burma. This approach, however, does not work in societies in which there is no word for a High God or where the local word for God is associated with many non-Christian meanings.

Other concepts can also serve as bridges of understanding, if they are close to biblical truth. Chhangte Lal Hminga (1987) notes that in Northeast India, concepts such as sin, salvation, sacrifice, heaven, and hell are similar to ideas in Scripture and can be used to communicate the gospel to non-Christians.

Another bridge is redemptive analogies. Most societies have practices that can be used to convey biblical truths by way of comparison. Richardson (1978) writes of the Sawi of Irian Jaya who give a "peace child" to the enemy to settle intertribal wars. F. Hrangkhuma (1989) points out that the Mizo of North East India have a concept of the "ideal man" that is helpful in communicating the biblical concept of righteousness to the people.

A third bridge is universal human experiences, such as birth, death, sickness, eating, and parenting. Which of these we can use depends on their meaning in the culture. In those where fathers are distant, drunk, and abusive, the idea of God as Father may be misleading until the people have a Christian view of the family. Appealing to the people's own norms, however, can be a bridge to communicating the gospel message of sin and forgiveness. Wayne Dye, working among the Bahinemo of Papua New Guinea, writes (1976, 39),

> I tried to translate Jesus' list of sins in Mark 7. As each sin was described, they gave me the local term for it. They named other sins in their culture.
>
> "What did your ancestors tell you about these things?" I asked them.
>
> "Oh, they told us we shouldn't do any of those things."
>
> "Do you think these were good standards that your ancestors gave you?" They agreed unanimously that they were.
>
> "Well, do you keep all these rules?"
>
> "No," they responded sheepishly.
>
> One leader said, "Definitely not. Who could ever keep them all? We're people of the ground."
>
> I took this opportunity to explain that God expected them to keep their own standards for what is right, that He was angry because they hadn't. Then I pointed out that it was because they fell short of their own standards that God sent His Son to bear their punishment so that they could be reunited with him.

This was a crucial step toward their conversion. The Bahinemo definition of sin is not fully biblical, but it is a beginning point for the communication of the gospel.

Bridges are precisely that, beginning points. Problems arise when we do not go beyond them. A Sawi Peace Child, a Mizo concept of the Ideal Man, and Bahinemo ideas of sin open doors of understanding. But we must move beyond these to biblical views of sin, righteous people, and an incarnate Savior.

Wholistic Evangelism

As we have seen, tribal cultures are wholistic in nature. They do not separate religion from the economic, social and political dimensions of life. Nor do they distinguish natural and supernatural realities, or this-worldly and other-worldly concerns.

We must, therefore, show that Christianity answers all the needs in their lives. Our entry point may be an economic need, such as food in times of drought. Or it may be a political need, such as peace between warring tribes, or land ownership as nations take over their territories. Or it may be a religious need, such as the desire for God's salvation and blessing. Whatever the entry point, the church must move on to deal with sin and salvation, and with other individual and corporate needs such as food, shelter, health, education, community building, justice, and reconciliation between peoples.

Even this, however, is not enough. As John Mbiti points out (1969, 3), Christianity must become the very center of the people's lives.

> Unless Christianity . . . fully occup[ies] the whole person as much as, if not more than, traditional religions do, most converts to [it] will continue to revert to their old beliefs and practices for perhaps six days a week, and certainly in times of emergency and crisis. The whole environment and the whole time must be occupied by religious meaning so that at any moment and at any place, a person feels secure enough to act in a meaningful and religious consciousness.

Basic Christian teachings about God, Jesus, and the Holy Spirit must be addressed. In many tribes, presenting God as creator and sustainer, as the loving parent who wants to be reconciled with wayward children, and as the present ruler of the universe who cares for his people is revolutionary. These doctrines destroy the people's fears and feelings of helplessness that spring from their pantheistic beliefs and distant High Gods.

This message grasped the Baganda of East Africa who, today, are the center of a spiritual renewal that has continued for fifty years. J. V. Taylor writes (1958, 252–53),

> The message which was received and implanted, and upon which the church in Buganda was founded, was primarily news about the transcendent God. "Katonda," the unknown and scarcely heeded Creator, was proclaimed as the focus of all life, who yet lay beyond and above the closed unity of all existence. This was in itself so catastrophic a concept that, for the majority of hearers, it appeared to be the sum of the new teaching. . . . The fact that they did hear it, and did not at this stage, for the most part, hear the message of the Saviourhood of Christ or the power of the Spirit, though these were the

themes that were being preached, suggests that this was the Word of God to them, and it was independent of the world of the preacher.

For the Baganda, the fact that the distant High God was concerned about them was revolutionary.

We must preach Jesus Christ as Savior, as founder of a new tribe made up of new people from all earthly tribes, as conqueror of the demons, and as ruler of God's new kingdom on earth. These messages, too, are revolutionary. Many tribals testify to their deliverance from the fear of the spirits and from intertribal wars.

We must preach about the Holy Spirit as God in our midst who teaches us the truth, guides us in our decisions, gives us power to live, and fills us with peace and joy. To people who feel powerless in a world of evil forces and spirits and overrun by powerful cultures from the outside world, it is indeed Good News to know that God is at work in and for them, giving them power to overcome sickness, fear, death, temptation, and sin, and to live joyful and holy lives.

Oral Methods and Concrete Thinking

Tribal people use oral methods of communication and think in concrete-functional terms. We must, therefore, present the gospel in stories, dramas, illustrated talks, and other narrative and visual forms. Most western missionaries find this hard to do because they are taught to think in terms of abstract theological principles.[2] We need to present abstract theological truth using illustrations, object lessons, and allegories (see reading 2, following page). For example, one missionary in a tribe with little sense of the past tried to teach them Old Testament history, but with little success. He then took a stick and stuck it in the sand. This, he said, was Adam. He put another stick in the sand and named it Seth. He added more sticks to the row, giving each a name. As the line of sticks grew, the people suddenly grasped the meaning of history.

We must also present the gospel in ways that make it easy to remember. Songs are particularly important. People who cannot read, sit for hours singing a dozen verses of one hymn and twenty of another. Songs capture people's beliefs in a lyric theology. One important sign that the gospel has become part of a people's lives is that they compose their own songs.

Reading 2

Witness in Tribal Societies

Christian Keysser

In New Guinea we often use missionary presentations to awaken people. They are based on the type and manner of the prophets and always portray Biblical truths . . . the simple, preached Word usually takes too much for granted. . . . The acted out Word, however, was not only better understood but it captivated the will and provoked it to decisive action, not rarely either. Sometimes the effect was of surprising force. The same divine truth may in one form leave no impression at all, whereas if presented in another form better suited for the people, it has a more immediately convincing impact.

At one of our outstations where work had been going on for eight years the population of the entire surrounding area was called in for a public meeting. That the people came was the fruit of years of preparatory work. They sat down in a circle at the mission station. In their midst all kinds of field fruit had been heaped which I had requested in lieu of later payment. The crowd was watching with expectation. The expectation turned to astonishment and finally to fierce indignation as the precious fruits . . . were beaten and trampled to a pulp by [the New Guinea Christians]. No sooner was this done than the helpers hurried away and returned with some junk, garbage, dirt and mire and completely covered the pulped field fruit with all this so that only a few root tips were sticking out. Then a mighty tree stump that had previously been made ready was with much trouble placed on top of the heap. To the further amazement of the onlookers this was now being richly decorated. After the work had been completed the Christians started dancing around the heap with such comical vigor that the crowd laughed heartily. The glee stopped suddenly, however, as the dancers began to sing. It was a well-known song from the pagan Ngosa festival in honor of the ancestors

Reprinted with permission from Christian Keysser, *A People Reborn* (Pasadena: William Carey Library), 1980.

which was the center of [the tribal] worship. The audience began to perceive that this dramatization had something to do with their chief festival. The explanation was not long delayed: the good field fruits were God's good gifts that your ancestors have disregarded, ruined and covered with folly and malice. Only slight traces are left. . . .

The effect was far more striking than any of us had expected. To the question as to whether they would follow the divine truth now, [the people] replied with a unanimous "Yes." "Your 'yes' comes fast and easy from your lips," was our reply, "but it is a hard thing to do and you are weaklings. It takes men full of strength and courage to remove this heathenism." In order to show their determination, the multitude immediately wanted to rush at the tree stump and straightaway throw it in the nearby abyss. We prevented them from doing so: "Nothing is accomplished by that. First you must quietly think it over in the villages as to what such an act means. All of you must first agree as to whether you really wish to give up the **Ngosa** . . . ?"

As a result of the presentation the whole area was aroused. Excited negotiations took place for days and nights, and after two weeks there was no holding back. The people came together again. "Heathenism with all of its murder, lying and infamies must go. We have recognized God's truth: Christianity shall have free course among us," the tribe vowed publically and solemnly. As a token of their earnest, sincere intentions, they stormed the heap. The men dragged the tree stump with immense shouting to the precipice and threw it down, and the women filled the rubbish into their netbags and threw it after it. And the people have actually kept their word. As strong as the rejection of Christianity had been before, so joyously appeared now the general openness toward God and His Word, and the readiness to follow Him.

(Note: Keysser wrote this in 1929, when western colonialism was at its peak, and some of his expressions reflect the general speech of his day.)

There are other mnemonic devises we should use. Tribes often have rich stores of proverbs, aphorisms, and sayings that contain the distilled beliefs of the people. We can use these to make a point and to identify with the culture. We should also use Bible memorization and simple catechisms. Sermons and theologies are soon forgotten, but people recall memorized verses and brief confessions of faith.

Creating Christian Rituals

Rituals are central to tribal life and should have an important place in the tribal church. We from modern societies have little understanding of sacred rituals. We think of them as dead traditions. But living rituals store and communicate our deepest beliefs, feelings, and values. Words speak of ordinary things. To speak of mysteries that transcend words we need songs, prayers, liturgies, and ceremonies. Our religious life is impoverished without them. The answer to dead rituals is not no rituals; it is living, powerful rituals that are constantly renewed.

Tribal Christians need lifecycle rites to give meaning to transitions in their lives and to maintain social order and morality. Christian birth rites should enact the sanctity of life. Twins must be blessed rather than killed, and girls honored equally with boys. Parents and relatives should commit themselves to rear the child to follow Christ.

Christian marriage rituals establish families and help maintain sexual morality. They teach chastity and faithfulness to one's spouse. The western idea of "love marriages" (as opposed to arranged ones) often comes with the missionary. Unfortunately, it often leads to immorality because courtship has few community controls and because marriages are based on personal choice and have little social reinforcement. Christian liberty without moral and community controls ends in license.

Funerals are powerful testimonies to the world of our fundamental beliefs about death, resurrection, eternal life, and heaven. In tribes with ancestor veneration, the church must help new converts differentiate between respect and worship. Christians need to make it clear to their non-Christian relatives that they do respect their ancestors but worship only God. Funerals are important evangelistic occasions. They are one of the few occasions when many of these relatives see Christian faith demonstrated.

The tribal ritual most misunderstood by western missionaries is initiation rites that transform children into adults. This is because the west has no such rites and because the rites often appear barbaric because of their widespread use of male and female circumcision. Westerners have often branded initiation rites pagan and tried to stamp them out. Consequently, in the eyes of tribal people Christians never become men and women. All their lives they remain boys and girls.

Churches need to introduce initiation rites for Christians in these societies. Some have used baptism as initiation, but this confuses a social transformation with a religious one. Churches need to create new Christian rites using symbols familiar to people.

Tribal churches make much of rituals. Christmas, Good Friday, Easter, Thanksgiving, planting time, and harvest are occasions to retell the story of God's presence among his people. Revival meetings, conventions, and other public gatherings bring together people from different communities for worship and fellowship. Rituals associated with crises such as droughts and plagues help people see God's presence among them. Prayer for personal sickness, guidance, and protection from witchcraft reassure people that the God of the Bible does indeed take care of them personally and removes the temptation to go to the shaman.

Rituals are important to teach new Christians the meaning of the gospel in their new lives and to proclaim the gospel to non-Christians who gather to see what the Christians are doing.

Power Encounters

As we have seen, power is a central theme in tribal religions: the power to defeat enemies, to be a successful leader, to heal the sick, to raise good crops, and to have many wives and children. Such power is acquired through magic or the support of powerful spirits and gods.

Alan Tippett (1971) coined the phrase *power encounter* for the confrontations of power seen in tribal societies. There are two types of encounter. One is public demonstrations of might, such as Elijah's defeat of the prophets of Baal. Here all Israel watched to see whose God was stronger, and Jehovah showed himself to be God alone in a great demonstration of power (1 Kings 18).

At times missionaries have challenged tribal gods to show the people that they are powerless before Christ. An example of this was Reverend Lowder's violation of the religious taboos of the Budu in southeast Africa. Lowder knew that the people believed in a powerful royal spirit said to reside in leopard skins. These were used only by tribal chiefs. Lowder obtained a leopard skin and went from village to village, trampling on it to show that he was immune to its power. This created much commotion among the people and drew large audiences. C. T. Studd ate plantains cooked in a fire fueled by the medicines used in witchcraft. The fact that he did not die instantly convinced people that he had superior powers.

In some instances, such demonstrations of power have persuaded people of the superiority of the gospel and led to conversions. In most cases, however, the response is mixed. Some believe in Christ, but the leaders increase their opposition to the gospel and persecute the Christians. This was the case for Elijah. After he demonstrated God's power and killed the prophets of Baal, he fled for his life. In the desert he experienced the most severe depression in his life. Jezebel appointed new prophets of Baal and there was no revival in Israel.

It is not wise for missionaries to precipitate such power encounters, for these often lead to strong opposition. When faced with such encounters, however, missionaries need to seek God's guidance and power. They need, also, to disciple those who turn to God at such times or they will retain a magical worldview and their faith will rest only on further demonstrations of power. Later, when they pray and God does not heal them, they will turn to other gods for help.

We need to show God's mighty works in the everyday lives of his people. We must pray for and minister to those who are sick, destitute, and demonized. We must exhort people to live holy, victorious lives. Demonstrations of power, however, bring no easy victory. Christ's miracles led to his crucifixion, and those who proclaim the gospel in power must expect persecution (1 Cor. 1:18–25). In many cases the deaths of Christian martyrs, native and missionary, have been the greatest demonstrations of power in tribal evangelism.

The second type of power encounter occurs when people want to become Christians. Here the confrontation is not between the missionary or pastor and traditional religious leaders. It takes place in the hearts of those who want to follow Christ but who fear the power of their old gods and fetishes. In these situations, people must publicly destroy their fetishes to show that they have turned to Christ and no longer put their trust in the old gods. Tippett writes (1971, 169),

> At the level of actual conversion from paganism . . . the group action (which is not mass, but multi-individual) must fix itself in encounter at some material locus of power at some specific point in time. There must be a psychological moment or experience when the persons involved actually turn from the old god(s) to the new. There ought to be some ocular demonstration of this encounter, some specific act of faith. Both Christian and pagan alike frequently demand some such act to indicate the bona fide nature of conversion.

To destroy one's fetishes and amulets is a fearful experience. There is always doubt. "Is Christ really more powerful than our tribal gods, ancestors, shamans and witch doctors whom we have rejected? Can he protect us from the evil spirits as our ancestors did? Can he provide for our needs and heal us as our old gods did?"

The power encounters accompanying conversion cannot be precipitated by the missionary. If he or she destroys the fetishes, people will remake them. If people say that the gods have gone away, the gods may return. Only destroying them will do. Tippett adds (1971, 203),

> None but the tribe can destroy the tribal fetish (with the chief as representative, acting in the presence of the group), none but the family (with the family head as representative) can destroy a family god, and a personal fetish can only be destroyed by the individual himself.

In some instances, when a whole community wants to convert, a few members destroy their charms and medicines as a test case, risking their lives for the rest. If they die, all believe that the old gods and spirits are angry and that the Christian God is not as powerful as they.

We need to be deeply sensitive to the inner conflicts and fears of those seeking to become Christians. Conversion to a new God is very stressful, and we must give people much pastoral care when they burn their old religious paraphernalia. Even after conversion, for months and even years people attribute sickness and disasters to the wrath of the old gods.

We must preach God's deliverance of his people from fear. Christians are freed from the power of old gods, spirits, witchcraft, and magic (Gal. 4:3–7). This is indeed good news to tribal peoples who live in constant fear of the spirit world.

Finally, we must challenge the beliefs and social structures of the old religious systems. There are important truths in tribal religions that can serve as bridges for communicating the gospel, but these religions, as systems, are in rebellion against God. If we leave them unchallenged, the young church is in danger of sliding into a Christian animism.

Adapting to Patterns of Social Organization

We must adapt our methods of church planting to the way the society is organized or we will find little response to the gospel.

Larry Niemeyer points out (1993) an example of the influence of social organization on the church. In patrilineal societies it is the women and children who first join the church. They are marginal to the power structure of the society and so can explore new ways of life that offer them status and power, which they do not find in their own society. In these societies we must also seek to win adult men, particularly the leaders of the lineages and clans.

In matrilineal societies, women have more power. The core of a community is made up of women who have grown up together. Men join their wives but are outsiders to the village. Men readily join the church because it offers them status and power, but they do not form a stable core for planting a church. They are marginal and transient. In such cases it is important to reach the responsible women of the community.

A third example of contextualized evangelism has to do with village organization. Elders and chiefs decide village matters after listening to the people. These leaders are the doorkeepers of tribal communities and we must seek their permission to share the gospel in their village. The leaders frequently give it, even though they themselves may not be willing at first to become Christians. If they give us permission to enter, the door is open for us to settle among the people. Moreover, people can listen to the message without fear of breaking with their community.

Group Movements

One dynamic of great importance in tribal churches is mass or people movements. In these, people become Christians in groups. In strong group-oriented tribes, all major decisions, such as marriage, migration, raiding, and use of land, are made by a family, lineage, or tribe acting as a whole. It should not surprise us that people decide to become Christians in groups.

An example of this is Lynn Barney's experience among the Hmong of Vietnam. People of a remote village invited him to tell them about the "Jesus Way," so he presented the gospel to the men in their long house. The men then broke up into clan groups to discuss the new way. After arguments, pro and con, the leaders of the clans gathered as elders to decide for the village. In the end, they told Lynn that they had all decided to become Christians!

Western missionaries, reared in a culture that stresses individualism and personal choice, often misunderstand such decisions. Many of them ask people to go back and then come to Christ one by one. In doing so they say to people that this is an unimportant decision, for only minor decisions are made by individuals. Moreover, people often feel rejected by the missionary and return to their old religion.

Other missionaries accept such group decisions as evidence that all the people do believe in Jesus and baptize everyone immediately. In group decisions, however, not everyone wants to become a Christian. Some agree to the decision to maintain the unity of their group.

We should allow the dynamics of group decisions to take their course. The initial decision is not so much a decision by all to follow Christ as it is to explore Christianity further. The community wants to know more about the gospel. It is imperative, therefore, that the church or the mission send an evangelist or a teacher to instruct people.

For the next months people discuss their decision. Some people reaffirm their desire to become Christians. This second decision is critical for their growth. Until it is made, the gospel, in a sense, is on trial. Later decisions further strengthen them in their faith. Other people choose to return to their old gods. Having affirmed the unity of the group by joining in its first decision, they are now free to reject the new religion. Only after this sorting has taken place, usually some months after the initial group decision, should missionaries and church leaders baptize the converts.

Decision making in a group society is often a multistep process (fig. 22). People who decide as a group to follow Christ need further decisions to confirm them in faith and to allow those who disagree to leave. Initial rejections are not final. People often say, "Maybe, but not now." We need to continue presenting the gospel for them to reconsider their decision. Only when they reject the gospel repeatedly do their hearts harden against it.

Figure 22
The Multistep Nature of Group Decision Making

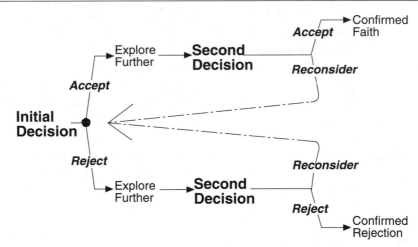

People movements are important in tribal evangelism. Converts who come to Christ one by one are often ostracized by the tribe. No one talks to them. No one marries their children. When a number of families become Christians together, the village cannot reject them without destroying the tribe. The Christians also have a community of fellowship and support in one another.

People movements also lead to "gossiping" the gospel along village trails. When one group of people becomes Christian, relatives and friends hear it and begin to think about converting themselves. When the preacher comes, people are ready to hear the gospel.

There are problems with group movements. If we do not follow up the initial response, the movement dies or the Christianity that emerges is shallow.

How can church planters foster people movements? Some evangelists announce that an invitation to respond to the gospel will be given on the last night of the campaign rather than at every service. They encourage people to go home and discuss their decision with their families. By the last evening people have talked about their choice together and are ready to make decisions that have family support.

One evangelistic team, holding one-night campaigns in tribal villages, asks those who want to follow Christ to discuss it with their families and to see the team the following morning if they decide to become Christians.

Indigenous Leadership Styles

How should tribal churches be organized? Should they have paid pastors or self-supporting elders? Should these be elected or appointed?

Too often we from the west have brought with us our understandings of leadership and imposed these on the churches we plant. Those from high churches ordain bishops and priests. Those from congregational churches want elections in which each church member has an equal vote. In many cases we have been more willing to contextualize the gospel than church organization.

The fact is that western leadership styles do not fit the social patterns of most tribes. Western forms of leadership tend to be hierarchical and bureaucratic in nature. They focus on getting jobs done, not on building a community. Leaders often feel the pressure to get things done, even if this damages relationships in the church. They ignore the importance of consensus, which is central to group-oriented societies. Elections and majority rule alienate the minority and split the group.

In tribes churches work best by consensus, even though forging it takes a great deal of time, skill, and patience. Left to themselves, people organize their churches like families and clans. Power is in the hands of elders and chiefs, but they rarely act without first listening to their followers. The advantages of this type of organization are obvious. People know how to work together in this way and respect for the elderly is retained.

Today, many tribal churches are caught between old and new worlds—between old and new styles of leadership. The elders are the keepers of the tribal identity and traditions. The young leaders bring the new ways they learn in modern schools. Unfortunately they often gain control through the power of modern education and ignore the wisdom of the elders.

Relationships Between Mission and Church

Too often we think of church planting in the short run. We assume we will plant new churches, turn the work over to national leaders, and leave, all in a few years. Earlier, missionaries thought the process would take generations. In a sense, both are wrong. If we abandon young churches too soon, they remain feeble or die. If we stay too long, we stifle their vitality and freedom. In another sense, both are right. We should train leaders as soon as possible and turn the work over to them. We should also continue to relate to the churches thereafter in new ways, as partners and fellow Christians. The church is a global church, not an assortment of isolated national churches, and God has called the whole church to evangelize the world, not merely a segment of it.

We need to understand the growth of tribal churches as a series of stages covering several decades, during which the relationships between younger churches, older churches, and mission agencies progress toward a full partnership in the gospel.

Dependence

In the first years, the missionaries take the lead. They proclaim the gospel, teach people, and model for them what a Christian is like. New converts do not know what a Christian is, so they imitate the missionary.

First-generation Christians often make a radical break with their old religious ways. They condemn witchcraft and magic and reject traditional rituals, dances, and other doubtful practices. This break is often accompanied by public destruction of charms and fetishes.

Independence

The second stage in the growth of a young church is independence. Now the Christians are established and no longer need the missionary to lead them. They can study the Scriptures for themselves and interpret it. They can organize their own activities.

It is important that missionaries recognize and affirm the church's desire for independence. This is not a rejection of the missionary, except when the missionary keeps control too long. Rather, it is a natural process of growth and maturation.

National leaders

Critical to independence is the emergence of national leaders. From the beginning the missionaries must look for leaders among the converts to take charge of the church. Too often, missionaries think in western terms and look for people with seminary training. Training such leaders, however, takes decades. Moreover, they are often alienated from their people. Natural leaders emerge in every group and it is these whom we must first trust and train to lead the young church.

Autonomy

Another area of independence has to do with the autonomy of the church. In the past, missionaries talked about the three selves. These related to the social autonomy of the young church: economically it should be self-supporting; politically, self-governing; and socially, self-propagating.

Today we speak of cultural autonomy. This is expressed in several ways. First, as it matures the church reevaluates its relationship to its own cultural past. First-generation Christians, as we have noted, often make a radical break with their old religious ways. For example, in parts of Africa they forbade the use of drums, which were frequently used in pagan rites. Third- and fourth-generation Christians, however, often seek their cultural identity by turning back to their traditional customs. They no longer associate these with pagan meanings. Churches in Africa, for instance, are reexamining the use of drums and many are using them in Christian worship services because they are no longer symbols of pagan but of African identity.

It is important that we understand and support this search for cultural identity and help the church to critically reevaluate its cultural past. At times, the greatest contribution we can make in the process is to support church leaders in such re-evaluations. They often hesitate to do so out of respect for the first missionaries, who many times condemned much of the people's culture.

Self-theologizing

Another expression of independence is the emergence of local theologies. At first, most converts know little about the Bible and its teaching. They accept with little question the theological teaching of the missionaries.

After a generation or two biblically trained leaders emerge who begin to ask difficult theological questions that arise out of their culture—questions such as, "What does the gospel have to say about ancestors and spirits?" "What should the church do about polygamy?" and "How should Christians respond to witchcraft?" They develop local theologies to answer these questions.

How should we respond to this "self-theologizing"? Our initial reaction is to reject it. We are afraid that the leaders may stray from our theological positions. If we deny them the right to theologize, however, we condemn the church to spiritual immaturity. The leaders have the same Scriptures we do and they have the right to read and interpret those Scriptures. Moreover, they are led by the same Holy Spirit. A second reaction is to withdraw and let the leaders develop their own theology unassisted. This denies them the theological heritage of the church and the insights gained by centuries of biblical scholarship.

It is important that we be willing to participate in the theological discussions of the young church as resource persons and as catalysts. Because we come from outside, we often see more clearly than the local church leaders where their theology is shaped more by their culture than by Scripture. They often see better than we where our theologies are more a product of western culture than of biblical teaching.

Independent churches

One expression of cultural independence is the emergence of African, Indian, Chinese, and other independent churches. These are denominations started by local leaders and are not affiliated with western missions and denominations. Often these leaders were trained in mission schools but have left the mission churches when their visions of indigenous forms of Christianity were spurned. David Barrett points out (1968, 139) that there is an incubation period averaging sixty years between the first planting of churches in a new culture and the emergence of independent church movements. There are now some eight thousand such movements in Africa alone.

Harold Turner (1981) notes that independent churches are part of a continuum of movements that emerge when tribal religions encounter Christianity (fig. 23).

The "New Testament" independent churches look to the Bible, particularly the New Testament, for their theological guidance. They look, however, to their tribal past for their cultural identity. They include such groups as Kimbangoists and Harrists in Africa and the Little Flock churches in China.

The "Hebraist" churches look for instruction to the Old Testament with its polygamy, sacrifices, and rituals. They identify closely with their traditional cultures but may see themselves as the descendants of the ten lost tribes of Israel. They include the Bayudaya of Uganda and the Maori movements of New Zealand.

The "syncretistic" churches mix traditional religion with Christian beliefs and practices in an attempt to mediate between the

Figure 23
The Interaction of Western Christianity and Tribal Religions

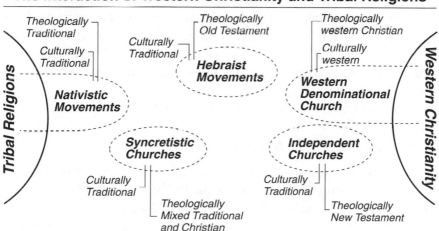

Adapted from Turner 1981, 19

two worlds. The result is syncretism. Such is the case of the North American Indian Church.

The "Nativistic" movements seek to revive the old tribal religions and reconvert Christians to the religion of their ancestors. Among these are the Religion of the Ancestors in Kenya and the Godians in Nigeria.

Interdependence

The goal of missions is not autonomous national churches but churches with a global vision working in partnership to win the world to Christ and his kingdom. This is possible only when the autonomy of different segments of the church is recognized and when these segments realize they are part of one body called to work together as partners to evangelize the world.

Working in partnership is not easy, however, particularly when some churches are large and others small; some rich and others poor; some well-established and others newly founded. What the large, rich, and established churches must discover is that they have as much or more to learn from small, poor, new churches as vice versa. The simple faith and vital Christian life of young tribal churches can help renew old, ingrown, and highly institutionalized churches.

Theological Issues In Tribal Churches

Tribes have been particularly responsive to the gospel and many of today's churches have their origins in tribal conversions. Like all churches, tribal churches face problems rooted in human sinfulness: greed, selfishness, quarrels, desire for power, self-centeredness, and so on. They also face unique theological issues that relate to their social and cultural organization—issues church planters in tribal societies must be ready to face.

Dealing with Old Beliefs and Customs

One important question facing all converts is what to do with their old customs. What music should they play? Whom should they marry? How should they bury their dead?

These questions are of particular importance in tribal societies, for religion is at the heart of their culture and touches every activity in the lives of the people. What should Christians do with their traditional dances and drums that were often used in spirit rites? Should they conduct fertility rites to assure them of good crops when these rites appeal to the ancestors for help?

Noncontextualization

In the past, missionaries rejected many tribal customs because they were associated with pagan beliefs and replaced them with western Christian practices. There were various reasons for this call for radical change in the lives of new converts. Some missionaries equated the gospel with western Christianity and "civilization" and saw tribal cultures as primitive, to be rooted out. Other missionaries understood tribal cultures well and knew that religion in them touches every area of people's lives. To continue using old customs, therefore, increases the danger of syncretism. Most emphasized the prophetic nature of the gospel and the need for a radical transformation in the lives and cultures of new Christians.

This wholesale rejection of old cultural ways created several problems. First, getting rid of old ways left a cultural vacuum that needed to be filled. Missionaries did so by introducing their own customs. Western music, clothing, food, marriages, and funerals replaced traditional practices. The western church became the model for tribal churches around the world. Consequently, Christianity was seen as a "white man's" religion. Christian converts were branded as traitors to their own people and treated as foreigners in their own land.

Second, when missionaries tried to suppress old cultural ways, these did not die—they went underground. Christians held Christian weddings in churches and then the traditional marriage rites in the village after the missionary and the pastor were gone. They prayed for healing in church but tied amulets and medicine bags under their clothes. The result was a mix of a public Christianity to get people to heaven and a private animism to protect them from the spirits, sickness, and death.

Over the years, the secret practices have resurfaced in Christian communities and led to syncretisms that have weakened the church. Today, church leaders are having to deal with the resurgence of witchcraft, magic, and spiritism.

Uncritical Contextualization

After World War II, western colonialism began to die. Moreover, through the work of linguists and anthropologists, missionaries began to see the good in other cultures. They learned to accept these cultures and not to judge them by western values and practices. They sought to fit the gospel into local cultural forms as much as possible. The missionaries realized that ethnocentrism had often closed the door to effective communication and that the "foreignness" of the gospel was one of the greatest barriers to its acceptance in many parts of the world.

We must deeply respect other cultures. However, an uncritical acceptance of them, like an uncritical acceptance of our own culture, devalues the transforming power of the gospel. First, an uncritical acceptance of any culture overlooks the fact that sin is both corporate and personal. It is found in social structures that oppress people and keep them from responding to the gospel. It is also present in cultural beliefs that keep people from faith, such as idolatry, ethnic pride, and fear of spirits.

Second, seeing human cultures as basically good and contextualizing the gospel in them uncritically makes the gospel captive to culture. The result is a cultural Christianity that has little power to transform societies or a Christopaganism that combines Christianity with old religious ways.

Critical Contextualization

An uncritical rejection of old cultural ways and an uncritical acceptance of them both lead to a syncretistic church, but what other alternative is there? A third approach is a critical contextualization of the gospel in which the old ways are evaluated in light of the gospel (fig. 24, following page).

The process may begin as people study Scripture and are convicted of their old practices, or it may be triggered by questions arising out of life, such as how Christians should bury the dead or what they should do with the drums they used to summon their old gods. The strategy has four steps.

Exegesis of the culture

The first step is to study the local culture phenomenologically. Here the church leaders and missionaries lead the Christians in

Figure 24
Critical Contextualization

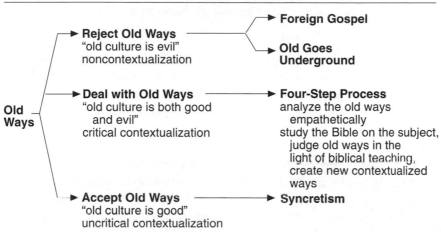

gathering and analyzing the traditional beliefs and customs of the tribe. For example, faced with the question of how Christians should bury their dead, the Christians should first examine their traditional rites. They should describe each song, dance, recitation, and rite of the old burial ceremonies and discuss the meaning of these.

It is important in this step not to judge the old ways. The purpose here is to understand them. If the leaders or the missionaries criticize the traditional ways, people will not talk about them freely for fear of being condemned. The old ways simply go underground.

It is important, too, to remember that the people themselves are the experts in analyzing their own culture. The leaders must listen and avoid telling people that they are wrong.

Exegesis of the Scripture

In the second step the pastor or the missionary leads the church in a study of the Scriptures related to the question at hand. In our example, the leaders should teach people the Christian beliefs about death and resurrection. Here the leaders play a major role, for this is the area of their expertise, but lay Christians must also be involved in the study because they must learn how to study the Bible for themselves.

It is important that the leaders be sensitive to the problems of cross-cultural communication, or the biblical message will be distorted. Linguistics and anthropology have much to offer here.

Critical response

The third step is for people corporately to critically evaluate their past customs in light of their new biblical understanding. The gospel is a call to change, but if the leaders make the decisions about change, they must become police and enforce their decisions. If people make the decisions, they will corporately enforce them.

To involve people in the process of evaluating their own culture in light of new truth draws upon their strength. They know their old culture better than do outsiders and are in a better position to accurately critique it after they have been biblically instructed. To include them also helps them grow spiritually by teaching them discernment and discipleship. Generally speaking, it is more important for new Christians to begin making decisions about their lives in the light of Scripture as they understand it than that they make what we may feel to be the right decisions.

The Christians may respond to old beliefs and practices in different ways. They will keep many old practices, just as we do. Through these, people reaffirm their cultural identity and heritage. But they will reject other customs as unchristian. We may not understand the reasons for this repudiation, but people know the deep hidden meanings and associations of their old ways. Sometimes we may need to question practices people have overlooked because these seem so natural to them.

The Christians may choose to transform old practices by giving these explicit Christian meanings. They may use their word for the High God for the God of the Bible; give new words to old melodies; and use traditional stories and proverbs to teach biblical truths.

Christians should also create new symbols and rituals to communicate Christian beliefs in forms indigenous to their own culture. One sign of spiritual life is this ability to create an indigenous Christian music, art, and culture.

The church should also adopt rites that speak of its new identity as part of the church universal. In becoming Christians, people acquire a new history and spiritual heritage. Baptism, the Lord's

Supper, church creeds, and hymns not only provide them with ways to express their new faith, but also symbolize their ties to the historical and global church.

New contextualized practices

After critically evaluating their old ways, people, led by their pastors, need to create new rites and practices that are both Christian and native. They are no longer pagans, nor should they live like western Christians.

This process of critical contextualization takes the Bible seriously as the rule of faith and life. It recognizes the work of the Holy Spirit in the lives of all believers open to God's leading. It also strengthens the church by making it a hermeneutical community in which everyone seeks to understand God's message to his people in the context of their everyday lives.

Critical contextualization must be an ongoing process. On the one hand the world is constantly changing, raising new questions that must be addressed. On the other, all our understandings of and obedience to the gospel are partial. Through continued study and response, we all can grow in spiritual maturity.

Dealing with Spirits, Power, and Witchcraft

Several areas of tribal culture require our special attention. One of these is the animistic worldview with its belief in spirits, magic, divination, and witchcraft. The initial response of many missionaries, especially from the west, is that these practices are not only pagan, but also figments of the tribal imagination that need to be eradicated. Westerners come from a culture that denies such spiritual realities.

Unfortunately, this view does not take the beliefs of people seriously. Even if their beliefs are wrong, people do believe and act on them. We cannot ignore or condemn these beliefs without explanation.

A second response is to accept the reality of the animistic worldview—to say that all the people's demons do in fact exist, that witchcraft and magic do command supernatural powers, and that divination does foretell the future. The danger is that we turn Christianity into a new and superior magic. The old worldview is not challenged. New tribal Christians often see Christian prayers as magic formulas, Bible verses as amulets, and preachers as magicians more powerful than their old ones. Christianity is perceived as a powerful witchcraft and spiritism, but the fear of witchcraft and spirits remains.

To deal critically with the animistic worldview, we must first understand it *phenomenologically* as a cultural system—as a system of beliefs that people believe is true. We must also examine carefully the functions divination, witchcraft, spirits, exorcisms, shamanism, and other beliefs serve in the social and political life of the tribe.

For example, in some tribes, belief in witchcraft serves as a social control, keeping people from deviant behavior for fear of being branded witches. In small, strongly group-oriented societies living in hostile environments and surrounded by unfriendly neighbors witchcraft serves as a release to pent-up hostilities. People dare not express their anger against one another for fear of disrupting the unity of the group, and that anger builds up until someone accuses another—usually a widow, a loner, a newcomer, or other marginal person—of being a witch. She or he is punished and the social tensions subside for a time. In this form, witchcraft may be a form of social pathology because it unfairly targets marginal people.

Second, we must evaluate the beliefs and practices regarding spirits and witchcraft *ontologically* in the light of biblical teachings. Here we must be careful that we do not judge them from a western secular point of view. We seek to understand God's response to these beliefs and practices.

Third, we must minister to people *missiologically*. We must start by ministering to people where they are in their understanding of reality. People do not change their worldviews overnight and we cannot wait until they do so. We can, in truth, proclaim that God is more powerful than all spirits, real and imagined, and that he delivers his people from fear of them. We should pray for those who are sick, possessed, fearful, and insecure and help them find their refuge in the God of the Bible.

We must, however, then begin the long task of changing people's worldview to a biblical one. Their ideas about evil must be Christianized, just as much as their understanding of the nature of God. An example of this worldview transformation is found in the Old

Testament. God ruthlessly condemns the belief and practice of magic (Exod. 9:11); witchcraft (1 Sam. 15:23); divination (Deut. 18:10); fetishism (Exod. 20:3–6); and shamanism (Lev. 20:6) practiced by the tribes surrounding Israel. He makes it clear that the other gods are no gods (Exod. 32:39; Isa. 44:6–20).

Spirits and Power

How do beliefs in spirits fit into this picture? Clearly each tribe must be examined separately. Many things that people consider to be spirits, such as the Spirits of Lightning, Smallpox, Eclipse, and Dustdevils, are better understood in natural terms. Other "spirits" are better understood as social and mental illnesses. Still others are real and demonic and must be handled through Scripture, prayer, and exorcism. This task of discerning what is caused by spirits and what is not is not an easy one.

We need also deal with people's focus on power. It is true that God often manifests himself to tribal peoples in demonstrations of power, but it also true that a fascination with power as a means to achieve our own desires is unbiblical. William Reyburn notes (1978, 273),

> The insipid nature of much of the African's Christianity stems from the fact that he joins a church and relies upon this association (church contagion) to place him nearer to the source of power. The step which is badly needed in the communication of the gospel to the African is that the presence of this power is realized in submission to the role of the humble servant to be filled with a power for service to others.

The church needs to present the biblical views of power and greatness. It must teach that we are to submit ourselves to God in worship and discipleship and not to try to control him by means of formulas and rites. It needs to honor servanthood and counter the traditional symbols of greatness such as many wives, political power, and wealth.

Facing evil requires more than responding to spirits and witchcraft. We need also to speak out against social and cultural evils that oppress and impoverish people and keep them from seeing the truth. Humans in authority are often the source of evil in a community and of resistance to the gospel. Shamans, witches and witchdoctors, village heads, and clan and family leaders have great influence. They can exploit people and keep them from following Christ, but if they become Christians, they can lead many to faith.

Witchcraft

Dealing with witchcraft raises other questions because it involves human beings accused of being witches. Some people indeed have committed themselves to evil and its attending powers. Many accused of being witches, however, are victims of social politics.

How we minister to witches and those bewitched depends on the situation. In each specific situation we must begin by discerning the nature of witchcraft we see. We must deliver those who have committed themselves to evil and witchcraft but want to renounce it, and minister to those who believe themselves, truly or mistakenly, to be bewitched. When the cause is social, however, we must defend those falsely accused of being witches.

In the long run, we must challenge the system of beliefs associated with witchcraft, and teach Christians that when they put their trust in God, they are freed from the dread and power of witchcraft. They must be taught to have no involvement in witchcraft, occultic powers, amulets, charms, and "medicines" connected with sorcery (Gal. 5:20–21). This freedom from fear is one of the most compelling and widespread testimonies to the power of Christ in the lives of tribal peoples who follow him.

We should also deal with the social roots that lie behind much of witchcraft, namely, tensions and hostilities in the group. The church must become a community of trust and support and have biblical ways for resolving jealousies and hostilities (Mulumba 1988). In group-oriented societies, it is impossible to overestimate the need for new Christians to have a new community of support. People's sense of identity depends on it, because they have not been taught to think of themselves as autonomous individuals. The best response to witchcraft is a caring church in which people share their anger and fears openly and deal with them by means of prayer and mutual support.

Finally, the church must address witchcraft in the larger non-Christian community of which it is a part. It must condemn the practicing of witchcraft as evil. It must defend Christians and others falsely accused of practicing witchcraft. It must also demonstrate the power of God to deliver when real witchcraft is involved.

Dealing with Ancestors and the Unborn

Few questions are more difficult to answer than those having to do with ancestors and the unborn. In the past missionaries often condemned rites associated with ancestors as worship and forbade them. People often thought, therefore, that Christians have no respect for their parents and forebearers. This idea was reinforced by the fact that people were encouraged to make their own decisions for Christ without asking their parents and relatives.

Unfortunately, the coming of Christianity and modernity have often led to the breakdown of extended family and kinship systems that were the moral foundations of a society. The result has been a rise in prostitution, divorce, and broken homes.

More recently second- and third-generation leaders in young churches have begun to reexamine the biblical view of ancestors. Some have reintroduced practices that border on worship. Others have sought to restore respect for parents but to avoid the worship of ancestors.

In societies with ancestor rites, the church needs to formulate a theology of ancestors. This should make explicit the similarities and differences between Christian and traditional beliefs on such matters as the nature of life after death, the relationship between the ancestors and God, the relationship between the living and the dead, and the connection between parents and children. It should also deal with the widespread fear that those who die untimely deaths through murder, suicide, or accident become ghosts that plague the living. The church needs to respond sensitively to the question many ask: "Will I join my ancestors if I become a Christian?"

The church must also create Christian rites that give public testimony to its beliefs. These should show that Christians do show great respect for their ancestors but that they do not worship them. Christian funerals should recognize sorrow but also bear witness to resurrection and eternal life. Annual memorial services may be organized to bear public testimony to the fact that Christians do honor their forebearers.

Finally, the church needs to instruct Christians on how to act when they attend non-Christian ancestor rites. In many ways this question is the most difficult to answer. On the one hand, great pressure is applied by the community on the new Christians to observe traditional practices when they attend the funerals of their parents, grandparents, and other close relatives. On the other hand, their behavior on such occasions can be a powerful evangelistic witness to their non-Christian kin.

In the modern world, the meanings associated with ancestor rites are changing. In many places people bow or burn incense not as religious acts but as cultural traditions. Some theologians believe that Christians should never participate in ceremonies some see as worship. Others argue that if acts are religious to some and secular to others, Christians can perform the rites provided they share beforehand their convictions and practices with non-Christian relatives and friends. That way, the latter will know that Christians honor but do not worship their ancestors.

Dealing with Polygamy, Widows, and Orphans

Another set of issues tribal churches face has to do with polygamy. For the most part, most western missionaries have condemned it, claiming that it is unbiblical.

Before we respond to polygamy, however, we need to understand its role in the social order. Contrary to western popular belief, polygamy often has little to do with men's desire for sex. Rather it serves important economic and social functions. Men seek power and vitality through polygamy. A man with many wives and children, numerous gardens, bountiful crops, and accumulated wealth has much life force and is an important person. Several wives also means more daughters who bring the man large bride prices when they are married—bride prices he can use to obtain another wife. In the end of life the man is honored and cared for as the head of a large family and is remembered as an ancestor.

Wives, too, may benefit by polygamy. Reyburn writes (1978, 259),

A woman who has more work than she can handle is often anxious that her husband take on another wife. This frees the first wife from much of her burden and gives her free time to take produce to a market, and sell it and perhaps spend her money. She will be free to go to her village and visit, to spend more time with her small children and to undertake other tasks in which she finds pleasure.

The first wife occupies a position of authority. She orders the junior wives and mediates between them. Frequently, she alone has direct access to their husband.

Polygamy serves another important social function: It resolves crises caused by the death of a husband (see pp. 88–89).

Polygamy is also used to cement relationships. Men have male friends and it is not uncommon for a man to marry his daughter to a friend to strengthen their friendship.

Finally, polygamy reduces adultery in societies where men are forbidden to have intercourse with their wives for two or three years after the birth of a child for fear of "killing the child."

New types of polygamy are emerging. With the rapid spread of industry and desire for money and modern goods, men go to the city to earn money. They leave their wives and children in the village to care for fields and old people. Away from their families for long periods of time, men are tempted to take a second wife in the city whom they support with their earnings. The rural family is left to fend for itself. Both rural and urban churches must address problems arising out of male urban migration.

What should be the church's response to polygamy? Given its important functions in tribal life, we cannot eliminate it by command. Even if we could do so, we would have to find other cultural ways to care for the widows, orphans, single women, and barren couples. Furthermore, to require men to put away all their wives but one is to teach them divorce, which is clearly unbiblical. People come to Christ as they are and we must begin with the social realities they bring with them into the church.

We must begin by teaching biblical views of marriage. These include the dignity of women, who are created fully in God's image, and the partnership of both sexes in marriage. Where these values are taught in the churches, polygamy declines. We need to deal also with barrenness and singleness and teach that childless couples are not cursed, nor are unmarried individuals half persons. Their fulfillment can lie in their ministry and in the spiritual children they beget.

So far we have looked at the church's response to polygamy, but what about the church's response to the polygamist? In the past, many missions refused to baptize a man with more than one wife. A polygamist had to put away all but one wife before he could join the church and few were willing to do so. Because all wives were married only to one man, they were allowed to join the church. Consequently, congregations often consisted primarily of women.

Putting away wives created many problems. Widows were left with only pagan men to care for them because Christian men with wives refused to marry them. Wives and children who were put away hated the gospel for what it did to them, and many of the women became prostitutes to survive. And, as one African leader pointed out, Christianity taught people that polygamy was worse than divorce.

In recent years, most churches have begun to baptize polygamists, recognizing that their marriages took place before they became Christians and that they have responsibilities to their wives and children. However, many churches prohibit polygamists from taking more wives or being leaders in the church.

This solution allows the shift to monogamy to take place over several generations, but it gives rise to another problem. Most Christian men whose wives bear them no children are under great pressure to take second wives. They know that if they take a second wife, they will be disciplined by the church. They also know that after several years they will be restored to fellowship with their two wives. The precedent was set when polygamists were admitted into the church.

Tribal churches continue to struggle with the care of widows. Old solutions such as polygamy have been abandoned, but no new solutions have emerged.

Marriage and Morality

The coming of Christianity has often challenged the traditional beliefs regarding marriage and sexuality. The result has been a moral confusion that threatens to undermine the church.

One area of moral confusion is based on changes in the nature and arrangements of marriage. One of these changes has to do with the selection of a spouse. In most tribes marriages are arranged by the family and the tribal elders. As modernity spreads, young people reject arranged marriages and choose partners on the basis of love. Many of these marriages lack the support of family and community and end in divorce.

In arranged marriages, the relations of the couple before marriage were carefully regulated by everyone in the community. Commonly those caught in adultery were killed and those caught in premarital sex were publicly shamed. When colonial governments came, they declared these to be crimes punishable by the state and forbade traditional tribal leaders from punishing sexual violations. People soon learned that adultery and premarital sex were rarely punished and then only with small fines.

Today, with the increase of "love marriages," the old constraints are gone and the church has no new ones to replace them. Consequently, there is often an increase in premarital sex, trial marriages, and other types of immorality.

One area needing particular attention is the escalation of marriage costs. Traditionally a man paid a fixed amount of animals or crops to the bride's parents to compensate them for the progeny she would bear. Today this progeny price must be paid in cash and modern goods and the amount is open for negotiation. Weddings, particularly in urban churches, are becoming costly affairs where families show off their status and wealth.

In many places, marriages are becoming too expensive for young men. Either they must wait until they are older before they can marry or they must elope with their lover and establish a common-law household. Rich old men, on the other hand, display their wealth by marrying several wives, and parents acquire wealth by offering their daughters to the highest bidders. Here the church must speak to the underlying problem of greed, pride, and the high cost of marriage.

As we have seen, most tribal societies have initiation rites in which children are transformed into adults. Those who are not initiated are seen as boys and girls, no matter how old they are. One important function of these rites is education. The children are taken to the forest or camp where they learn the secrets of tribal life and knowledge. Old men teach the boys about sex, hunting, bravery, family life, and what it means to be a man. Elderly women teach the girls about sex, pregnancy, childrearing, cooking, and what it means to be a woman.

Another important function is reaffirming tribal unity. This is often done by the rite of circumcision of males and sometimes females. In many tribes, circumcision speaks of bravery and virility; of union with the tribe and its ways; and of identification with the ancestors. John Mbiti writes (1969, 161), "the shedding of blood in the ground binds [the young African male] mystically with the living dead who are symbolically living in the ground, or are reached at least through the pouring of libation on the ground."

Early missionaries generally forbade initiation rites in the church. They did so because they did not understand them (there were no comparable rites in the west) and because of pagan elements in the rituals. Christian men and women, therefore, were looked upon in the tribe as children throughout their lives.

Tribal churches now realize the need for a Christian ritual of initiation. This should not be equated with baptism, for then people seek baptism to become adults and not for reasons of faith. Nor should it be the old rite with its pagan associations. What is needed is a ritual in which Christians publicly mark their transition to social and religious adulthood.

Churches are also discovering the urgent need for education in sex, morality, family relations, and other aspects of adult living to replace those lost when the traditional initiation rites were dropped.

Identity Crisis

Today, around the world, tribal societies are on collision courses with modernity. Few are so isolated that they are able to retain their old ways. Most are being swept into the stream of modern, global life, often against their will. It is not uncommon to see a man or a woman raised in a tribal hamlet, flying around the world in jets and participating in international conferences.

These changes have affected tribes in different ways. Some have managed to survive and adapt to a globalized world. Tribal political parties, cultural centers, businesses, and churches help people retain their tribal identities in cities, often at the expense of national loyalties and stability. Work, education, business, and government, however, draw them into the modern world of individualism and material comforts. Many end up as cultural schizophrenics, caught between traditional and modern worlds.

Cultural Schizophrenia

For a few people in tribal societies, modernity has brought prosperity and new ways of life. For many it has brought the collapse of families, villages, and old ways of life. For all it has created an identity crisis of enormous proportions.

Modernity attacks the group orientation of tribal societies. The traditional morality that linked individuals to the family at large—the clan and the tribe—is dying. Increasingly there is only law, which is obeyed only for fear of physical punishment. Elders wise in the ways of the world are replaced by young leaders who have western education. Sharing and concern for the well-being of the community are replaced by personal material gain. The individual is encouraged to find his or her own self-fulfillment. The devastation in terms of people's corporate identity is incalculable. Modernity has come and people cannot go back to their traditional ways which were sounder because of an overall unity achieved by a respect for power far greater than that of the modern police force with its jails and firing squads.

Modernity also destroys the core of traditional beliefs and values. These are rejected as irrational myths. Tribals often attempt to completely adopt the new ways or to recapture the old, but both are impossible. Their life has been changed and is going to change increasingly and inevitably. People are faced with the question of how to reconcile this change with a belief in the past to which traditionalists still cling, or the acceptance of a foreign belief that is usually superficial. The result has been a profound spiritual crisis. Tribal people no longer can "go home" to their past cultures and they do not belong mentally to the new world around them.

As Colin Turnbull points out, the problem is most acute in the westernized city.

[There it] results either in the abandonment of all belief, which is perhaps the most logical solution, or else in the adoption of the outer form of western belief without any inner conviction. This applies not only to religious belief, but also to political and economic and social life. And in each case it leaves either a terrible spiritual void and emptiness of purpose, or else the desperation of sheer materialism, both of which threaten to destroy the Africans as a people in their own right (1968, 68).

Unfortunately, Christian missionaries in the past did little to alleviate the situation because they often saw modern "civilization" as part of the gospel. Most did not encourage tribal people to keep what was good and valuable in their own culture. Jon Bonk notes, "Missionaries could not be expected to match in scientific sophistication the racist-imperialist thinking of the leading intellectuals of the time, but they could hardly have been unaffected by it" (1980, 299).

It is urgent that the church in tribal societies help people find a new identity in Christ, who meets them in their own cultural context. It is the Christians who must provide the moral and spiritual roots that can help tribal people maintain their cultural identities in lands overrun by modernity.

Political Rivalries

Today in many young nations carved out of tribal lands by colonial rulers, tribal rivalries have emerged. Often one tribe gains political power and excludes the others from key government offices. The result is periodic civil wars in which those out of power try to gain control. Even if they do, they generally replace rule by one tribe with that of another.

In such situations, the church has a special responsibility to work for intertribal harmony and to exercise its power for justice and peace. This is not easy, for it pits people's Christian identity against their tribal loyalties. The extent to which Christians are willing to participate in intertribal wars is an indication that Christianity has not yet become their deepest identity. In this, however, they are no different from many Christians in the west who are willing to kill Christians of other countries in the name of national defense.

Cultural Disintegration

With the spread of modernity and urbanization, many tribes are decimated as their young move to cities for work and excitement. There, caught between the promises of the city and its stark realities, the young eke out a bare living without a community and cultural tradition that give them an identity and support. Relatives and friends come from the countryside expecting extended hospitality, believing everyone in the city is rich. The urban dwellers are caught between traditional tribal demands to share what they have and their need to accumulate wealth to buy houses and start businesses.

Migration also ravages tribal villages. Young gifted adults go to the cities and men go to work in mines and factories, leaving the aged, the wives, and the children to maintain life at home. Some tribes disintegrate in their confrontation with modernity. Their members end up living on the edges of towns and cities, marginal, alienated, and drunk.

The church, so far, has done little to reach tribal peoples caught in the backwaters of modernity. To do so, it must offer them dignity and hope. It must offer them salvation, a new identity, a new community in Christ, and a new life.

We will look further at tribal peoples as they assimilate into peasant and urban societies.

6 | Peasant Societies

During early human history most people lived in bands and tribes. Today, more than two billion peasants live in more than a million villages. These rural communities form the backbone of the great civilizations of China, India, Central and South America, Europe, Russia, and North America.

The massive numbers of peasants lead to great diversity. Peasants live in low, hot, flat, coastal areas and in high, cold rugged mountains. Some work full-time on their own land; others rent, sharecrop, or work part-time as artisans. Still others, especially in recent times, spend much of their time working for wages in distant places, returning periodically to help with the crops.

Peasants are rural cultivators, fishers, or craftsmen associated with agricultural production. Most use animals to plow and irrigate their fields. But peasants do not operate agribusinesses for profit, unlike many farmers in the United States and Europe. They use farming and animal husbandry as a means of livelihood. Even so, the economic surpluses that peasants produce make possible through trade and taxation the growth of cities and nations.

Peasants live in two worlds. On the one hand, they are poor, subsistence-oriented, rural people often living in relatively isolated communities. They care most about what is going on in their families, fields, and villages. Their community life reflects this inward-looking orientation. On the other hand, peasants are tied to the world outside their communities. Peasant societies are subject to outside governments and markets, and their taxation, military control, and market forces intrude on peasants' everyday concerns.

The distinction between tribal and peasant societies is not a sharp one. Tribal societies, too, are not isolated. They often have symbiotic economic and ritual relationships with one another and with peasant communities. The primary distinction is not the degree of outside involvement but the character of that involvement. Tribal societies are more or less politically and economically autonomous and share their economic resources among their members. Peasants are subject to outside rulers who tax their surplus production to maintain courts, cities, armies, and a ruling elite. They must also sell their products or their labor to outside markets to survive. Peasants differ from city dwellers, however, because they are tied to the land and produce their own food.

Eric Wolf (1955) makes a useful distinction between closed and open peasant communities. The former are more inward-looking than the latter. Closed communities tend to produce basic grains for food rather than commercial crops and are more isolated from the cultural, historical, and political life of the larger society with which they are linked. Open communities have more economic, political, and cultural ties to that outside society. The influences of the outside world are more direct and more important in the everyday lives of the peasants. Today Coca-Cola, transistor radios, fertilizers, and sewing machines are found in many peasant villages. Land shortages have also led many rural people to migrate in search of work. All these connections to the outside world undermine the peasants' ability to determine the course of their own lives. The peasants are subject to outside forces beyond their own control.

Society

Still, compared to cities, peasant villages are relatively autonomous communities. They provide most or all the essentials necessary for the community to survive. Many also strive to prevent outsiders from becoming members of the community and discourage their members from having close relationships with the outside world.

But the fact that peasant villages are tied economically and politically to a larger society influences the way they organize life. To understand them, we must examine both their internal social organization and their ties to the larger states of which they are a part.

Social Structure

Most tribes are homogeneous groups. Apart from visitors, everyone speaks the same language, shares the same culture, occupies the same land, and has the same blood. Most importantly, all families do the same work.

Peasant societies are often heterogeneous. They are made up of different groups of people, often with different cultures and languages. Internally, each of these operates like a homogeneous group. Externally, these groups are held together not by blood or shared culture, but by social, economic, and political systems that regulate relationships between groups. As we will see, these systems constitute a higher-level social organization.

Two types of social groups appear in peasant societies: ethnic groups and classes. In some villages one type is dominant; in other villages the other is primary. But both are generally found in most peasant communities.

Multiethnic Communities

Tribalism continues in many peasant societies in the form of ethnicity. Like tribes, ethnic groups are based on ties of blood and marriage. Consequently, much of what has already been said about kinship-based groups, marriage, and descent holds true for ethnic groups in a village. Families, extended families, lineages, and kinship ties take care of most of the primary needs of an individual. Polygamy among the wealthy, levirate marriages of widows to their husband's nearest male relative, and the adoption of a son of a relative to continue the family name are not uncommon occurrences. Nor is the enforcement of important decisions made by the heads of families and lineages.

What is different from tribal settings is the presence of more than one sizeable ethnic group in the same village. This raises questions of relationships between two or more ethnic groups and calls for a higher level of organization to maintain social order.

An example of a simple polyethnic society is found in Rwanda, East Africa, where three tribes—the Tutsi, the Hutu, and the Twa Pygmies—live scattered across the same countryside. The Tutsi are pastoralists. In the past they were the patrons, political rulers, and military leaders who controlled the labor and economic surpluses of the other groups. The Hutu are agriculturalists who worked the fields of their Tutsi patrons, kept the Tutsi huts in repair, carried their patrons in litters when they traveled, and attended them at night. In return, the Hutu clients counted on the economic profit of the cattle loaned them by their patrons, help in times of distress, and protection in all spheres of their lives. The Twa Pygmies, dependent on hunting and food gathering, lived in nearby mountain forests. Some were potters who traded their wares with the Hutu and Tutsi. Others gathered honey and brewed honey beer, which was the favorite drink of the Tutsi (d'Hertefelt 1965, 407–40). In exchange they received grain from the Hutu and milk and skins from the Tutsi.

In the past, relationships, particularly between the Tutsi and the Hutu, were often close. Tutsi men occasionally took Hutu women as wives or concubines and Tutsi men made blood-brother compacts with Hutu men. Nevertheless, the ethnic groups remained distinct. The Tutsi were the ruling aristocracy and the Hutu the commoners. The disruption of the traditional relations (see chap. 4) between the Hutus and the Tutsi by colonialism has caused bitter rivalries and killings in recent years.

Caste-Based Communities

The close interdependence between the Tutsi, Hutu, and Twa constitutes a higher form of social system—a simple caste system. Castes are ethnic groups that form an integrated part of a larger society in which they retain their distinguishing identities. Castes usually take on economic specialization and are valued differently. In other words, they are organized along a hierarchy of status and power.

The classical case of a caste system is peasant society in India. Here many ethnic groups, or *jatis*, are integrated in a common social system on the basis of specialization, hierarchy, and hereditary ties.

Specialization integrates castes into a single economic system. Many castes have monopolies on certain essential occupations. There are blacksmith, rocksmith, goldsmith, carpenter, barber, and laundryman castes, as well as castes of priests, winetappers, weavers of fine cloth, weavers of coarse cloth, fishermen, tanners, musicians, dramatists, bards, and snake charmers. Not all castes in India have occupational monopolies and not all work belongs to certain castes. Day labor, farming, general trade, and other tasks are open to everyone. So also are modern occupations such as tailors using modern sewing machines, aluminum workers, taxi drivers, and factory workers.

Hierarchy regulates relationships between people of different castes. Each caste has a rank based on its ritual purity. At the top are the priestly castes, or Brahmins. Beneath these are Kshatriya castes, which once were the rulers and warriors; the Vaishya castes, which handled banking and trade; and a great many Sudra castes, such as farmers, craftsmen (weavers, potters, ironsmiths, carpenters, rocksmiths, goldsmiths), and service people (barbers and laundrymen, to name two). At the bottom of the social scale are "untouchable" castes (sweepers, leather workers), which keep the village clean.

A person must show respect for persons from higher castes by standing, bowing, and not touching them and by eating food they offer. A person must also show superiority to those of castes beneath him or her by not eating their food or doing their jobs.

Reading 3

The Sweeper

Mulk Raj Anand

[In peasant societies, with the emergence of multiethnic and multiclass communities and of systems of social hierarchy, some people are in positions of power and dominance; others are powerless and oppressed. This passage by Mulk Raj Anand describes the experiences of Bakha, a member of the Sweeper caste in an Indian village who is discovering as a young man the harsh reality of his status at the bottom of the society.]

Reprinted with permission from *Untouchable* by Mulk Raj Anand (London: Bodley Head, 1933).

[Bakha's] mouth was watering. He unfolded the paper in which the jalebis [sweets] were wrapped and put a piece hastily into his mouth. The taste of the warm and sweet syrup was satisfying and delightful. He attacked the packet again. It was nice to fill one's mouth, he felt, because only then could you feel the full savour of the thing. . . .

'Keep to the side of the road, you low-caste vermin!' he suddenly heard someone shouting at him. 'Why don't you call, you swine, and announce your approach! Do you know you have touched me and defiled me, you cockeyed son of a bow-legged scorpion! Now I will have to go and take a bath to purify myself. And it was a new dhoti and shirt I put on this morning!'

Bakha stood amazed, embarrassed. He was deaf and dumb. His senses were paralysed. Only fear gripped his soul, fear and humility and servility. He was used to being spoken to roughly. But he had seldom been taken so unawares. The curious smile of humility which always hovered on his lips in the presence of high-caste men now became more pronounced. He lifted his face to the man opposite him, though his eyes were bent down. Then he stole a hurried glance at the man. The man's eyes were flaming and red-hot.

'You swine, you dog, why didn't you shout and warn me of your approach!' he shouted, as he met Bakha's eyes. 'Don't you know, you brute, that you must not touch me!'

Bakha's mouth was open. But he couldn't utter a single word. He was about to apologize. He had already joined his hands instinctively. Now he bent his forehead over them, and he mumbled something. . . . The man was not satisfied with dumb humility.

'Dirty dog! Son of a bitch! The offspring of a pig!' he shouted, his temper spluttering on his tongue and obstructing his speech, and the sense behind it, in its mad rush outwards. 'I . . . I'll have to go-o-o . . . and get washed-d-d- . . . I . . . I was going to business and now . . . now, on account of **you** I'll be late.'

A few other men gathered around to see what the row was about. The poor lad, confused still more by the conspicuous place he occupied in the middle of the crowd, felt like collapsing. His first impulse was to run, just to shoot across the throng, away away, far away from the torment. But then he realized that he was surrounded by a barrier, not a physical barrier, because one push from his hefty shoulders would have been enough to unbalance the skeleton-like bodies of the Hindu merchants, but a moral one. He knew that contact with him, if he pushed through, would defile a great many more of these men. And he could already hear in his ears the abuse he would thus draw on himself.

'Don't know what the world is coming to! These swine are getting more and more uppish!' said a little old man. 'One of his brethren who cleans the lavatory of my house, announced the other day that he wanted two rupees a month instead of one rupee, and the food that he gets from us daily.'

'As if he owned the whole street!' exclaimed the touched man. 'The son of a dog!' . . . .

To Bakha, every second seemed an endless age of woe and suffering. His whole demeanour was concentrated on humility, and in his heart there was a queer stirring. His legs trembled and shook under him. He felt they would fail him. He was really sorry and tried hard to convey his repentance to his tormentors. But the barrier of space that the crowd had placed between themselves and him seemed to prevent his feeling from getting across. . . .

Luckily for Bakha, a tonga-wallah came up, goading a rickety old mare which struggled in its shafts to carry a jolting, bolting box-like structure and shouted a warning (for lack of a bell or a horn) for the crowd to disperse as he reined in his horse in time to prevent an accident.

Bakha hurried away. He felt that everyone was looking at him. He bore the shopkeeper's abuse silently and went on. A little later he slowed down, and quite automatically he began to shout, '*Posh,* keep away, *posh,* sweeper coming, *posh, posh,* sweeper coming!'. . . . 'Why are we always abused? . . . They always abuse us. Because we are sweepers. Because we touch dung. They hate dung. I hate it too. That's why I came here. I was tired of working on the latrines every day. That's why they don't touch us. . . . For them I am a sweeper, sweeper—untouchable! . . . A shock of which this was the name had passed through his perceptions, previously numb and torpid, and had sent a quiver into his being, stirred his nerves of sight, hearing, smell, touch, and taste, all into a quickening. 'I am an Untouchable!' he said to himself, 'an Untouchable!' . . . Then, aware of his position, he began to shout aloud the warning word with which he used to announce his approach. *'Posh, posh,* sweeper coming.' The undertone, 'Untouchable, Untouchable,' was in his heart; the warning shout *'Posh, posh,* sweeper coming!' was in his mouth.

Castes are also integrated into a system through hereditary ties. People in one caste are hereditary patrons to people in other castes who are their clients. For example, a well-to-do farmer is a patron to the families of carpenters, ironsmiths, laundrymen, barbers, leatherworkers, and sweepers who work for him. These clients work all year without cash payments, but when the crops are in they receive their shares of the harvest (fig. 25).

Boundaries between ethnic groups are maintained largely by regulating the social relationships between them, rather than by maintaining their cultural differences. Of particular importance is caste endogamy, because interethnic marriages break

Figure 25
The Indian Caste System

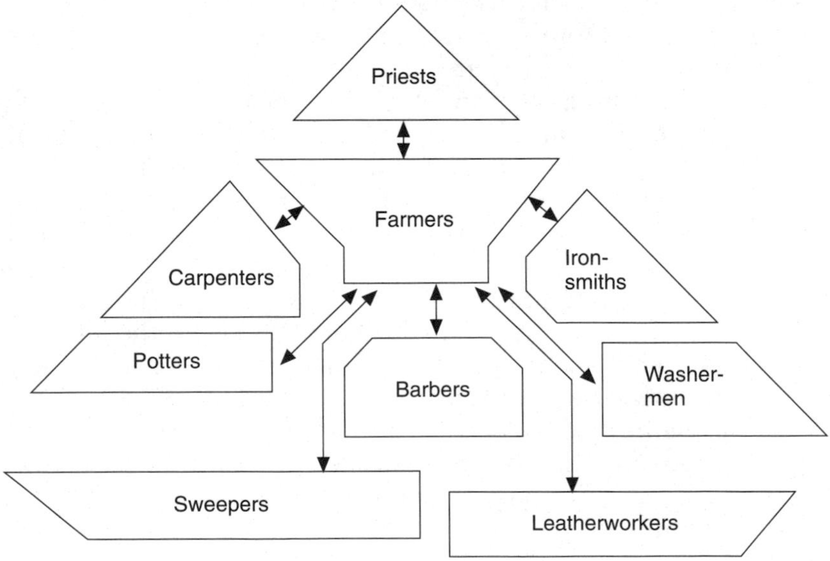

down ethnic differences. Consequently, engagements are arranged by the parents, often when their children are young, and marriages occur at early ages to prevent premarital affairs and "love marriages."

Sexual liaisons between men of the dominant caste and women of lower groups are not uncommon and offspring of these relationships belong to the mother's group or drift as half-breeds on the margins of the village. Sexual relationships between women of the dominant group and men of lower groups are vehemently condemned.

Individuals of one ethnic group may try to "pass" as members of a higher group. This does not destroy the ethnic boundaries, because the "passer" takes on the values of the new group and marries in it. Villagers, however, tell stories of the terrible fate of those who were caught trying to pass. The message is clear: "Don't try to change castes." Racial pride is common in caste societies. It maintains the walls that keep ethnic groups apart.

Class-Based Communities

A second type of grouping to emerge in peasant societies is "class." Various definitions of this slippery concept have been given. For our purposes, we will define it as a stratum of people who share a common culture and rank in a social hierarchy based on wealth, power, and social prestige.

Theoretically, classes are not social groups but societal categories. They are the categories people use when they think about their community: "rich landlords," "small farmers," and "hired laborers."

Societal categories give rise to social groups. For example, people from low classes often form their own clubs and churches, just as people from higher classes do. The ties between the people in a class, however, are rarely as strong as the blood ties between people in ethnic groups.

In contrast to tribal societies, which are essentially classless, most peasant societies have at least a two-class system: a dominant elite and the commoners. Many have three or more classes (see fig. 26, following page).

Unlike the hierarchy in ethnic societies, which is based on identity based on birth and so cannot be changed, hierarchy in class societies depends to a great extent on personal achievement.

Figure 26
Class Societies

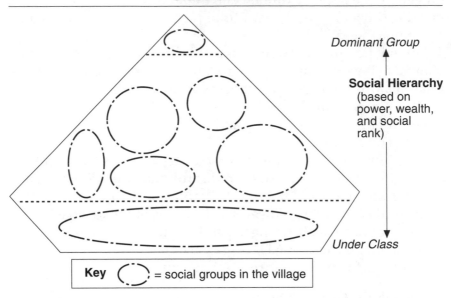

People are born into a class, but they can rise or fall in the social order, depending on their actions.

Lifestyle and rank are determined by a number of factors. Wealth is important because it not only enables people to live well and acquire symbols of status such as better houses, food, and clothing, but it also gives them power. Occupation is also important. Universally, field workers and manual laborers rank below landowners, political leaders, and religious priests. Education also is important because it opens doors to higher occupations. Finally, urban life in general ranks above rural life because city people are nearer the social centers of power.

In villages where class is the dominant form of organization, people with similar incomes, occupations, education, residences, and authority tend to live in the same area, join the same associations, share common cultural symbols and practices, exchange meals, marry one another, and possess the same values. They often have similar child-rearing practices, courtship habits, speech patterns, food, and dress. In other words, they share a distinct subculture.

Unlike caste boundaries, which are clearly demarcated, class lines are blurred. People in one class may share a number of characteristics with those in another class, but they know that they are a "different kind of people" with dissimilar cultural identities. Social mobility contributes to this fuzziness. Because classes are based primarily on achievement, individuals and families move up or down the class hierarchy.

Class/Caste Systems

Many peasant villages have several classes and several ethnic groups. The relationships between the two types of groups are often complex. One ethnic group tends to dominate the society, even though it has low-class people in it. Other ethnic groups are in the middle or at the bottom, but may have a few high-class members (see fig. 27).

Figure 27
Multiethnic and Class Society

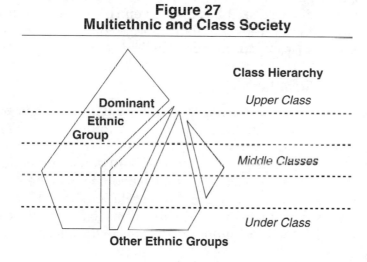

In such societies, individuals may move to higher classes in their ethnic group through personal accomplishment. Ethnic groups may also move up as they gain status within the society.

Dominant Elites and Pariahs

Hierarchical societies have *dominant elites*—people and groups at the top of the society. They generally have not only social status, but also the political and economic power to enforce their decisions on the village. Their lifestyle is often idealized by the lower groups who emulate them.

Such societies also have underclasses and untouchable castes. These are the powerless within the society. In some cases these bottom groups are excluded from the society and form isolated social subsystems with their own values and culture. Their identity is assigned them by the society as a whole and they have little hope of assimilation into it. Examples of such pariahs are the untouchables in India, Eta or butchers of Japan, and plantation slaves in the southern U.S.

In recent years, the spread of modernity, with its values of freedom and equality, has fostered tensions in many peasant societies as under classes and castes demand equal rights and dominant groups struggle to preserve their reign of power and wealth. This has made the former receptive to modern ideologies such as Marxism and to flight to the cities where they are less known and branded. As we will see, it has also given rise to liberation theologies, base communities, wholistic mission programs, and other Christian responses to oppressive social systems.

Economic Structure

Peasant economies, in general, are more complex than tribal economies, but both are built on the same foundation, namely, that they are best understood as a "livelihood" (Polanyi 1957). In "modern" societies, people seek money and consumer goods as ends in themselves. In peasant societies, people focus their attention on subsistence and on maintaining relationships. Economic concerns are subordinate to social obligations to the family, caste, and community and to religious obligations to the ancestors, spirits, and gods.

Land, Technology, and People

Peasant villages are basically subsistence societies. People produce much of the food they eat. Unlike tribes, however, peasants have developed elaborate agricultural technologies. Human energy is replaced by that of oxen, horses, and other draft animals; and digging sticks are replaced by plows and harrows. Many peasant societies use animal fertilizers to replenish the soil. Some have developed elaborate irrigation systems that assure them of good crops and enable farmers to permanently cultivate arid land. All of these advances help peasants to produce surpluses of food.

One result of new technologies is sedentary living and larger and denser populations. Hunting and gathering food can sustain little more than one or two persons per square mile of land. Horticultural methods can raise this to five to ten. Dry farming can maintain from twenty-five to one hundred persons and more per square mile of land (Barth 1963). Advanced methods such as irrigation, fertilization, crop rotation, and weeding have led to 1,980 persons per square mile in the Yangtse Valley in China (compared to 254 for China as a whole) and to 5,000 per square mile in north-central Java, compared to the Indonesian average of 155 (Geertz 1963, 13, 33).

Above all, agricultural surpluses give rise to cities and states. The peasants themselves are rural, but they live in symbiotic relationships to market towns, urban capitals, and ruling aristocracies. Peasant villages are only partial societies because they are linked by complex ties to a much larger world through trade and taxation. As we will see, the use and allocation of agricultural surpluses is controlled largely by the ruling elite who reside, for the most part, in cities.

In some places land is owned by the peasants who farm small plots. In others land is owned by a few rich landlords or patrons in the village who supervise laborers who are little better than serfs on the land. In either case, the state or the ruler exercises domain or ultimate ownership and control over the use of the land. This gives the state or the overlord the right to tax people and to confiscate land whenever it wishes to do so.

The relationship between peasants and rulers is asymmetrical. The overlords tax the farmers. In return they promise the peasants protection from enemies by their armies and internal order by police. In the balance, however, the rulers take more than they give, squeezing the peasants for more revenues to support their court life and to build their monuments and maintain their armies.

Since the demands of magistrates and municipalities is unending, there is the ever-present pressure to increase taxes. To avoid taxation, peasants must consume what they produce and spend surpluses in ceremonies and feasts. They must also hide their wealth. If they display it, they are liable to be taxed even more. Consequently, there is little initiative to save or to change. Traditional ways are proven ways to maintain life.

Peasant Households

The fundamental characteristic of peasant agriculture is that it is a family economy. The family is both a home and a "factory." This explains why the concept of profit in peasant economies differs from that in capitalist economies and why the capitalist concept of profit cannot be applied to peasant economy (Chaianov 1931, 144–45). The fundamental goal of the family is not to make money, but to stay alive and to maintain its place in the society.

In peasant societies, survival is the fundamental economic value. Consequently, where land is limited, farmers spend great amounts of time and effort to increase their production of crops even a little. They do not calculate the value of their work by how much economic gain each hour produces. Rather they work until they have enough to survive.

Peasant families do not calculate their time in terms of the money they earn per hour. All members must work until they produce enough food for all of them to live. Some family members must clean the house, gather firewood, cook meals, and care for children and the aged so that others can work in the fields. No track is kept of how much each one works, nor are family members paid for what they do. The sick, aged, and slow cannot be fired because they are economically unproductive.

In such a system, a house and a field are not merely resources used in production. They are the "home" and "livelihood" of the family and have been for the past hundreds of years. Here great-grandfather first tilled the soil and grandmother kept seven children alive during the famine. Family jewels are not economic commodities that can be sold for economic gain; they are heirlooms rich with memories.

With the aid of animal power, most peasants raise more than they need to survive, but much of what they produce is taken from them in the form of taxes and rents. The latter often cost tenant farmers a third or more of what they raise.

Social obligations and religious duties have first claim on what is left over. Marriages, funerals, family gatherings, gift exchanges, offerings to ancestors, and festivals for the gods are costly affairs. There is often little left to save and invest for economic purposes. The result is that the peasant household is not controlled primarily by economic values such as productivity and profit, but by social and religious values that emphasize the importance of maintaining relationships with people, ancestors, spirits, and gods.

Peasant Families

In China, India, and parts of Europe, extended families, made up of parents and their married sons and their families, are held up as the ideal. These are found largely among well-to-do peasants and landlords, but rarely among poor peasants and farm laborers. Extended families provide many hands to do different tasks and to do work requiring much labor, such as clearing forests and cultivating large fields. For example, in the South Slav *zadruga* or extended household the women garden, cook, clean, embroider, and make lace. The men plow, mow, cut wood, make furniture, and work in vineyards and orchards. Men help women in weaving and women aid men in hoeing and reaping. Children and unmarried girls care for the livestock, and old people do work around the house.

Extended families, however, are often full of tensions. Aged fathers may refuse to turn authority over to their grown sons who want to introduce changes. Daughters-in-law resent the dictates of their mothers-in-law who control the household. These tensions may lead family units in the household to start separate kitchens and to divide cash income. Finally, the land is divided and the families split when the patriarch dies (Minturn and Hitchcock 1963).

In many peasant societies, such as Japan and parts of Europe, the land is passed on to the oldest son, in others to the youngest son. The other children must then find work elsewhere. In other societies, the sons (or in a few cases the daughters) inherit the land equally. Daughters often receive a share of the estate in the form of dowries.

Nuclear families made up only of parents and children are found where land is in short supply and where family members depend on wages for a large share of their income. They are more vulnerable to droughts, floods, and other disasters. If the husband is sick, the family starves. If the mother dies, there is no one to take care of the children. Nuclear families have fewer family ties on which they can count in times of need.

Specialization

Peasants are not engaged in agriculture alone. They need to build houses, make containers, manufacture tools, and trade their products for other commodities. Each peasant household can do some of these tasks for itself. Some households, however, cannot make a living by farming and must turn to part-time skills to supplement their livelihood. In East China some farmers raise rice and silkworms to manufacture thread for the market. In Nicaragua farmers weave baskets and make pots. As technologies become more complex and tasks more demanding, some people become full-time specialists and live off the fees peasants pay them for their services.

Specialization takes place on two levels. The first to emerge is specialization in occupational roles. Political leaders such as chiefs and religious leaders such as priests appear early on. Technical specialists arise later: blacksmiths, carpenters, weavers, potters, shopkeepers, and barbers ply their trades full-time and pass them on to their children through apprenticeships. Often these workers form guilds to provide mutual assistance. The result of this specialization is further technological development as specialists develop new techniques and products.

The second type of specialization to emerge is institutional specialization. Peasant societies often have temples, local palaces, and markets. Still, banking systems, transportation services, factories, universities, and other complex specialized organizations emerge largely in urban societies.

Patrons and Clients

The production of economic surpluses, the emergence of class differences, and the development of technological specialists lead to complex, asymmetrical relationships between landowners and their workers. Land, wealth, and power are increasingly concentrated in the hands of a few.

This division of labor often leads to an economic system based on patron-client relationships. Rich landowners become the patrons and their workers, such as the ironsmiths, carpenters, potters, launderers, and field laborers who serve them, are their clients. Clients are expected to provide the essential services needed to produce the crops and maintain the life of the patron;

the patron is responsible for the total well-being of his workers. This is not a system of economic contracts, but of symbiotic exchange in which the subsistence needs and social aspirations of all are met through a network of social obligations.

An example of the patron-client system is the *jajmani* system found in Indian villages (fig. 28). In its classical form, the system centers around a high-caste landlord (*jajman*) and the raising of crops. To farm the *jajman* needs the services of other specialist castes: priests to assure the favor of the gods; ironsmiths and carpenters to maintain the plows; potters, barbers, and laundrymen to serve his household; and untouchable laborers to work the fields. All these are hereditary workers who perform their services throughout the year without cash payments. Rather, at harvest they receive a portion of the grain that their joint effort has produced (Hiebert 1971).

The first measures of the crop heaped on the threshing floor are sent to the high-caste priests as offerings to the gods and to the village officials in respect of their authority. To the craftsmen who share a rank just below him, the landlord gives a payment. To his clients ranked well below him, he presents a *gift* of grain based on the amount of their work.

Figure 28
Distribution of the Harvest
(patron-client system)

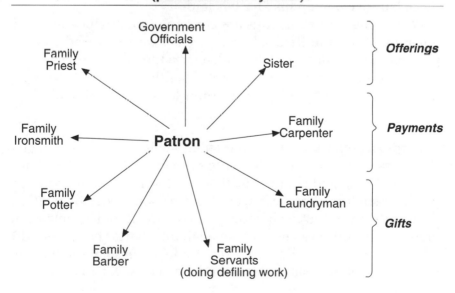

The relationship between a *jajman* and his workers is more complex than that between an employer and an employee. As their patron, the *jajman* is responsible for the survival and well-being of his workers. In addition to the grain he gives them to keep them alive, he must give them blankets when they are cold, shoes when these wear out, places for them to build their huts, and fodder for their cows.

Clients, in turn, have the hereditary right and responsibility to carry out the work the patron assigns them. In addition to work in the fields and home, they must be willing to carry his luggage, help in family weddings and funerals, and fight for him if his rivalries erupt in open violence.

Economic activities in the patron-client system are not calculated in terms of profit and loss or equal exchange. In a year of bad crops, the landlord gets little more than his own subsistence because he must provide enough for his workers to live, whether there is work or not. But in good years, the landlord makes a handsome profit because he has to give the workers little more than a subsistence portion of the crop. For the workers, the system provides security in times of want. For the landlord, it provides laborers, power, prestige, and occasionally wealth.

Relationships between clients are often based on exchange. The barber shaves the men in a laundryman household. In exchange those laundrymen do his family's laundry.

Patron-client relationships are common in many peasant societies. In some, the field laborers are serfs indentured to their patrons because of their debts or because they have nowhere else to go. In other societies, the poor and landless are free to move to new lands or to other villages, so their lot is not as difficult.

Markets and Money

Surpluses, specialization, and technological development give rise to trade and markets. Peasants raise crops to feed their families, pay taxes, and conduct festivals. What is left they barter for products such as plows, carts, clothing, ornaments, and furniture.

With the introduction of money the nature of trade changes. As more goods and services become available, barter becomes difficult. Cash, however, allows for freer trade. It does not rot, it is easily transported to distant places, and it can be saved to make large purchases at a later date. The result is an ever-expanding network of trade.

Many peasant communities develop their own economic specialty. In one village, people farm and also make pots, in another they farm and weave cloth, and in a third they farm and produce tile or work leather. People from these communities gather at markets to trade their products. These play an important role in the social and economic life of peasant villages. In smaller villages markets are held every four, five, or seven days. Local farmers bring their produce and outside traders come with their wares. The focus, however, is social. People come to visit friends from neighboring villages and to listen to the latest news.

Shops and daily markets appear in larger towns. Here economic relationships become increasingly independent of other relationships. The farmer no longer buys from a friend if he can get the products cheaper elsewhere. He trades with anonymous buyers and sellers who have no moral obligations to him based on kinship, friendship, or other social ties. Consequently, exploitation and "cheating" become increasingly common.

As marketing grows, traders and middlemen arise who transport local commodities to distant places for sale and import outside wares. Today, coffee raised in Colombia is used for coffee breaks in Chicago, Danish butter for Latin American breakfasts, and German aspirin to cure the headaches of Indonesian peasants. Eric Wolf writes (1966, 42):

> The peasant may thus find himself not merely dealing with a large number of middlemen and processors, but also becoming involved in a market system with many levels of ever widening scope. Moreover, the peasant involved in such far-flung systems may discover that prices are no longer regulated by custom and by local exigencies, determined by the many-stranded relations of his local world, but by even stronger forces of demand and supply which he may not entirely understand and which he certainly does not control.

In a traditional style of exchange, prices are fixed by tradition. With the coming of open markets, they are not determined in advance, but are subject to fluctuations according to supply and demand. This has increasingly put peasants today at the mercy of world markets.

One consequence of this peasant involvement in regional and global markets is the production of crops for cash rather than for subsistence. Traditionally peasants produce food for themselves and a surplus that is taxed. Due to colonial pressures and to the incentives of profits, more and more peasants are now producing crops such as coffee, sugar, or bananas for sale in the world market. When prices are good, they succeed, but when prices drop, they often starve because they no longer produce food they can consume.

Most peasants live close to nature and are dependent upon the rains and sunshine for their crops. Poor peasants are particularly vulnerable. Many do not have enough food to wait for the harvest and must cut the grain green or borrow against their harvest at a low price. In East China, for example, farmers borrowed rice from the rice merchant at $4.00 per bushel, and had to repay their loans from their harvest four months later at $6.30 a bushel, an interest rate of more than 100 percent per year (Fei 1939, 276–77). Oppressive money lenders play a major role in many peasant societies.

Markets and money also lead to an increasing individualism. The family, rather than the lineage or clan, becomes the important unit of production. As long as the old patriarch lives, the extended family made up of his married sons and their families may remain together. But this generally breaks down into nuclear families at his death. Among the poor even this mutual assistance may break down as each family seeks to fend for itself.

Political Structure

The historical emergence of peasant societies is closely tied to the emergence of nations. The state replaces the tribe as the ultimate authority. The state is an autonomous integrated political unit based on territory, encompassing many communities in its land with a central governing authority.

With the rise of states the basis of political organization shifts from kinship to geography. Many different ethnic groups are incorporated into the same political unit and membership is based on where people live, not on whom they are related to.

The state is sovereign over the lives of individuals. It can draft them for military service, tax their production, expropriate their land, prevent their leaving, and take their lives. The state is also ultimately responsible for keeping peace between different groups and making provision for the welfare of the public.

Power and authority in states are concentrated in the hands of a few people. Most citizens have little say in the government. Moreover, power and authority are institutionalized. By that we mean that they are vested in official roles or offices rather than in charismatic individuals who are able to persuade others to follow them. Succession may be based on birth, as is the case in kingships, or it may be based on age and political power as in oligarchies and autocracies. What is important is that the ruler justify his or her leadership by showing that he or she has the right to hold the office of ruler. When political revolutions occur, the new rulers must legitimate their accession to office.

Laws are also institutionalized. In tribal societies, there are traditional ways of doing things, but the decisions of the leaders tend to be more particularistic—that is, they deal with specific situations in the light of precedents. In nation states, general laws are formulated that apply whenever a particular situation arises. For example, inheritance laws may decree that all sons inherit equally. If an ethnic group in the state customarily gives all the inheritance to the oldest son, the other sons may appeal to the state and claim their shares. State rules are often codified in systems of written law.

Government itself is also institutionalized. Courts are established to try cases, bureaucracies developed to handle finances and regulate order, and armies and police organized to enforce it. In small states, political leaders are recruited largely on the basis of birth and kinship. As states grow and the number of offices increase, recruitment and promotion are increasingly based on the expertise, performance, and seniority of the individual, rather than on birth, personal ties, or influence. The result is some form of civil service.

Leadership on the village level is sometimes vested in officials appointed by the central government. Often, however, it is based on local political dynamics. Different ethnic groups in the village have their own leaders who call councils of the elders in their groups to deal with internal affairs and negotiate with one another when intergroup disputes arise. Leaders of the dominant group call village councils made up of the leaders of different groups to settle village affairs. The outside rulers generally intervene when these local systems of government fail.

Culture

The historical change from a tribe to a state-based peasant society has a deep effect on the people's beliefs and the way they view their world. The coexistence of several groups introduces questions of cultural pluralism and how people of different cultures relate to one another. Trade, markets, and state officials bring in new ideas. The move of political power from the local community to outside governments transforms a group's image of itself and of others. In other words, social changes lead to cultural changes.

But cultural changes also lead to social changes. New technologies give rise to specialists and communities of craftsmen. New religious beliefs lead to new social groups. New values, such as the acceptance of hierarchy, lead to a restructuring of social relationships.

What are some of the characteristics of peasant cultures? Again, we must note that there is a tremendous variation from one to another. Nevertheless, some patterns emerge that are common to many or most peasant cultures.

Symbols

With peasant societies comes social and cultural pluralism. This is true with the Javanese, who have four or five levels of language with different words used by different social classes. It is also true of caste systems, in which different ethnic groups may speak different languages; dress in different clothes; eat different foods; perform different birth, marriage, and burial rites; and worship gods in different ways. It is less obvious between classes, but language, dress, food, house styles, rituals, and a great many other sets of symbols do mark class distinctions. We can no longer speak of a peasant village in terms of a single culture. Instead, we must examine it in terms of its cultures.

New symbol systems are also generated. Without these the production of food surpluses and complex state organization are impossible. These new systems include land surveying, writing, and money, which profoundly affect both the social and cultural life of peasants.

Writing

One basic distinction we must note in symbol systems is between oral and literate cultures. Most peasants are oral people. Like tribal people, they use mnemonic devices to store ideas in their minds. They tend to think in concrete, functional ways. For them the spoken word and enacted rite carry great weight. The forms and meanings of symbols are closely tied to each other. When one person curses another, the words themselves are thought to bring about destruction. When the village performs rain ceremonies, the rituals themselves are believed to produce rain.

Literacy introduces new ways of thinking. Information is stored on paper and in books. This enables people to read about distant places and new ideas. It also freezes ideas into set forms. Oral versions of local stories are told and retold and in the retelling are changed. Written texts remain the same over time. What does change is the interpretations of these texts, which themselves may be written down in the form of commentaries and commentaries on commentaries.

More important, literacy enables people to store and retrieve vast amounts of information. It thereby facilitates abstract thought. While the spoken word is gone the moment it is spoken, the written word can be reexamined and organized in complex ways. This makes records of complex business and government transactions possible. Imagine, for a moment, trying to run an airline or an automobile factory without the use of writing.

Finally, writing enables people to communicate widely. The spoken word is heard only by those in earshot of the speaker. The written word can be copied and distributed widely. This ability to communicate to many people in distant places was essential to the formation of the state. Without writing it is impossible for rulers to rule large kingdoms. Early feudal states often consisted of many local rulers who served rulers of rulers, who in turn served the king, who ruled the rulers of rulers. As writing and rapid, long-distance communication spread, however, kings were able to exercise a direct control over distant lands.

Literacy is power. Not only can the literate communicate with people in distant places, particularly with government officers and businessmen in cities, but also their information committed to paper takes precedence over oral testimony in village disputes and in courts of law.

An example of this on the local level is the relationship between literate businessmen and oral peasants. At planting time, the farmers borrow seed from the businessman, who records the amounts in a ledger. The farmers cannot read and do not know what figures he has written down. They are at his mercy. When farmers come to repay their loans, lenders often claim the loans were larger and back their claims with their written documents. In court, the farmers have little defense. Similarly, poor peasants often lose land because they do not understand and cannot read land deeds and bills of sale.

Finally, writing facilitates a sense of history and of general, abstract, and universal ways of thinking.

Money

Another symbol system that changes the lives of people is money. Barter is adequate for simple, small-scale, immediate, personal transactions. With cash, traders convert goods into symbols of value that are easily stored and that can be converted into other goods at a later time. The appearance of money, as we have seen, has led to a rapid spread of trade, which in turn led to more manufacturing and specialization.

Mathematics

The power of writing to assist abstract thoughts is readily seen in mathematics. Oral societies find it difficult to calculate anything beyond small numbers and simple arithmetic. Without writing it is impossible to determine land ownership accurately, to calculate the value of trade goods in a large market or, for that matter, to send a person to the moon.

The appearance of writing and the need to keep track of land boundaries and money transactions led to the rise of formal mathematics. This was a new language that enabled people to measure their world accurately. It also pushed them toward the standardization of units of measurement and accounting. The emergence of mathematics was also the basis for the rise of formal science.

Rites and Myths

Community ceremonies, festivals, and fairs play an important role in peasant life. On a cultural level, these reinforce people's beliefs about the nature of reality. On a social level, they are public dramas portraying the order of relationships in the community. Village leaders organize the events and in doing so show that they are leaders. Others take part according to their stations in the society. Those vying for higher status and power must legitimate their claims in public ritual displays. The performance of community rites, therefore, becomes an arena in which social rivalries and hostilities are manifested and changes sought. The staging of a successful ceremony both testifies to the local beliefs and reinforces the social order.

Myths, too, are important in peasant life. A number of themes are particularly common in peasant societies. One of these has to do with a better world. Peasants often protest the harsh conditions of their lives by telling stories about justice and equality. One common story is about the bandit-hero who stands in open defiance of an oppressive social order. These include Robin Hood in England, Janosik in Poland, Pancho Villa in Mexico, Stenka Razin in Russia, and the bandits glorified in Chinese peasant lore. These are champions of the peasant. They exact revenge, redress wrongs, and claim land for the landless.

Closely related to stories of bandit-heroes are myths of a coming millennium in which the world will be perfect. These myths may speak of a return to a golden age of justice and equality, or of a new age on earth. This new world will come through the judgment of the gods or through peasant revolutions. It is not surprising that in recent decades, Marxism, with its promise of a new world, found a ready audience in peasant societies.

At times myths of bandit-heroes and imminent millenniums give rise to peasant revolts that are bloody and cruel. The peasant revolts in Europe after the eleventh century, the Taiping Rebellion in China in the nineteenth century, the uprisings of the Spanish anarchists in the same century, and the Mexican peasant revolt of 1917 are examples of this.

Myths of a future golden age provide the people with a common vision and unite them in common action, but they do not give the people an organizational framework for action. Generally, the peasants do not know how to mobilize their forces, and they are wiped out. E. J. Hobsbawm (1959, 24–25) points out that such myths and revolutions are protests, not against the fact that peasants are poor and oppressed, but against the fact that they are excessively poor and oppressed. Bandit-heroes are not expected to create an equitable world. They can only right wrongs and prove that sometimes oppression can be turned upside down. Beyond that the bandit-hero is merely a dream of how wonderful it would be if times were always good.

A third type of story concerns the fall of a particular group of people in the village from a high status and their return to it. For example, most untouchable castes in India have stories showing that they once were high castes and that their current low status is due to the deceitful actions of others or the mistakes of their ancestors.

These stories of fall and rise serve two functions. First, they give dignity to the untouchable who can claim, at least among themselves, that they are not what they publicly appear to be. Second, they justify actions by the community designed to raise their social status. As untouchable castes gain power and wealth and take on the symbols and practices of high castes, they can claim they are not upsetting the social order, but instead are restoring it to its original condition.

Beliefs

As specializations develop, knowledge becomes increasingly fragmented. Smiths develop highly technical knowledge to extract and shape copper, brass, iron, gold, silver and other metals—knowledge not accessible to other members of society. Similarly, potters, weavers, administrators, and soldiers perfect sophisticated techniques known only to themselves.

A second result of specialization is the growing interdependence among people in the society. To farm, the farmer needs smiths, leatherworkers, carpenters, and traders. They in turn need the farmer and one another to maintain their lifestyles. Whereas in tribal societies people relate to one another primarily as persons, in peasant societies they increasingly relate to each other in specialized roles such as buyer and seller and craftsman and customer. These *monoplex* relationships, in which people relate to each other only in specialized roles, often seem impersonal. Personal relationships in which people know each other intimately and share many role relationships are increasingly confined to homes and friends.

Science and Technology

Critical to the rise of peasant societies is the development of new technologies that enable one person to raise a surplus of food that can be used to support rulers and specialists. One such technology is the plow drawn by oxen, buffalos, horses, or other draft animals. As long as people depend on human power, they can produce little more than their families consume. With animals, they can cultivate large fields and increase their power tenfold. The obvious superiority of these methods in producing food has led peasant agriculture to displace tribal horticulture.

As agricultural production becomes more labor-intensive and land availability shrinks due to population growth, ownership of land becomes significant. Shifting horticulture gives way to permanent cultivation. This is accompanied by the determination of precise boundaries of fields and clearly established ownership.

A second major technological development that fosters the rise of widespread trade and the state is the invention of carts and large ships. Horses and donkeys enable people to cover more ground at higher speeds. The ability of these beasts to carry large quantities of food and materials, however, is limited. Caravans of oxen, llamas, camels, and elephants and fleets of small boats increase the mobility of goods. Wheels, carts, roads, and ships make large-scale and distant trade possible.

Internal peace enforced by the state and agricultural surpluses freed people to develop other trades. The result was a technological explosion. Pottery, weaving, metal work, and rock cutting were improved. Large palaces, temples, and public buildings were constructed. Roads were built. Furniture, jewelry, and the arts were perfected. The net result is that material commodities and the comfort these things afford grew in importance, particularly in the urban centers.

Religion

Religion plays a central role in the life of peasants, just as it does for tribal people. The emergence of literacy and specialization, however, gave rise to new, formally organized religious systems that extend over large territories, including Buddhism, Hinduism, Christianity, and Islam.

The spread of these universal or high religions did not displace traditional animistic beliefs. Rather, in peasant societies, two levels of religious explanation developed that coexist in uneasy relationship to one another: formal, institutionalized religions with explicit theological systems; and animistic practices such as magic, divination, witchcraft, and spirit worship that continued to occupy much of the common people's attention.

Formal religions

Most peasants belong to one of the world's great universal religions such as Christianity, Islam, Buddhism, Hinduism, Confucianism, and Sikhism. These high religions address cosmic questions regarding the ultimate origin, meaning, and destiny of the universe, of groups, and of individuals. They speak of high gods who are powerful creators or of cosmic energies that coalesce to form the material world. But these beings and forces are often remote, and high religions such as Hinduism have lesser deities and spirits who are involved in human affairs. In contrast to the particularism of tribal religions, many of these formal religions claim to be universally true.

The institutional centers of a formal religion are found in the cities and capitals of the state. Here emerge *great traditions* led by religious specialists—priests and prophets who are the keepers of the religious tradition. They interpret the sacred texts, debate orthodoxy, and run the central institutions of the religion: the great churches, temples, and mosques that symbolize the movement; the schools where young leaders are trained; and other religious organizations.

Formal religions also have *little traditions*—the many local beliefs, practices, and organizations of the peasants scattered in villages throughout the countryside. They know little of the theological debates of the great tradition. For them, Buddhism, Islam, Hinduism, and other faiths are expressed in worship at the local shrines led by a local priest, in performance of lifecycle rituals such as births, weddings, and funerals, and in participation in traditional festivals.

Festivals and religious fairs play an important role in peasant religion. They dramatize the people's beliefs about the nature of reality. They also provide the people with excitement in a world that is often harsh and dreary.

Pilgrimages are also part of many peasant societies. Peasants spend much of their lives near home tied to the land. Visits to famous religious centers help reinforce their religious convictions, but also give them a legitimate way to see new and exciting places.

Animism

Formal or high religions often leave unanswered the questions of everyday life. How can we prevent calamities such as drought and plagues? Why did my child die so suddenly in an accident and not someone else's child? How can we guarantee success in crops or business, and whom should I marry?

People know they need to care for their bodies to be healthy and to plant their fields to produce crops. Their formal religion tells them how to get to heaven or gain nirvana. But how do they deal with the droughts, plagues, disasters, and uncertainties that neither their science nor their high religion can prevent?

To deal with these problems the peasants turn to animistic beliefs and practices that they retain despite the coming of formal religions. They use magic, divination, witchcraft, and offerings to spirits and ancestors to deal with illnesses, bad fortune, sudden death, and other crises and to gain success in love, farming, business, and school. They turn to diviners, fortune-tellers, shamans, and oracles for guidance in making important decisions.

In contrast to formal religions, which often have detached, cosmic deities who deal with ultimate concerns, peasant animism is full of local gods and goddesses, nature spirits, demons, and ancestors. These beings live on earth in the village or in its surrounding fields, not in heaven. Most are limited in their power to a specific territory, but in that space they possess great power over humans. For example, in India, there are thousands of local goddesses who have power within ten miles of their homes. Beyond that, they are impotent.

Dealing with spirits is part of everyday life. In Burma, for example, household *nats* and village *nats* are thought to bring illnesses and other evils and must be kept away through proper offerings and rituals. A yellow string may be worn on the left wrist to avoid cholera; or the house may be sprinkled with holy water; or food may be left at special shrines devoted to the *nats*. If sickness strikes, it is treated with rites of expulsion. In Thailand, *phi, cao,* and *devata* are placated out of fear of the harm they can cause. In Japan, *kami* and other native spirits are appeased.

Most local spirits are neither all good nor all bad. Rather, like humans, they are idiosyncratic. Some are known to be more cantankerous than others, but all of them help those who propitiate them with sacrifices of food, clothing, and blood. Those who neglect them are plagued with illnesses, accidents, and barrenness. The peasants try to keep them happy and serve them not out of reverence but out of fear.

The people set demon traps and use spirit repellents to protect themselves from ghosts and other malevolent spirits. Most spirits are powerful but simple-minded. Fortunately, they can easily be distracted. In parts of China, for instance, spirits are believed to go in straight lines, and people build bridges with zigzags so that the spirits will fall into the river. In India, spirits are thought to run along white lines, so patterns of endless white lines are used to decorate entryways for the purpose of snagging demons. Gypsy women wear mirrors so that attacking spirits will be frightened away when they see their own reflections.

Fertility is the focus of many peasant animistic practices. Lesser goddesses are propitiated when crops are planted, animals are blessed, and rice and other symbols of fertility are used at weddings to ensure offspring. Underlying many of these customs is a pantheistic view of nature in which everything is alive and all life is sacred.

Another belief found in the peasant societies of the Near East, Mediterranean lands, Europe, South Asia, and North Africa is that certain people have an internal power that can harm others through their sight, word, or touch. The belief that some people have evil eyes and can harm those they look at is particularly widespread. Infants, brides and grooms, cows, and ripe crops are particularly susceptible to this power. So too is freshly cooked food. Those who eat it after it has been seen by someone with an evil eye get stomach cramps and fever. In many countries, the evil eye is associated with envy. People who are jealous of others are often accused of harming them.

People use many ways to protect themselves from the evil eye. No one talks about a baby boy lest this draw the attention of a person with the evil eye and the child get sick and die. Black spots are put on the babies' faces and they are given denigrating names such as Unwanted, Worthless, or even Dung so that people will not notice them. In the extreme, baby boys are given female names and raised until three or four as girls to protect them from the evil eye. Brides and grooms wear protective tinsel headdresses to attract the attention of those with evil eyes and draw away their power. Color-spotted pots are put in fields to attract the gaze of passers-by and protect ripe crops.

Animistic beliefs are not organized into logically consistent philosophical systems. Rather, they consist of loosely related sets of beliefs and practices, often mutually contradictory, that are not used to present a coherent view of reality but to produce immediate results. Peasants are not concerned whether magic, amulets, and divination are true explanation systems or not, nor with how they work. All the people want to know is *whether* they work. Do they have power?

Folk religion

Peasant religion is a mix of the beliefs and practices of formal religions and those of animism (see table 5, following page). The result is folk Islam, folk Buddhism, folk Hinduism, and folk Christianity.

The relationship between formal and folk religion varies greatly from region to region. In some places the formal religion has assimilated traditional beliefs and practices with little change in meaning. In Sri Lanka, for example, a hierarchy of gods and spirits evolved, ranging from the localized guardian spirits of village and field to regional gods like Skanda and Vishnu, who were absorbed from Hinduism. Finally, the Buddha was added to rule the universe. Guardian spirits stand guard at Buddhist temple entrances. Similarly, in Japan, *kami* are seen as *bodhisattvas* or manifestations of Buddha.

In many parts of the world, however, there are tensions between the leaders of high religions and the practitioners of folk religions.

Table 5
Formal and Folk Religion

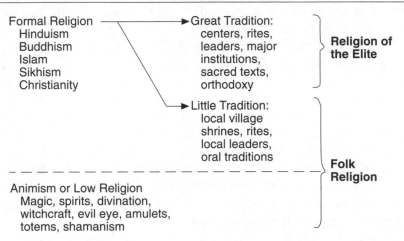

In India, Hindu priests despise the low-caste shamans who perform blood sacrifices to village and nature spirits. In Iran, Iraq, Pakistan, and other Muslim countries, the *mullahs* reject the folk Muslim practitioners with their amulets, charms, and divination. In China, the Buddhist monks are critical of the animistic practices of the villages. In Latin America, many Christian leaders oppose the magic and spiritism of the common folk. In short, from the point of view of the religious specialist, the peasant's application of animistic beliefs to the concrete problems of everyday life is often seen as full of magic and empty of ethical principles and higher-order meanings.

The same tension is seen in the history of the church in the west. The official doctrine of the medieval church formulated by Thomas Aquinas treated peasants as Christians of a lower rank and tended to disdain them. The peasants lived in the countryside (*pagus*) and were referred to as pagans (*paganus*).

In times of crisis, relationships between the leaders of the church, mosque, or temple and the peasants frequently break down. The result is "protestant" movements—crusades of protest. Examples of such religious peasant uprisings include the millenarian and Protestant sects in Europe since the late Middle Ages, the popular Taoist reaction to Buddhism, and the popular movements such as Sufism in Islam.

Worldview

In peasant societies the multiplicity of social groups produces cultural pluralism. This is particularly true in multiethnic peasant communities but is also characteristic of communities in which class differences emerge, particularly that between rulers and administrators linked to urban centers and peasants tied to the land. This pluralism has far-reaching consequences at the worldview level.

Land and State

Like horticulturalists, peasants are people of the land. As a result, the theme of fertility and the focus on crops and the rhythm of the seasons play a central role in people's minds. So too do the concerns with power and with pragmatic solutions to the concrete problems of everyday life.

These similarities to tribal worldviews, however, mask a fundamental shift in how land is perceived. In most tribes, land belongs to God and is given to clans, lineages, and families for use. It cannot be bought or sold. The opposite is true in peasant societies: land ultimately belongs to the state. Individuals may own it but the state can tax it and confiscate it through its right of eminent domain. Furthermore, individuals can buy and sell land. Land becomes an economic commodity and not a divine heritage.

This shift leads to worldview differences between the peasants and the rulers of the state. The peasants are close to the land and look to it for their sustenance; the rulers consider land to be a political and economic means of exploitation for personal gain. If their control of the land and peasants is lost, the state is finished. Consequently, ruling bodies must maintain armies to defend their land, attack other states to expand their own territory, and dominate their peasants to prevent insurgence.

Subsistence and Trade

Many peasants divide economic activities into two mental domains. Land, agricultural labor, crops, animals, plows, hoes, and other goods and activities associated with farming are associated with subsistence. These produce the food necessary to keep the people alive. Buildings, beds, clothing, baskets, pots, and other nonsubsistence goods are associated with cash and trade. They are not essential to staying alive.

In some societies the two domains are kept separate. Subsistence labor is paid not in cash but in grain and other food that the workers store to keep alive. Other work is paid in money. A farmer may go into debt to build a house, but the money lender cannot take his land away to pay for this debt because land belongs to subsistence, not trade. To take a person's land is to kill him or her.

Modern development agencies rarely understand this separation between subsistence and trade activities. The result has often been devastating to the peasants. When governments take land and give the peasants cash for it, the money lenders, relatives, and friends come to get a share. Soon the peasants have neither land nor cash. Even if the peasants want to buy land elsewhere, their creditors will first collect their debts and their relatives ask for help, because they now have money.

Accumulation of Wealth and Social Status

The change in land ownership is only one factor in the growing secularization of society. Religion is fundamental to tribal life and permeates all of culture. In peasant societies it becomes one segment of life alongside political and economic realities, which are increasingly divorced from religious significance. This is particularly true at the state level, where conflicts between ruler and priest are common.

Another expression of secularization is the emphasis on acquisition. In tribal societies, wealth is important not as an end in itself but as a means for building relationships and gaining status through sharing. In peasant societies, particularly among the ruling elite, wealth above that needed for livelihood is hoarded because wealth in and of itself is regarded as a measure of status and power. This accumulation of material goods is fostered by the production of agricultural surpluses that make sedentary life possible. Unlike nomadic societies, in which an excess of material goods is a liability, in permanent villages, goods are transformed into symbols of social status.

The effect of this switch from sharing to accumulating is far reaching. The manufacturing of nonessential goods such as jewelry, fine clothing, palatial homes, and other luxuries increases dramatically. These goods are consumed by the ruling elite.

The difference in wealth in peasant societies is often great. The rulers and urban administrators, in particular, often live in great luxury while their peasants live on the edge of starvation.

Rulers parade their wealth. They build great palaces, employ large entourages of guards, servants, and attendants, and live in luxury. State functions such as coronations, victory celebrations, and visits by dignitaries from other states are special pageants—exhibitions that showcase the rulers' greatness, wealth, and might.

The growing economic and political inequality compounded with the peasants' awareness of this imbalance fuels hostility and resentment on the part of the commoners. Often peasant revolts explode. Lacking organizational skills and military technology, these insurrections generally end in appalling bloodshed and further repression of the peasants.

Limited Good

Village life is public—everyone and almost everything is known by all. This is conducive to a sense of mutual responsibility in times of crisis. The negative side is that intimacy often leads to envy of and gossip about the good fortunes of others, particularly of those who belong to another ethnic group or class.

The fact that the village is a small, closed system often leads to a view of reality that George Foster has called the "image of the limited good."

> By "Image of Limited Good" I mean that broad areas of peasant behavior are patterned in such fashion as to suggest that peasants view their social, economic, and natural universes—their total environment—as one in which all of the desired things in life such as land, wealth, health, friendship and love, manliness and honor, respect and status, power and influence, security and safety, exist in finite quantity and are always in short supply, as far as the peasant is concerned. Not only do these and all other "good things" exist in finite and limited quantities, but in addition there is no way directly within peasant power to increase the available quantities. . . . If "Good" exists in limited amounts which cannot be expanded, and if the system is closed, it follows that an individual or a family can improve a position only at the expense of others. (Foster 1965, 296–97)

Because one person's advance is thought to take place only at the expense of the others, ambition becomes a threat to other members of the community. Someone's advantage implies someone else's disadvantage. A person, therefore, should be content with what he or she has, and not strive for more. There is a great deal of gossip about who has gotten what and how he or she has acquired it.

Those who do get ahead through enterprise and work are targets of gossip, hatred, and ostracism. In extreme cases, their crops are destroyed at night and their newly-built houses are vandalized. The lesson is clear: do not try to get ahead because to do so you must rob others and they will turn against you.

People jealously guard what they have, including relationships. They zealously guard and cultivate their relationships to powerful individuals and seek to reserve the attention of these patrons for themselves. They assume that the bounty of a generous patron is easily spread thin. They also do not want to admit that they have learned anything from someone else (Pike 1980). To do so means that they are in debt to that person. Consequently, the people learn most of what they know by casually watching and imitating others. There is little formal education.

The notion of "limited good" contributes much to the conservatism of most peasants. People are afraid of the response of their neighbors to new ways. It also adds to an envy and mistrust of one's neighbors and to gossip as a powerful means of social control.

There is one exception to the concept of limited good. Goods that come to a person from outside the system are not seen as a threat to the village but as a windfall. Others feel jealous but not threatened if someone is given a gift from the government, inherits wealth from a distant relative, or finds a pot of gold. Buried treasures are a common theme in peasant societies. They serve as a way of legitimizing wealth. A person can hide his or her savings and then suddenly "discover" a pot of gold. Others may accept this as a blessing from the gods.

Traditionalism and Risk Taking

Peasant societies have often been called "traditional" by outsiders, particularly those who want to change the peasant ways of life. They accuse peasants of being suspicious of new ideas and practices. This emphasis on tradition is due partly to the belief that good is limited and partly to the oppression of rulers. Peasants have a deep distrust of outsiders, a distrust that is well founded. Government officers tax their produce, traders exploit them, and urban folk look down on them.

Peasant traditionalism is also due to the risk inherent in any change. Because their life is a precarious balance between survival and meeting family needs on the one hand and heavy taxation on the other, peasants cannot afford to try new ways because the risk is too great. If these ways fail, people lose their land and starve. They know that their old ways have worked; these methods have provided the necessities of life in good times and bad.

Outsiders from capitalist economies often criticize peasant farmers because they seem to lack economic motivation. This only shows that the outsiders misunderstand completely the nature of the peasant economy and peasant family life. In modern welfare states, the government must take care of the people if they have nothing. In peasant states, there is no such safety net for the destitute. When they run out of food, they die.

Pluralism

The integration of several groups into one society and the emergence of specializations raise the question of pluralism. People in the same society or village do not share the same cultural symbols and beliefs. They may not even speak the same language.

At the worldview level this pluralism has profound consequences. People must include in their worldview the fact that there are other worldviews and that these other worldviews make sense to other peoples. This raises difficult questions. Whose worldview is right and how can people with different worldviews live together in harmony?

Most peasant groups answer the first question by affirming the rightness of their own beliefs compared to other groups on their social level. However, they often emulate the beliefs and practices of the dominant elite in their village and the rulers, because these have high status.

The answer to the second question is that culture and worldview become less and less the integrator of peasant societies. We must speak now of the worldviews, not worldview, of the village. There are common public elements to be sure. There is usually a trade language all use in public affairs. People also know how they should behave toward those in other groups and toward the rulers. But they share a full worldview only with members of their own group. This is particularly true in India, where different castes living in the same village often have different language styles, marriage customs, festivals, and religions. This cultural pluralism is also found in peasant communities in Europe and Latin America.

In societies that acknowledge cultural pluralism, evangelism, like intergroup marriage, is seen as disruptive. Each group seeks to preserve its own beliefs and its identity. No one is allowed to publicly declare his or her ways superior to other ways or to seek to convert and assimilate other people. To do so is to undermine social harmony. Consequently, groups tend to insulate themselves from one another at the level of beliefs.

What holds these communities together is larger social structures. Politically, they are part of one system ruled by a central authority. Economically, people are dependent on one another for marketing their produce and for specialized services. Socially, they relate to people of other groups in prescribed ways that reflect and reinforce the differences between groups.

As we will see, this fragmentation of cultures and worldviews within the same society becomes more pronounced in urban societies.

Hierarchy, Dominance, and Oppression

The emergence of social pluralism in peasant villages raises the question of social integration. How can different groups live in harmony with one another? The almost universal answer is hierarchy and domination. One or more groups gain wealth, power, and status and rule the village. On the state level, a small group of people control the villages under them by means of armies and police.

The social fact of dominance leads often to a worldview that accepts hierarchy not only as a fact of life, but also as right and necessary. A family, village, and state must have a head who has power to rule and maintain order. Disorder is seen as evil.

Hierarchy in peasant societies is often justified by religion. In Indian villages, the hierarchy of castes is seen as divinely ordained. One's standing in it is determined by the good and bad deeds of one's previous lives. In medieval European and Russian societies, the rulers were believed to be divinely appointed. In Chinese villages, wealth and power are often seen as the blessing of the gods.

With dominance comes the acceptance of violence as a necessary means to maintain the social order. The dominant value is maintaining order, and the leaders must maintain it at any cost. To do so they must have police to control the people and armies to hold off enemies. The greatest sin is treason—to reject the authority of the state and its rulers.

Tribal societies raid one another for property, women, slaves, and vengeance. Peasant societies are often involved in long-term wars that mobilize the whole of the society to conquer a neighboring state or to defend the nation against an attacker. Young men are expected to die for their country and obedience and valor are highly valued. Young men volunteer or are drafted to fight the wars of the state.

Dominance leads in a fallen world to injustice. The powerful do not care for the poor but exploit them. Those with high status do not seek to include those with low status. Rather they despise the lowly and exclude them from their social circles. On the worldview level, this oppression is usually justified by blaming those at the bottom for their plight. They have sinned against the gods, they live impure lives, they have earned their suffering through the misdeeds in their previous lives, or they are less than fully human. Slavery, too, is justified by one means or another as morally right.

Peasants in Cities

The cities of the world are growing rapidly and much of their growth is due to rural immigration. When peasants reach the cities, they do not become urban people. It is their grandchildren and great-grandchildren who will be true city folk.

Peasant immigrants often settle in urban villages—pockets of village life located within the city boundaries. In many ways these rural enclaves operate like peasant villages despite their surroundings. Leadership, family and kinship ties, social obligations, hierarchy, gossip, and community discipline are often imported from the rural settings.

There are, of course, differences. The impact of the city on these urban villages, particularly in economic affairs, is strong. Nevertheless, peasant culture patterns survive in proximity to the metropolis and many urban culture traits fail to diffuse through these pockets of peasant society.

Peasant Networks and Associations

Peasants come to the city to find work. Many hope to earn some money and then return home. Most end up immigrating to the city because there are few opportunities in the village or because they cannot adjust again to rural life.

New immigrants often find a relative or someone from their village who already lives in the city. These put them up for a few nights and help them to find jobs and places to stay. The result is regional peasant associations. People from one part of the countryside help those who come from their region to assimilate into urban life.

Some of these regional associations become formal organizations. They organize sports teams, local newssheets, and fiestas. They contribute to the weddings of their members and raise money to help their home town. In short, they become the community in which peasant immigrants find social fulfillment.

Invasions and Squatter Settlements

One of the greatest problems peasant immigrants face is housing. Those seeking work cannot afford the high rents of city housing or dream of buying land to build their own. Their only hope is to squat on some unused land.

Around the world this has led to squatter invasions. A dynamic leader organizes a group of his relatives and friends and on a given night they move to an open piece of land and start building shanty houses. Often this is government land and the government may send police to clear them off. But they return a few nights later. Many, in time, are finally permitted to stay "until another place can be found" for them.

With the rise of democratic governments, many political leaders are hesitant to push the people off land on which they have squatted for fear of bad publicity in the newspapers and on television. The leaders of the invasion often know this and invite the press and populist-minded politicians to see the founding of a new "people's democratic" township. With their support, it is almost impossible for the government to drive the squatters off the land.

Sometimes the land is privately owned. The owners call the police, but the police are often hesitant to intervene for fear of being accused as oppressors. The owners may finally resort to lawsuits, but these are costly and take years to settle. Many give up claim to the land for promises that no new land will be taken.

Once on the land, the people begin to make improvements on their shanties. Tin roofs appear, brick walls rise around lots, and appeals are made to the city officials for water and electricity. In time the settlements often become stable urban communities. This pattern of settlement by invasion has been the basis of the *favelas* of Rio, the *barriadas* of Peru, the *callampas* of Chili, the *bidonvilles* of North Africa, the *barongbarongs* of the Philippines, the *bastis* of India, and the shantytowns of Puerto Rico, Hong Kong, Ankara, and Athens.

Rural-Urban Circulation

Most city peasants keep ties with their home villages. Occasionally they may send money home to support family members and return home for weddings and funerals.

In this circulation, city peasants are caught in a bind. On the one hand, costs are high in the city and wages are eaten up by essentials. On the other hand, because they come from the city, their rural kin expect them to be rich and to bring presents for relatives and friends, near and far. Pleading poverty is not a good defense, because villagers believe that anybody who can't make money in the city is obviously weak in character, dissolute, a spendthrift, lazy or incompetent, and generally useless. Moreover, the city peasant wants to impress his or her rural cousin. If the city dweller ever really hopes to come back to the village, he or she must put up with these obligations.

There is also circulation from the village to the city. Country folk come to the city to experience the excitement of urban life. They expect their city relatives to house and feed them and to cover their costs during their stay.

No matter how generous city peasants are, village folk are distrustful and jealous of them. Rural people are suspicious that they have sold out to the morals and lifestyle of the city. The city peasants are also alienated from their rural folk. The city does change them and they get impatient with the traditionalism and closed-mindedness of village folk.

The costs of this circulation to city peasants are often so high as to keep them from saving money and getting ahead. Those hoping to return to the village manage as best they can. Some decide the cost is too high and cut their ties with their villages. Their action confirms what the villagers have suspected all along, that the city takes their young and destroys their way of life.

Modern Problems

We have stressed that peasants now are inextricably bound up with modern, global systems. They grow crops in order to sell them on the market, rather than to feed themselves, and have more and more of their production conditions, such as supply of loans or technology and prices for the commodities, determined by forces beyond their control. In order to understand modern peasant problems, then, we must understand world systems.

In chapter 4, we investigated some of the political implications of the colonial era for tribal societies. With peasant societies, the economic implications of that era and of the associated Industrial Revolution are relevant.

Colonialism began as a result of the adventurous energy that the Renaissance fostered in Europe. But it ended up a stable, and for Europeans, profitable, economic enterprise. In general, Europeans traded manufactured goods and civil rule for raw materials and labor with their colonies. The exchange was very much to the rulers' advantage, because manufactured items were sold back at a handsome profit to the colonies that had provided the raw materials. When colonial peoples attempted to initiate manufacturing themselves they were put down with military force.[1] Of course, taxation also benefited the rulers. The result was up to four hundred years of wealth transfer from what is now the Third World to England, France, Spain, Belgium, Holland, and Germany.

It was this era that set up the modern global economic system. Better and better transportation and communication facilities made worldwide trade possible. A new class of capitalists in Europe, people with surplus money to invest, fueled the expansion. The colonial military supported trading companies, such as the British East India Company, by "pacifying" those local kings who would not cooperate. In perhaps the most shameful event of this period, in 1839 and 1856 the British declared war on the Chinese, and won, forcing them to reopen their markets to the lucrative opium trade despite serious problems in China with opium addiction.

Colonialism broke down politically in the late nineteenth and early to mid-twentieth centuries, with many colonies gaining their independence after World War II. But the exchange between rich and poor countries continues. Immanuel Wallerstein (1979, 1974) has suggested that modern nations can be divided, based on the roles they play in the global economic system, into three groups: core nations, semiperipheral nations, and peripheral nations.[2] Core nations, such as the United States, Germany, England, and France, have the highest complexity of economic activities and the greatest capital accumulation. They are rich and powerful. Peripheral nations, such as Bolivia, Honduras, or Jamaica, are less wealthy and so must rely more heavily on labor than on machines in production. As in the colonial era, they export mostly agricultural products, which do not fetch a high price compared to manufactured ones. Semiperipheral nations, such as Mexico, Venezuela, and the countries of Eastern Europe, are intermediary between these two types.

As with the exchange between European countries and the colonies under colonialism, the exchange between core and peripheral or semiperipheral nations now is unbalanced, resulting in a net transfer of wealth from periphery to core. Modern Third-World nations, in which most peasants live, are not naturally poor. They are being made poor. And it is peasants specifically who usually bear the brunt of this poverty.

In fact, there is a sense in which poverty is a modern invention. According to archaeological evidence, previous to the rise of cities, food-producing peoples lived in small, egalitarian communities. They had little formal leadership and families were largely self-sufficient. An ethic of reciprocity no doubt prevailed. So when hard times came, such as crop failures due to natural disasters, all suffered together. Under normal circumstances all were able to feed themselves and live comfortably.

With the rise of cities, however, sometimes vast differences in wealth developed. Just down the road from the Egyptian pyramids, which were elaborate tombs for kings full of buried wealth, are large pits into which hundreds of malnourished bodies were thrown at about the same time. Other archaeological sites, such as Mohenjo Daro of Pakistan, have some huge homes, full of frescos, furniture, and other objects, and many little hovels where poor people resided. Evidently, it was the centralization of power that caused wide divergences in wealth and effectively prevented people from being able to feed themselves.

Likewise, the modern global economic system, though it has produced enormous amounts of wealth, has not distributed that wealth evenly, either within nations or between them. The Bolivian economy illustrates the problem. Highland Bolivian peasants have done intensive agriculture since their ancestors, the Inca, ruled. But in the 1980s many of them switched suddenly to cocaine production. Why did this happen?

As always in a market economy, the story starts with demand. Though illegal, cocaine had swept across the United States as the drug of choice. The price of coca leaves soared on the global market. As a result, many Bolivian peasants, under the influence of a network of criminal overlords, took up coca production as a cash crop. Even those villages whose climate could not support coca lost most of their young men to labor on the coca plantations. The urban Bolivian overlords became enormously wealthy and took effective control of the Bolivian government, but the peasants became hooked on cocaine themselves, lost control of their land to criminals, and now face hunger and a destroyed economy (Weatherford 1994). It seems the larger and more elaborate our human systems are, the larger are their failures.

The disruption in the Bolivian economy has been due to the boom in coca demand. But, over and over again, history has made clear that every economic boom will be followed by an economic bust. Bananas in Central America and rubber in Brazil are examples (Weatherford 1994, 189). When the coca bust occurs, Bolivian peasants will lose their cash income. They may also lose the pressure of traders from the outside as well, though, and may return to healthier forms of production. A subsequent boom might disrupt life again. The point is that the global market is volatile, in even the best of commodities, and provides a precarious existence for peasants.

Still, when they are free to choose entry and exit into the market, and when alternative forms of subsistence can be quickly accessed, peasants can profit from their connection to the larger world. William Roseberry's (1989) account of the Venezuelan peasant town of Bocono illustrates this. In the late nineteenth century, Spanish and Italian migrants came to the Bocono area and started coffee production. In addition to setting up their own plantations, the migrants purchased coffee from local farmers, who had previously been growing subsistence crops, and transported it out to the global market. The coffee trade is notoriously volatile. In boom years, Boconoans had cash and could purchase outside goods. In bust years, particularly during the Depression, they had to raise production to meet their financial needs with the new lower cof fee prices.[3] Eventually, however, Boconoans turned to other means of subsistence, such as regional trade. Their contact with the world market "loosened" (116) because it was no longer profitable. Roseberry stresses the flexibility of peasants in adapting to oscillating external market circumstances.

Planned economic development efforts with peasants have sometimes been disastrous because of the assumption that integration with the global market is inevitable and ultimately beneficial to local farmers. In general, development experts have assumed that increasing global supply of needed commodities will automatically provide for their distribution to those who need those commodities (in spite of the poor's lack of ability to pay).

In the 1960s and 1970s, a worldwide development effort known as the "green revolution" swept across agricultural countries. It combined highly specialized varieties of rice, maize, and wheat with chemical fertilizers, pesticides, and new cultivation techniques, and resulted in a dramatic increase in the world's food production. But the expected decline in global hunger did not occur. In fact, there is more hunger today among both rural and urban poor around the world than there ever has been previously. Clearly, hunger is not the result of our inability to produce enough food. It is the result of our inability to control power structures that inhibit the distribution of that food.

For instance, in Java (Kottack 1994, 346), the rice program under the green revolution was initially highly successful because the development workers, who were students from local universities, were careful to insure that all peasants received seed, fertilizer, pesticides, and technical help. After 1966, however, a new government in Indonesia allowed foreign multinational corporations to manage the rice program. As a result, wealthy landowners were able to hoard the assistance for themselves, and many poor farmers lost their land and were forced to migrate to cities. Kottack concludes,

> Peasants stopped relying on their own subsistence production and started depending on a more volatile pursuit—cash sale of labor. Agricultural production became profit-oriented, machine-based, and chemical-dependent. Local autonomy diminished as linkages with the world system increased. Production rose, as the rich got richer and poverty increased. (348)

Kottack, who is an applied anthropologist with extensive development experience, suggests that there are two reasons that development efforts with peasants fail (1994, 351). First, he identifies the problem of "overinnovation." This refers to development plans that try to change too much too quickly. The result is either resistance from local people or damaging unexpected results. Planners, working with paper models, are inclined to think they can anticipate all results, when real situations are more complicated than this.

Second, Kottack identifies the problem of "underdifferentiation." This refers to the application of the same development plans to very different circumstances. Kottack complains that "the aim of many agricultural development projects . . . seems to have been to make the world as much like Iowa as possible" (372). Highly educated in economic theory and in agribusiness, planners have not been taught to take culture into account. If they are aware of local traditions, they are inclined to consider them irrelevant to economic development efforts. More than one project of this type has failed due to the "irrational" beliefs and practices of local people. In one case, an Indonesian rice farming community happily accepted a high-yield variety of seed to plant, only to have most of the harvest eaten in the field by the rats (who also preferred it to the previous variety). When the development planners then wanted to exterminate the rats with pesticides, local people refused on religious grounds.[4]

Clarence Maloney (1988), in his analysis of why Bangladesh is poor, makes the startling, if somewhat pessimistic, suggestion that the same cultural characteristics of peasant life that cause peripheral nations now to suffer from poverty may prove successful in a coming ecological disaster produced by the overindustrialization and wastefulness of core nations. These peasant characteristics include a high value on fertility, social interconnectedness, and the patronage system. Maloney suggests that it is the global system's maladaptation to its natural environment that will cause serious crises in the future, not the peasant culture's maladaptation to the global market.

There is, however, much good development, defined in terms of the enhancement of local peoples' lives, taking place among peasants. According to research by Ewert, Yaccino, and Yaccino (Ewert, Clark, and Eberts 1993, 2), the most successful development projects typically have the following characteristics: the participation of people in their own development, local ownership of the decision-making process, commitment of local resources to the community development process, outside agents playing the role of facilitators of change, a belief in people's capacity to effect change, a value on peoples' indigenous knowledge, the transformation of limiting structures (such as authoritarian leaders) that impede local initiatives, and the primacy of process over projects.

In chapter 2, we suggested that change is not only inevitable, but also necessary, and that it is the nature of the change that must be evaluated. In chapter 4, we mentioned that giving material assistance, of the right kind, can be seen as "giving a cup of cold water in Jesus' name." Here, where peasant societies are concerned, we must add that our material and spiritual assistance to others must be informed by an understanding of the dangers of concentrations of power. The global market economy has concentrated power in the hands of a few wealthy nations. Consequently, local peasant landlords are often able to gain power over their neighbors. The result is poverty, not due to lack of resources, but due to the hoarding of wealth.

It is difficult for Christians to know what part they can play in alleviating local, much less global, suffering from unjust power structures. We are inclined to feel helpless in the face of such large systems. Jesus' response to such structures, such as the Roman Empire, seems to have been characterized by a kind of humility, love, and cooperation that produced tremendous liberation. He always called people to examine their own consciences and to be willing to die, if necessary, for the Truth. Such a call for personal moral behavior from the Christian community to peasants, traders, and officials at every level must go out. If even moderately successful, a call to personal morality, properly demonstrated by Christians themselves, would radically transform the morality of social, economic, and political structures as well.

Peasants still make up the majority of the world's people. How effective have Christians been in planting churches in the millions of small villages of peasant societies and how can we be more effective in doing so? These are questions we must now examine.

7

The Church in Peasant Societies

In some ways peasant societies are like tribal societies and in some ways they are radically different. Church planters in peasant societies need to understand both similarities and differences if they want to be effective in their ministries. Just as they translate the Bible into local languages, so also they must use methods of evangelism and church planting that are adapted to the social and cultural contexts in which they serve.

Planting Churches

How do we evangelize and plant churches in peasant societies? Most of the principles of church planting we examined for tribal societies (chap. 5) apply equally to peasant societies. We need to identify with people, learn their language, and understand the deep longings of their hearts. We need to take time to bring people to Christ, help organize them in churches, and nurture them to maturity. Other principles emerge, however, that are unique to rural communities. It is these we need to examine in greater detail.

Building Trust

Peasants live in tight-knit communities in which trust is essential to relationships. They are wary of outsiders because their experiences with strangers are usually negative. Tax collectors and other government officials oppress them, and traveling traders take advantage of them because they do not know the ways of the outside world. Most of them are nonliterate and at the mercy of those who can read and write. Many of them do not understand the ways of the outside world and are afraid of them.

We must, therefore, take time to build acceptance among people. We need to learn their language well and live among them so that they learn to know us as trustworthy and steadfast. We must adopt a lifestyle compatible with that of the people, and extend hospitality to them.

A crucial test of our identification with people is what we do in our spare time. It is all too easy to associate with other missionaries for friendship and relaxation. But this speaks loudly of our real affiliations.

One important bridge in building relationships is our children. People know we love them when we share with them our most precious possessions by allowing our children to play with theirs. Another bridge is sickness and even death. When a missionary is ill, people meet him or her in their common humanity. There is no greater testimony than when they realize this stranger has given her or his life for them. Our lives and deaths are as powerful testimonies of the gospel as our words.

Itinerant and Resident Evangelism

One area of considerable debate in peasant evangelism is the way evangelism should be done. In the nineteenth and early twentieth centuries, mission leaders thought in terms of geography. They wanted to evangelize the whole earth, so they divided it into territories. Missionaries were assigned to different mission fields and were expected to evangelize the several hundred villages in their field. The strong emphasis on letting everyone hear the gospel in their lifetime compelled the missionaries to tour the villages, preaching in each two or three nights and then moving on. During the days they visited in homes and held Bible studies for national evangelists on the team. In the evenings they held evangelistic services, often in the public square. Converts were organized into small congregations supervised by native preachers who visited them about once a month. This method gave birth to many small congregations scattered around the land. Often, however, these churches were spiritually weak due to lack of discipling (Luke and Carman 1968). Moreover, the churches often depended on missionaries to evangelize other communities.

In recent years some leaders have stressed the importance of planting mature, reproducing churches. Missionaries are assigned to single communities and given four or five years to plant a strong autonomous congregation with its own leaders and evangelists. Then the missionaries move to a second place.

This method is slower in evangelizing a country. In the long run, however, the outreach multiplies as churches join missionaries in evangelizing the region. In this approach it is the church, not the missionaries, that are the center of evangelistic outreach.

Working in Communities

Most peasants live all their lives in the same community. The result is enduring, stable relationships, a strong sense of community, and a loyalty to traditions.

Community Life

Unlike urban people, who have little understanding of true community life, peasants have a strong sense of their corporate identities and strong networks of relationships that hold them together. Their groups provide them with enduring communities of relatives and friends and support in times of need.

A barrier to church planting

Strong community life often acts as a barrier to church planting. Group pressures keep people from accepting the gospel and taking public stands of faith. In Muslim, Hindu, and Buddhist villages, converts to Christianity are frequently ostracized and even killed by their kinsmen and religious compatriots. We must not underestimate the power of social and cultural systems to keep people from Christ.

In such cases, the missionary must be ready to provide places of refuge where new converts can stay. In the past missionaries have often created Christian settlements, not because they wanted the new Christians to leave their villages but because the Christians were thrown out of their parental homes.

In some cases, missionaries may need to defend the Christians before government officials and courts to protect the lives of the

Christians. This raises difficult questions of how far the missionaries, who are usually guests in the country, should use political
means to defend their Christian brothers and sisters in the land.

A bridge to church planting

People's strong sense of community can also be a bridge to
church planting. It is the basis for people movements in which
whole families and communities come to Christ together.

It is very difficult for single converts to stand alone in a village against the opposition of their relatives and neighbors. It is
important, therefore, to encourage family decisions, for then new
converts are not forced to leave their homes when they become
Christians. When several families convert together, they have a
community of support that helps them withstand the opposition
of others.

An example of reaching families is the work of the Baptists in
South India. The missionaries sought to win adults, and when a
person became a Christian, they urged him or her to go home and
win the spouse and family to Christ before taking baptism. Bap-
tisms were often delayed a few years, but when they took place
they often involved whole families.

It is important to recognize that baptism in most peasant societies is the public ritual that, more than anything else, marks a
convert's break with the non-Christian family and community. So
long as wives or husbands are not baptized, they are generally
allowed to remain at home and to practice their new faith privately. Normally we should encourage baptism only when young
Christians are ready and able to stand and when there are enough
converts to form a new community of support.

Social groups in one village are linked by ties of marriage to
groups in other villages. Consequently, people often hear about
the gospel long before the evangelist or the missionary arrives.
People may have heard that their relatives in another village have
turned to Christ and they are discussing the advantages and dis-
advantages of doing so themselves. These webs of relationships
lead to the conversion of clusters of related families. If a significant number of families become Christian, it is harder for the others to throw them out of the community and it is easier for the
Christians to stand in their new faith.

Finally, we need to minister to converts until a strong church is in place. In doing so, we can build upon the sense of community that characterizes village life. The church needs to become a new community in which people find worship, fellowship, mutual support, and security. Unlike urban settings, where the church must strive to build true communities, in peasant villages Christian communities will emerge naturally if they are nurtured.

The fact that people in peasant villages do not move often makes church planting easier. Converts, their children, and their grandchildren attend the same church over the years. Members in the congregation know each other intimately and provide one another with a strong community of support.

This does not suggest that the Christians always get along smoothly with one another. In village life there are rivalries, jealousies, and gossip. People know, however, that they must live together for many years in the same local church and there are local procedures in place for dealing with conflicts and misbehavior.

Caution must be exercised, however, to keep the church from turning in on itself. The same sense of community that nurtures Christians can cause them to shut the doors to outsiders. For example, in many Indian villages Christians have become an endogamous caste (*jati*). They no longer seek to win other people to Christ and to assimilate these people into their churches.

Indigenous Patterns of Church Organization

When a number of converts form a church, questions of organization arise. Along with the gospel, we bring our own culturally shaped ideas about church polity. Some of us introduce democratic procedures in which all members, mature and immature, have an equal say. Others of us institute presbyteries or clerical orders based on succession. All of these modes of organization are characterized by formal rules and bureaucratic forms of management.

In peasant societies, state governments organize formal bureaucracies to rule the people. In the village, however, the peasants depend much more on consensus and ad hoc organization to get things done. They often hold informal councils and discuss matters for hours, even days, until some general agreement is reached. The people who make up a majority do not impose their decision on others, because they know they must live together with these people in the village for the rest of their lives.

An example of these informal councils are the *panchayats* in Indian villages. The elders of a caste or of the village gather to discuss disputes and community actions. These elders are not elected. They are older, more mature individuals who have earned people's respect by their wisdom and even-handed judgment in settling disputes. Anyone, however, may throw in a word. The discussion continues until the elders and those involved reach a consensus. There are no police to enforce their decisions, no jails to hold the offenders. Enforcement depends upon everyone complying with the group decision. Punishment is social criticism and ultimately ostracism.

Given the *panchayat* system, it should not surprise us that in the rural areas of India, the strongest churches are normally those organized around recognized elders and church *panchayats*. Where democracy and *Robert's Rules of Order* have been introduced, church business meetings often become political arenas in which the young and the powerful seek to gain power by inviting their friends in to vote, whether these friends are Christians or not. Village Christians with their Indian worldview that draws fuzzy rather than sharp boundaries in life hesitate to exclude non-Christians from business meetings. Some may be seekers. Others may be interested in joining the faith. To exclude them from participating in the meetings would drive them away.

Adapting the church polity to the way peasants normally organize things is generally effective. In South India, those churches that use democratic procedures are torn by rivalries and factions. Those organized around elders and church councils have been strong and continue to grow. Unfortunately, western missionaries today are often more willing to contextualize the message of the gospel than patterns of church organization.

Multiple Groups

One important difference between tribal and peasant societies is that the latter are made up of two or more groups. These may be different ethnic communities or they may be different social classes.

The presence of several groups in the same village has significant implications for church planting. If we plant a church in one group, people from other groups may not be willing or permitted to attend. Consequently, to effectively evangelize a village we may initially need to plant separate churches in the different communities. Social distances are as important as geographic ones. People may live a few yards from each other but socially be a hundred miles apart.

Several factors reduce the complexity of church planting in peasant societies. First, worship groups are often broader than marriage groups. For example, in a South Indian village, people from different castes worship in the same temple. There may be twenty or more castes or ethnic groups (*jatis*) in an Indian village, none of which will intermarry with the others. However, these belong to four or five worshiping communities. People from the clean castes gather together in the central Hindu temple, untouchables in their shrines, and Muslims from different castes worship at the mosque. The Gypsies and other semitribal castes have their own places of worship. We do not need a separate church for each caste but for each religious community. If people of different castes gather together to worship as Hindus, we can certainly expect them to do so as Christians.

Planting separate churches in each religious community in a village raises important theological questions that must be answered biblically. Should we divide churches on the basis of fallen human social structures such as class and caste? Where is the unity of the church and the oneness of the gospel and Holy Spirit? These are not questions that can be put off until the church is planted and strong. If bridges of fellowship are not built between groups from the beginning, the church will be captive to social systems and will contribute to the segregation and oppression that characterizes these systems.

The first bridges often come between leaders of different churches meeting together for prayer and fellowship. Later their congregations can hold joint celebrations at regional gatherings and build bridges of fellowship. Reconciliation between people of different classes and ethnic groups in the church is not peripheral to salvation. It is at the heart of salvation itself.

Going to the Top or the Bottom

When we deal with societies made up of several groups ranked in a hierarchy of prestige and power, we face a dilemma. To whom should we go first: the dominant elite, the middle-class commoners, or the untouchables, serfs, poor, and other marginal peoples on the bottom of the society?

Going to the Rich and Powerful

Many missionaries have argued that we must go first to the dominant group. If the community leaders become Christian, they argue, the others will follow because the elite serve as their example. This strategy, however, has met with limited success in peasant societies.

First, peasant elites have been more resistant to the gospel than the lower classes and castes. Priests, village headmen, and wealthy landowners have a vested interest in maintaining the religious system in which they have power and prestige. The church planter must not only persuade them to follow Christ, but also help them brave the strong institutional opposition that invariably occurs when people of importance become Christians.

Furthermore, most peasant societies, such as those in China, India, and Latin America, are parts of old civilizations with great philosophical and cultural histories. The great difference in power that exists between western civilization and tribal societies and that attracts many tribal peoples to the gospel, does not exist between the west and other civilizations. Church planters cannot appeal to cultural and theological sophistication as evidence of the truthfulness of Christianity.

A second reason why the "trickle-down" theory has not worked well is the high walls that separate the elite from the common people. Even if people in the dominant group become Christians, they are rarely willing to associate with and evangelize the lower classes. This is seen in the relationship between white slave owners and their slaves on U.S. plantations and between middle-class churches in North America and the inner-city poor. The lower classes may equate Christianity with oppression and reject it, as they have in parts of Latin America.

Going to the Poor and Oppressed

Other missionaries have gone first to the poor and oppressed. This has frequently occurred not because of conscious planning but because of the widespread response of the downtrodden for whom the gospel has a special attraction. For instance, in South India, Protestants started their work among the high and middle castes, but it was the untouchables who began to come to Christ in great numbers. The missionaries knew that if they opened the door for these outcastes, the church would be branded as untouchable. After a long debate, they decided they could not turn the untouchables away. The result was a flood of the poor and oppressed into the church.

At first the high-caste people turned away from the church because they equated it with untouchability. Today the picture is beginning to change. The first-generation Christians were poor, but they somehow managed to send their children to school and these became clerks and grade-school teachers. They sent their children for higher-level training. Many of the third-generation Christians are seminary and university professors, doctors, and lawyers. Seeing the transformation that has taken place in the Christian community, high-caste people are beginning to turn to Christ.

This socioeconomic rise in Christian communities is sometimes referred to as redemption and lift. It has two sides to it. Positively, the church gains respect and economic resources that enable it to better evangelize its neighbors. Negatively, as the church rises in socioeconomic status it disconnects itself from its old community and loses its ability to evangelize it.

Going to the Middle Class

Many peasant societies do not have middle classes, at least not in the contemporary sense of the term. With the spread of modernity, however, educated, relatively independent, middle-class people have begun to appear in many rural communities. In recent years, evangelicals have increasingly gone to them to plant churches because they are open to change.

It has been easy to build bridges to middle-class people elsewhere because western evangelical missionaries are usually educated, middle-class people themselves. The result is a growing middle-class Protestant church that is literate and economically powerful. Moreover, as democracy has spread and traditional aristocracies have disintegrated, middle-class people, including Christians, have gained political power. In these lands, Christianity is increasingly being identified with wealth, power, success, and other middle-class values.

Modern, middle-class churches often ignore the poor and oppressed. Today it is the Pentecostals with their gospel of hope and some Roman Catholics with their gospel of liberation who have an effective witness among the masses of poor peasants.

Using Oral and Literate Methods

Peasant societies have both oral and literate communities. We must, therefore, use both oral and literate methods of communicating the gospel to reach these two audiences.

Most peasants are nonliterate and, therefore, our primary means of communication must be oral. In the past, western missionaries have often assumed that literacy is essential to evangelism and Christian maturity. Great efforts were made to promote literacy. In the process, oral communication methods were largely ignored. Today we recognize literacy as a powerful tool in helping Christians study the Scriptures, yet people do not need to learn to read in order to become Christians.

There are many ways to evangelize oral people. In one region of Africa, church planters are recording Bible stories on audiotapes using the traditional narrative forms of the people. In India, Christians are experimenting with native bardic performances and street dramas. In Thailand, they are adapting classic forms of drama and dance to evangelize village peoples. Bible societies are beginning to use picture and cartoon books to present Bible stories. Radio, movies, and videotapes are other important ways of communicating with oral peoples.

Church planters must also use literacy to evangelize literate peasants. Printed portions of the Bible, tracts, magazines, newspaper ads, correspondence courses, and books have all been used with varying results, depending on the content of the materials, the audience, and the ways the materials have been presented. A New Testament given personally to a seeker or sold for a low fee, for example, is more effective than tracts distributed to strangers, although God can use such tracts to bring people to himself. It is best if literate methods are incorporated with other methods in larger evangelistic strategies.

Literacy plays a particularly important role in another area of church planting, namely, in nurturing the church to maturity. Ultimately, Christians, and especially leaders, need to read the Bible for themselves in order to grow and to understand God's message to them in their particular sociocultural context.

Using Whole Ministries

In peasant societies, with their strong sense of community, the gospel must be presented as a whole way of life. The church must present the way of salvation, but also respond to immediate human needs such as sickness, starvation, spirit possession, and sorcery. Jesus preached the coming of God's kingdom on earth and he showed us the nature of that kingdom when he taught, healed, and liberated people.

In the past, missionaries started schools and hospitals around the world. These ministries opened the door for many to hear the gospel and trained the leaders of nations. Christian schools and hospitals are central to the educational and medical services of many countries.

While recognizing the immense contributions Christian schools and hospitals have made globally, we must admit that they were not always the effective witnesses for Christ that we thought they would be. There are two reasons for this deficiency: one is cultural, the other social.

A Split Worldview

On the cultural level, many western missionaries unconsciously took with them the western worldview that makes a sharp distinction between natural and supernatural realities. The former is seen as the domain of science; the latter as the realm of religion (table 6, following page).

The missionaries preached eternal salvation and planted churches. They also built schools and hospitals on the foundations of science. Bible classes were taught in schools and prayers offered at the beginning of each hospital day, but these rarely challenged the essentially scientific nature of education and medicine.

Table 6
The Dualism of the Western Worldview

Supernatural Realities	Christianity	Churches	Evangelism
Natural Realities	Science	Schools, Hospitals	Social work

Algebra and chemistry were generally taught with little reference to God and the gospel.

The consequences of this dichotomy were far-reaching. In missions it led to a destructive division between evangelism and social concerns. In the church it led to a focus solely on other-worldly concerns, leaving this-worldly concerns to the state and secular institutions. In the society it led to the spread of secularism as young people studying in Christian schools accepted the sciences but rejected Christianity.

There are many notable exceptions in missions to this dualism. There have always been missionary doctors, teachers, and preachers who viewed all of life as a unified whole under the care of God. They saw medicine as one way God works in this world and the sciences as discovering truth about God's creation. In their hands hospitals and schools became powerful means whereby people were converted and ministered to in their needs. These people must be our models. Like them, we must rid ourselves of the dualism that leaves human earthly needs to the care of a secular science.

Bureaucratic Organization

On the social level, western leaders have a culturally shaped drive to create formal, highly organized institutions. We create roles such as teacher, doctor, nurse, and preacher, organize committees, set goals, pay leaders, and formulate rules.

This tendency to high organization can have a negative effect on church planting. First, we are in danger of creating specialized institutions the people cannot maintain. Big schools and hospitals are often a great burden on young churches. Even missionaries and church leaders can become so busy running institutions that they have little time to be with the people.

Second, the hidden message behind bureaucratic organizations is that life is divided into segments and specialists are needed in each. Medical care is entrusted to doctors, education to teachers, and church ministries to trained pastors. There is little room in this model for an empowered laity.

There is a place for schools, hospitals, and other institutions in peasant churches, but they must serve the church and not become ends in themselves. The church must focus on people, not programs.

Models of Wholistic Ministry

Several models show us what a wholistic ministry might look like. One is the African Independent Churches. These indigenous churches are centers where preaching, worshiping, ministering, teaching, fellowshiping, and healing are combined. A second model is the Base Community movement that started in Latin America. In this lay Christians gather together to study the Bible, pray for one another, and decide how to apply the gospel to their everyday lives. A third is the charismatic churches among the poor in Latin America. These churches become centers of hope and help to those without hope or vision.

All these models stress an integrated ministry at the local level in which leaders and informed lay persons empower the common people to minister to one another and to the needy in the world.

Theological Issues in Peasant Societies

What are some of the central issues the church faces in peasant societies? Some of the concerns we examined in tribal societies reappear here because peasant societies are often made up of ethnic groups that act in many ways like tribes. We face people movements in which extended families and networks of families turn to Christ together. We also face questions of polygamy, animistic beliefs, and traditional customs.

In peasant societies, however, we face other theological questions that emerge out of the nature of peasant sociocultural organization. Many of them are the center of much debate among church leaders and have no easy solution.

Marriage and Mistresses

Like tribal societies, peasant communities often have polygamy, but many peasant villages also have socially accepted liaisons between men and women outside formal marriage. These are often stable, lifelong relationships, with children and second homes. A wife often knows of her husband's mistresses, but can do little about them since these relationships are tolerated by the public.

In Indian villages liaisons are generally secretive and occur most often when high-caste men take advantage of low-caste women. Children of these affairs belong to the caste of their mother or are rejected as illegitimate. In Europe and Latin America, mistresses often belong to the same class as the men.

The theological problem becomes more difficult in Roman Catholic countries. Because the Catholic church rarely grants annulments and divorces, most couples who separate must enter into common-law marriages if they wish to remarry. What should we do when people who have lived together for twenty years and have children want to join the church? In most cases, they cannot go back to their legal spouses because these have their own common-law families. In such cases, it is normally best to recognize that when people come to Christ, they come with their sinful backgrounds. When they turn their lives over to Christ, it makes them new people and gives them a new beginning.

Multiple Groups

The fact that peasant villages are made up of more than one group raises several theological problems. Two of these have to do with Christian marriages and with the unity of the church.

Questions of Marriage

One question new Christians in peasant societies face is where to find husbands and wives for their children. They often belong to endogamous groups in which there may be no Christians for their sons and daughters to marry.

For example, in recent years high-caste families in India have been turning to Christ, only to find there are no Christian spouses in their caste for their children. One solution is to marry their children to Christians of other castes, but then their non-Christian kin cut them off for having broken the fundamental rule governing castes and they lose their Christian witness among their own people. Others, too, reject them for fear of the stigma associated with intercaste marriages.

Another solution is for parents to marry their children to Hindu young men and women who are willing to become Christians to marry the children. Are such conversions genuine, or is this a case of being "unequally yoked with unbelievers"? Such marriages are powerful means for evangelism and maintain ties between Christians and their non-Christian relatives. They also prevent the church from becoming another endogamous caste. But has the "converted" spouse truly found Christ? In many cases they have, but in some cases they have not.

The problem is more difficult in Muslim countries where Christians must convert to Islam when they marry Muslims. The result is a constant loss of Christian young people and an accentuation of the problems related to marriage.

Questions of the Unity and Diversity of the Church

More difficult are questions about unity and diversity within the church. In tribes, all converts in a village belong to the same group and naturally go to the same church. In peasant societies they come from different classes and ethnic groups. Should Christians from different groups in the same village form one church or should they organize separate churches along ethnic and class lines?

Early Catholic and Protestant missionaries treated classes and castes as social realities that needed to be changed. This transformation, they argued, was part of Christian maturation and would take decades to accomplish. They planted separate churches in each of the ethnic and class communities or allowed these communities to meet separately in the same church.

Beginning in the nineteenth century most Protestants began to stress the unity of the church. This was less of a problem in China, where most of the people in a town belonged to the same ethnic group and where sharp class distinctions did not divide people into different worshiping communities. All went to the same Buddhist temple, so all could attend the same church. Class did play an important role in relationships within a congregation, but usually did not divide it.

In India the picture was different. Each caste had its own caste gods, and untouchables and Muslims were not allowed into the temples of the clean castes. If Christian converts from the high castes attended the same church with the untouchables, they were put out of their castes. If they met in different churches, they would give in to the caste system that is an essential part of Hinduism. The caste system is not just a form of social organization. It is first and foremost a religious hierarchy rooted in Hindu theology.

After 1800, Protestant missionaries in India argued that all Christians should be in one church because they are a new people in Christ and because caste distinctions should be rejected as being part of Hinduism. As a result, multitudes of untouchables joined the church, for it freed them from the tyranny they had suffered so long. However, few high-caste people became Christian because Christianity became identified with the untouchables.

In Latin American peasant communities the social divisions are based both on class and ethnicity. Latin American Indians live alongside mestizos and European immigrants. There is also a great distance between the rich landowners and the poor. How can the churches show to the world the love and reconciliation that Christ brings to a broken and hostile world?

In recent years the issue has been revived. Advocates of the Church Growth school of thought argue that forcing unity on the church has kept many high-caste people out of the kingdom of God and leads to ostracism and problems of marriage for those who do become Christians. They argue that separate churches should be started in each major social group to encourage people to come to Christ without having to change their social system and to develop a sense of community in congregations. They add that in time these churches should begin building bridges of fellowship.

Critics of this approach argue that to organize churches along caste lines is to compromise the essence of the gospel. If caste divisions are not challenged at the beginning of the church, reconciliation between ethnic groups will never be achieved. They point out that Paul did not permit Jews and Gentiles or rich and poor to form separate churches. For him the fact that all of them worshiped together was itself a sign of the powerful transformation they had experienced in Christ. These critics also contend that starting separate churches in homogenous groups does not guarantee growth. It is true that more high-caste people might have become Christians had they been permitted to start their own churches. However, fewer untouchables would have done so because the church would then not deliver them from the tyranny of caste.

The best answer probably lies between these positions. It is hard for us to expect all young converts to make a radical break with their social past, particularly when class differences are still deeply embedded in western churches. It may be necessary for them to meet for a time with others from their people in homes and small assemblies to build Christian maturity and fellowship. At this stage they should be permitted to choose leaders from their own group, and encouraged to maintain relationships with their own people to win them to Christ.

Early in the life of these young churches, however, the Christians must be taught that those who are in Christ belong to one body. This is not a by-product of the gospel. It is at the heart of the gospel itself. Through the cross, Christ has reconciled us unto himself and made us one family. Poor Christians and rich, dark-skinned and light, are our sisters and brothers whether we like it or not. They are closer to us than our unsaved biological siblings. Our identity as Christians is deeper than our identities of class and ethnicity and we need to demonstrate this to a divided and strife-ridden world.

From the beginning, young churches need to build ties of fellowship with other Christians. At first this should be done by teaching the unity of the body of Christ and by the mature leaders of different churches gathering in worship and prayer. Then relationships need to be built between congregations so that the world may see a new community shaped not by the values of this world but by God.

Missionaries in peasant societies must face the tension between the existing social order and God's call that the church be one community of reconciliation. We must allow people to be different but affirm the oneness we all have as Christians in the Spirit.

Justice and Liberation

A third theological issue we face in peasant societies is justice and liberation. In tribal societies, the rich share with the poor and there is little systemic oppression of one group by another. In peasant societies, hierarchy and social divisions are not only present but also affirmed, particularly by those with status and power who feel themselves to be better than the poor and powerless.

As we have seen, in class societies the poor form an underclass that is cut off as a group from power, status, and wealth. Often these are landless serfs and tenant farmers who work for wealthy, literate patrons, *kulaks,* and other landed gentry. Where there is surplus land, the peasants have some power—they can move to another village or start a new hamlet by clearing and tilling the soil. In many cases, however, they have no option but to remain, living at the mercy of their landlords who keep them in debt by lending them money at high interest rates and by controlling the shops that sell them goods. After debt payments and taxes, there is little on which to live.

Small landowners fare better, but only slightly. Most are in constant debt to moneylenders who charge exorbitant interest on small loans. Peasants often borrow seed at planting time and must pay 50 percent interest or more at the harvest four or five months later. Many also borrow heavily for weddings and funerals and spend a lifetime paying off these debts. Children often inherit the wedding debts of their parents.

It should not surprise us that liberation theology was born and thrives in peasant societies among the poor, dispossessed, and oppressed. Today it is found in Latin America, but is spreading in Korea (as Minjung Theology), India, and Southeast Asia.

Much of contemporary liberation theology is based on a Marxist analysis of social systems. Christians cannot advocate solutions that have only material goals, that advocate the use of force, or that in any way underestimate the power of God to work apart from human effort. But the questions that liberation theology raises are important and as Christians we cannot ignore them. We must offer biblical answers to injustice, oppression, and poverty, because these are of deep concern to God.

We must address two issues: freedom from poverty and oppression and the empowerment of people. Some Christians argue that the only solution to the first of these is violent revolution, but, as Christ points out, violence only breeds more violence. Missionaries and church leaders often find themselves defending the rights of the oppressed before courts. They also organize programs of food distribution, basic health care, agricultural development, and small business improvement. These approaches, however, do not change the fundamental social structures that oppress people and impoverish them. The church as a whole needs to speak out for justice and compassion and work for the peaceful transformation of the society.

One important way to bring about freedom and justice is to help people to organize themselves and to take responsibility for their lives. The hierarchical model of church organization that concentrates power in the hands of a few leaders is being challenged today on the frontiers where the church is growing rapidly. In much of the Third World it is impossible, numerically and economically, to train enough professional leaders to meet the needs of the exploding church. Moreover, many of the young churches cannot afford and do not want elaborate organizational structures. Consequently, new forms of church organization are emerging that give power to the laity.

One such form is the congregationalism of the Pentecostal and charismatic movements. They give power to lay leaders, men and women, to use their gifts of church planting and leadership. In many ways, these leaders resemble the Methodist circuit riders and the Baptist farmer-preachers of rural America. The Pentecostal and charismatic movements, base communities, and independent churches already described are examples.

What is clear is that the church in much of the world will need to depend on lay leaders, simple organization, and flexible evangelistic strategies if it is to grow. The same characteristics give the church great power in confronting oppressive social systems.

Folk and Formal Religion

We saw in chapter 6 that there are several layers of religion in peasant societies. The coming of literacy and of universal religions, such as Islam, Hinduism, Buddhism, and Christianity, give rise to formal structures, sacred texts, orthodox theologies, professional leaders, schools and churches, mosques and temples.

These give answers to the ultimate questions of life, but their coming does not displace the local animistic beliefs. Witchcraft, spirit possession, divination, ancestor veneration, and many other beliefs and practices persist, providing answers to the many questions of everyday life concerning sickness, guidance, justice, and meaning.

Ordinary peasants mix the local customs of formal religion with animistic practices. The result is folk Islam, folk Hinduism, folk Buddhism, and so on. Muslim villagers go to the mosque to worship Allah, but stop under a tree to venerate a saint or put the imprint of a hand on their door to protect themselves from the evil eye. Hindu villagers call the Brahmin priest to their home to conduct their rites of passage and worship at the temple in the village, but also placate the local spirits with blood sacrifices and turn to the shaman and the magician for healing.

When we deal with religious beliefs and practices in peasant communities we must examine and respond to each of these levels of religious expression.

Responding to Formal Religion

The great religions of Islam, Hinduism, and Buddhism have sacred texts, sophisticated philosophies, and elaborate religious organization that hold their followers in tight control. To leave these religions, particularly in small peasant communities, people face ostracism, persecution, and even death. Consequently, the large peasant populations of Asia have been less responsive to the gospel than have tribal societies around the world.

We need to know the basic beliefs of the formal religion of people to know how to communicate the gospel to them so that they understand it. If we do not do this, we will fail to present a true picture of the gospel.

Our study of the formal religion must go beneath its explicit beliefs and practices to the level of worldview. The fundamental beliefs of a religion are written most deeply in its categories and its basic assumptions about the nature of reality. For example, *deva*, the word for "God" in South Indian languages, means the highest of living beings. But *devas* are part of creation, not creators. The word for the origin of all things is Brahman or Cosmic Force Field. If we use *deva* in translating the Bible and preaching, people think of the word with its Hindu meanings. If we use Brahman, the Force, we distort the gospel. There is no word in these languages that captures fully the biblical idea of God.

If we fail to deal with worldview issues in the teaching ministry of the church, we will soon face syncretism. People may believe our biblical teaching, but will associate the words with their Hindu, Muslim, or Buddhist meanings. In time the words distort the teachings. The result is a syncretistic mixture of Christian and non-Christian ideas (fig. 29).

Figure 29
The Subversion of Christianity
by a Non-Christian Worldview

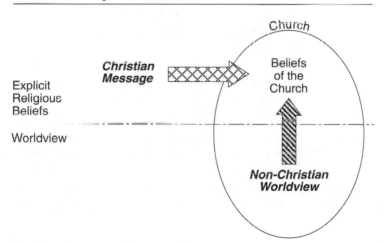

We also need to study the formal religion in order to prepare new converts for the type of persecution they may face. Young churches seek to define themselves over against the religions around them. The gospel calls the church to be a new community that is in the world but is not of it. When the church adapts uncritically to the world around it, it becomes captive to that world. First-generation Christians generally reject completely their old religious ways and often suffer severe persecutions as a consequence. Second- and third-generation Christians are more established in their identity and must decide how they should relate long-term to the others in their village. Often Christians constitute only a small minority in a community controlled by Muslims, Hindus, or Buddhists.

The simplest solution, particularly if there is persecution, is for the church to become a quiet, countercultural community. Christians cease to evangelize their neighbors for fear of being beaten. They become an isolated community and adopt a religious relativism that allows each community to have its own religious beliefs.

It is difficult for the church to take a strong stand on the uniqueness of Christ and to continue its evangelistic outreach. This often leads to opposition and even martyrdom. Yet only as the church takes this stand is it faithful to the gospel. Many young churches have been willing to suffer greatly and in their suffering they have grown in maturity and number. It is often the old established churches that are more willing to compromise their evangelistic stance to avoid persecution.

The difficulty we face as church planters and missionaries is that we come from the outside and can leave when the opposition grows strong, but the local Christians must stay and suffer the consequences of a bold witness. How can we teach them faithfulness to Christ when we ourselves do not have to bear persecution? When persecution begins, should we stay with the Christians or should we leave for the safety of our families? Does our presence strengthen the church or does it lead to greater persecution of the Christians? These are difficult questions we must face.

Finally, third- and fourth-generation Christians face another challenge, namely, the reevaluation of their cultural past. First-generation converts often make a radical break with their old ways. They reject their traditional drums, dances, art, and music because they associate these with their pagan past. Many of these practices are indeed closely tied to the old religion. The Christians two or three generations later grow up in the church and no longer associate past customs with paganism. Today pride in one's cultural past is supported by the anticolonial reaction to the western ways formerly brought by missionaries. To affirm their identity with their cultural past, many churches around the world are now turning back to their traditional names, clothes, drums, dances, and other practices. The church must help people reaffirm their cultural heritage, but guard lest this affirmation of their past lead them into syncretism.

Responding to Folk Religion

As church planters and missionaries we focus on the formal religion of the people we serve, but we often overlook their folk religious beliefs and practices. We study formal Islam, Hinduism, and Buddhism to evangelize people, but we are largely unaware of the fact that most of them are folk Muslims, folk Hindus, and folk Buddhists. They are more concerned with witchcraft, spiritism, divination, ancestor veneration, magic, the evil eye, and other animistic beliefs than with formal religious orthodoxy.

This blindness is due in part to the fact that western Christianity is embedded in a western worldview. Central to this is a deep faith in progress. In religion this led to the widespread belief that when Christianity and science came, old animistic beliefs would die out. However, this did not happen. Christianity in much of the world has been added as another layer of religion over the old animistic ways. The result is Christopaganism. Where animistic beliefs have been displaced by science, the result has often been the spread of secularism.

It is not enough to simply condemn witchcraft, spiritism, magic, divination, and other animistic practices. We must provide Christian answers to the everyday needs of people, or they will continue their old ways. They attend church on Sundays for eternal salvation, but during the week they go to the shaman and the magician for protection, healing, power, and guidance. We must develop in the church biblical answers to these human concerns.

If our gospel provides an answer to the concerns of everyday life but fails to deal with the ultimate issues of sin and salvation, we are in danger of presenting Christianity as a new and superior magical power and destroying the heart of the gospel.

In peasant villages we must respond to both the formal and the folk religious beliefs and practices of people and present a whole gospel that deals with both their ultimate and immediate needs. We must continue to preach the message of salvation, but we must also deal with the issues of witchcraft, spiritism, ancestors, and magic, which are reemerging around the world.

The great peasant heartlands of Islam, Hinduism, Buddhism, and Sikhism are among the most resistant areas to Christian faith, despite centuries of mission work. They also are one of the great challenges to Christian witness today. There are growing signs of responsiveness in peasant societies in different parts of the world, including China, Korea, Thailand, and South India, but much must be done before all villagers hear the gospel in such a way that they can understand and respond to it.

8   Urban Societies

Cities! These are the last type of sociocultural organization we will examine. They are a radically different way of organizing human life. Robert Bierstedt (1970, 411) writes, "[The city person and the country person] do indeed adhere to two different views of the world, have different rounds of activity, sustain in different ways the progression of the seasons, indulge in different kinds of work and play, and spend their span of life in different surroundings." What is the city? How does it function? How can so many people with such diverse cultures live together in some measure of order?

Many of us live in cities, but know little about how they operate. Until we do we will not be able to minister to people in them in relevant ways. Too often we try to plant country churches in urban areas, and we don't know why we fail.

The explosion of cities has taken place largely in the twentieth century, but cities themselves are not new. In the middle of the third millennium B.C. cities such as Eridu and Thebes emerged along the Tigris-Euphrates and Nile rivers. In the second millennium B.C. they appeared in North India at Harappa and Mohenjo-daro and in Chengchou, China. In the first millennium B.C. Teotihuacan and other cities appeared in Central America. Cities emerged in West Africa after the coming of Christ.

Most of the ancient cities were not large by modern standards. Ur had a population of about 24,000 in 2000 B.C. and Athens about 180,000 in 300 B.C. Rome emerged as the first great city in Europe. It had about a million people in New Testament times. When Rome fell to the invading barbarians from Inner Asia, Europe reverted to peasantry with small episcopal cities rarely larger than 3,000 people with their lords and bishops, walls, cathedrals, and religious institutions.

In North India, the cities of Harappa and Mohenjo-daro were destroyed about 1500 B.C. Large cities reemerged in South Asia only a few hundred years before the coming of Christ. In China, cities have flourished and decayed, but urban life never collapsed so completely as it did in Europe or North India.

Ancient cities, for the most part, were political and religious centers. Here kings established their courts, taxing the peasants around them to maintain their affluency. They built walls to protect themselves and their entourages from enemy attacks. Here

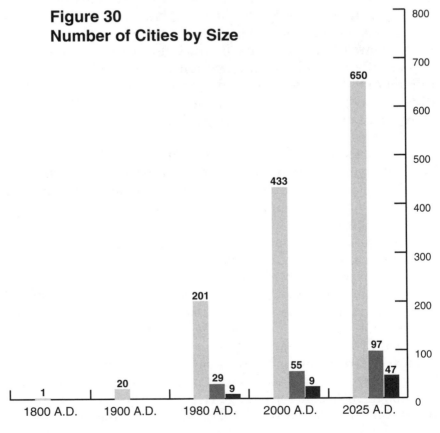

Figure 30
Number of Cities by Size

Source: David Barrett

bishops and priests built great cathedrals, temples, and mosques as centers of their religious power.

Cities depend on surplus food for their existence. The first cities emerged after the invention of ox-drawn plows, wheeled carts, iron and steel tools, irrigation, sailboats, and new breeds of plants and animals. Modern cities depend on "factories in the fields" that produce not only subsistence for the farmers, but also for city people. They are also dependent on carts, trains, ships, and planes to transport goods to and from their markets. Today, in many countries, less than 10 percent of the people produce the food that feeds them all.

Modern cities emerged after 1000 A.D. They were centers of economic activities such as manufacturing and trade. Business, not government or religion, was their driving force. They were not refuges in times of war. They thrived in times of peace and walls became hindrances. These cities emerged first in northern Europe but they soon spread around the world as commerce and manufacturing increased.

In our century, modern cities have exploded. In 1900 only one city, London, had more than a million people. Today there are more than 380 cities larger than that, including little-known urban areas such as Ibadan and Lagos in Nigeria, Nagpur in India, Bolo Horizonte and Recife in Brazil, Shen-yang in China, Kitakyushu in Japan, Meshed in Iran, and Omsk and Kuybyshev in the former U.S.S.R. There are now at least 12 cities with more than ten million people (see fig. 30, preceding page).

The massive flow of people from the countryside to cities continues. Never before in history have so many people moved from one place to another. In 1800, less than 3 percent of the world's people lived in towns with more than 5,000 people. By the end of this century more than 55 percent will do so. More than 48 percent will live in cities of more than 100,000 people. Today urbanization is taking place faster in China, India, Africa, and Latin America than in Europe and North America. By the end of this century, only three of the ten largest cities will be in North America (including Mexico City), and none in Europe (fig. 31, following page).

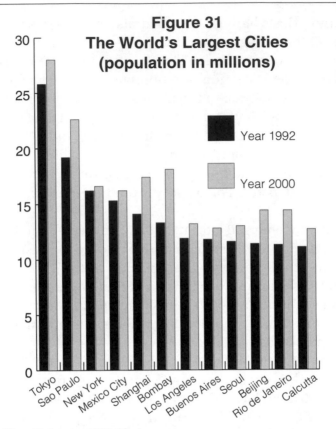

Figure 31
The World's Largest Cities
(population in millions)

■ Year 1992

▢ Year 2000

Source: *Time*, 11 January 1993, 38.

Analyzing Cities

The sheer size of modern cities makes it difficult for us to understand them. The population of Tokyo is more than five times as large as all of Papua New Guinea with its nearly one thousand tribes. One high-rise in Bombay may have more people than ten Indian villages.

How do we study such large and complex sociocultural systems? Sociologists have taken one approach. They try to understand the city as one operational whole. To do this, they must take a "helicopter" view of the city, looking at it from above. They map the physical, social, and cultural features to understand population densities, ethnic and class compositions, migration patterns, transportation and communication systems, religious distributions, and so on. They compile statistics on a great many demographic variables. And they look at how cities change over time.

This helicopter view is valuable in helping us to get an overall picture of the city and its many layers of social and cultural systems. In the process, however, we lose sight of living human beings. We think in terms of maps and numbers.

Anthropologists have taken another approach to the study of the city. They use the ethnographic methods they used to study tribes and peasant societies to examine the city from the street level. They live with people and hear their life stories. They participate in neighborhood activities and observe life in its everyday flow.

This approach to the city helps us to understand everyday life. We learn what it is like to be members of a street gang; single mothers trying to rear their children in high-rises; business tycoons lunching on the top floors of their skyscrapers; suburban families busing their children to schools, doctors, music lessons, and sports activities; immigrants trying to find a new life; and the thousands of other kinds of people who inhabit the city. In the process, however, we lose sight of the larger systems that structure the lives of ordinary people and make the city possible.

We need to use both micro and macro approaches—both helicopter and street-level views—to help us understand this great, complex, and confusing thing we call a city.

Social Order

How can we understand the city? Early analysts focused on the number of people, population density, and geographic layout to define a city. But these do not capture the essence of the city. Some rural areas, such as parts of Bangladesh, are more densely populated than many urban areas, but they remain rural in character. Small towns, such as those in the Amazon forest, often provide the major functions of a city for the surrounding territories. Furthermore, cities no longer have sharp boundaries separating them from the countryside. The city changes from skyscrapers and high-rises to suburbs and exurbs as one moves out from the center.

Later analysts focused on the city as a new type of social organization. They contrasted the social life of cities with that of peas-

Table 7
Redfield's Rural-Urban Continuum

Rural Life	Urban Life
established, traditional	mobile, free
homogeneous	heterogeneous
group-oriented	individualistic
ascribed roles	achieved roles
community	intersecting communities
harmonious	managed conflict
status quo, little change	rapid change
egalitarian	hierarchical
wholistic life	segmented life
human in scale	impersonal
sacred cosmos	secular cosmos

ant villages and noted marked differences between them. Robert Redfield (1947, 1955), for example, placed tribal hamlets, peasant villages, and cities along a continuum. In particular, he focused on the movement from rural to urban communities (table 7).

There are grains of truth in the rural-urban continuum, but we now know that the model is far too simple to help us understand the city. The city does not exist in opposition to the countryside. It is symbiotically linked to the peasant communities around it by complex social, economic, and political systems. Moreover, it often encapsulates peasant, even tribal, communities in its boundaries. And, increasingly, city-minded folk commute from small towns to the city or carry on their work through phones, faxes, and modems.

The rural-urban continuum forces us to think in polar contrast. We develop broad stereotypes both of villages and cities on the basis of a few experiences. Harvie Conn (1987) points out that many of us see the city as a place of crime, poverty, and secularism that depersonalizes people and reduces them to powerless pawns in the grips of powerful social systems. He shows that we may exaggerate this view and not see that people can live happy lives there. Before we study the city, we must examine our own stereotypes of it, for these too often determine what we see.

When we examine the social order of cities, we must constantly remind ourselves that cities are not a single, uniform organization. Internal structures vary greatly from one area of the city to another. Even in one area, such as the inner city, there may be a great variation from one street to the next.

Cities also vary greatly around the world. Most of the work done on cities has been done by sociologists studying cities in the west. Much less has been done on cities in Asia, Africa, and Latin America. What is clear is that cities differ from country to country depending on their distinct histories and cultures. For example, many Indian and African cities were once colonial cities that had separate areas where the colonial rulers lived. The legacy of their colonial past colors the present configurations of these cities.

We must recognize, too, that cities vary greatly in their reason for existence. Some cities such as New Delhi, Moscow, Beijing, Brasilia, Nairobi, and Washington, D.C., are primarily governmental cities. Other such as Mecca, Jerusalem, Varanasi, Kyoto, Vatican City, and Lourdes are religious centers. Others, such as New York, Bombay, Shanghai, Sydney, Amsterdam, and Cape Town, are centers of trade, business, banking, and transportation. Others such as Las Vegas, Pataya, and Acapulco are built primarily around tourism and conferences. Some cities combine several functions, such as business, government, and tourism. While the special focuses of a city shape its life greatly, all cities must provide the basic social functions for those who live in them.

General Characteristics

Despite the great variation in and between cities, some generalizations can be made that apply to most, if not all, cities. These apply equally to the social, economic, political, legal, and functional dimensions of urban social organization.

Scale

The social organization of a city is shaped, to a great extent, by the vast numbers of people of different cultures living in the same place. It is impossible for ten or twenty million people to live together without very complex social, economic, and political systems to make their common life possible. Thus, to understand cities we must look at the effect of size on human organization.

Bands make life possible for a few hundred people by organizing them into families and camps. Tribes order life for as many as twenty or thirty million people by imposing higher levels of social organization, such as clans and age grades, over families and local communities.

Peasant societies assimilate tens and hundreds of millions of people into one social system by adding even higher levels of social organization, such as class and caste systems, feudal and national states, and extensive trade networks. People continue to live in families, but these families are aggregated into classes and castes and these into villages, regions, and nations.

As societies grow in complexity, more levels of social organization are added and on each level new social structures emerge that encompass the social systems below them (fig. 32). Furthermore, there is constant interaction between levels. What happens at the *village level* affects family organization. What happens at the national level impacts *regional and village* structures. Changes in family and community life profoundly affect the higher levels of peasant organization.

To understand the city, we must recognize that here too there are many levels of social organization. For example, urban Americans belong to families, associations, and neighborhoods. Neighborhoods are served by city-wide organizations having to do with transportation, electricity and gas, garbage removal, hospitals, schools, parks, police, courts, and central government. The city, in turn, is part of the larger state and national structures. At each

Figure 32
Levels of Social Organization in Cities

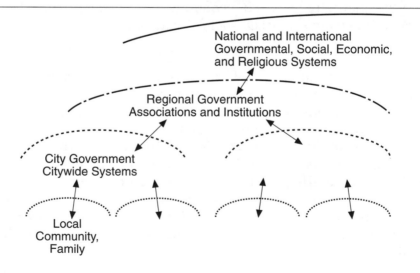

level new systems of government, trade, and association emerge that coordinate the activities of the units below it.

These new systems, however, are not just larger in size; they are also different in kind from the systems below them. Bands and tribes are relatively homogeneous communities held together by ties of kinship and association. Kinship groups and associations continue in peasant villages, but now people from different social and cultural groups live together in the same community on the basis of class and caste systems. These systems are based on ties of status and power.

Cities encompass even greater social and cultural diversity and maintain order by the addition of bureaucratic governments, police, armies, complex business, religious, and social institutions, and intricate networks of communication, travel, and trade. Moreover, their very life depends on structured relationships with rural areas that provide them food, on transportation networks that bring and take their goods, and on state and national governments that maintain regional order and peace. Complex and stereotyped patterns of interaction guide people's behavior in these new systems, each of which may be based on a different function.

Today, cities are also part of a growing global order. They are centers of business, education, research, travel, communication, and religion, having networks and organizations that reach around the world. It is impossible to understand Los Angeles, for instance, without understanding not only its city organization and national ties, but also its links to Japan, Korea, Southeast Asia, and the rest of the world. At the global level too, new and more complex systems, such as the United Nations, international banking, relief and development organizations, and the international scholarly, community have appeared. These all have their own rules for operation and are integrated vertically with the appropriate systems below them.

Centers

If we chose one word to characterize the city, it might be "center." Cities attract power, wealth, knowledge, and expertise. In them we find the centers of government, banking, business, industry, marketing, learning, art, transportation, and religion.

Cities dominate the countryside around them. In many ways we can understand the world better if we focus on cities and their hinterlands rather than on nation states (Jacobs 1984). For example, Bombay dominates west India; Calcutta, northeast India; Jakarta, Indonesia; Paris, France; and Los Angeles, Southern California. Urban alliances and rivalries are important in shaping regional cultures.

The relationships between cities and the rural and tribal communities around them are complex. Food raised by farmers is shipped to cities for processing and packaging and then sold back to the farmers with a high mark-up in price. Young people from the country flock to urban universities and many never return to take over their parents' farms. City-based television and radio stations shape the worldviews of rural audiences. And land developers carve fields up into residential tracts.

The relationship, however, goes even deeper. As Michael Lipton (1988) shows, power lies in the hands of modern governments and business and they have a strong urban bias, causing them to exploit the rural areas to the advantage of the cities. Most governments see rural areas as sources for food, foreign income (through the sale of cash crops), and revenues. They tax agricultural lands and crops heavily and spend most of their income on cities—on industry, housing, and infrastructural systems of water, sewers, electricity, transportation, and communication. The result is the impoverishment of rural areas. Lipton writes, ". . . less than 20 percent [of the world's] investment for development has gone to the agricultural section, although over 65 percent of the people of less-developed countries, and over 80 per cent of the really poor who live on $1 a week each or less, depend for a living on agriculture" (1988, 43).

Businesses and rich farmers, too, see the countryside as the source of cheap food and raw materials for urban industry and seek to keep the price of these down. They also invest in cash crops that they can sell abroad, rather than in subsistence crops that raise the quality of life for the poor. City people commonly earn twice as much as their rural relatives. It is not surprising, therefore, that poor people flood to the cities.

Walter Christaller (1966), a geographer, notes that the size of the city creates a cycle in which big markets attract more institutions and these in turn attract more people. For instance, in a small town of a thousand, there is room for one general physician. The city is large enough to attract not just doctors, but plastic surgeons, osteopaths, and otorhinolaryngologists who need populations of a hundred thousand or more to sustain their professions. Similarly, cities can support symphonies, professional sports teams, major research universities, and stock markets. The presence of these institutions attracts more people and makes even more services possible.

This enrichment of city culture attracts both rich and poor. From their beginning, cities have attracted the rich and powerful who want to participate in the life of the elite. The poor are attracted by the hope of jobs, excitement, and government assistance. Criminals and social deviants are attracted because of the anonymity of the city and the many ways they can cheat people. In short, masses of people attract more people.

Diversity

A third characteristic of cities is diversity. As societies grow larger, they attract different kinds of people who form their own cultural communities. People no longer interact daily with everyone else as they do in a tribe or a village. They relate closely to people in their own groups and only superficially to others in the city. Most of the people they pass in the street or sit with in a bus are strangers.

Distinct communities rise based on ethnic, class, cultural, and residential differences. Many of them maintain their own languages and cultures. Consequently, side by side in the city we find Chinese, Thai, Italian, French, Persian, Indian, and other restaurants; Roman Catholic, Orthodox, Protestant (of many varieties), Hindu, Sikh, Buddhist, and Muslim churches; and mansions, highrises, row houses, slums, and sidewalk shelters.

Not only is the city of necessity a place of diversity, but also its people relish difference. They try different ethnic restaurants, look for new kinds of cars, visit other lands, and try new fashions. The enjoyment of variety is characteristic of the urban mindset.

Ethnic diversity

Cities attract traders, politicians, immigrants, and tourists from many different ethnic groups. For example, Bombay attracts people from all over India who live in caste and linguistic enclaves. It also has sizable foreign colonies made up of diplomats, business-men, and traders. Los Angeles has more than seventy-five distinct ethnic communities and teaches classes in public schools in more than seventy languages.

Relationships between ethnic groups in cities vary greatly. For example, in Ibadan, Nigeria, the conservative Hausa have main-tained their ethnic distinctiveness for generations by maintaining their language at home, discouraging interethnic marriages, and living apart. The Ibos, by contrast, have assimilated with the domi-nant Yoruba, learning their language and marrying their sons and daughters (Cohen 1988).

Class differences

Classes emerge in peasant villages, but in the city they explode into a great many different lifestyle enclaves made up of people who share similar cultural practices, values, and interests (Bellah 1985). These cultural neighborhoods vary greatly from one part of the city to another.

The large number of people in a city also fosters the formation of a great many special-interest groups. People organize clubs and promote specific cultural interests such as cars (racing, monster trucks, antique automobiles), the arts (dance, opera, theater, music, sidewalk shows, museums, antiques), recreation (bridge, fishing, hunting, camping, kayaking), sports (football, basketball, baseball, hockey, tennis, golf, soccer, polo, yachting, billiards), academics (sciences, humanities, history), jobs (construction workers, factory workers, doctors, lawyers, businessmen), and religions (Christians, Muslims, Hindus, Jews, Sikhs, secularists). In time conferences are held and associations formed to cultivate these interests.

Subcultural communities emerge around these special inter-ests. For example, in an American city there are sports subcultures associated with specific sports. Many of these have their own clubs, magazines, and professional and nonprofessional teams.

Degree of urbanization

One of the most fundamental differences in cities has to do with the mindset of the people. Not all city folk have an urban men-tality. Many are peasants who visit or move to the city but keep

Figure 33
Tribal and Peasant Communities in Cities

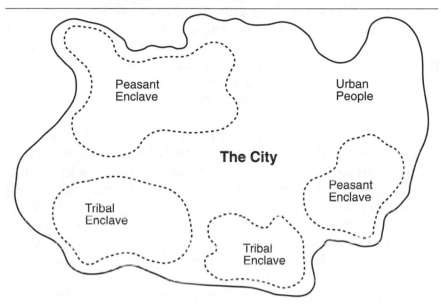

their small-town attitudes. They join people from their hometown and form small village enclaves in the city where they try to maintain life as they knew it in the countryside (fig. 33). This is particularly true in Asian cities.

There are also city tribals—people from a tribe who move to the city and live with others from their own people. They return to their hometowns regularly and maintain ties with their tribal relatives.

In time, most tribal and peasant people become true city folk. This may take generations, but the city ultimately reshapes the mentality and the lives of the people who live in it. In new cities, the number of country people is often high. In old urban centers, most people have been thoroughly acculturated to an urban way of life.

Residence

Another dimension of urban diversity has to do with residential areas. Most cities have one or more central zones where the main government and commercial offices are found. Markets, industry, and transportation often occupy other zones, with human residences scattered around them.

Homes in the inner city vary greatly. Some areas have run-down rental housing occupied by transients and recent immigrants, and others have small tract houses where laborers live. Still others have posh high-rise buildings or apartments along the coasts where affluent executives and professionals live.

Further out the suburbs begin. These are often "bedroom" communities of homes and children. Here people seek to find a quiet, orderly life away from the rush and crime of the city. Many of them commute to the city and are home only at night and on weekends. Suburbs, however, provide only temporary refuge. As they grow, they become major regional business and employment centers with tall buildings and traffic jams. In other words, they acquire the characteristics of the central city. Those who can move out further into exurbs and small towns and commute to the suburbs for work.

One form of suburb common in countries that were once under western rule are the colonies and cantonments. These were formerly areas where British, German, French, or other rulers lived. While the old cities are crowded and have narrow winding roads, the colonial suburbs are spacious and have broad straight roads. Today they are home to city elites.

Another form of urban settlement are the squatters' communities. Annually, thousands of the poor move to the cities in hope of work, excitement, and a better life. With no money to rent even the poorest of apartments, they are forced to build cardboard, wood, or tin shelters wherever they find unused land. Often this is along railroad tracks, on steep mountain slopes and river flats, near the garbage dumps, on sidewalks, or in alleys and empty fields.

Squatters generally organize themselves into local settlements with their own leaders, who serve as intermediaries between the squatters and government officials. Frequently they invade vacant lands as a group. The landowners complain and file lawsuits and the government occasionally clears squatters off by force. Having nowhere to go, they find another vacant place to build their temporary shacks. Often, however, the government wants their political support and is willing to bring in water, sewers, electricity, and the other infrastructures necessary for community life.

Slum life does provide millions of people with the necessities for bare survival. There were an estimated 715 million such squatters around the world in 1993, up from 260 million in 1970. This amounts to 13 percent of the world's population. Some estimate that this will increase to more than 15 percent by the end of this century. An estimated 100 million of these squatters are children who live, work, and die on the streets of the world cities. World Vision estimates that this number will double by 2000 (*Together* 32:1). But slum life also breeds gangs, crime, and prostitution among people deprived of the basic necessities of life.

Impact of diversity

The effects of diversity are far-reaching. Claude Fischer (1984) argues that the size of the city itself encourages and strengthens the formation of subcultural groups by drawing together enough people to form them. These may be based on ethnicity, class, religion, occupation, institutional affiliation, or common interest. For example, there are enough Iranians in Los Angeles to form an Iranian community, enough computer specialists to develop computer networks, enough violinists to organize a violin association, and enough taxi drivers to organize a union.

These subcultural communities coexist side by side in the city and interact with one another. Fisher argues that this interaction both strengthens these communities and gives rise to new subcultures as people from different groups intermarry. For example, Koreans move to cities in the U.S. and create Korean communities with Korean restaurants and Korean churches. In time, however, some marry American whites and create a new community different from either the Korean or the white American subcultures.

We must see the city, therefore, not as a homogeneous place, but as hundreds of subcultural groups living and interacting with one another in the same geographic area.

Specialization

One general characteristic of the city is the emergence of specialized roles. In the country, most people are involved directly or indirectly with raising food. They must be generalists. A farmer must know how to cultivate different kinds of crops, tend different kinds of animals, mend fences, dig wells, and do a hundred different tasks around his or her farm.

The city person has an almost limitless range of ways of making a living. If we look at the "employment opportunities" section of a large metropolitan newspaper the chances are great we will find advertised jobs so different from our own experience that we have never heard of them before. Umpires, diamond cutters, engineers, brokers, detectives, anthropologists, computer programmers, and many more make their livelihood in the city performing their job day after day, all year.

As the city grows, tasks are divided and new specialties emerge. To take a look at doctors again, physicians specialize in neurology, urology, pediatrics, radiology, otorhinolaryngology, and surgery. Surgeons become experts in abdominal, colon, ophthalmologic, orthopedic, and plastic surgery. Plastic surgeons may specialize in certain techniques or parts of the body. Similar specializations can be found among teachers, those who make and repair machines, or office workers.

Specialization is a function of size and complexity. Complex technology requires people with specialized knowledge. A group of people with general knowledge cannot build an airplane. In factories and bureaucracies activities are broken down into tasks that individuals can do. An airline hires pilots, navigators, mechanics, baggage handlers, flight attendants, sales personnel, and many more to transport people around the country.

Specialization begins with roles, but expands to institutions. In small towns there are general stores. In the city, shops specialize in groceries (general, health foods, Hispanic, Polish, Indian), car parts (tires, mufflers, windows), bicycles, bridal boutiques, floor coverings (rugs, tile, linoleum), foods (catering, restaurants—Chinese, Thai, Indian), and so on. There are banks, insurance agencies, stock markets, trade centers, railroads, hospitals, high schools, universities, and technical schools. This specialization contributes to the break-up of the city into subcultural communities.

Hierarchy

The sheer size and complexity of cities and their centralization of power give rise to internal hierarchy. The distance between the rich and the poor, the powerful and the powerless, the high status and the low in the city is almost incomprehensible. Heads of modern corporations earn more playing a game of golf with other executives than their lowest-paid workers earn in two or three years of hard work! The rich do not see the lives of the poor and the poor do not know what it is like to be a billionaire for whom money is not a matter of livelihood or consumption but a counter in games of power and status.

Hierarchy dominates most public urban relationships. In factories, business, governments, and even in the church vertical roles determine the interaction between those who lead and those who serve. In relationships between ethnic and class groups, hierarchy helps preserve order by maintaining the status, wealth, and power of the dominant group.

The oppression of hierarchy on those in the middle and the bottom of the society is tempered by the individualism and freedom found in most cities. Many poor believe that if they work hard, they, too, can move up the ladder. This belief may keep them from blaming the rich and powerful for their present conditions.

Change

A final characteristic of most cities is change. All human societies change, but the rate of change in cities is faster and more radical than that in peasant and tribal societies. A major reason for the increased rate of change in the cities is that specialization allows people to give their full efforts to specific jobs. This promotes the growth of technology, science, services, and information. Another reason is the constant input of new ideas from the outside.

Change is also due to the urban mentality that sees change as good and values highly what is new. Peasant and tribal immigrants are often attracted to the city by the hope of a new life it promises.

Social Organization

Having looked at some of the general characteristics of urban societies, we need to examine in more detail the dimensions of their social organization.

Roles

Most relationships in peasant societies are multiplex in nature. Those in urban settings are simplex.

Tribal and peasant communities are small, usually less then two or three thousand in population. Consequently, everyone meets everyone else on many different occasions and in many different roles. The result is multiplex role relationships (fig. 34, Gluckman 1944).

Figure 34
Multiplex Role Relationships

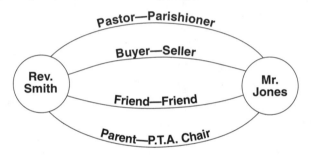

Relationships are multidimensional, intimate, and complex.

For example, look at the relationships between Rev. Smith and Mr. Jones in a small American town. Rev. Smith is the pastor of the local church and on Sunday morning he preaches to Mr. Jones, his parishioner. On Monday morning, Bob Smith goes to Harry Jones's grocery store to buy supplies. That afternoon they golf together as friends, and on Tuesday night Mr. Smith attends a Parent-Teacher Association meeting where he is a father and Mr. Jones is the P.T.A. chairperson.

The strength of such a multiplex relationship is that Rev. Smith and Mr. Jones learn to know each other intimately, not as pastor and lay person, nor as buyer and seller, but as whole persons. They see behind the social masks each plays in particular social contexts. Such relationships are often enduring, sometimes lasting a lifetime. Moreover, each member can count on the other for help in times of personal need.

There is a price to pay in multiplex relations, namely, role overlap. Rev. Smith dare not preach too harshly against the sins of Mr.

Jones because on Tuesday night Mr. Jones will criticize him for having missed the last two P.T.A. meetings. On the other hand, Harry dare not sell questionable produce to Bob because he will hear about defrauding customers on Sunday. So he sells it to a stranger passing through town. In the past Mr. Jones was often expected to give Rev. Smith a 10 percent discount on all his purchases because he is a minister.

Village-wide, multiplex relationships lead to a strong sense of community (fig. 35). The same people show up at the local basketball games, the hardware shop on Saturday night, and church on Sunday morning. The church does not need to build a sense of community among its members—they already are a community. The church, therefore, can focus mainly on worship and religious teaching.

Most roles in city life are simplex (fig. 36, following page). Mr. Peterson in Seattle teaches at the university. There he meets the other economists in his department as colleagues. None of them are Christians, so he can share his faith with them only on a very elementary level. In the evening he visits with his neighbors about lawns, cars, and children. They know nothing about economics and little about Christianity. Sunday he goes to church where he worships with people he meets only at church. He cannot share

Figure 35
Multiplex Relationships and Community

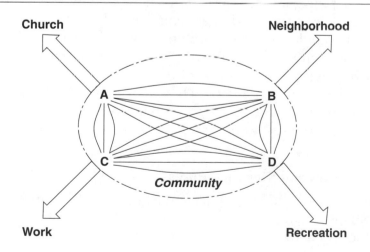

Figure 36
Simplex Role Relationships

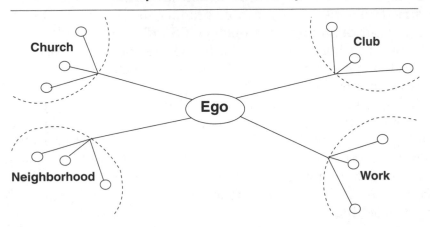

with them his new economic theory and how it relates to a Christian view of responsibility for the poor and oppressed because they would not understand it.

Such simplex relationships are task-oriented and efficient. They allow Mr. Peterson to deal with the task at hand in each situation without being sidetracked by the personal needs of those he meets. In none of these relationships, however, do people look behind the social mask Mr. Peterson puts on in each setting. They see him primarily in terms of the role he plays when they meet him: as economist, neighbor, or Christian. There are few real, enduring relationships in which Mr. Peterson can fully be himself and on which he can depend when problems arise in his life.

People in cities who do not belong to village or tribal enclaves and who have cut themselves off from their broader kinship ties often feel alone and alienated. They meet more people than their country kinsmen. In fact, they are often tired of meeting people. But their relationships are superficial and functional and they do not feel that others see them as real persons.

Families and Kinship Groups

Families and kinship groups persist in urban life, but they take new shapes under the pressures of the city. In western cities, a split occurs between the public and the private spheres of life.

Public life is the world of government, business, politics, and work. Here people must play roles assigned them by their jobs. Private life is where they can "be themselves." This is found in their homes, neighborhoods, and churches. Apart from small family businesses where work and home overlap, most urban family life is limited to the private domain.

In general, there is a tendency for the nuclear family rather than the extended family to be emphasized in cities. Relationships in this small family may have an intensity to them that is not part of larger rural families, particularly since city people expect nearly all of their deep social and emotional needs to be met at home. When such a family is doing well, the experience can be a good one, but when trouble comes there is no one to intervene to prevent family members from harming one another.

The internal structure of the family varies greatly in the city. Among the poor we often find families made up of mothers and their children. Women can often find low-paying work more readily than men can. Men visit the home and may stay if there is enough money to feed the whole family. Blue-collar families tend to be strongly patriarchal. Children go to work after a minimum education to contribute to the family finances. In many countries, wives in these families often carry on petty trade and work in service jobs. Many urban white-collar and high-class families are more egalitarian. Women are educated and take professional jobs. In Islamic cultures, they are kept at home but may manage businesses and carry on trade through male assistants or even their children (Schildkrout 1990, 221–28). In Hindu settings some enter politics and become doctors and lawyers.

Urban mobility, individualism, and freedom are acids that erode family stability. Divorce and remarriage are more common than in most peasant societies. The result is single-parent families and blended families made up of husbands and wives who bring with them children from previous marriages. The anonymity of the city also affects the family. It makes it easier for men to keep mistresses. This is particularly common in Latin American cities. Despite the onslaught of urban life, however, families continue to play the dominant role in the private sector of city life.

Networks

Networks are a major form of middle-level social organization in cities. News may spread rapidly through the networks. People ask neighbors and friends where to find a good doctor or repair shop. Couples invite their friends and neighbors to family celebrations. Mothers call each other to find their children and in time they visit one another and organize family barbecues.

C. Douglas McConnell (1990) analyzes the role of networks in cities and in city churches and points out that most city folk develop core networks made up of people with whom they like to associate, discuss personal problems, and share in social recreation. They tend to choose others similar to themselves. In peasant communities this similarity is generally based on ties of kinship. In urban settings people tend to associate with nonkin who share similar occupations, personal interests, and belong to their class and ethnic group.

Geography plays an important part in the formation of networks because people who live too far apart find it hard to meet regularly. Modern technology, however, is changing this as people link up with one another by means of phones and computers. Networks restore a personal face to impersonal city life as people form intimate relationships with other like-minded people.

Networks also provide real, practical support for city people. They allow the elite to politic and do business with one another. John Galbraith points out that top government officials circulate with the heads of business, banking, academia, and church at banquets and symphonies, exchanging information, making deals, and hiring one another.

Larissa Lomnitz (1988) argues that networks are also important in shanty towns. The city systems of medicine, welfare, and police do not reach them, so people must rely on one another for their elementary needs. People borrow from friends when they are out of work and lend when they have an income. They exchange information, loan food, blankets, tools, clothing, and other goods, care for one another's children and aged parents, and run errands for each other. They share televisions and latrines and offer moral and emotional support, particularly at weddings and funerals. Above all, they gather to socialize.

In many parts of the world, fictive kinship networks provide economic and moral support for urban dwellers. In Latin American cities, young people become compadres, in Papua New Guinea young males form wantok relationships, and in North America they organize gangs that provide them with support and camaraderie.

Most rural immigrants follow their kinship networks to the city. They move in with a relative, but often have little to offer the market—no assets and no skills except their devalued labor. Their relatives give them simple training and help them find work. In time they move out and establish their own household, usually near their kinsmen with whom they continue to have regular contact. Other country relatives join them later and the cycle begins again.

Associations and Institutions

The dominant social structures of public life in cities are associations and institutions. Their great flexibility and ability to organize large numbers of diverse people in multifaceted tasks makes them much more functional than kinship groups in complex societies. They enable newcomers to enter with remarkable ease into the activities of a group. For example, surgeons can perform emergency operations in hospitals in which everyone else is a stranger, and students quickly enter into the complex activities of college life by attending classes and joining its clubs.

Associations

Associations proliferate almost endlessly in cities. They are groups of people who organize themselves initially informally around a common interest or cause such as chess, hiking, music, education, and electing a government official. Some are based on friendships, such as a bridge club; others on gender, such as the Boy Scouts, Daughters of the American Revolution, and football teams; others on age, like associations of retired people and teenage gangs; and others on prestige, such as yacht and country clubs.

Associations have certain common characteristics. Most are organized to serve some specific purpose, whether that be social, economic, political, religious, or recreational. They create symbols to express their identity such as names, logos, and songs. These reinforce their members' sense of belonging and personal worth. They coordinate tasks and formulate roles like president, treasurer, and secretary. They develop their own cultures and norms which they enforce through social pressure.

Institutions

Informal associations may evolve into formal institutions: casual friendship groups become elite country clubs, political parties create governments, religious revivals give birth to denominations, and small colleges grow into universities. In the process, tasks are divided and specializations formed, informal practices are regularized and codified, property is acquired, and salaries are paid.

Institutions are the major form of social organization in the public sector of most cities. They include governments, banks, businesses, factories, schools, churches, airlines, railroads, and utility companies, to name a few. Institutions are subcultural communities or "cultural frames" (to use Clifford Geertz's term) in which people find their public identities. Doctors live much of their lives in hospitals, teachers in schools, bankers in banks, business people in shops, and pastors in churches. Each of these institutions has its own language, membership, roles, networks, associations, social hierarchies, economic resources, power structures, symbols, systems of belief, and worldviews. In short, each operates like a subcultural community.

Most city folk find their public home in one institution, but they draw on other ones for specific services. In the former, they are "insiders"; in the latter they are visiting "outsiders" drawing on what those institutions have to offer.

Let us look for an example at Dr. Matthews. She is a professor in the state university and spends most of her days on the campus. There she has a role with status and power (professor of biology), property (an office, lab, and library), symbols of identity (diploma; hood and robe at graduation), and economic rewards (salary). The university is her cultural community. It has its own language, values, goals, and activities. Although it is primarily an educational institution, the university has social, economic, political, and legal dimensions to it. In short, it is a fully defined society with its own culture and worldview.

On her way home in the evening Dr. Matthews stops at the local grocery store, another institution. She is an outsider buying the goods it has for sale. Mr. Zigler is manager at the store. He finds his primary public identity in his role at the store and in the symbols and rewards it gives him. The store is another clearly defined society with its own language, values, goals, and activities, which are very different from those of the university.

That night Dr. Matthews and Mr. Zigler attend the local professional baseball game. Here they are both outsiders drawing on the services of yet another institution. For Mr. Davis and his teammates, however, the local professional team is their social and cultural home. Dr. Matthews, Mr. Zigler, and Mr. Davis find their primary identity and home in a single institution or culture frame, but draw widely on other culture frames for specific services.

Urban institutions are increasingly linked together to form complex social systems. The local restaurant becomes part of a chain of restaurants. Airlines hire pilots, navigators, attendants, baggage crew, and ticket clerks, forge links to companies and unions that provide it with fuel, food, planes, and personnel, and work with the government that runs the airport. The interlocking webs of such institutional relationships provide much of the social structure that keeps the city going.

Institutionalization

The processes that lead to the growth and development of institutions are known as institutionalization. Several changes occur in the structure of associations as they become institutions and then grow into large social systems.

First, informal, personal relationships give way to formal social roles. When a new organization is formed, members volunteer to type correspondence, handle finances, welcome newcomers, and do the other work of the club. As it grows, formal, specialized roles are created and people hired to do specific jobs. Relationships now are based not on friendships but on formal roles. For example, in an informal house church we may ask Tom to preach, but when we organize and make him the pastor our relationship to him changes. We may feel that we must treat him with a little more respect and, particularly if he is paid a salary, also feel we have the right to voice our opinions on his use of his time.

Second, ad hoc arrangements are replaced by rationally formulated rules, management manuals, and constitutions that standardize and regulate activities. For instance, in a newly formed church the leader may ask someone at the last moment to lead the singing or take the offering. Later, as formal order is instituted, such arrangements must be made well in advance so that the names can be put into a bulletin.

Third, the charismatic leadership style normally found in new organizations must give way to a managerial style that administers the many complex activities of a large institution. Charismatic leaders are necessary to motivate people to action initially. But a charismatic leader with great vision and no organizational skills can quickly destroy a large establishment.

In part, institutionalization is a function of size. It is necessary to help social life function smoothly. It is also a function of culture. With their obsession for control, efficiency, and rationality, western societies tend to organize institutions along the lines of bureaucracies. In these, tasks are divided into specialties and allocated to different roles that are linked to one another by lines of command. The result is a mechanical approach to human organization, in which people become standardized parts in a factory or bureaucracy that has production and profit as its goals (Berger, Berger, and Kellner 1973).

Institutions in nonwestern cities are often more organic in nature. For example, businesses in Japan are organized on the pattern of parent-child relationships (*oyako*). Subordinates are expected to be loyal to the leaders and much time is spent in building trust with outsiders before decisions are made. Although such institutions do have rules, relationships are more important, so many decisions are negotiated on the basis of the particular persons involved, rather than by company policies. One can get things done if one knows the right persons and formalities.

Institutions are work groups. They make complex urban life possible by enabling leaders to mobilize a great many people to accomplish a common task. Moreover, they are efficient. Nonformalized social groups spend a great deal of time and energy on deciding what to do and how to do it. New decisions must constantly be made for each activity. Formal organization reduces the effort necessary to operate an institution by routinizing its activities. Institutions are even "homes" for their members with a measure of stability that more casual associations do not have.

But institutions can also be prisons. At first, working in them is exciting because there is vision and purpose. In time the work can become meaningless and routine. For example, a church organizes a committee to evangelize the neighborhood. The committee sets up an office and hires a secretary to carry on the paperwork. If she is not involved in the vision of the committee, her job becomes routine secretarial work that she does mainly for pay.

An institution can also lose its vision and become concerned primarily with maintaining itself. Young churches get along with the simplest of facilities in order to focus their efforts on their mission to the world. Older churches spend most of their time and resources on administration and on beautiful sanctuaries and parking lots for themselves.

As institutions grow, they also lose their flexibility and suffer from a hardening of their categories. Early on, decisions are made on an ad hoc basis. As rules and procedures are added to establish order and increase efficiency, flexibility is lost. Pressures build to keep the rules, because too many exceptions to the rules are threatening to the leadership and to people's general sense of order.

Just because formal institutions tend to become rigid, bureaucratic, and self-serving does not mean we should reject them. Urban life is impossible without them. Even the church in the city must be formally organized if it wishes to carry out large projects such as missions. The answer is to know how institutions work, to provide for the renewal of their vision, and to keep them flexible by means of loose organization.

Ethnic Groups and Classes

Ethnicity and class are the two fundamental city-wide identities of most city folk. The first has to do with ties of blood and kinship, the second with similarities of status, wealth, power, and lifestyle.

Ethnic groups

Cities are made up of many different ethnic groups, all competing for power and resources. Large ethnic groups generally form their own communities and maintain their cultural distinctives for generations. Individuals and families who come alone, however, are soon assimilated into the larger urban society.

Ethnic consciousness is found most among minority groups and immigrants. They are most aware of their lack of status and power and the subtle oppressions of the dominant population. Moreover, they must compete with one another for a share of the city's resources. Interaction with other ethnic groups in the city may solidify ethnic group boundaries and formalize ethnic institutions in the competition for power and resources. People from different cultural backgrounds may be amalgamated into the same ethnic group as leaders try to draw the boundaries wide to create a powerful bloc.

An example of this is the category *Hispanic* in the United States, a cateogry that includes people from Mexico, Central America, South America, and Puerto Rico and has been formed as a separate ethnic group primarily to get strength with large size. In so doing, Hispanics are set off from the dominant culture and assimilation is resisted both by the members of the group and by the dominant majority. In places like Africa, Eastern Europe, and the Middle East, this kind of ethnic politicking causes a great deal of conflict: conflict that usually takes place in the cities.

Urban life, however, with its emphasis on individualism, freedom, and mobility, is a strong counterforce to the bonds of ethnicity. People are forced to work together in government and business, marriages between people of different ethnic communities take place, and mixed neighborhoods spring up. To understand the city we must understand the forces of ethnicity and class that pull people in different directions.

Tribal and peasant immigrants

To understand ethnicity in the city we must also understand immigration. There are two types. One is the immigration of country people to the city. The other is the immigration of city people from other parts of the world. Both find that their ethnicity is the first identity assigned them by their new neighbors.

Until recently it was assumed that tribal and peasant immigrants to the city lost their ties to their country kin through the process of detribalization. We now know that most of them keep ties to their home villages for long periods of time, returning home for important festivals and family functions. As we saw earlier, this circulation puts great pressures on rural immigrants in the city.

Cross-cultural immigrants

Immigrants from cities and towns in other parts of the world face other adjustments. Many of them are refugees, driven off their

Figure 37
Generations and Identities in Immigrant Communities

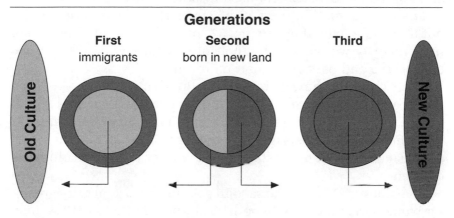

lands by war and violence. Others are attracted by the opportunities in the more affluent cities of the world.

Intercultural immigrants who come in small numbers are generally absorbed by the city in a generation or two. When large numbers come, however, they form a community that enables them to preserve their language, intermarriages, and ethnic identity for generations. This is particularly true if people are not well accepted by the dominant community.

First-generation immigrants—people who come as adults—generally identify closely with their home culture and never fully assimilate into the new city (Hiebert and Hertig 1993). They develop survival skills that enable them to function in their new setting, such as learning the language, taking unskilled jobs, and establishing an ethnic enclave. Many suffer status shock because they cannot do the work for which they were trained, like medicine and law, and must settle for more menial jobs such as janitorial services and cooking.

In most immigrant communities it is the men who go out to work. They assimilate most easily into the life of the new society. Women who stay at home alone or work in family businesses face the greatest cultural isolation and loneliness. Professional women may take jobs and so acquire a measure of financial and social independence. They assimilate rapidly. But their husbands may have patriarchal views of the family and be threatened when the wives have independent incomes. In this case, the result is alienation and conflict between husbands and wives.

The first-generation immigrants are foreigners in a new land, but they know who they are (fig. 37, preceding page). The core of their identity was shaped by their old culture, which they hope to preserve and pass on to their children.

Their children, however, face a deep identity crisis. At home they learn the beliefs and values of their parents. In school and in public they are enculturated to the surrounding beliefs and values. Their identity crisis is compounded by the fact that their parents usually do not understand them and try to impose old ways on them.

The identity crisis of the second generation is generally greater for women than for men. In both western and oriental cities, men are expected to assert themselves, but women face role confusion. Many of their old cultures pressure them to be subordinate to their parents and husbands, while city life encourages them to be independent and self-reliant. Many immigrant women prefer the new culture but find it hard to get husbands within their own community who share their views of equality. If they seek husbands outside the community their parents will be very upset.

Some second-generation immigrants seek to solve their cultural schizophrenia by rejecting their old culture and seizing the new. A few find security at home and reject the surrounding culture. Most compartmentalize their worlds, following their old ways at home and the new ways outside. A few are able to integrate the best of both worlds in their lives.

The cultural differences between the first and second generation often cause strong family conflicts. Many parents try to force the old culture on their children, who rise up in rebellion. Some parents, overwhelmed by the problems, become apathetic and exercise little discipline on their children, who then may descend into drugs or alcohol to handle their pain.

The tensions between second-generation (first generation to be born in the new setting) and third-generation immigrants are usually less severe. Both have grown up in the new urban context and share at a deep level in its worldview.

When a great many immigrants gather in the same area, they can form a critical mass that delays assimilation into the new culture. They preserve their cultural identity for several generations and the tensions of assimilation are distributed over a longer period of time, making them less stressful on any one generation.

Classes

Classes emerge in peasant societies as occupational specializations emerge, but they are few and the differences between them are not great. In European feudal cities the main classes were rulers, priests, and common folk. A medieval jingle said,

> God hath shapen lives three,
> Boor and priest and knight they be. (Bierstedt 1970, 437)

In modern cities, occupational and cultural differences increase greatly and lead to a variety of subcultural communities based on cultural differences. In the first major study of class in U.S. cities, Lloyd Warner (1941) differentiated three major classes: upper, middle, and lower. He divided each of these into two sections: upper and lower. He concluded that there were six classes: upper-upper, lower-upper, and so on.

Subsequent studies have shown that there are many more than six distinct subcultural communities in a city. Moreover, the boundaries between them are not sharp. There is constant flux in their ranking as different communities compete for power and wealth.

Robert Bellah (1985) refers to classes as "life-style enclaves." A lifestyle enclave is a group of people who share basic beliefs, values, and lifestyles. Michael Weiss (1988) defines some thirty-five distinct enclaves in North American cities (table 8, following page). In a sense, these are arbitrary groupings, and we can argue with his categories. They illustrate, however, the fact that people in modern cities do live in a great many different sociocultural groups.

Classes are societal categories. They are not groups of people who know and relate to one another. They are taxonomies we use to mentally organize our whole society. We use them to locate people we meet in the social order so that we know how to relate to them. Classes do, however, give rise to social groups. People with similar occupations tend to form professional associations and to form social clubs that reinforce their shared interests and values.

Table 8
Some of the Lifestyle Enclaves in American Cities

1. **Blue Blood Estates: 35–44.**
$40,307. Wealthy, white, college-educated families. Posh big-city townhouses, Mercedes, the *New Yorker,* and natural cold cereals.

2. **Furs and Station Wagons: 35–54.** $50,086. New money in metro suburbs. College-educated families. Country clubs, second mortgages, BMW 5 series, *Forbes.*

3. **Pools and Patios: 45–64.** $35,985. Upper-middle-class couples with grown children. Cruise ships, health clubs, the *Wall Street Journal.*

4. **Young Suburbia: 25–44.** $38,582. White college-educated, child-rearing families. Swimming pools, mutual funds, frozen waffles, vans, *World Tennis.*

5. **Blue-Chip Blues: 25–44.** $32,218. High-school educated, wealthiest blue-collar suburbs. CB radios, frozen pizzas, unions, Chevys, *Golf, and 4 Wheel & Off Road.*

6. **Gray Power: 55-plus.** $25,259. Upper-middle-class, retirement communities. Movie projects, corned-beef hash, Cadillacs, *Golf Digest.*

7. **New Beginnings: 18–34.** $24,847. Middle-class, urban apartment dwellers. Slide projectors, jazz records, whole wheat bread, Mitsubishis, *Scientific American,* and *Rolling Stone.*

8. **Heavy Industry: 55-plus.** $18,325. Lower-working-class ethnic families. Wall paneling, nonfilter cigarettes, canned spaghetti, *The Star.*

9. **Emergent Minorities: 18–34.** $22,029. Lower-middle-class, single-parent families. Canned orange juice, Chevy Novas.

10. **Hispanic Mix: 18–34.** $16,270. Singles, families, grade-school education, blue collar. Use buses, canned chicken, Chevys.

11. **Smalltown Downtown: 18–24, 65-plus.** $17,206. High-school educated families and singles. Gospel records, hair tonic, canned meat spreads, instant potatoes, Chevettes, *Sporting News.*

12. **Public Assistance: 19–24, 65-plus.** $10,804. One-parent families, city ghettos, blue collar, burglar alarms.

Note: The first number is age range, the second is annual income. Excerpts throughout from *The Clustering of America* by Michael Weiss. Copyright © 1988 by Michael J. Weiss. Reprinted by permission of Harper-Collins Publishers, Inc.

Social classes combine social status, economic wealth, and political power in complex ways. Lloyd Warner (1960) suggested that the four visible symbols of class in the U.S. are occupation, income, house, and location of house. In varying degrees these apply worldwide. For example, we find people in most cities making a distinction between independently wealthy people who do not need to work, white-collar workers, blue-collar workers, and paupers.

Important as they are, however, economic variables alone do not explain class differences. Power is also a factor. Top politicians and high government officials gain recognition beyond that based on their personal wealth. So, too, do public figures in sports, art, entertainment, and higher education.

Social status is determined primarily by wealth and power, but sometimes it is more. The old bluebloods at the top of the social life are often those who have history and descent. They are offspring of the elite who founded the city. One cannot join them on the basis of wealth and power; one joins only by invitation to their homes and intermarriage with their children.

Reading 4

Class in an American City

Sinclair Lewis

[In Sinclair Lewis's famous novel, George F. Babbitt is a rising realtor in a small city. One day he meets Charles McKelvey, a college classmate who is now the owner of a successful construction company, a politician, and member of the town's aristocracy, inferior only to the haughty Old Families. Babbitt, hoping to rise in the city society, invites the McKelveys to dinner. Lewis writes:]

The Babbitts invited the McKelveys to dinner, in early December, and the McKelveys not only accepted, but after changing the date once or twice, actually came . . . .

The McKelveys were less than fifteen minutes late.

Babbitt hoped that the Dopperbraus [his neighbors] would see the McKelveys' limousine, and their uniformed chauffeur, waiting in the front.

The dinner was well cooked and incredibly plentiful, and Mrs. Babbitt had brought out her grandmother's silver candlesticks. Babbitt worked hard. He was good. He told none of the jokes he wanted to tell. He listened to the others. He started Maxwell off with a resounding, "Let's hear about your trip to Yellowstone." He was laudatory, extremely laudatory. He found opportunities to remark that . . . Charles McKelvey [was] an inspiration to ambitious youth, and Mrs. McKelvey an adornment to the social circles of Zenith, Washington, New York, Paris and numbers of other places.

But he could not stir them. It was a dinner without a soul. For no reason that was clear to Babbitt, heaviness was over them and they spoke laboriously and unwillingly.

He concentrated on Lucile McKelvey, carefully not looking at her blanched lovely shoulder and the tawny silken band which supported her frock.

"I suppose you'll be going to Europe pretty soon again, won't you?"

"I'd like awfully to run over to Rome for a few weeks."

"I suppose you see a lot of pictures and music and curios and everything there."

"No, what I really go for is: there is a little **trattoria** on the Via della Scrofa where you get the best **fettuccine** in the world."

"Oh, I—Yes. That must be nice to try that. Yes."

At a quarter to ten McKelvey discovered with profound regret that his wife had a headache. He said blithely, as Babbitt helped him with his coat, "We must lunch together some time, and talk over the old days."

When the others had labored out, at half-past ten, Babbitt turned to his wife, pleading, "Charley said he had a corking time and we must lunch—said they wanted to have us up to the house for dinner before long."

[The invitation never came, of course, and after a while "they did not speak of the McKelveys again." This, however, is only half the story. Babbitt also met his old classmate Ed Overbrook, who had been a failure and who admired Babbitt for his success. To his embarrassment, Overbrook invited him and his wife to dinner some night. He boomed, "Fine! Sure! Just let me know," and promptly forgot it. But Ed Overbrook did not.]

[Finally Babbitt] accepted Overbrook's next plaintive invitation, for an evening two weeks off. A dinner two weeks off, even a family dinner, never seems so appalling, til the two weeks have astoundingly disappeared and one comes dismayed to the ambushed hour. They had to change the date, because of their own dinner to the McKelveys, but at last they gloomily drove out to the Overbrooks' house in Dorchester.

It was miserable from the beginning. The Overbrooks had dinner at six-thirty, while the Babbitts never dined before seven. Babbitt permitted himself to be ten minutes late. "Let's make it as short as possible. I think we'll duck out quickly. I'll say that I have to be at the office extra early tomorrow," he planned . . . .

Babbitt tried to be jovial; he worked at it; but he could find nothing to interest him in Overbrook's timorousness, the blankness of the other guests, or the drained stupidity of Mrs. Overbrook, with her spectacles, drab skin, and tight-drawn hair. He told his best Irish story, but it sank like a soggy cake. Most bleary moment of all was when Mrs. Overbrook peered out of her fog of nursing eight children and cooking and scribbling, tried to be conversational.

"I suppose you go to Chicago and New York right along, Mr. Babbitt," she prodded.

"Well, I get to Chicago fairly often."

"It must be awfully interesting, I suppose you take in all the theaters."

"Well, to tell the truth, Mrs. Overbrook, thing that hits me best is a great big beefsteak at the Dutch restaurant in the Loop!"

They had nothing more to say. Babbitt was sorry, but there was no hope; the dinner was a failure. At ten, rousing out of the stupor of meaningless talk, he said as cheerfully as he could, "Fraid we got to be starting, Ed. I've got a fellow coming to see me early tomorrow." As Overbrook helped him with his coat, Babbitt said, "Nice to rub up on the old days! We must have lunch together, P.D.Q."

Mrs. Babbitt sighed, on their drive home. "It was pretty terrible. But how Mr. Overbrook does admire you!" . . .

For a week they worried, "We really ought to invite Ed and his wife, poor devils!" But as they never saw the Overbrooks, they forgot them, and after a month or two they said, "That really was the best way, just to let it slide. It wouldn't be kind to **them** to have them here. They'd feel so out of place and hard-up in our home."

Central to class is the notion of hierarchy. Obviously we cannot rank everyone in a city, nor even all subcultural enclaves. Rather, we have mental maps in which we rank occupations, institutions, neighborhoods, houses, cars, dress, and other symbols of status (fig. 38, following page). For example, we rank Federal Supreme Court justices higher than physicians, physicians higher than electricians, and electricians higher than garbage collectors. We rank Harvard University over the University of Illinois and that over a local community college. We value Mercedes over Buicks and Buicks over Chevrolets; Rolex over Seiko watches and Seikos over Timexes; the *Wall Street Journal* over the *National Observer*; *Atlantic Monthly* over *Readers Digest*; country and yacht clubs over bowling leagues and bingo parlors; and Saks Fifth Avenue over Sears, K-Mart, and thrift shops. We even mentally rank churches: Episcopal, then Presbyterian, Baptist, and Pentecostal.

Class ranking is not sharply defined like steps on a ladder. Rather, there is considerable overlap between similar cultural enclaves. Top administrators of the University of Illinois rank higher than the assistant professors at the University of Chicago though the latter school has more prestige. Small homes in a wealthy area of town rank lower than mansions in a slightly poorer part of town.

Obviously, not everyone shares the same class map. Some groups see themselves as being higher than others in society see them. In their relationships with outsiders they are looked down upon. They, therefore, must live with a measure of cognitive dissonance, as they juggle other peoples' treatment of them with their own view of themselves.

Figure 38
Hierarchy of Class Symbols

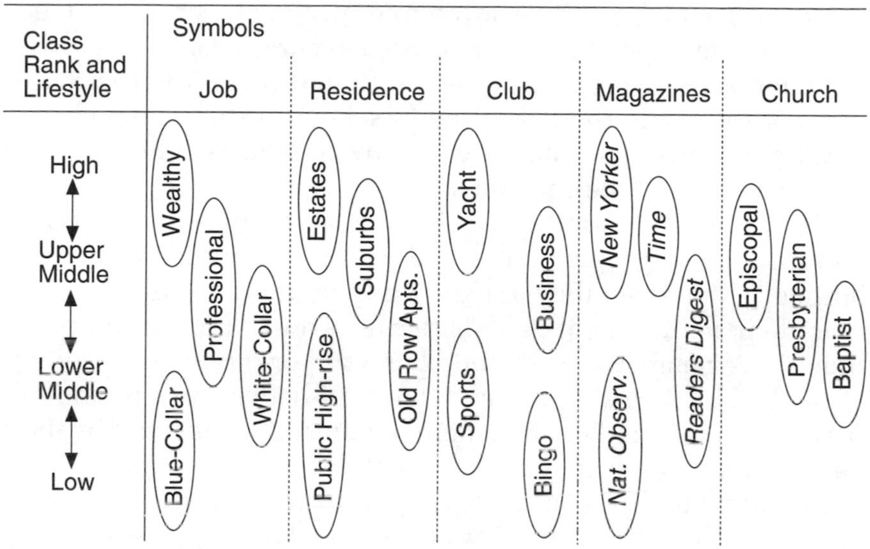

Class Rank and Lifestyle	Symbols				
	Job	Residence	Club	Magazines	Church

Class Rank and Lifestyle (top to bottom): High ↕ Upper Middle ↕ Lower Middle ↕ Low

Job: Wealthy, Professional, White-Collar, Blue-Collar

Residence: Estates, Suburbs, Public High-rise, Old Row Apts.

Club: Yacht, Business, Sports, Bingo

Magazines: New Yorker, Time, Readers Digest, Nat. Observ.

Church: Episcopal, Presbyterian, Baptist

Lifestyle enclaves emerge as people associate with others who share their social and cultural ways. They develop their own subcultures and feel out of place when put in the unfamiliar settings of another class. High-class people are uncomfortable in low-class bingo and bowling clubs, just as low-class people are in expensive yacht and country clubs.

People also seek congruence in their lives. If they live in a poor neighborhood and eat in poor restaurants but attend an affluent church where everyone dresses in stylish clothes, they will have to learn the rules in two places and may experience some real pragmatic problems. They will be afraid that after church they may be invited by upper-class members to go to a restaurant and the tip will be more than they usually spend for a whole meal. Most are content to associate with their class peers: living in the same part of town in similar houses, going to the same clubs, eating at the same restaurants, shopping at the same stores, and going to the same churches.

Social mobility

Classes are different from ethnic groups in one significant way; their boundaries are porous. Because classes are based on achievement, not on blood, it is possible for people to acquire wealth, power, and status and to move to a higher class. It is also possible for them to lose these and drop to a lower class.

Upward social mobility or moving up the class scale is fairly common over a period of two or three generations. Parents work hard and acquire a business, which they turn over to their children, or they send their children to school to study medicine or law. Downward social mobility is also common as children fail to keep the status of their parents.

Upward social mobility in cities is facilitated by geographic mobility. Often people do not find better jobs in their old neighborhood. Moreover, they are known there more for their history than their achievements. No matter how much they accomplish, they are remembered as the butcher's son or the former waitress at the local coffee shop. They often find better work in another part of town or another city where people judge them not by their past but by their current achievements.

Upward mobility also creates cognitive dissonance in the lives of people. They must learn new cultures and new values and reject old ways. They will become estranged from relatives and friends in the old class who now seem uncouth and who mock their upper-class ways.

It is not easy to gain acceptance in a higher class, particularly when people know one's background. Not only must one acquire the necessary symbols to identify with the new crowd but also one must avoid the shibboleths that would betray his or her lowly background. A current television advertisement portrays an uncouth Texan at a high-class dinner party asking for "jelly" instead of "fruit." One of the dinner guests faints. People tend to aspire to higher status and to avoid association with those below them.

One result of hierarchy and class differences is that the highest group sets the trends for lower ones. People in this group often control power and wealth in the city. Many people below them imitate their cultural ways in what is referred to as "the emulation of the elite." To rise in the social hierarchy, people must adopt the ways of those above them, especially those who define what is "civilized" and what is not.

The urban poor

Another consequence of hierarchy and class is the emergence of underclasses. These are the people at the bottom of the social order. In megalopolises around the world there are emerging whole communities of poor that are largely outside the systems of the city. They have no city water and sewers, few jobs in the "formal sector" of the urban economy, little police protection, and no political power. Moreover, they and their children have little hope of ever entering the mainstream of urban life.

What is urban poverty? It is important for us to distinguish between relative poverty and absolute poverty. The former is found at all levels of society. For example, a man may complain that he has only one yacht and his neighbor has two. The latter is when people lack the basic needs of life—food, water, clothing, housing, and rest. Our concern here is with this kind of poverty.

The urban poor do not form a single sociocultural group. Nor are they all poor in the same sense. Some, if given an opportunity, will improve their conditions. Others appear to be trapped in cultures of poverty that are more difficult to transform.

Squatter settlements

We have already described how some immigrants to the city form squatter settlements. Squatters tend to be conservative. They work hard and try to improve their living conditions by replacing wood walls with brick ones, putting on better roofs, and planting flowers in their yards. Many commute long distances to work in the city.

Squatters are usually marginal to the formal systems of the city. Most do not have jobs in modern factories or businesses. They do not turn to the police or the city welfare systems in times of need. They earn their living in the alternative economic system known as the "informal economy" consisting of small-scale manufacturing and crafts, small-scale trade, and many varied services. For instance, in Brazil, many poor women and children collect scraps of paper or metal to sell. In Mexico and the southwest United States, burritos are made in the home and sold door-to-door. In India, a poor person will "guide" you around the temple for a few pennies. And in many Two-Thirds World countries, people live by scavenging in garbage dumps. Squatters are often very creative in their ways of earning a living (out of necessity) and they support one another within the settlement with a variety of kinds of mutual assistance.

The most immediate needs of the squatters are ownership of the land on which they have built their houses. They also need water, sewers, power, transportation, clinics, schools, and other technological infrastructures necessary for a decent life. Many squatters live in the real fear that they will be driven off their land on short notice and that they will have to start again somewhere else. For the longer term, squatters need to be incorporated into the formal economy with better-paying and more stable jobs.

Culture of poverty

A second type of urban poor are found in old tenements, housed in decaying buildings around the inner city and exploited by slumlords who prey on their need for shelter. Some are ethnic immigrants from other cities around the world who start in the inner city and work their way up to better neighborhoods. But many, particularly in the large cities of Asia and Latin America, have lived in the inner city for generations and have little hope of ever leaving their slum.

Oscar Lewis (1961) suggests that these communities are rational adaptations to the realities of city life for those on the bottom of society. In other words, the people create a culture that enables them to live with chronic underemployment and lack of resources. In this "culture of poverty," whoever earns something today must share it with those who have nothing because tomorrow he or she may have no job and will need to borrow from others. Lewis argues that people in the culture of poverty are neither dumb nor lazy. Nor are they innocent victims of the deeds of others. Rather they are people faced with the very real fact of chronic poverty and deprived of opportu-

Reading 5

Life in a Slum

Oscar Lewis [as told by Manuel]

My mother-in-law and her husband lived in one room and a kitchen on Piedad Street, No. 30. At that time all four of her children, with their families, were living with her . . . .

From *The Children of Sanchez*, by Oscar Lewis. Copyright © 1961 by Oscar Lewis. Reprinted by permission of Random House, Inc.

The room had one bed, in which Faustino and his wife slept. The rest of us slept on pieces of cardboard and blankets or rags spread on the floor. . . . That is the way the thirteen of us, five families, arranged ourselves in that little room.

When so many people live together in a single room, naturally there is a break, a restraint, on one's liberty, right? As a boy in my father's house I didn't notice it so much, except when I wanted to talk to my friends or look at dirty pictures. But as a married man, I had more bitter experiences. Living together like that, never, never can there be harmony. There are always difficulties, like the time my brother-in-law insisted on removing the light bulbs whenever he left the house, because he paid the electricity bill.

We really had it rough for a long time. Even when I found a temporary job, we were very poor, because I earned only a miserable low wage, and I had to wait a week to get paid . . . .

When Paula [Manuel's wife] was five months pregnant, Raul Alvarez asked me to come to work in his lamp shop . . . . The first week I drew two hundred **pesos**, just like that. . . . I worked there for a month, when my brother-in-law Faustino, the one who treated me like dirt when I wasn't working, became sick. He was paralyzed from the waist down. He said to me, "**Compadre**," (I'm the godfather of baptism for his two children) "be a good fellow, go and help out in the cafe, brother, won't you? If I don't go to work, I'll lose my job. Take my job for two or three days, until I get better."

"Man alive, **compadre**," I said, "you can see I'm just barely getting on my feet. I've just gotten this job with **Senor** Raul. How am I going to ask him to let me off for a couple of days?"

"Aw, come on, be a good fellow," and he looked at me so sadly that my conscience got the better of me.

"O.K., I'll go; but only for two days; here's hoping you get well soon!"

I went to work in the restaurant. But Faustino recovered slowly and the two days stretched out and became a week, then two weeks. I earned fifteen **pesos** a day and of this I gave my wife only five. The rest I turned over to my **compadre** to pay for the doctor, medicine, rent and food. I thought, "Well, I'm lending him money; it's like a saving. He'll give me back the whole amount in a lump sum and I'll be able to pay my wife's hospital bills."

Well, it didn't turn out that way. One time, while my **compadre** was still sick, my godson Daniel became ill and at night I had to go every two hours to get a woman to give him penicillin injections. After that my **compadren** Eufemia got sick, and so there I was taking care of all three of them and paying for everything. But I would think, well, I'm actually saving money. . . . The situation dragged on like that for more than a month and a half. And so I lost the job with **Senor** Raul.

Santos, my daughter's godfather, suggested that I open up a shoe shop; I took to the idea. Santos said, "Get hold of two hundred **pesos**. You can make shoes and sell them at a profit of five **pesos** a pair." I thought, "Suppose I make five-dozen pairs of shoes a week. That makes sixty pair . . . that makes three hundred **pesos** profit a week. Why that's wonderful!"

Santos loaned me the lasts and a stitching machine, and I borrowed two hundred **pesos** from my father . . . .

So I went into business. Santos went with me to buy the leather, and we started making shoes. But I knew nothing about shoes or business then, I worked only by God's good will . . . .

I don't remember exactly what happened. . . . One of my finishers, Chucho, went on a binge for two or three weeks, getting drunk every day. He later died in the street, abandoned and drunk, poor thing. But I took pity on him, thinking that the workers kill themselves to earn so little, so I raised the finishers twenty **centavos** for each shoe, and the machinists ten **centavos**. I wanted to show others how a boss should treat workers.

Instead of making a profit, without knowing it, I was actually losing on each pair of shoes. Then I sent someone, I don't remember who, to deliver twenty-five pair of shoes, and he took off with the money. To make a long story short, my business went broke.

After my business failed, I gave up trying to plan my life and get ahead. I lost the little confidence I had in myself and lived just from day to day, like an animal . . . . To me, one's destiny is controlled by a mysterious hand that moves all things. Only for the select, do things turn out as planned; for those of us who are born to be **tamale** eaters, heaven sends only **tamales**. We plan and plan and some little thing happens to wash it all away.

nities for advancement. They develop a set of strategies that are rational, given their circumstances, and that enable them to survive.

Among the characteristics of these enclaves of poverty is a mistrust of the police, government, people in high positions, and even the church, which is identified with wealth and power. The people make little use of banks, hospitals, large stores, and government services. They face underemployment, low wages, lack of food reserves, and a chronic shortage of cash. Consequently, they must borrow at usurious rates of interest or get temporary loans from neighbors, make frequent purchases of small quantities of food at high prices, and use second-hand clothing. The children do not go to school and must learn to fend for themselves early in life. There is little adolescence. Initiation into sex comes early and there is little privacy in the home.

If Lewis is right, it is not enough to give money to those who live in the culture of poverty. Nor is social revolution the answer. What is required, along with new opportunities, is teaching them a new worldview and new cultural ways that enable them to participate directly in the systems of the dominant society.

Pavement dwellers and street children

Many of the poorest of the poor have no home at all. An estimated forty-eight thousand people live on the streets of Calcutta alone, occupying a few square yards of a sidewalk or roadside and building cardboard and tin shelters to protect themselves from the weather. Thousands of children roam the alleys of Sao Paulo (estimates range from eight thousand to three hundred thousand) living by odd jobs, begging, and petty theft.

Street children often form gangs for mutual support and sidewalk dwellers aid one another when they can, but there is little formal organization among them that would enable them to mobilize political pressure on the government or society or to form cooperatives to keep their costs down. These people are truly marginal, living their lives outside the formal social, political, and

economic structures of the city. Unfortunately, they are also marginal to the church. With some exceptions, city churches are not
involved in ministries to them.

Drug addicts and prostitutes

Another type of urban poor is drug addicts and prostitutes. For
example, there are more than a half million prostitutes and a half
million drug addicts in Bangkok (Grigg 1992, 97). These are not
problems unique to that great city. Around the world, travel and
tourism have created subcultures of entertainment that often cater
to the human vices. Those who are desperately poor may be forced
into these services to survive themselves.

Refugee settlements

One kind of urban poor that has multiplied in recent years is
refugees near cities. There are now more than eighteen million
refugees around the world, driven from their homes by wars, political unrest, ethnic hostilities, and droughts. Many are confined to
camps that breed hatred and militancy. They must organize meaningful lives without work or permanent homes.

Causes of urban poverty

Why do these communities of the poor and disenfranchised
exist surrounded by the great riches of the city? Some argue that
these are defective communities of people who do not want to
work and live off government dole. With few exceptions, this view
is false. Others argue that the rich and powerful exploit the poor
for their own gain. This is true to some extent, but it is not the
whole picture either.

One reason for the urban poor is the constant migration from
the countryside of people attracted by the amenities and glamor
of city life. Rural life is hard for millions of small and tenant farmers. Some are driven off their land by drought and economic misfortunes. Others are drawn to the city by the hope of access to hospitals and education for their children. In time, many of these
immigrants do rise economically.

Another reason for urban poverty is the emergence of the international economic inequalities that we examined in chapter 6.
Modernity and industrialization took place first in western cities
and they today control much of the world's wealth. Cities in poor
countries have few resources to expand the roads, sewers, water

systems, hospitals, and schools needed to better the lives of their people. The countries to which they belong are saddled with great debts and have little to sell on the world market to earn money needed for development. Until more equitable systems of world trade are developed, these countries and their cities will be plagued by unremitting poverty.

Class and ethnicity

The interactions between ethnicity and class in a city are complex and vary greatly in and between cities. In some, particularly young cities, ethnic identities are stronger than class ones and people marry and live within their ethnic communities. In others, class plays the central role and people of different ethnic groups mix freely within class-based communities.

Generally speaking, urban life erodes ethnic loyalties over the generations and class identities grow stronger. This is true even in caste-based societies like India. Caste boundaries are more fuzzy and fluid in cities than they are in villages. The major exceptions are ethnic communities whose identities continue to be reinforced by immigration from rural areas or other countries.

City people tend to rank not only individuals but also ethnic groups. In North America, "whites" are ranked by the general public as higher than African-Americans and Hispanics. In the Middle East, Arabs, as a whole, have a higher status than Filipinos and Indians.

Complex social structures can organize ethnic groups in one of three ways: in nonranked groups, in ranked groups, and in majority/minority groups (Barth 1963, 9–38). When class is weak and ethnicity strong, nonranked groups will be in competition and sometimes conflict with one another for resources such as jobs, positions in government, or city services. Much of urban Africa is characterized by this structure. Ranked ethnic groups will have less competition and conflict, but more real oppression, with the elite group being able to effectively control the groups underneath. South Africa, until recently, and the caste system of traditional India are examples of this. Majority/minority ethnic group systems are unique in that the dominant group is able to fill all its own economic and political needs, leaving the minority groups without a legitimate position.

In ordinary, peaceable times class increasingly modifies the impact of ethnicity on interpersonal urban relationships. In a majority/minority system, higher-class members of minority ethnic groups rank above lower-class members of the majority. For instance, high-class African-Americans and Hispanics may rank above middle- and low-class whites in America, and Filipino diplomats and business tycoons above ordinary Arabs in Middle Eastern cities (fig. 39).

In a nonranked ethnic system, higher-class members of different ethnic groups may associate more comfortably with one another than they do with the lower-class members of their own groups; urban-educated Masai with urban-educated Kikuyu in Kenya, for instance (fig. 40, following page).

In a ranked ethnic system, the higher-ranked ethnic groups will be more firmly entrenched in higher-class positions and lower ethnic groups in lower-class positions. Still, a white South African laborer may rank below a Black South African political leader in certain restricted contexts, causing both of them to feel no small amount of fear and confusion (fig. 41). The ideologies of class and ethnic group conflict with one another and create some of the complexities of urban life that stand in such contrast to village life.

Figure 39
Ethnicity and Class in Majority/Minority Urban Settings

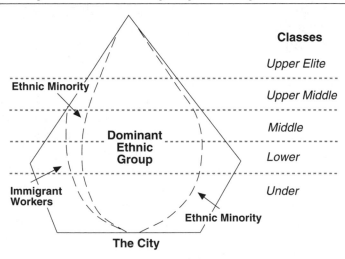

Figure 40
Ethnicity and Class in Nonranked Urban Settings

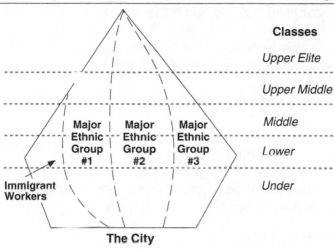

Economic Structures

The city is characterized by the tremendous growth of technology and of economic structures. In fact, economics and politics become the glue that holds the diverse subcultures of the city together.

Figure 41
Ethnicity and Class in Ranked Urban Settings

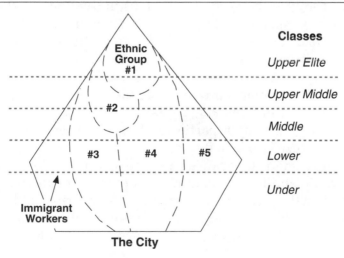

Technology

The city is a product of human technology. It is a world of asphalt, concrete, brick, glass, and plastic. Even the trees, flowers, and grass are confined to peripheral spaces and shaped by human engineering. Without roads, railroads, electricity, gas lines, sewers, phones, and other infrastructural systems the city could not exist.

The city is also a creator and distributor of technology. Factories, research centers, businesses, banks, insurance companies, markets, ports, and service agencies are the dominant institutions of urban life, and when they are not controlled by central governments, they generate a bewildering array of goods and services. People must choose from a great many kinds of shops, restaurants, entertainment, cars, soaps, and medicines.

Commercialism

As we have seen, the city is a center of commerce. This is true especially of modern cities. Early cities were often centers of government and of religion that peripherally attracted traders and supported weekly markets. The heart of many cities later became industry, business, trade, and transportation.

Karl Polanyi (1957, 127–32) defines three forms of exchange of goods and services: reciprocity, or exchange of gifts; redistribution, or the gathering of goods and services by a center of power that are then disbursed to the community; and market, or the exchange of goods and services between anonymous individuals on the basis of supply and demand. In the first of these, reciprocity, the primary reason for exchange is to establish social relationships. Our own giving at Christmas time is of this type. In the second, redistribution, the reason for exchange is to mark and maintain power relations. Taxation and government programs are the way that we experience this type. In the third, market, exchange is strictly for the purpose of economic gain to both parties and personal relationships are explicitly expected to be left out.

Foraging societies, because they are small and personal and because their families are economically quite self-sufficient, function with just the principle of reciprocity. Even tribal and peasant societies, though they have important redistribution through their chiefs, are subsistence communities in which people work for food and shelter and give priority to maintaining relationships over the accumulation of goods. The exchange of gifts, the celebration of lifecycle rites, and community festivals consume any surplus the people accumulate.

Redistribution was the underpinning of governmental cities. Many ancient cities were built by kings who taxed the countryside to sustain their regal courts and who doled out protection, roads, relief during famines, and religious pageantry. Monarchs and priests and under them corps of officials and soldiers controlled a broad stratum of peasants in the surrounding region. Redistribution is also the basis for the economies of modern cities controlled by Marxism. Major resources such as land, factories, and housing are owned by the state and allocated to people on the basis of need and status. In all of these, relationships of power are more important than producing goods.

The dominant form of economic transaction in most cities today is market exchange. The market mentality, which minimizes power relations and emphasizes the accumulation of things over the accumulation of relationships, expands to cover most areas of life. Few things in the city do not have their price. Almost everything becomes a commodity that can be bought and sold. Child care, nursing of the aged, marriages, funerals, companionship, and sex, which in tribal and peasant societies are functions of the family and community, are marketed in the city by strangers. Jobs, too, are valued primarily in terms of their salaries and economic security.

If patron-client relationships are prevalent in peasant societies, contracts are the hallmark of urban life. These are agreements in which the exchange of goods and services are carefully specified solely on the basis of their economic worth and which can be easily terminated. In contracts, neither party is concerned about the well-being of the other as persons. Both sides are involved for what they get out of it themselves.

Money

Modern markets depend on complex systems of money, credit, and banking. In large cities, the capitalist sector of the economy becomes increasingly important (table 9, following page). The market focuses on the production and accumulation of commodities such as land, buildings, cars, and other consumer goods. The capitalists focus on making and accumulating money. They start with money and use it to build factories, businesses, or service agencies in order to earn more money. They do not care which of these they pursue, only that it makes money. Money no longer is of value because it can buy goods. It becomes a way to keep track of wealth in the economic game. In the late stages of capitalism, money is used to speculate on money to make more money. For example, bankers trade on the international money market in hopes of making millions of dollars on the fluctuations of exchange rates. There is no connection to the production of goods or offering of services, much less to people who might need these things.

Table 9
Emergence of Capitalism and Consumerism

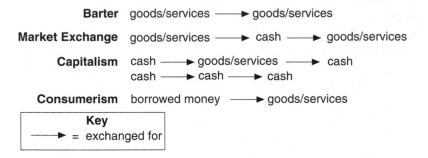

In recent years, cities are increasingly being linked to one another by global economic systems. People in Madras now invest in the stock market, not only in Bombay but also in New York, Tokyo, London, and Paris. Multinational corporations belong to no nation, but have multiple headquarters in cities around the world. This global networking is rapidly leading to the internationalization of markets and monetary structures that will shape the cities of the future.

Political and Legal Systems

The city is about money. The city is also about power. These are the two social glues that hold the city together. We cannot understand the city until we understand the nature and structure of politics and authority in the city and how these relate to wealth and social status.

Power in the City

Political power is the dominant motif in many modern governmental cities such as Beijing, Washington, D.C., Moscow, New Delhi, and Lhasa. Religious power dominates ceremonial centers such as Varanasi, the Vatican, Mecca, and Jerusalem.

Modern cities are closely tied to the emergence of the modern nation state. The nation state is the broadest unit of political organization in the world today. It differs from earlier forms of government in two significant ways. First, it is based on geography, not kinship. Land is of vital importance to nations and they frequently fight for territory. Citizenship, for the most part, is based on the place of one's birth.

Second, there is a shift from loyalties to local, kin, and tribal groups to identification with the population of the nation as a whole. The ability of a state to unify its people and mobilize its resources depends heavily on its ability to develop a national consciousness among its people. Consequently, state governments frequently control educational and communication systems in an attempt to indoctrinate the people to obtain ultimate allegiance. On the one hand, the nation is a welfare state. The people look to it to solve all their major problems: education, health, welfare, and protection. On the other hand, the nation demands that they die to preserve its own interests.

The emergence of states means that cities are no longer the highest level of formal political organization. They are now parts of nations that pass laws regulating the life of the city. It also means that multiple levels of governmental organization emerge: national, regional (state, province, district), city, and neighborhood. The relationship of city to state is symbiotic. Each needs the other to survive.

Social control in peasant societies is characterized by a moral order that appeals to tradition. There are sets of commonly accepted values and rules that dictate appropriate behavior in various situations. Conformity to these is enforced largely by informal social sanctions, such as gossip, rebuke, and community action. The ruler living far away in the city intervenes locally only if things get too bad.

Social control in urban life is based on formal political structures such as laws, police, courts, prisons, administrators, and the bureaucracies that uphold them. Informal means of control continue to operate in kinship groups and many of the small subcultural communities. But the sheer size and diversity of cities means that most relationships people have are with strangers and cultural foreigners. It is on this level that formal governmental systems are needed to keep order and peace.

We would be naive to equate power in the city solely with government. Power is exercised in every family, association, and community. Above all, it is exercised by ethnic groups, classes, and institutions to keep their privileged positions.

In nongovernmental organizations, power is closely linked to social status and the control of economic resources. It is exercised not only through the ability to make and enforce decisions, but also to command symbols of power and prestige such as membership in clubs, social and political office, and control of the media.

Power of the City

As we have seen, cities hold power over their surrounding hinterland by virtue of their central control over the instruments of power, such as government and the military or the police.

As the city grows, it exercises another power over the rural hinterland, namely, it begins to urbanize the surrounding countryside. Trade, roads, railroads, radios, and television bring the city into rural communities and transform them into urban outposts. Farmers sell their wheat to urban millers, eat bread baked in the city, and identify with the sports teams of their nearest metropolis. They are no longer peasants but urban people living in the country.

Cultural Systems

The city is culture par excellence; the epitome of human creation. Nature surrounds the tribesman and the peasant. Humans create the environment of city folks. It is bricks, steel, mortar, and cement; streets, sidewalks, bridges, and tunnels; and elevators, cars, buses, trains, and airplanes. Even the plants and trees are planted and trimmed. Nature sends rain, snow, searing heat, and heartless cold, but in the city these are managed by means of heating, air conditioning, subways, and road crews.

Even the night in the city is transformed into day by electric lights and round-the-clock services. There are all-night markets, restaurants, taxi services, radio and television broadcasting, and gasoline stations. Hospitals, hotels, police stations, continuous-process refining plants, three-shift factories, and electrical generating plants operate around the clock. The city never sleeps (Melbin 1978).

The city is also the climax of human culture because it contains in it the riches of many cultures. On its streets are restaurants, newspapers, and products from many countries. Its radios broadcast music from around the world. Its libraries and computers store the accumulated knowledge of humankind down through the ages.

Symbols, Myths, and Rituals

If diversity is the hallmark of city cultures, it is also the characteristic of city symbols, myths, and rituals. Each subculture has its own language, symbols of identity, and stories to tell. Above these are the trade language, money, uniforms, ballots, mass media, and other shared symbols that communicate to everyone in the city and unite them, on one level, into a single community.

Symbols

The city is rich with symbols. Talk, print, pictures, logos, icons, sirens, bells, and smells assault our senses. Signs tell us to go, stop, walk, buy, sell, yield, and watch out for danger. Shop signs, billboards, phones, radios, television stations, and computer networks clamor for our attention. City folk are addicted to stimulus and stress. They find it hard to sit still for long periods of time.

On another level, the symbols of the city manifest its values. Food, language, and dress mark different ethnic neighborhoods. Money, houses, cars, penthouses, boardrooms, golf clubs, and private jets speak of economic wealth. Police uniforms, patrol cars, legal gowns, and presidential insignia exhibit legal power. Priestly robes, temple spires, minarets, and ceremonial rites proclaim religious authority. Music halls, theaters, art galleries, museums, stadiums, parks, and gardens exhibit the culture of the urban elite.

Finally, the city is a place of mass media. The leaders of government, business, education, and religion cannot communicate with the millions living in the city using word-of-mouth, public announcements, and street dramas. These continue in urban neighborhoods, but above them are the newspapers, magazines, books, theaters, radio and television broadcasts, cassettes, CDs, billboards, and store windows that reach the masses. These media provide people in different groups with both areas of common discourse and ways to reinforce their subcultural differences.

Myths and Rituals

In one sense, the city is secular. It has little place for myths and rituals that speak of transcendent, cosmic realities. The city is also existential. Life is focused on the here and now. City folk have little time for things having to do with eternity, at least not in public life.

In another sense, people cannot live without myths and rituals that order and give greater meaning to their lives. This is true of city folk. A careful look at city life shows many ritual occasions.

One example in American cities is sports, which fulfills important ritual and mythological functions for people. Not only does ritual rule the game, but as a whole, the game is a cultural enterprise that gives identity, meaning, excitement, and hope to those who attend. In many ways it functions like a secular religion that dramatizes the vision that life is a competition in which both sides compete equally and fairly and infractions are punished by godlike umpires. It shows us a world in which things are just and the victor reigns because of talent and achievement.

The myth that we see operating in sports is the same one that guides managed competition in the market, in politics, and elsewhere. Sometimes the ideals of the myth are realized, and sometimes not. People come to the city with the hope that they can better their lives if they work hard. This is true for some, but for the masses who come life in the city is hard and dehumanizing. Still, sports illustrate in microcosm the macrocosm in which city people live (Geertz 1973, 412–53), including the fact that there are winners and losers. Perhaps this is why the Olympics have been able to gain international cooperation and attention.

Another common urban myth is "civil religion" (Bellah and Hammond 1981). The nation invests itself with symbols of the divine and demands the ultimate allegiance of its citizens. The name of "God" is invoked, prayers are offered, and festivals commemorating independence and the war dead are celebrated to legitimize the authority of the state and to indoctrinate the citizens in complete obedience to the state.

There are numerous other hidden myths in the city, many of them tied to the dominant cultures of the region. We need to study these carefully because they reveal the hidden order that gives meaning to people's lives.

Cultural Knowledge

The city's reliance on specialists and its roots in many different cultures make it the storehouse of rich and diverse bodies of cultural information. Its libraries store the wisdom and the folly of all ages. Its museums and archives document the histories of past cultures. Its universities and research centers generate new knowledge that constantly reshapes the city itself.

Science and Technology

The city is a creation of technology and science. Technology enabled the city to produce goods through industry and to transport these goods from place to place. It made possible the infrastructures of roads, water, power, sewage, and waste-disposal systems that enabled millions of people to live together. In this century, the rationalization of commerce and mass advertising has shaped the city as a consumer society.

But the impact of science on the city goes deeper than technology. In a pluralistic society, some things become part of the public domain and are enforced on all people. For example, in North American cities, everyone must go to school, stop at stop signs, and obey the same set of civil and criminal laws. Other things are left to the private domain of life—to the family, class, and ethnic community to decide. People are free to choose their food, dress, and personal lifestyles within limits set by the law.

The organization of the city is possible only through the application of rationalized planning. Today few cities operate without growing bureaucracies that gather a vast array of statistics and formulate regulations to help maintain order in the city. As Jacques Ellul points out (1964), engineering and management are applied to all areas of public life to bring them under human planning and control, a goal that is an essential part of the urban worldview.

Religion

It should not surprise us that religion in the city is influenced by the social and cultural systems of city life. The diversity of the city is reflected in the proliferation of religions. In most major cities, one finds not one or two believers from foreign religions, but many different religious communities. Christians, Muslims, Hindus, Buddhists, and Sikhs live side by side. Temples, mosques, churches, synagogues, *gurudwars,* and *stupas* are found along the same streets.

The city also gives rise to a diversity of expressions in a single religious tradition. For example, Protestant churches in North American farm communities are relatively homogeneous. In the city we find store-fronts, house gatherings, suburban sanctuaries, megachurch auditoriums, and great cathedrals. We also find a bewildering variety of denominations, worship forms, and theological positions.

The development of specializations in urban settings affects religious institutions. Peasant communities may have full-time pastors, priests, *mullahs,* or other clerics and sometimes a religious school associated with the church, temple, or mosque. In the city, religious specializations proliferate. Administrative centers emerge with denominational leaders and bureaucrats, advanced schools arise with theologians and other religious scholars, central shrines are built that attract pilgrims from afar, and local churches hire pastors for different ministries.

The rise of professional religious leaders in cities leads to the formation of religious "great traditions" (see chap. 6). These are the bureaucracies, bodies of teachings (theologies, commentaries, and interpretations), and practices (rituals and organizational procedures) that the religious leaders and seminaries declare to be orthodox and that are communicated to the common people by means of preaching, teaching, and modeling and that are enforced by threats of excommunication and force.

The "little traditions" of the local religious communities (fig. 42, following page) are made up of lay people with little religious expertise. Consequently, they contain a great many interpretations

Figure 42
Great and Little Religious Traditions

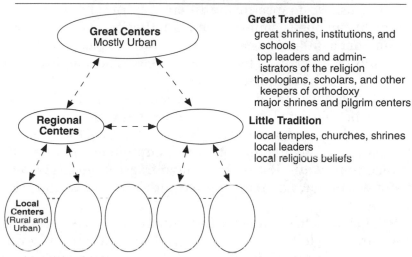

Great Tradition

great shrines, institutions, and
schools
top leaders and admin-
istrators of the religion
theologians, scholars, and other
keepers of orthodoxy
major shrines and pilgrim centers

Little Tradition

local temples, churches, shrines
local leaders
local religious beliefs

not always considered "orthodox" by the religious specialists of the great tradition. These beliefs focus more on the problems of everyday living than on cosmic stories and ultimate truths, which are the primary concern of the specialists.

Practitioners of the little traditions have a tendency to mix orthodox religious beliefs with local animistic practices. For example, a Hindu layman will stop at the temple to make an offering to the god Vishnu on his way to consult a local magician concerning the barrenness of his wife. Similarly, many North American Christians worship Christ on Sunday morning and follow their astrological charts in the Sunday afternoon paper.

Worldview

We first think of the city as a geographic area with a great many people. Later we see it as a place of complex social and cultural systems. Ultimately, however, the city is a way of looking at reality, a worldview.

Worldviews, Mazeways, and Fragmented Mazeways

A. F. C. Wallace (1956) raises an important question when he asks whether we can speak of the worldview of a city. Does Bombay, or Beijing, or Paris, or Cairo have a worldview? Is the ethos of Los Angeles different from that of San Francisco or Tokyo? In a broad sense we do speak of the different spirits of different cities. We might say one is sophisticated, another an overgrown town, and another a Buddhist or a Hindu city. But it is clear that the very sociocultural diversity of the city keeps it from developing a single worldview in any simplistic sense.

Wallace argues that, given the diversity and individualism of city life, people develop their own personal worldviews, which Wallace calls their "mazeways." Reginald Bibby (1987) suggests that many city people do not have comprehensive, integrated, rational mazeways. Rather they have fragmented mazeways— bits of worldviews that are applied piecemeal to various situations in life.

Perhaps even here there are individual differences in the city. There are people in the city with well thought-out mazeways. These include people with strong ideological views, such as committed Christians, Muslims, capitalists, secularists, and naturalists. But other urban people give little thought to formulating a coherent set of beliefs. They have particular ideas about politics, business, religion, and recreation, but do not integrate these into a consistent view of the world.

In the city there are also subcultural communities in which people do share common worldviews. Ethnic, class, and immigrant groups enculturate their young in their basic pictures of reality. Major institutions, such as business corporations, hospitals, schools, and bureaucracies, create their own worldviews based on fundamental assumptions about the nature of things. Members in these organizations must accept these worldviews, at least at work.

For certain purposes, it is useful to think of each city as having a particular ethos or spirit based on its historical and cultural distinctives. In general, people in Bangkok look at things differently than do those in Singapore or London. The former is influenced by its Buddhist context, the others by their business orientation and particular histories. Obviously such differences are subtle and hard to pin down and we must not make too much of them, but such comparisons may help us see things we might otherwise miss.

Urban Worldview Themes

While we recognize the great diversity between cities, it is helpful to speak of the worldview themes found in most cities. There are many exceptions, of course, and we must hold our conclusions lightly. Nevertheless, in some ways urbanites in Bombay are closer to those in Sydney and Chicago than they are to their rural and tribal compatriots in the Indian countryside. At the risk of overgeneralization, we will examine a few themes found among city folk in many parts of the world.

Acceptance of diversity

Urban people are raised in the midst of cultural pluralism and they come to accept and even celebrate it. They enjoy eating in different ethnic restaurants, visiting other neighborhoods, and touring other countries. Diversity becomes a part of the stimulus and spice of urban life. Such people find it hard to return to the sameness of small-town life. Peter Berger and his associates write (1973, 66–67),

> Since its inception in ancient times the city has been a meeting place of widely different people and groups, and thus a meeting place of discrepant worlds. By its very structure the city pushes its inhabitants to be "urbane" with regard to strangers, and "sophisticated" about different approaches to reality . . . [U]rbanization has not been only a matter of physical growth of certain communities and the development of specifically urban institutions; urbanization is also a process on the level of consciousness. . . . It is the city that has created the style of life (including styles of thinking, feeling and generally experiencing reality) that is now the standard for the society at large. In this sense it is possible to be "urbanized" while continuing to live in a small town or even on a farm.

The difficulties of living in a pluralistic society can lead to dogmatism and intolerance of diversity. This is true in some Muslim cities where new ideas and practices are viewed with suspicion by the keepers of orthodoxy. It is also true of certain communities, often religious in character, in modern secular cities.

Public/private split

The acceptance of diversity as a legitimate way of life has a profound effect on the urban worldview. No group in a city can live totally as it wishes. There must be some common ground that holds the various groups together in a single society. A division takes place, therefore, between what is enforced on all communities and what is a matter of personal or community choice (Berger, Berger, and Kellner 1973). The former constitutes the public sector of life, the latter the private sector.

In most modern cities, the public sector includes government, business, and public education. The laws of most cities apply to everyone—at least in principle. Everyone in New York must drive on the right side of the road, pay taxes, and obey government regulations. Similarly, the workplace is part of public life. People interact with people of other communities in factories, businesses, banks, markets, and public buses. Public schools are for everyone and what they teach is held by the society to be the truth that everyone needs to know. In modern cities this content is the humanities and sciences.

The private sector generally includes the home, community life, and entertainment, so long as these do not violate the laws. A family may eat American, Thai, or Chinese food and in its own ethnic fashion. In the community people are allowed to build churches, mosques, or temples, to celebrate their own festivals, and to worship as they please. They may choose to be involved in sports, dramas, movies, television, art, music, or dance.

The place of religion varies greatly. In some cities, religion is part of the public sector. For example, in the cities of Iran, Saudi Arabia, and Pakistan, the Muslim *shariat* is public law and one religion is the official religion of the people. Those not belonging to this religion are consigned to marginal communities with little or no political power. In these cities, religion plays a central role in the political and economic activities of the city.

In modern secular cities, however, no one religion is recognized as the official religion of the city or state. In these cities, religion is assigned to the personal sphere of life. It is something people are free to pursue for themselves. It is not seen as universal truth that is taught to everyone. Science and public doctrine, by contrast, are truth for everyone (table 10, following page).

Table 10
Domains of Secular Urban Life

Public Domain	Private Domain
government, law, economics, work, public institutions	religion, entertainment, home, subcultural community, customs
science as universal truth	theology as personal belief
men in control	women in control
emphasize rationality and order	emphasize feelings and creativity
absolutes	relatives

Splitting life into public and private spheres separates the sacred from the secular and the supernatural from the natural. It reduces religion to feelings and matters of private belief. In secular public schools children are taught mathematics, physics, chemistry, and the social sciences, but not religion. Private schools may include religion but they must teach the same sciences and humanities taught in public schools.

In the long run this relegation of religion to personal beliefs, not public truth, leads to religious relativism. People in the city are encouraged to keep their religious beliefs to themselves and not to seek to convert others to their faith. It also leads to the secularization of the city as a corporate system. Religion may flourish in the private sphere, but have little influence in the public sphere where power, resources, and prestige are concentrated. Pragmatism, not principle, becomes the dominant value in modern public life. The danger here is that interethnic and interreligious peace may be bought at the price of trivializing religions.

Individualism

The size of the city fosters anonymity. In a tribe or a village, everyone knows the kinship ties, stories, and personal idiosyncracies of everyone else. In the city, individuals can escape these and acquire status and power based solely on their achievements. This shift from ascribed (or inherited) roles to achieved roles attracts many of the best young people to the city. There they do not have to be a blacksmith like their father or a housewife like their mother. Nor are they remembered for the failures of their youth. They can be doctors, lawyers, professors, and politicians.

Anonymity and achievement foster freedom and mobility. To move up in the society, people must be freed not only from their histories but also from social structures that keep them in their old places. For many, this means moving to the city to get away from their class and caste identities. In the city they can begin life anew.

In the modern urban context, the autonomous individual becomes the center of life. Concern for the group or for the other gives way to self-interest. Self-fulfillment becomes an unquestioned value, self-promotion the way to achieve this. For some the city is a place of liberation and personal achievement. Many, however, have only the hope that someday this will become true for them.

Individualism and freedom have their price, namely, a sense of depersonalization. City dwellers cannot avoid having segmented, impersonal, superficial relationships with many people they meet. They do not have enough time or energy to relate to everyone intimately. Ulf Hannerz notes (1980, 105),

> One manages a traffic relationship by avoiding sidewalk collisions; by following the rules for standing in line, taking the end position of the queue as one arrives, without crowding the individual immediately in front; by not causing offense through unnecessary claims on the other's senses, as through odor or noise (however these may be defined); by not seeking eye contact, except possibly momentarily in order to determine how more intensive forms of contact can be forestalled.

Similar descriptions could be given of relating to people in the grocery store, theater, bus, and elevator.

But the impact of individualism on relationships goes deeper than public arenas. In local groups, such as at school, church, and work, people often restrict their relationships to courtesy because they are more interested in their own tasks than they are in each other as people. Relating to others takes self-denial and time away from work.

In the end, extreme individualism leads to loneliness and alienation. Escape from social bonds is liberating but also disturbing. People have no social nets to catch them when they fail and they must try to find meaning in life apart from belonging to a community.

Consumerism

The city celebrates technology and material well-being. Its streets are full of wares from around the world crying for the passer to buy. Its magazines, newspapers, billboards, radios, and televisions preach a message of happiness through material comfort. The right toothpaste will brighten our romance. The best car will gain us status. The chief symbols of the city are the symbols of material consumption: the dollar, yen, or rupee, the car, the fine home, the sumptuous food, and the luxuries of life. The public values of the city are the values of affluence, luxury, and leisure.

Consumption often means more than living a good life. For many in the city, particularly in the middle classes, it becomes a religion and a worldview. It provides them with their deepest values: self-absorption, focus on this life, and comfort. It promises salvation not in the next world but in this one through therapeutic self-realization (Fox and Lears 1983). It offers love, social acceptance, a dazzling smile, passionate romantic experience, health, abundant vitality, and intense experience through the buying of the right products. It gives meaning to life: buying a new stereo gives us a reason to exist for several weeks, a new car for several months. It also threatens the consumer that he or she will fail in life if he or she does not buy.

Consumerism stresses the now. There is little place for delayed gratification or for self-sacrifice. It emphasizes feelings— "if it feels right, do it"—and defines morality in material terms. The problem, it says, is not morality but morale. People are not evil, they are deprived and depressed. The solution is consumption and therapy. What we need is self-worth and fulfillment and these can be gained through material success.

Ultimately, consumerism turns everything into a commodity. Time, traditional heirlooms, companionship, even sex can be bought and sold. Politicians and religion are marketed. In the end, it commodifies the self. We sell not only our labor and skills, but also our image and personality. We calculate our time in terms of its worth in dollars, rupees, or won.

Time- and future-oriented

As we saw, tribal and village life is determined by the cycles of day and season. Land and relationships are their dominant values. By contrast, the city never sleeps. Time is its most precious commodity. Watches, daily schedules, calendars, time management, overnight post, faxes, high-speed computers, jets, satellites, and, above all, hurry are part of everyday life in the public sector, particularly for people in the upper and middle classes.

Tribal and rural societies often focus on the past. The city looks to the future. The rapid advances in technology in the past century promise even greater progress in the future. There are communities in the city that hope to maintain their past traditions, but the lure of the city is to the new, the latest, the fastest, and the best. The hope of the city is that more technology and more human engineering will provide answers to the tremendous problems confronting people.

This future orientation cuts people off from their history and tradition and leaves them with no enduring cultural foundations. The result is a sense of rootlessness and emptiness that create a great deal of anxiety. People in the city often feel lost.

Modern Problems

Cities are not in danger of extinction, at least not immediately. While there are enormous disparities among the different populations within cities, city people usually are the ones with power and wealth compared to peasant, tribal, or band peoples. Still, cities are nodes in the larger network of global systems. These global systems are, at present, primarily economic in nature. But political links, such as the United Nations, are being developed to support international trade and cultural links. Similarities in public culture, like airports, media, and fashion, are following.

Will a dominant global culture be established parallel to the "public" arena in cities? If so, will the hegemony of that culture suppress the "private" cultures of particular regions, classes, or religious groups? Although we do not recommend a simplistic application of biblical symbols to modern developments, the Book of Revelation does seem to point to such a time. Furthermore, it indicates that living as a true Christian will be difficult when world systems have so consolidated as to force high levels of conformity on everyone.

Much good has come, and no doubt will continue to come, from world systems. Most notably, the establishment of political links at higher and higher levels has brought peace between warring political groups. Bands have united into tribes. Tribes, incorporated into states, have put down their arms. States have sometimes made peace with one another by intermarrying their royalty, leading to consolidation. And now, nations, such as the western European ones, are putting aside differences, establishing economic interconnections, and preparing to unite in political cooperation. The United Nations, World Court, and other international institutions have been established and are gaining in strength and ability to foster the well-being of people everywhere.

A second good effect of world systems has been the increasing regulation of trade. The market system, whether local or global, is prone to wasting resources and to producing disparities in wealth. But when properly regulated, it can harness human energy and ingenuity to create and distribute new things that enhance the quality of life. Medical care, transportation, and better housing are examples. It can free specialists to pursue an understanding of God's created universe. Space research, ecology, and the social sciences are examples. The invention of machines to do monotonous tasks can provide jobs for people that are less difficult, more interesting, and more personally rewarding to do. Writers, teachers, pastors, and missionaries can use technology to enhance tasks.[1]

But the market system does not only produce these good things. Our natural tendency to evil as fallen beings causes us to exploit one another very easily. And thus the unregulated market system has also produced slavery, both literal and figurative, as we have seen.

World systems that place ethical constraints on trade are a tremendous benefit. These constraints might include the removal of protective trade barriers from rich countries and their (at least temporary) installation in poor ones; the prevention of trade in unhealthy commodities, such as in narcotic drugs; or the insistence on proper distribution of loan money in poor countries and the resistance to rich countries' demands for exorbitant repayments on those loans. In any case, just as ethical regulation is needed in one's personal moral life, so it is needed at the highest levels of human interaction.[2] World systems are beginning to provide this kind of regulation for the world market. Perhaps they will be able to improve the functioning of the international market in the way that nineteenth- and early twentieth-century regulation of business alleviated the worst effects of internal markets (in Europe and the United States).

Still, the Bible does not predict a humanly created utopia on earth. If anything, it suggests the opposite. God had to destroy all his previous creation at the time of Noah. The tower of Babel, the first humanly built world center, had to come down. In the end, God will have to destroy this earth in order to create a new one. It seems that the larger, more complex, and more effective our human systems become, the more we forget God.

Consumption, for instance, which we have noted as a characteristic of cities, has now become a global phenomenon. Kottack (1994, 378) speaks of a "transnational culture of consumption." Business, through advertising, is actively creating a "craving" for things we never previously thought necessary. By playing on our desires for comfort and stimulation, we can be persuaded that we will be miserable, and worse, oppressed, if we do not have these things.

If we decide to simplify our lives and reject these extra objects, people somewhere will lose their jobs and governments will have to try to "stimulate" the economy to growth. All this is taking place at an increasing pace internationally, causing Arjun Appadurai (1991, 194) to portray a modern world in which, "money, commodities, and persons unendingly chase each other around the world."

To what end are we pursuing economic growth? At what point will we have enough material goods? If we cannot answer these questions adequately, we have allowed money to become god, just as the people of Babel allowed their tower to become god.

Global political systems carry the same inherent danger. The peace they bring us is a welcome relief from the horrors of war. We are all inclined to give up a little of our political freedom to a government, if it means freedom from fear of our neighbor's hostility (Colson 1974). But Paul Tournier (1978) reminds us that a superficial lack of conflict does not mean that no violence is occurring. Governments have oppressed their own people throughout history, and in modern times, due to superior weaponry and surveillance technology, governments have been able to abuse their subjects more viciously than ever before (such as in some Central and South American countries).

Only the true God, who sent his son Jesus to save us from these and all other ill fates, can work through historical events and transform them such that "all things work together for good. . . ." But the later half of that verse (Rom. 8:28), "for those who love God, and who are called according to his purpose," seems to indicate that we must be following God's call in order to see the good that he is doing. Christians must not be cowardly in pointing out the evils of this world. But Christians need not be pessimists about the final outcome. Christ is our Redeemer, not only in the next life, but in this one as well. He wishes to end suffering, to bring hope, and to create a new world. The Christian message to the world is: if you put away all other gods, including the gods of power and money, you will be redeemed.

How do we evangelize people living in these complex social systems? How do we theologize in the context of the urban worldview? These are questions we must now address.

9 | The Church in Urban Societies

How can the church not only survive but also thrive in the city? This is a critical question because cities are the centers that control the future of the people. If the church captures the cities for Christ, it will grow. If it loses the cities, it will become a movement on the margins of modern life.

The early church was an urban movement. It began in Jerusalem and spread through persecution to the cities of Samaria (Acts 8:5), Damascus (9:2), Caesarea (10:1), and Antioch (11:19).

Paul saw the importance of the city. His strategy was an urban strategy. He did not go to the many small villages in Asia Minor but to the cities; when he had planted churches in them, he declared his work finished in that region (Rom. 15:23).

The Reformation, too, was an urban movement. It began in the cities of northern Europe and captured the urban centers. From there it spread to the surrounding countryside. In the past the growth of Christianity was connected with cities. The Protestant church has since become largely a rural movement. This is due in part to the growth and adaptation of the church on the American frontier. It is also due to the fact that many Protestant missions focused their work on rural communities around the world.

Today, missions around the world are focusing on planting urban churches, but too often they start peasant-style churches and, therefore, are unable to reach city folk. Many church planters misunderstand and fear urban life. They succeed best in the suburbs because these maintain some rural characteristics.

What has kept us from seeing, studying, and loving the city? Harvie Conn points out that Christians often have an anti-urban bias. They see the city as a place of evil. Jacques Ellul (1970) expresses this fear in theological terms. He points out that the first city was built by Cain (Gen. 4:12) and that Babel was the city of corporate rebellion against God (Gen. 11:1–9). Sodom, Gomorrah, and Babylon are symbols in the Bible of the concentration of evil in human hands.

Harvey Cox (1965) criticizes the anti-urban bias of the church. He sees the village as a place where people are bound by the tyranny of tradition and by Hinduism, Islam, and other religions. To him the city is a place where people are free to discover and believe the living God of the Bible.

Both views express certain truths and both are reductionistic. The city is indeed a place where sin abounds. Because it is the center of human activity and because humans are sinners, evil grows freely in urban settings. The moral checks of traditional societies on excessive evil are gone and people are free to sin openly. Furthermore, where there is power there is the potential, at least, for corruption and oppression. The hierarchical structure of the city, along with its generally impersonal nature, allows for the ill treatment of a great many people.

The city also is a place where God is mightily at work establishing his rule over human societies. An often quoted adage is that "the Bible begins in a garden and ends in a city." In the Old Testament, Jerusalem stands in contrast to Babylon and the cities of refuge to Sodom and Gomorrah. In the New Testament, Jesus was associated with the city. He was born in the "city of David" (Luke 2:11), preached in the city (Matt. 9:35), wept over the city (Luke 19:41), and was crucified and rose near a city (John 19:20). Paul, too was a city person. He was born in Tarsus (Acts 22:3), set out on his mission from Antioch (Acts 13), and used an urban strategy, planting churches in the main cities with the expectation that they would spread the gospel to neighboring towns and villages (Acts 16:11–40; 17:16–33; 18:1–11; 19:1–10; 28:16–31). The writer of Hebrews looks for a new city whose builder is God (Heb. 11:10).

In early church history, Jerusalem, Antioch, Ephesus, Alexandria, Constantinople, and Rome became, successively, the centers from which the church reached out to the tribes of Europe, to the villages of South India, and to the towns of China.

The city is a place where the wheat and the tares both ripen to maturity. Above all, it is the place where the church must proclaim the message of God's salvation and his reign. We can be assured that God is already at work in both hidden and visible ways. But to take this stand, we must overcome our anti-urban bias and learn to understand and love the city and its people.

Planting Churches

Obviously no chapter, or book, can fully explore the issues involved in planting urban churches, given the diversity of cities. No single set of principles can be formulated. The methods for planting churches among the Baluch immigrants in Karachi must, of necessity, be radically different from the methods of planting churches among the urban elite in Rio de Janeiro or the suburbs of Chicago.

Another reason is that our understanding of church planting in urban settings is still so new and incomplete that any generalizations we make now will soon be revised.

Our purpose here is not to explore exhaustively the methods for planting churches in urban settings. Rather it is to make us aware of the need to study and understand the specific urban setting in which we minister and to be sensitive to the way the social and cultural contexts of people influence the ways in which they hear and believe the gospel.

Moreover, we must remember that the work of evangelism is the work of the Holy Spirit, who is already at work in the city. We need to train people who do not trust in their techniques and strategies as much as they do the leading and power of the Spirit.

The Church and Diversity

As we have seen, one of the hallmarks of the city is diversity. This raises a serious question: how should the church respond to these differences?

One of the great obstacles to effective Christian witness in the city is our own preconceptions of what constitutes a church. We often believe that it must have a seminary-trained pastor, a church building, hymns, offerings, and sermons because these were characteristics of the rural and suburban churches in which many of us grew up. While some strong churches in cities do fit this pattern, most will not. Too often we are peasants seeking to plant rural churches in urban settings. We need to break from our stereotypes of the church if we want to be effective church planters in the city.

One thing is clear. There will be no one form of church that serves as the model for all the others. There will be house churches, store-fronts, local congregations, and megachurches; ethnic churches and integrated churches; churches that stress high ritual order and those that emphasize informality. No one of them can serve the spiritual needs of all people. And each of them has its own temptations and faults.

One thing many urban congregations are learning is the need to incorporate diversity into the local church itself. Different worship services with different worship styles are often held in the same sanctuary at different times on Sunday morning, or they may be incorporated in the same service. Different ethnic groups may form congregations that work together and use the same facilities. In one North American case, three small churches, composed of whites, African-Americans, and Hispanics respectively, merged to form a single church so that they could afford a pastor.

Probably less understood is that many urban churches are made up not of one congregation but of several intersecting congregations. In rural churches, everyone is expected to attend all the church services and social pressure is put on members to do so. In urban churches, one group meets for the Sunday services but other groups, equally a part of the church and its ministries, may attend Bible studies, counseling sessions, and fellowship groups during the week. Each group should have a place and a say in the life of the church. In such settings there may be few ways to build a sense of common community. Rather, each group in the church needs to be nurtured and fed in its own gathering.

Finally, the church will take different shapes in different communities. Megachurches appeal largely to middle- and upper-class people seeking multiple ministries. They can be effective if they have multiple subcongregations and small groups to provide people with a place for fellowship and personal sharing. Storefronts and missions reach out to the poor and street dwellers, small churches to those seeking intimacy and a strong sense of community, and cathedrals to those wanting ritual expressions of their faith.

Decision-making in the City

How do urban people make decisions? As we have seen, in tribal societies major decisions are made by families, kinship groups, and tribal leaders. In peasant societies decisions are made by families that belong to ethnic or class groups in the village. Here family networks often process a major decision together. In both cases the result is often group movements to Christ. But what about the city?

We must avoid reducing decision-making in the city to a single stereotype. As in other areas of city life, we face here a bewildering diversity. In tribal and peasant enclaves in cities, group decisions still take place. People shop at family-owned stores where personal ties are important, and they discuss choices with their neighbors. Outside their neighborhood, however, they learn to make decisions as city folk do, and this fact begins to change their lives.

People in ghettos, bustees, favelas, shanty towns, and other enclaves of the poor have their own ways of making decisions. As Oscar Lewis shows (1961), economic decisions must be made on the basis of survival. Whoever gets some money must share it with others who have nothing because in the future he or she will be the one who needs help. Decisions are often made at the last moment. It is hard to make lasting commitments and long-range plans. Consequently relationships are of necessity fragile and the future uncertain.

Planting suburban-style churches in such contexts is almost impossible. Services must be based on last-minute arrangements because those who promised to serve do not show up. Leadership often lies in the hands of a few unpaid persons who can inspire others to participate. Missionaries to these communities must be very flexible and not become upset when things do not work out the way they planned. They must be able to choose another course of action on the spur of the moment, something many from the west find hard to do. Charismatic churches have been successful in such communities, in part, because they are ad hocracies rather than bureaucracies.

Middle- and upper-class urban people tend to make individual decisions based on reason and feelings. They ask the advice of knowledgeable friends and neighbors, the "opinion leaders" whose advice they trust in the matter at hand. They ask one friend about cameras, another about doctors, and a third about religion. In such settings, the gospel often spreads along networks of friends and associates.

Window Shopping the Gospel

One way truly urban people gain information to make decisions is by window shopping. People in small towns go regularly to the same store and buy what the shopkeeper recommends because they trust him or her. In large cities, shops have large display windows where passing strangers look at the merchandise. They make their choices on the basis of price, quality, and appeal, rather than on personal trust in the merchant.

Window shopping is closely tied to the concept of "territory." Edward Hall (1966) and others have argued that all people have a sense of territory—a sense that different geographic and social space "belongs" to different people and groups and is used for different functions. The concept of ownership is far broader than legal possession. People living together often feel that they own their neighborhoods even though the streets and parks belong to the general public.

City shops are semipublic. Strangers may enter to purchase goods but the space "belongs" to the owners and salespeople are free to talk to the strangers about buying goods and services. Consequently, to enter a store is a tentative commitment to buying something. People do not expect to go to a shop just to visit or to argue about religion.

Similarly, a church is a semipublic place and people who enter it generally have some interest in Christianity. But they also realize they have entered territory owned by Christians. What about people who are only casually interested or curious? Where can they look at Christianity without being pressured to convert?

Neutral territory is public space not owned by any particular interest group. It is sidewalks and markets where people can look at commodities on display. It is public roads with their billboards and parades, and stadiums and public auditoriums where one can remain a spectator lost in the crowds. In all these places people can examine new ideas and products without a pressure to "buy."

What implications does this have for evangelism in the city? One thing is clear: many city folk will not come to a church, even for evangelistic meetings. They see the church building as religious territory. To enter it is to make a first positive step to becoming a Christian, a step they are not ready to make. They may be willing to look at Christianity, but they will do so only in the safety of some neutral territory where no precommitment is needed. They just want to window shop the gospel.

What are some of these neutral territories that the church should explore in evangelistic outreach?

Streets, parks, stadiums, and auditoriums

Streets, parks, stadiums, and auditoriums—these are public spaces and although they are used for specific functions such as rock concerts or trade fairs, they are generally thought of as neutral territory. The sheer size of large gatherings in them also guarantees a person's anonymity. Moreover, the fact that different types of functions are held at the same site prevents it from being identified closely with any one of them. In North America, a stadium may host a football game one day, a music festival the next, and a gospel crusade the third.

The church in the city has long used empty lots, parks, and streets for public meetings. In many parts of the world, these are important places where films can be shown and the gospel preached. For example, the Christian and Missionary Alliance churches in Lima, Peru, have developed a cycle in which evangelistic meetings are held in tents near a church, then several weeks are given to incorporating new converts into the church, and then another set of evangelistic meetings follows.

More recently stadiums and civic auditoriums have become important places for public rallies where people may come to window shop the gospel. For instance, the Eagles Communication Team in Singapore stages modern musical concerts in public auditoriums. Each concert is followed by an evangelistic challenge and appeal. The team regularly fills auditoriums with young people, many of them non-Christians.

In many cities congregations have bought theaters and converted them into churches, attracting people who would not enter the door of a building that looks like a church. Others use shops for store-front churches and shopping malls for large meeting halls.

Restaurants and banquet halls

City folk eat out regularly. It should not surprise us, therefore, that churches are discovering that restaurants and hotels are good places for evangelism. For years the Christian Business Men's Fellowship and the Full Gospel Business Men's Fellowship in North America have used restaurants to make non-Christian businessmen feel at home. Others are using them as meeting places for young adults and seekers' groups.

In Singapore the Eagles Communication Team ministers to upper-class professionals by organizing banquets in top-rated hotels. They encourage Christian doctors, lawyers, teachers, and business people to buy tickets and invite non-Christian friends as guests. The banquet is followed by a musical concert and a brief evangelistic presentation. Most of the guests would feel uncomfortable in a church, but at the hotel they can enjoy a meal together with their friends and look at Christianity without the pressure to convert.

Retreats, festivals, and pilgrimage centers

In recent decades, evangelicals have discovered the importance of camps and retreats, but the idea is not new. Throughout history the church has made extensive use of retreats, not only as places for spiritual formation but also for people to explore faith. Some in Asia are exploring the use of ashrams and other retreat centers where people, harried by urban life, can get away for times of reflection and decision.

In many cities of the world, religious festivals are celebrated in public with street parades and mass rallies. Christians in some of these cities are beginning to do so as well, making the public aware of the Good News.

Neutral Territory and Sacred Space

Neutral territory is public space where secular people can look at Christianity without being pressured to convert. It is a place of evangelism, similar in ways to the Court of the Gentiles in the Jewish temple. But the church also needs "sacred" space where it gathers to worship and fellowship. Outsiders are welcome, but here the church reaffirms its identity as the body of Christ.

The form of the sacred place will vary. Some congregations seek to express the greatness, mystery, and providence of God in all creation by building large cathedrals. Others emphasize the presence of Christ and fellowship in the congregation and build churches. Still others symbolize the power of the Holy Spirit in the life of each believer by constructing chapels and informal auditoriums. The forms also vary according to the social class, ethnic tastes, and culture of people. What is common is a sacred place where the congregation as congregation gathers regularly to meet God. Without sacred places and times to give expression to our experiences with God, we are in danger of being drawn into the secular world of the city and forgetting God's magnificent presence among us. Or we are in danger of becoming social clubs in which Christ is only a member.

There is another reason why the church needs sacred space. It is a testimony to the world of the presence of the church. Non-Christians may be unwilling to enter a church building, but its very existence reminds them of Christianity. In Seoul, Korea, the rapid proliferation of church buildings with crosses on them is seen by non-Christians and Christians alike as witness to the growth of the church. Muslims are aware of the importance of sacred symbols in the city and are investing great amounts of money in building impressive mosques in cities around the world. Likewise, many Christian communities around the world want church buildings that publicly symbolize their presence in the city.

The tension between neutral space and sacred space reflects the tension the church faces between being in a secular world and yet not of it. In the world it is a witness; apart it renews itself. If it lives only in neutral territory, it is in danger of losing sight of its Lord; if only in sacred territory, of becoming ingrown and old. The church needs to be present in both territories.

Ministry in Mobile Communities

As we have seen, urban people are mobile. They travel long distances each day. They move to find jobs and better lives, or are forced out of their squatter settlements by police. Many are part of the flood of peasant and tribal immigrants that streams to the city to find a new life. How can the church evangelize and minister to such people?

Ministry to Mobile People

City people are people on the move. Buses, cycles, rickshaws, trains, elevators, and cars are part of their daily lives. This mobility changes the shape of the church in the city. Those in poor communities are less mobile and so retain a sense of the neighborhood parish. The church building is a place not only for worship but also for visiting and community activities. The members share in the needs and joys of each other's daily lives.

Churches in affluent parts of the city are often commuter congregations that draw together people, not on the basis of geography but of common interest. Unlike neighborhood parishes, these churches are often socially and culturally homogeneous and find it hard to reach out to people of another class or ethnic community.

Commuter churches need to work hard at building a true sense of Christian community in their congregations. This is difficult because commuting prevents their members from developing the multiplex relationships necessary for intimate fellowship. Many seek to build a sense of community by extending the range of church activities beyond worship and evangelism to informal gatherings, recreation, and even neighborhood projects. So long as members in a congregation see each other only in religious settings they are reduced to simplex relationships. Meeting together in other settings helps them to learn to care for one another.

Ministry to Migrant People

City people migrate. Some estimate that in North America people move to new locations an average of once in five years. This means that the urban church can count on losing 20 percent of its members each year! How can the church survive with such turnover?

It is clear that the urban church must absorb people rapidly into the life of the church. They need to be incorporated into programs of worship and lay ministry where their gifts are effectively used. Leadership, too, needs to be flexible and creative. Prolonged leadership apprenticeships and bureaucratic traditions built around maintaining programs rather than ministering to people can kill the urban church.

The church must learn to minister to people at their own particular levels of spiritual development. In tribal and peasant churches, people spend their whole lives in the same congregation. An urban church has people for only a few years before they move on. Consequently, it cannot assume that it will help its members from their cradles to their graves. It must find out quickly where newcomers are in their spiritual maturity and build on that. Some are new believers in need of basic indoctrination and support. Others are mature saints who need discussions of deeper spiritual matters. Still others may be experiencing stagnation in their faith. The urban church must help them to grow and it has little time to do this.

Finally, the city church must reach out to newcomers to its area. People are most open to religious change when they move to new settings. Nominal Christians, having lost their old ties, are in danger of dropping out of the church. Secular people may be looking for a meaningful community. The urban church must make special effort to find and contact those who move into its area.

Ministry to Immigrant Communities

People who immigrate to the city from tribal and peasant societies often build small ethnic enclaves that serve as halfway houses between their old ways and urban life. To reach such people, we must use the methods of tribal and peasant evangelism, namely, living among the people and building trust. Here the gospel often follows kinship lines and decisions are made after discussions with others in the community.

But urban immigrant communities are in transition. Their children and grandchildren are city folk. As we have seen, this leads to tremendous intergenerational stress, tensions that may be brought into immigrant churches. Mark Mullins points out (1987, 322–23) that churches made up of first-generation immigrants are ethnically conservative, but that "the history of immigrant churches reveals that the tendency toward conformity is ultimately the dominant force shaping their character. The process of assimilation forces the churches to choose between accommodation and extinction."

In the long run, churches that remain tied to ethnicity die out. By the third and fourth generations, ethnic churches in the city must de-ethnicize their identity and open the doors to outsiders if they want to survive. M. J. Yinger notes (1970, 112), "What will give one generation a sense of unifying tradition may alienate parts of another generation who have been subjected to different social and cultural influences."

First-generation immigrants want to hold services in their native tongue and style. For them the church is a haven where they can preserve the old ways with which they are comfortable. They choose pastors who reinforce their ethnic distinctiveness. Often such pastors are entrenched in their old ways and do not understand the next generation in their church. They are part of the problem, not of the solution to ethnic assimilation. When challenged by young elders to adopt new ideas and customs, they often resort to dictatorial ways to defend their positions.

Second-generation urban immigrants struggle with problems of language and cultural identity. At home their parents maintain old ways. In public they learn the new. The result is a breakdown of relationships between parents and children and an identification of Christianity with old ethnic ways that drives the young from the church.

It is critical that immigrant churches understand the forces of assimilation into city life or they will lose their children. They need to minister to the first generation with its anxieties about urban life. They need to minister equally to the second and third generations that are trying to find their way in the city. This requires leaders who are able to bridge the generations and provide the people with hope. It requires bilingual or separate language services and pastoral ministries that help the old understand the young and the young understand the old. Above all it requires a vision of a new life that draws on both old and new and gives the people a strong sense of their own identity as Christians in the city.

Ministry to Foreign Enclaves

The movement of people is not only to the city and in the city, it is global. Cities today have enclaves of people from other lands. Some are immigrant communities. Others are businessmen, diplomats, students, and tourists whose stay is temporary. The modern city is not an autonomous community, it belongs to a global network of systems and relationships.

To evangelize the world today, we can begin by reaching out to the foreigners in our own cities. Many of the top leaders around the world have received training in other countries. Urban churches in these countries can reach out to international students in the universities near them, and top Christian businessmen can share Christ with their associates around the world.

Network Evangelism

As we have seen, networks provide one of the major forms of social organization on the middle level of the city. People link up with other people through word of mouth, references, meetings, phones, faxes, and computers.

Ray Bakke (1984, 86) points to three kinds of networks: those based on kinship, on geography, and on vocation. To these we can add networks based on common interest and shared information. Each of these can serve as a means of evangelistic outreach.

Unfortunately, in an effort to build community or out of fear of the world around them, many churches encourage their members to form their friendships only inside the congregation. Soon then the church members have few networks they can use to witness to the lost. Urban churches must encourage their members to form friendships with non-Christians. Moreover, Christians must make these friends feel at home when the latter visit the Christians' homes. If Christians are offended when such friends smoke in their homes or use off-color language, they will destroy the bridge of communication between them.

How can networks be used in reaching the city? We will explore a few of the many ways that networks can serve the church.

Home Fellowship Groups

One way to mobilize networks is through home fellowship groups. The membership of the church is divided into groups of three or four families. Once a month these families meet in one of their homes and invite non-Christian friends for an evening of fun and fellowship. The evening is spent playing games, visiting, and possibly going to a restaurant or theater.

The object of these gatherings is not evangelism, but if occasions arise, members are encouraged to answer questions and witness openly to their faith. These are opportunities for neighbors and friends to window shop Christianity and to see that it is not strange or cultish but genuine and compassionate. Preferably, the majority of those who attend should be non-Christians, so that they do not feel they are the target of high-pressure salesmanship. Through such gatherings friendships are built that, in time, may lead people to faith.

Linking Church Members to Evangelistic Teams

A second way to mobilize networks for outreach is to link people in the church to members of an outreach team. Elmo Warkentine, a successful urban church planter, points out that the old motto of "each one reach one" rarely works in a local congregation. Most Christians do not know how to effectively lead people to Christ or are uncomfortable in doing so.

When planting new churches, Warkentine chose a few members with the gift and motivation for evangelism and trained them as an outreach team. He then linked everyone in the church to one of the members of this team. When the people came across opportunities for evangelism, they contacted their team member and he or she responded to the need (fig. 43, following page).

For example, imagine Mr. Jones, a solid member at church but unsure and inexperienced in evangelism. Through the church program he is linked to Mrs. Thomas, who is an excellent personal evangelist. One day Mr. Jones's neighbor, Mr. Peterson, dies. Over the next weeks Mr. Jones goes over to offer sympathy and help to Mrs. Peterson. He knows that Christ could help her in her sorrow, but feels uneasy about sharing the gospel with her in this time of her need. For one thing, he does not want to exploit her when she is vulnerable. For another, he does not want to break fellowship with her. If he points her to the gospel and she rejects it, their relationship is estranged. What should he do?

In Warkentine's program Mr. Jones helps Mrs. Peterson however he can and in the process tells her that he knows a woman who can help those going through times of grief. Mrs. Peterson can reject his offer without straining their relationship, because she is not rejecting him as a person. If she accepts his offer, Mr.

Figure 43
Evangelism by Network Referrals

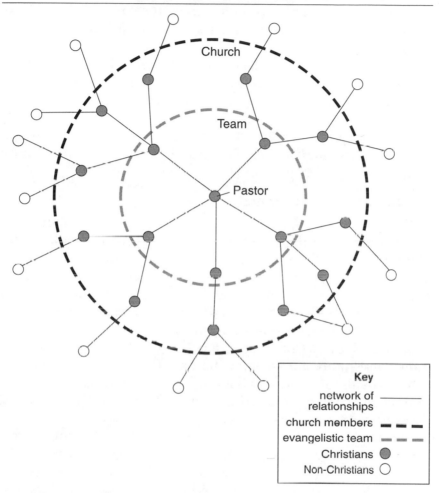

Jones contacts Mrs. Thomas immediately and in a day or two she calls Mrs. Peterson to arrange a visit. She comes because she has been invited through the trust Mrs. Peterson has in Mr. Jones. Mrs. Thomas is, therefore, welcome. She can share about Christ with Mrs. Peterson and Mrs. Peterson can accept or reject the invitation without threatening her relationship with Mr. Jones.

Church members have many occasions when they can recommend help to friends and neighbors. People need help when illnesses, deaths, family conflicts, divorces, loss of jobs, and other crises strike and the church needs to be there to offer them assistance. Some churches have accountants, counselors, electricians, and mechanics who volunteer their time to help those who request their services and share their faith in the context of their aid.

Warkentine's approach has a second step to it. If Mr. Jones is willing to go with Mrs. Thomas to visit Mrs. Peterson, he sees ministry modeled. After a few such occasions, he, too, may become interested in joining the outreach team. He then is discipled and assigned people who refer others to him for help. It is important not only to reach people in the world but also to multiply those who are involved in personal evangelism.

Special Interest Groups

A third way to use networks in the church is to organize special interest groups that nurture Christians in their particular walks of life and bring others to faith and spiritual maturity. An example of this is Christian business associations. Christians in the marketplace gather in a neutral space and invite their non-Christian friends. The services are generally built on issues that interest people in the business world. Because of their common business experiences, these Christians are better able to share Christ with their non-Christian associates than are Christians in other specialized fields. Similarly, Christian doctors, nurses, academicians, politicians, construction workers, and other specialists can and do reach out to those in their vocations.

Special interest groups go beyond vocational associations. Single parents, young singles, old people, parents whose children are on drugs, women whose husbands are abusive or drunkards—all these need Christian friends who understand and help them through their particular trials. Churches need to be sensitive to their special needs, and stand by them with love and friendship.

One group has been particularly responsive in cities around the world, namely, students. Students are exploring new ideas and so are often more open to hearing the gospel than when they become established in their cultures and careers. Student ministries in high schools and universities have not only won many to Christ but also produced many strong leaders for the church.

Starting New Churches

One effective method of outreach has been to mobilize churches to start new congregations in new areas. In the New Testament, the church in Jerusalem grew into a megachurch. Some estimate it had more than ten thousand members. The Antioch church, by contrast, reached out by starting new churches and became the center of God's outreach (Acts 13).

One important reason for churches to plant new churches is that the city is so large that one church cannot minister to the needs of everyone. In hamlets and villages one or two congregations are enough to serve the community and everyone knows who is a Christian and who is not. In the city, a great many congregations are needed to reach all the people.

Another reason is the diversity of modern cities. City churches tend to serve their own kind of people. Who reaches out to groups of people who have no churches? Unless the church intentionally plants new congregations among unreached groups and neighborhoods, they will not hear the gospel.

A third reason for planting new churches is the rapid growth of cities. Local churches look at their own areas. No one looks at the city as a whole. The result is a great neglect of entire areas of the city. Whole shanty towns and suburbs rise with not a church in them—and the surrounding churches are totally unaware of this.

Discipling the whole city requires that somebody, whether denominational leaders or coalitions of churches, examine the city as a whole to find where congregations are most urgently needed and work toward establishing congregations in these areas.

Carrying Out Relevant Research

Planting new churches, whether through outreach by mother churches or by teams of urban missionaries, must begin with careful research. If we do not study the city and the area where we plan to work, we will be blind to many of the social and cultural forces that can help or hinder our work.

First, we need to gather demographic data on populations, ethnic communities, class differences, and so on. Cities require extensive planning and the information gathered by government offices and businesses is available through libraries, city planning offices, police agencies, schools, hospitals, and business bureaus. Data on

religious affiliation are available through city and national cen-
suses. There is no need for the church to duplicate what the world
already has done.

A second step is to select an area for ministry and to study it in
depth. This requires ethnographic research methods. If a mother
church is planting the new church, it is important that the elders
and laity be involved in this research to sensitize them to the needs
and opportunities of this new ministry. Using the existing church
as the base, they should organize and train research teams; survey
neighborhoods to determine ministry needs; visit the neighborhood to distribute tracts, visit people, show films, and become
known and trusted by the local residents; start Bible studies; gather
and instruct new believers; and form the new congregation in a
home, school, or public building.

It is important not to separate research from ministry. If we think
of first doing research and then ministering, we will either become
mired down in research and never move on to ministry, or we will
stop doing research and lose touch with the people. Research itself
opens doors to ministry and ministry raises further questions that
requires more research. A second danger is to confuse our own
methodology with the work of the Holy Spirit. God has given the
important work of evangelism to us and expects us to do it dili-
gently and intelligently. We must not, however, imagine that a perfect technique can be found that will coerce others to believe, or
in any way replace the work of the Spirit in converting them.

A third step in research is to examine our own preconceptions
as individuals and as churches about people and the work. Our
deepest attitudes, hidden to ourselves but clear to the people we
serve, are often the greatest barriers to effective outreach in the
city. Frank discussions of our own prejudices against city life and
other kinds of people is essential if we want to truly learn to love
and minister to them.

Gathering People Together

After preliminary research, steps are taken to gather a group to
form the nucleus of a congregation. Sometimes a team is sent to
hold tent meetings and show Christian films for a week or more.
A follow-up team then disciples the new converts and organizes
them into a Bible study and fellowship group. The team must con-

tinue to assist the new congregation until it has its own identity and leadership.

A second, probably more effective, method is for a church to intentionally divide and send a nucleus of its members to start a new congregation elsewhere. The mother church assists the daughter church with finances until it is strong enough to stand on its own. Sometimes a mother church organizes a number of preaching points and sends its members to help organize a new work.

In most of the world there are not enough seminary graduates to plant and pastor new congregations. Consequently, it is important to disciple and empower the natural leaders that emerge in any human group. As a young congregation grows, there will always be some members who arise as leaders in the group. Properly discipled, they often become good pastors for the new church. This method has been effectively used by the Pentecostals in their rapid growth in Latin America.

These methods are effective in starting new churches among people of the same ethnic and cultural communities as the mother church. Planting churches in other ethnic and class communities calls for another approach. One way is to find a few Christians in those communities and to support them as they plant churches among their own people. This has been particularly successful in starting ethnic churches in the cities of North America. For example, parent churches find and help Vietnamese, Laotian, Hispanic, and Indian Christians to gather and organize churches. They assist the young congregations and often let these use their facilities.

Unfortunately, parent churches often take a paternalistic approach to the young churches, assigning them odd hours for services and making strict rules for the use of the sanctuary. It is hard for established churches to truly accept young congregations as full and equal partners, particularly when the former contribute most of the finances for church upkeep. Parent churches do not realize that the young congregations contribute much to the spiritual and social life of the church and that they, as old established Christians, have much to learn from the life and vitality of new converts.

These methods can help us plant churches where Christians exist. But many, if not most, people in cities around the world live in communities where there are no churches or Christians. To reach these we must send cross-cultural urban missionaries who are willing to live in non-Christian communities, build trust with people, and share the gospel in culturally appropriate ways. This is an area in which we need much study. We know more about planting churches in tribal and peasant societies than we do about reaching urban communities in other cultures.

One thing is clear: there is a strong and growing resistance to Christian missions in many cities, particularly those in which Islam and Hinduism are dominant. Muslim and Hindu fundamentalist movements, centered in cities, are systematically organizing opposition to urban Christian missionaries and seeking to win Christian converts back to their old faiths. The battle to win the cities for Christ will not be an easy or a bloodless one.

Using the Media

In small communities, basic information is communicated by word of mouth. In cities, people depend on the media for general knowledge. Newspapers, magazines, books, billboards, radio, television, and computers flood the city with news, commentary, advertisements, sermons, music, and talk. To inform the city about Christ, the church must make effective use of the media available to it.

One effective method for reaching people is campaigns. Evangelistic crusades and mass rallies reach many who otherwise would never hear the gospel. But such campaigns often serve more as pre-evangelism than as effective evangelism. People hear the gospel and respond personally to the invitation, but many of them are never incorporated into the ongoing life of a community of faith. Consequently, their commitment dies through lack of nourishment. It is essential, therefore, that there be a systematic, long-term follow-up of the new converts to help them join living churches and grow in faith.

Another use of media is correspondence courses. This has been particularly effective in countries such as India and Africa where literacy is rising rapidly. Advertisements in newspapers invite people to write in for Bible study courses. The response is often overwhelming. Through well-designed courses, people are led to faith and to Christian knowledge. Many of them, however, do not join a church that can help them grow in faith.

Films, radio, and television, too, are powerful media that the church can use. In countries with open communication systems, these serve two major functions. They provide people with an awareness of the gospel. This is particularly true when Christian programs designed specifically to reach non-Christians are broadcast on secular stations. They also nourish Christians in faith. This is true particularly of Christian broadcasting stations. In countries where the government opposes Christianity and controls the media, radio and television broadcasts from other parts of the world in the languages of these countries do have an important role in spreading the gospel.

Often we overlook mail as a means of letting people know about the church. Letters to visitors let them know that the church is interested in them. General mailings to a neighborhood keep people aware of church programs.

The phone, too, is a means of reaching the general public. Chinese churches in North America call people in the directory with Chinese names and let them know about Chinese gatherings. Some church planters use mass calling to invite people to the first services of a new church. A number attend and some join and form the core of a new congregation.

There are many other ways Christians have used media to plant and nurture the church. Billboards, newspaper advertisements, posters, cassettes, and videos have been tried with varying degrees of success, depending in part on the culture in which they are used.

Despite their power, modern media will never be the primary means of leading people to faith and to growth in Christian maturity in a congregation. These critical steps are most often taken through personal witness and invitation to fellowship in the church. Ervin Hastey writes,

> New believers and new churches must be nurtured to Christian maturity if they are to reproduce themselves. Seed sowing and church planting without confirmation and follow-up stands no chance of impacting today's cities with the gospel of Christ. Strong churches grounded in biblical doctrine, energized by the Holy Spirit and filled with evangelistic zeal are needed today in our urban centers. (1984, 158–59)

Wholistic Ministries

The church in the first century proclaimed the divine message in public, taught from house to house and in public places, gossiped the gospel through informal witness, ministered to the sick, demonstrated the transforming power of the gospel in the lives of the people, formed fellowships of believers that showed the world a new kind of community based on love for one another, performed miracles, and cared for the poor.

The medieval church in the city saw itself as the refuge for the poor and needy. Protestant churches gave birth to the first public hospitals, schools, and orphanages. Only in the last century, with the emergence of the modern welfare state, have people looked to government as the body responsible for the well-being of everyone, including their education, medical care, retirement benefits, and welfare. This is particularly true in the west with its elaborate public programs administered by the government.

Today the church in the city must proclaim and live the whole gospel. It cannot relegate concerns for everyday human needs to the government and expect to be relevant to people. It must provide for the care and nurture of its members, help feed the poor, heal the sick, counsel the distraught, care for the widows and orphans, and preach the Word with boldness. It must avoid the mental dichotomy that separates evangelism from social ministries and see both as ways to bear witness to the transforming power of the gospel.

Theological Issues in Urban Societies

Urban churches have great opportunities. They also face great challenges that vary greatly from one city to another. In many cities in the Third World, Christians often constitute a small, powerless minority in hostile settings. Moreover, they face incredible poverty and oppression. Churches in the west face other challenges, many of which spring out of modernity and its fruit. We can look here at only a few of the issues urban churches must deal with in doing their theology and ministry.

Building Community

The city is a place of alienation. People meet more and more people but they feel less and less a part of intimate communities. How can churches provide a sense of community in the midst of the depersonalizing systems of the city?

There were numerous kinds of clubs and institutions in the Greco-Roman society that the first Christians could have emulated. Rather, the New Testament writers chose the term *ekklesia* to describe the church. An *ekklesia* was not a voluntary association or a corporation. Its members were seen as children in the same family (Eph. 5:23; Acts 11:29), parts of the same body (Rom. 12:4–5; 1 Cor. 12:12), and citizens of the same colony (Phil. 3:20). In other words, the church was a true community that was more than the sum of its members.

The early church was a new kind of society characterized by *agape* and *koinonia*. Above all, however, it was a community with Christ in its midst. Stanley Hauerwas and William Willimon write,

> Christian community . . . is not primarily about togetherness. It is about the way of Jesus Christ with those whom he calls to himself. It is about disciplining our wants and needs in congruence with a true story, which gives us the resources to lead truthful lives. In living out the story together, togetherness happens, but only as a by-product of the main project of trying to be faithful to Jesus. (1989, 78)

The church is always in danger of borrowing from the social models around it to organize itself. In so doing, it risks losing its distinct character as the body of Christ.

The Church as Crowd or Club

Churches in the city are in danger of becoming religious clubs. As we saw in the last chapter, clubs are single-purpose gatherings that people join on the basis of self-interest. Relationships in them are easily broken and members leave to join other clubs.

When a church organizes itself using the social principles of a club, it soon becomes a club, no matter how much it preaches community. It is a group of people who gather only to fill personal needs to worship God or experience fellowship. People join because of what the association can do for them, not because they are contributing to Christ's kingdom. They do not want the church to meddle in their private lives or to be asked to sacrifice their own interests for the sake of others.

Club-style congregations tend to be homogeneous, held together by the same ethnicity and social class. Members must constantly reaffirm the beliefs and practices of the congregation to show that they are in good standing and hide their disagreements for fear of ostracism. Open differences between members often lead to splits in the church because participation in the church is voluntary.

Club-style churches are not true communities in the biblical sense of the term. Their underlying assumptions prevent them from creating the new life of *koinonia* as a reality.

The Church as Corporation

The second dominant form of social organization in the city is the corporation. This is an institution with a formal organization, specialized professional roles, and bureaucratic management.

Large urban churches often take the shape of a corporation. They have formally organized management with specialized paid professionals. Relationships are based on contract. For those hired by the church, the contracts are formal and can be legally enforced. Promotions and rewards are based on performance and achievement. For the laity contracts are informal. Voluntary service is encouraged but is generally seen as having less value than paid ministries. The laity is the audience or the consumer. There is little participation in what goes on on stage and little personal commitment other than paying to keep the church going. The church is run by specialists.

The primary services offered by many corporate-style churches is entertainment. Regarding televised services, Neil Postman writes,

[R]eligion, like everything else, is presented, quite simply and without apology, as an entertainment. Everything that makes religion an historic, profound and sacred human activity is stripped away; there is no ritual, no dogma, no tradition, no theology, and above all, no sense of spiritual transcendence. On these shows, the preacher is tops. God comes in as second . . . . (1985, 116–17)

Like businesses, this style of church is concerned primarily with what it "has to sell" the public and "how to make it attractive" to the people. It is concerned with planning and building programs, achieving quantitatively measurable goals such as attendance and contributions, increasing efficiency, and managing by objectives. As Peter Berger (1973) and Jacque Ellul (1964) point out, in such cases the concern with technique dominates church life. Os Guinness (1993) points out the great dangers megachurches face as they seek to bear witness to the gospel while adopting many of the trappings of modernity.

Church as Covenant Community

How can the church truly remain the body of Christ in the midst of the urban pressures to reduce everything to economic models and associations based on self-interest?

Clearly the church must avoid acting like a club or a corporation. Rather it must provide a radical alternative—a covenant community in which Christ is the head and the desires of the members are second to the building of the kingdom of God. In one sense the church is a community like other human communities, a living reality fleshed out in the concrete human relationships and experiences of life. In another sense, it is unique because it is a gathering in which God is present and at work (Phil. 1:1–11).

Membership in the church as community is not optional for a Christian. Nor is it based on contracts with the church as a corporate body. It is based on a person's relationship to Jesus Christ. Everyone who is Christ's follower is a member of the church. No one can exclude such a follower from the church on the basis of class, ethnicity, culture, or gender.

The church ultimately does not exist for the well-being of its members. C. Norman Kraus writes, "[The goal of Christianity is not] the self-sufficient individual secure in his victory through Christ enjoying his own private experience of spiritual gifts and emotional satisfaction" (1974, 56). It exists to glorify and obey its Lord. Hauwerwas and Willimon write, "[The church is] a place, clearly visible to the world, in which people are faithful to their promises, love their enemies, tell the truth, honor the poor, suffer for righteousness, and thereby testify to the amazing community-creating power of God" (1989, 46). The church also exists as

God's prophetic voice calling the world to repentance, salvation, and reconciliation.

Because they follow the same Lord, members of the church are committed to each other. The inner bond and essence of life that holds them together is love—the commitment of each member to "be for" the others in self-giving service. This love transcends all social, economic, gender, and racial distinctions that divide human societies (Gal. 3:26–28; Col. 3:10–11). The result is a new family, a new race, a gathering of those who share the same Lord and Spirit and who devote themselves to one another's well-being (Acts 2:42–34). In such a community, members cannot leave when they are dissatisfied. They must learn to live together in harmony, to sacrifice their personal interests for the sake of the body, and to respond to the call of their Master.

Life in the community church is multidimensional. There is no division between spiritual, social, and economic needs. Members minister to one another as whole persons. Moreover, this reciprocity is not based on a quid pro quo. Members contribute according to their gifts and receive according to their needs. There is no calculation of an equality of exchange.

Is it possible for local churches to truly be covenant communities in an urban setting? The early church was and it drew the lonely and lost into its fold. If the church today loses its battle against being a religious club or a corporation, it will be or it is in danger of becoming just another human organization captive to its times. If the church wants to reach the city, it must first be the church in the biblical sense of that term—a place where Christ is in the midst and the Holy Spirit is present in holiness and power.

Church Buildings

One major problem urban churches face is finding suitable facilities for worship and ministry. The high cost of land and construction, particularly in inner-city areas, and the poverty of most Christians around the world make it impossible for them to build a large building and support a fully paid pastor.

One solution is to meet as house churches in the homes of the members. This has been an important solution, particularly in cities where Christians are not allowed to meet openly, such as in parts of China, Bangladesh, Afghanistan, and Saudi Arabia.

House churches are also an answer in other cities, particularly in the early stages of organizing a new congregation. The problem is that house churches tend to be transient. One study of a number of denominations found "that families will not stay with the house church more than two years" (Maroney, Hill, and Finnell 1984, 127).

There are other solutions to the problem of buildings. Congregations in Singapore have bought theaters and converted them into churches. In many cities they buy or rent shops and have store-front churches. Increasingly, several congregations from different language groups share the same building. Despite these creative alternatives, church buildings remain a major problem in cities around the world, and parent churches and missions involved in urban church planting must generally help new congregations find and finance places to meet.

The issue of buildings goes beyond places to meet. In cities, buildings are powerful symbols. It is significant that the tallest and most impressive buildings in most cities are owned by banks, businesses, and insurance companies. Large churches with prominent buildings are public signs of the presence of Christ in the city. However, we do need to be aware of the message they convey. Most appeal to upper- and middle-class people. Some speak of the gospel as an import from the west. We need indigenous but clearly Christian architecture.

Ethnicity and Linguistic Diversity

Ethnicity is a strong force, both in uniting people from the same language and culture and in dividing them from others. What is the proper place of ethnicity in the church?

The sociocultural realities are that people belong to different communities and that they like to associate best with their own kind of people. It is natural for people to wish to associate with others who think, talk, and act in familiar ways. Consequently, they are most easily evangelized by building different churches for each sociocultural group.

But no church can keep people out for not being of the "right" ethnic group. The Bible is clear that the followers of Christ belong to a new people that takes priority over their old worldly identities. If Christians do not learn to live and express their unity, the church will become a part of the world's structures that perpetuate poverty, divisions, hostilities, and wars. Christian growth means that we must challenge our existing sociocultural systems, what the Bible calls *cosmos* (world) and *sarx* (flesh), and be transformed into God's new order.

The urban church may begin by evangelizing different ethnic and class groups, but it must also build bridges of reconciliation and love between them. In many cities, the church is the only body that can bring reconciliation between hostile gangs and ethnic communities.

Reconciliation often begins first with the leaders and pastors, but it must spread to the congregations. Paul writes that the fact that rich and poor, Jew and Gentile, males and females worship together in love and harmony is itself the sign of God's transforming power on earth.

Finally, we must help Christians to mature to the point where they see that their primary identity is Christian, not upper-class, or white, or male. When we truly realize that a Hispanic or an African-American or an Egyptian Christian man or woman is closer to us than our biological brothers and sisters who are not Christians, then we can celebrate our diversities because we know that underneath we are truly one. If, however, our earthly distinctives are our most fundamental identities, we know that no matter how much we enjoy each other's company, we will stand divided when things go wrong.

Poverty and Shattered Dreams

The city is a place of dreams. It attracts the rural poor, the refugees, and the young seeking a better life, and many who come to the city do find a better life. But the city is also a place of shattered dreams. Between one-half and two-thirds of the populations of many cities in the developing world live in slums and squatter settlements. Over three-fourths of the population of Calcutta live in overcrowded housing, with 57 percent of the families living in one room and an estimated one million living on the streets (DuBose 1984a, 55). What is the church's responsibility to these multitudes of urban poor? Clearly, God loves all people, including those who are poor.

The early church saw ministry to the poor as an essential part of its mission. Paul took up an offering for needy Christians in Jerusalem. The medieval urban monastic orders, led by Francis of Assisi, ministered to the destitute. The evangelical church of the nineteenth century began hospitals, schools, orphanages, and homes for the needy. It was the church, not the state, that first took care of those adrift on the margins of society.

America has long had a church of the urban poor. This is seen in the many store-front churches, inner-city missions, and industrial missions. It is also seen in the vital African-American church that has emerged in the cities since World War II. But the urban poor have been marginal to the central stream of American Protestantism, both mainline and evangelical.

For the most part, Protestant churches have failed in their mission to the poor. Viv Grigg (1992) gives a number of reasons for this. One of these is our failure to really see poor people around us. We keep away from the areas of our cities where the needs are greatest. Another is our belief that if economic growth takes place in the city, the poor will rise. With this goes the myth that the poor can improve their condition if only they work harder. Most poor people do work hard and little of any economic expansion trickles down to them.

A third reason Grigg gives for the failure of the North American church to reach the urban poor is spiritual. "A church trapped by cultural perspectives on affluence rather than adopting the biblical stance of opposition to the 'god of mammon' has exported this into missions." In missions we stress identifying with people culturally, but we have not been willing to identify with people in their poverty.

In most cities of the Third World the church is mostly poor. In this sense, we are coming full circle to the apostolic era when most churches and Christians were poor (DuBose 1984a, 70).

Toward a Theology of the Urban Poor

Before the church can effectively minister to the urban poor, it must develop a theological foundation for such ministries. In a word study of the Old Testament, Thomas Hanks concludes: "Oppression is viewed as the basic cause of poverty (164 texts). In the case of the other 15 to 20 causes for poverty indicated in the Old Testament the linguistic link is much less frequent—not more than 20 times" (Grigg 1992, 89). The writers of Scripture do not blame people who are poor for their poverty or see them as inferior and lazy. Rather, they are people whom God loves in a particular way because they have been crushed (Deut. 24:14, 19–22; James 2:1–7; 5:1–6).

A theology of the poor must begin with Christ. His incarnation among the poor, his miracles, and his suffering model for us what our ministries should look like.

This theology must also proclaim the kingdom of God that has invaded the cities of the earth wherever God's people gather to worship him and live together in peace and reconciliation. The kingdom outlines the scope for our ministry, which should include preaching the good news of salvation, healing the sick, feeding the hungry, educating the ignorant, and seeking to transform the structures of society that oppress people and keep them poor (Luke 4:18–19).

The kingdom also determines our attitudes in ministry. We must not serve people who are poor from positions or attitudes of pride and superiority. If we do so, we only add to their oppression. We must be aware that we, too, are sinners and paupers. It is only the grace of God that has transformed us, and we did not deserve that grace any more than others. Nor can we ourselves save the poor. It is God who must do so. We can only share what we have experienced of his deliverance. We must come as paupers, pointing people to God, who can transform their lives. We must join as brothers and sisters those who follow Christ. We need to realize that we have more to learn from people who are poor about faith and dependence on God than we have to offer them by way of material aid.

Ministry among the Poor

Our goal in ministry is not simply to help poor people to meet their daily needs, but to see them transformed by the power of God and empowered to be people of dignity and worth in society. We may need to begin with food, clothing, and shelter, but we must move on to the transformation of people and social structures. If we do not, our ministry can exacerbate the cycle of poverty.

There is no single way to minister among the poor. They are widely diverse in their needs, cultures, and abilities to help themselves. Our ministry must begin by learning to know people and identifying ourselves with them. Then, in partnership with them, answers can be sought to meet their needs. They must have the say in what needs to be done and how to do it, or we keep them powerless and dependent.

How can a church help? In part, the answer depends on the social position of the church. The ministry of affluent churches outside the communities of the poor must be different from that of the churches of poor living in the midst of such communities.

Mobilizing affluent churches

In a sense, the problem of poverty is not so much a problem of the poor but of the rich and powerful. Transformation must begin with a change in the attitudes and actions of prosperous Christians and churches. They must reject the urban environment's tendency to evaluate people by wealth and see, as the Bible does, the dignity and worth of every human being. They must see themselves as members of the same body with their poor sisters and brothers in faith. They must know deep within themselves that sharing is greater than accumulation of wealth and that the well being of others is as important as their own.

How can well-to-do churches serve the poor? Some middle-class churches have felt the particular burden to begin ministries to help feed, educate, and befriend the needy. Downtown churches in increasing numbers open their doors in winter to provide temporary lodging for the homeless. Church agencies have engaged in economic and community development projects.

But the church must go beyond relief and development. It must call people to be transformed by the gospel. Only as people themselves are changed will there be a change in their conditions.

The church must also work to transform the social structures that keep the poor poor. It can begin by establishing cooperatives and lending associations that free poor people from the high prices of shopkeepers who come from outside and from the usurious interest rates of money lenders. It can help squatters to get legal titles to the land on which they live and mediate between them and the police whom they distrust. It can speak out publicly for the rights and dignity of poor people and lobby the government to provide them with water, sewers, and roads. It can work to change structures that oppress.

Roger Greenway points out that there are particular obstacles to helping the homeless (1989, 187). Many of them are transient and live isolated lifestyles. They mark out little circles of space where they guard their meager possessions and are resentful of outsiders who approach them.

Another obstacle is recidivism. Individuals come off the streets, or out of jail, only to "run" after a time of success. The entreaties of old friends and drug pushers and the freedom of street life are appealing when pressures rise. The marginalized live with a sense of failure, and those who minister among them must be willing to live with frustration and disappointment.

Ministry among the homeless cannot be done out of duty. It must be born out of love for people. If we come as saviors to those in need, we provide immediate help, but in the long run we only add to their despair. We need to look them in the eyes and see not their sin and squalor. We must see them as God sees them, created in his image, redeemable and potential saints in eternity. Above all else, we must remember our own broken, sinful state and the redemption we ourselves have found in Christ. Only then will we be willing to share with them as brothers and sisters and not as paternalistic philanthropists.

Our love must be unconditional. Certainly we want people to receive the Good News and become Christians, but we should not use ministry to manipulate people. We must love them even if they reject Christ, just as God continues to love us even when we sin.

Identifying with the poor

Ministry by affluent churches in poor communities is essential, both for the well-being of the poor and the spiritual vitality of the rich. But this is not enough. There need to be teams of Christians who are willing to live and plant churches among the poor. In the Middle Ages, preaching friars and monks planted churches among the poor in the cities of Europe. In more recent years Roman Catholic orders have ministered among the poor and helped them establish base communities. Protestants, too, have begun work in the slums and squatter settlements of the world's great cities (Grigg 1992). The great Japanese Christian Toyohiko Kagawa went to live in the slums of Tokyo and Agnus Lieu serves in the sweatshops of Hong Kong.

It is important that missionaries to the poor go in teams. In many ways missionaries raised in affluent lifestyles find it harder to adjust to living with the poor in their own society than with tribal and peasant people abroad. The shock is even greater when they identify with the poor in Calcutta, Lima, Manila, or other cities where massive poverty exists.

Because the demands on the family are so great in such ministries, some, such as Grigg, recommend that the teams be made up of single people and young couples who delay having children for the sake of ministry. In any case, fully incarnational ministries to people living in poverty are needed.

Church movements among the poor

Church planting teams are not the end of the story. Today churches among the poor are beginning to plant other churches. In Latin America, in particular, poor churches, many of them charismatic, are reaching out to their neighbors and establishing new congregations.

Local leaders are essential to such movements. These churches cannot wait for leaders who have finished formal theological education. Moreover, such education often alienates students from poor communities. The most effective leaders are those who emerge in the context of everyday life and have vision, zeal, and the gifts of organizing and guiding people. Most of them must earn their own living and minister out of their passion for Christ. They need Bible training, but can get it only through personal discipling, night courses, or ongoing seminars.

Many church movements among poor people have been accompanied by an emphasis on God's miracles. People look for visible demonstrations of God's transforming power. A wholistic ministry does not consist of preaching the gospel and dispensing medicine in separate contexts. This only reinforces the western dualism between spirit and matter, evangelism and social concern. Ministry consists of preaching and teaching, praying for the sick, providing medicine, sitting with people to comfort them when they are bereaved, and celebrating with them when they are healed in an integrated fashion. We need to demonstrate the power of prayer and of God's extraordinary healing and provision. All healings are God's healings and are miraculous. Some seem more ordinary than other, but we must expect and affirm them all.

Poor people need dignity and hope. On a daily basis, they are despised by the society in which they live. The sense of power-lessness breeds hopelessness and despair. The church must pro-vide people with a sense of their dignity and power as new creatures in Christ. With this comes hope, joy, and the ability to change conditions.

Finally, it is worth repeating that urban poor Christians have much to offer to rich suburban Christians who have difficulty with spirituality because their lives are too comfortable. Rich churches need to hear the prophetic voices of their poor sisters and broth-ers, and learn again what it means to trust God in the happenings of everyday life.

Dealing with the Urban Worldview

The church must learn to live in the city and speak its language, but it must never sell its soul to the urban worldview. The gospel must be good news to those trapped by the alienation, hedonism, greed, oppression, and poverty of the city. It must challenge the values of the city that destroy people.

Extreme Individualism

The city nurtures individualism. The effects of this are both positive and negative.

On the one hand, the city frees people from the tyranny of small, ingrown communities and of traditions. Hindus, Muslims, and Buddhists are more open to the gospel in urban settings. It is eas-ier there for them to get away from the persecution of relatives and neighbors. (Weak Christians, however, often drop out of the church when they move to the city.)

On the other hand, the stress on individual freedom rather than on group responsibilities cuts people off from enduring relation-ships of kin and community and leaves people alienated in large impersonal institutions. The urban church must continually fight against this extreme individualism that tears down communities of support and accountability. It is hard for an urban church to preach against sin and to discipline its members if they have no loyalty to it and are willing to leave and join another church. The result is a weakening of morality not only in the city but also in the church.

The church must oppose the self-centeredness, materialistic narcissism, and hedonism that thrive in urban settings and are fostered by high mobility. It must also resist the tendency to turn worship into entertainment, fellowship into racism and classism, and service into self-gratifying paternalism.

Human Engineering

The heart of public urban structures is a mechanical view of order (Berger et al. 1973; Ellul 1964; Guinness 1993). The city is the product of human engineering and engineering presupposes that the world is determined by predictable laws of cause and effect. This is what makes planning and human control possible.

Rural people are aware of rains, droughts, plagues, seasons, and other forces beyond their control. City people turn night into day, winter into spring, and bring faraway places into their own neighborhoods via the media. Through science and technology they control diseases, create amazing new products, and gather vast storehouses of knowledge. In such a worldview it is hard to see the place for God. The temptation for city folk is to be self-reliant—to think that with proper knowledge, planning, and effort they can achieve their goals by themselves.

This dependence on human engineering also spreads to the churches, especially upper- and middle-class urban churches. There, long sessions in prayer and waiting for the leading and power of the Holy Spirit are replaced by planning boards, goal setting, strategy sessions, and mobilization of the people. The life of the church becomes a program imposed from outside the Christian, not a vision and life that springs up from within.

Certainly there is a place for planning and human effort, but we must remember that the growth and vitality of the church are not founded on human might, power, planning, or management by objective. They are founded on the Spirit of God. The church is Christ's body, not our human organization. Its life has his life flowing through it, not mere enthusiasm generated by human programs.

This tendency to human engineering is particularly strong in western cities with their modern worldview. They have much to learn from the powerless Christian minorities in cities around the world who have had to learn from experience that all that they have comes from God.

Pluralism

One set of problems urban churches face emerges out of the pluralism of the city. People of many different religions gather here. How can Christians affirm their faith, while working together in the same society with people of other faiths?

One solution is to make one religion dominant and to tolerate other religious communities so long as they do not disturb the majority community or convert others. This is the policy in cities where Muslim law is enforced. There, Christians face a great deal of harassment and are often prohibited from having church buildings. Above all, they are prohibited from evangelizing their neighbors, especially Muslims, on pain of harsh persecution. Many of these Christians have a strong faith forged by suffering.

Another solution is for a nation to declare itself a secular state and to let all people practice their religions so long as they do not violate the public rights and disturb the peace by upsetting people in other religious communities. The question then arises: what effects does this split between public and private spheres of life have on the country and on the church?

The first consequence of establishing a secular government is that morality in the state is reduced to law. There is no sense of sin in the public sphere. Christians must consequently struggle with the tension between the ethics of the gospel and the commonly accepted practices of the society around them. It is hard for the church to take a strong stand against premarital sex, greed, shady political deals, questionable business practices, and materialism. The awareness of sin is eroded and virtue is reduced to doing what is good for one's self. This loss of a sense of sin and morality leads to the rise of crime and evil in the city.

With this loss of a sense of sin comes a loss of the need for repentance and salvation. The church's message often becomes one of developing a sense of self-worth in people and of denying their real guilt and damnation. The gospel becomes a gospel of therapy and healing, not of forgiveness and salvation. The city church must begin by dealing with the felt needs of the people they serve, but it must then move on to their real eternal needs.

A second consequence of the public-private split is the privatization of religion. Religion is rarely discussed in public. People keep their religious beliefs to themselves. Even if local governments don't restrict evangelism, there may be monumental social pressure not to disturb the public peace by trying to convert others. Public witness and evangelistic outreach are often difficult in secular societies.

A third consequence is religious relativism. Living in a secular society, many Christians begin to question whether Christ is the only way to eternal life. They ride to their jobs with Hindus and work with Muslims and Sikhs who are very good people, better than some Christians they know. They wonder what right they have to claim that other religions are false and only theirs is true. They are tempted to maintain their faith at home and to avoid witness in public.

It is helpful to remember that the temptation to relativism comes not because of a flaw in Christianity or its reasonableness. The temptation is a social one, resulting from our own timidity and desire not to antagonize people of other persuasions. Logically, it is not possible for all religions to be true, because they contradict one another. If our religious beliefs are not just private opinions on an unimportant subject, if they are as real as science and far more important, then it is foolish to think that we are being loving in allowing our neighbor to follow any god. We believe deeply that salvation comes through Christ and wish to share that message because we do not want our neighbor to be lost. We may indeed need to work on our tactfulness when living and working in a plural setting, but the message we have should remain strong.

The urban church must allow pluralism in its patterns of organization and worship. It must affirm differences in cultures and social structures. But it must also declare the truth of divine revelation in Jesus Christ that addresses all human needs and judges all human cultures.

The city is a paradox. It is a place of great good. Here are the great culture centers where human thought and creativity find full expression. Here are found many of the great Christian churches, denominational headquarters, mission agencies, seminaries, and colleges. From here the gospel goes out around the world. The city is also a place of great evil. Here secularism, materialism, violence, poverty, and oppression abound.

This paradox reflects human nature—created in the image of God, yet fallen and sinful. It reflects Christ's parable of the wheat and the tares that grow together in the same field awaiting the day of harvest (Matt. 13:25–40). Until that day, the city church faces great opportunities and great dangers. If it is faithful and bold, it can, by God's power, win the cities of the world to Christ. If it sells its soul to the city, it will fail its divine mission.

10   Incarnational Ministries

Bands, tribes, peasant villages, and cities: we have examined four types of human society. These are ideal types—constructs based on a comparison of many societies. We must not reify them or force real societies to fit their categories. No society fully conforms to any one of them. We must study each society we serve in terms of its own organization and not simply fit it into one or another of these types.

Ideal types, however, can help us in missions. First, they help us understand the particular society we serve by giving us categories and methods for the study of human systems and by helping us see things we might miss.

To understand a society we must first seek to understand it as the people themselves do. In other words, we must begin with an emic analysis (Headland, Pike, and Harris 1990). People act on the basis of their perceptions of reality, not of reality itself. If we want to understand their actions, we must know their thoughts.

Emic studies help us to understand the issues involved in contextualization. How do people perceive the missionary? How do they understand the gospel? What theologies do they construct when they read and interpret Scripture in the light of their sociocultural settings? What sins do they struggle with? How does the gospel transform people and their social and cultural systems?

Finally, emic studies help us to understand the worldview and beliefs of the missionary. Too often we are unaware of the categories and basic assumptions about the nature of reality that we bring with us, many of which we have learned not from the Scriptures, but from our culture and history.

Second, ideal types enable us to compare societies and develop general theories of human social and cultural organization. These etic theories offer new insights into human systems by way of comparison. The presence of a trait in one society raises questions of its counterparts in other societies. Etic theories also help us examine questions of our common humanity, cross-cultural communication, universal truth, and morality.

In missions, etic analyses help us understand the Scriptures better. Bible scholars rarely see the cultural biases they bring with them when they study Scriptures. They see the biases of others more clearly than their own. They therefore need Christians from other cultures to point out their biases to them so that they can free themselves from the control of their own cultures. Christians from different cultures studying the Bible together can understand it better than those from only one culture.

Emic and etic analyses complement one another. Etic analyses are built on comparing emic studies. Etic studies raise new questions that require further emic analysis.

History and Social Change

In this book we have taken primarily a synchronic view and focused on the structure of human communities. We looked at social structures and cultural systems and how these shape the way people hear and respond to Scripture. These understandings of both the biblical text and the context of the hearer are crucial to our everyday ministry among the people we serve.

There is a second, and equally important, way to study missions, namely, a diachronic approach that looks at God's work in human history. This approach tells the stories of outreach and of the people and churches transformed by the gospel. History provides us with the big story of missions. Synchronic analysis helps us to understand what happens in history.

Synchronic and diachronic models complement one another. Given our human limitations, when we focus on one, the other is out of focus, on the periphery of our vision. Together they give us binocular vision.

History

We need to say a word about our understanding of history. The four types we have outlined have often been put in anthropological and popular thought into a sequence of complexity and then seen as the evolutionary emergence of human cultures. This theory assumes that less complex societies, such as bands and tribes, represent fossilized remnants of early human societies that have remained largely unchanged over the millennia and that peasant and urban societies emerged out of them more recently through the processes of cultural evolution. This belief in evolution is closely tied to the idea of "progress." We read of the discovery of "stone-age" peoples and "primitive cultures" and equate these with our ancestors before they became civilized—of course, we are among the civilized.

This view of progress influenced missionaries in the nineteenth and twentieth centuries. Many equated Christianity with western civilization. People who heard the gospel often rejected it not because it called them to faith in Christ, but because it meant adopting foreign practices.

As Christians we reject this view that explains history only in terms of cultural evolution. We see history primarily as the arena in which God works out his purposes for humankind. We, therefore, must take history seriously. For us, history originates in God and his divine purpose in creating and redeeming the universe. It begins "in the beginning," and moves toward an end in eternity. It is not the random record of human activities. It has a direction to it.

The hand guiding this history is God's hand. It is he who superintends the overall events and the outcome of history. Within this larger history, God gives us as humans the freedom to act as people created in his image. Consequently, we create cultures and societies. But we have also rebelled against God, and all the cultures and societies we create are disfigured by sin.

In Scripture we see bands and tribes as the first forms of human organization. Adam and Eve and Abraham and Sarah lived in small, kinship-based societies. These were not "primitive" or backward. They made meaningful life possible for countless humans throughout much of history.

Peasant societies emerged as humans began to cultivate the earth and build political centers. This was true of Cain, Babylon, and Egypt. It was true of Israel after the period of the judges. Large urban societies appeared during the reign of Saul, David, and Solomon.

There is an overall movement in human history from smaller, less complex societies to larger, more complex ones, but this movement is not linear. Urban societies, such as the northern and southern kingdoms of Israel and the Roman Empire of Paul's time, collapse. People are forced to rebuild peasant or tribal societies to sustain themselves.

Furthermore, this movement of human history will not lead us to an earthly utopia. No advance in morality parallels the development of complex societies and technologies. The bad news is that evil flourishes in complex societies. The good news is that God is also at work in them, establishing his kingdom through the church and transforming the lives of the people of God.

If, as we affirm, history has a plot, a story to it, it appears that we are approaching its culmination. The world cannot continue long with its current rate of population growth, depletion of natural resources, and urban decay.

The exciting news is that Christ will return to restore righteousness and bounty on earth. The crises of our day should not lead us to despair, but motivate us to greater prayer and obedience in the tasks to which God calls us, knowing that human beings are the focus of God's redemptive work.

Social Change

In the past, there has been a false dichotomy in the west between culture preservationists and advocates of change. The former, many of them anthropologists seeking to respect and protect local cultures, saw all change as bad. They condemned missionaries and others seeking to change other peoples' cultures. The latter, many of them missionaries, sought to offer people salvation and a better way of life.

While secular scholars do not recognize the hand of God in history, they are increasingly recognizing the fact that change is essential for any society to survive. Some even admit that Christianity has been the best bridge whereby traditional societies can enter the modern world while retaining their cultural identities (Mead 1956).

Missionaries are learning to respect local cultures when they bring the gospel. Not all changes are good. Modern technology can improve some areas of human life, but often at a great cost—broken communities and alienated individuals. Our task is to share the gospel, not import our cultural ways.

Anthropology and Missiology

How can we incorporate the insights of anthropology in our missionary task without losing sight of the gospel? Many involved in missions are discovering the power of social science analysis. They believe that if they understand sociocultural realities such as corporate decision-making, receptivity, and good cross-cultural communication and if they "do it right," they can lead multitudes to Christ. This view presupposes that missions is what we as humans do for God and that the people we serve are controlled by social and cultural forces beyond their control. Both of these assumptions are false.

There is a danger in missions today of replacing the biblical foundations of missions with the social sciences. As we use the assumptions and categories of modern science, we can easily become captive to them. How can we draw on the insights of anthropology without subverting the divine nature of the missionary task?

The Text

Before we address this question, we must look again at the foundations of Christian mission. The vision and motivation for missions is rooted in the history recorded in the Scriptures, not in our human desire to help others. Missions is first God reaching down to save humans from sin and its consequences and restoring them to perfect life in fellowship with him. It is God establishing his kingdom on earth as it now is in heaven. In this mission, God calls us, his disciples, to proclaim and live his gospel throughout the earth.

If the source of missions is God, our understanding of that mission must be based on the assumptions and categories of a biblical worldview, not those of the social sciences. We begin with the fact that all humans were created perfect, in the image of God, that they sinned, individually and corporately, and are under the judgment of death, that God came in the person of Jesus to die to save them, and that those who follow him have eternal life. This new life transforms not only Christ's followers, but also gives rise to the church. Hauwerwas and Willimon write, "The confessing church seeks the **visible** church, a place clearly visible to the world, in which people are faithful to their promises, love their enemies, tell the truth, honor the poor, suffer for righteousness, and thereby testify to the amazing community-creating power of God" (1989, 46). The church is God's prophetic voice to the world, calling it to repentance, salvation, and reconciliation.

These truths are based not on human discovery, but on divine revelation, disclosed in the words and works of God in history, manifest supremely in the person of Jesus Christ, and recorded in Scriptures. They are the text of missions. They are the message we preach and the power of God unto salvation.

Our understanding of the gospel must emerge out of a careful study of the Scriptures. We may use different methods in doing so. We may use philosophical reflection, historical analysis, and social science examination, because each of these can contribute to our understanding.

There are two dangers in studying the Bible. The first is to equate our understanding of the Bible with the Bible itself. All of us begin by reading the Bible in terms of our own worldview, its categories, and its assumptions about reality. We must recognize that our understanding of Scripture is always partial and biased. This does not mean that we cannot know biblical truth. We may see through a glass darkly, but we do see. The more we are aware of our own cultural biases and the more we read the Scripture and let its categories and assumptions shape our thinking, the closer we come to understanding its full truth.

The Scriptures are our foundation in mission and we must be willing to look at them in fresh ways. We must also encourage young converts to study the Bible for themselves and formulate their own theological understandings of it, flawed as these are by their cultural biases. Then together with them we must form a hermeneutical community in which we listen and share our insights, correcting one another's biases and seeking together to understand and follow the Scripture more fully.

The second danger is more subtle. It is to let the methods of our study limit our understandings of the biblical text. When we use the rational, systematic approaches of philosophy we gain certain insights into Scripture, but we lose sight of other truths. Similarly, the methods of history and science can help us see some truths, but blind us to others. These approaches are complementary. We need all of them to gain a fuller understanding of the text.

Finally, the gospel is not simply a message we need to understand. It is a command we must obey. Only when we ourselves are transformed by the gospel does it give birth to missions in our lives.

The Context

Mission is more than a text. It must take flesh in human contexts. We must make the gospel known not to humans in general, but to real people who live in particular times and places in history, who are members of real societies and who share common languages and cultures.

How can we learn to know these contexts—the languages people speak, the social systems in which they live, the cultures and worldviews that shape the way they see reality? Here the social sciences can help us. Anthropology and sociology help us study people's social and cultural contexts by living with people, observing them, and listening to what they say. Psychology helps us examine people's personal contexts—their deep emotions and inner conflicts. History gives us insight into the events that have shaped their present.

The social sciences can also help us understand human change—the factors that influence people's response to the gospel, the methods of evangelism most appropriate in a particular society, and the effects of conversion on the lives and beliefs of new Christians.

These sciences can also help us understand young churches and the problems they face living as God's community in a fallen world. How are they responding to the beliefs in spirits, ancestors, magic, witchcraft, and divination of their surrounding culture? How are they dealing with social oppression and corporate injustices?

Finally, the social sciences can help us understand ourselves and our own contexts better and the ways in which these shape our study of Scripture and our missions. Too often we equate Christianity with our particular understandings of it and make the gospel captive to our culture. When we see our own cultural biases, we are freed to see the radical, transforming nature of the gospel in new ways.

Contextualized Ministry

In mission we must go beyond understanding the divine text and human contexts. We must proclaim divine revelation to people in their diverse settings.

Here the incarnation is our model. Just as the infinite Creator became incarnate as a human to reach finite people, so the divine revelation must take flesh in human languages and cultures. Just as Christ chose to live in a particular time and setting, so we must incarnate our ministry in the contexts of the people we serve.

Some refer to this embodiment of the universal gospel in particular human settings as "contextualization," others as "inculturation" (Shorter 1988). Both refer to more than a simple translation of the gospel into different languages and cultures in the way that one translates a history book or a science text. Rather, they point to the embodiment of the living Word in human cultural and social settings in such a way that its divine nature and power are not lost. True contextualization is more than communication. It is God working in the hearts of people, making them new and forming them into a new community. It is his Word transforming their lives, their societies, and their cultures.

There are dangers in contextualization. If we overcontextualize the gospel, we make it captive to the local culture. It loses its divine character and becomes human ideas about God, not God living, acting, and revealing himself in their midst. The result is Christopaganism. If we do not contextualize the gospel, but proclaim it in our language and live it in our cultural forms, the people cannot understand it, or reject it as a foreign culture. Inculturation takes place when the gospel and the messenger become a part of the life of a community.

Social Contextualization

The incarnation serves as our model in human relationships. First, as missionaries it means we must identify ourselves with the people we serve. We must live among them, learn their language, adopt cultural ways, and work alongside them. Becoming one with people enables us to build trust and earn the right to be heard.

But Christ remained fully God even when he became fully human. Missionaries, too, are to reflect this. They are both sociocultural insiders and outsiders. They must be insiders to be heard and trusted, but they must also be messengers sent by Christ to announce his salvation and his kingdom. They are representatives of the new transformed humanity Christ is bringing to life on earth.

The inculturation of the gospel must take place not only in the life of the missionary, but also in the church. Too often in the past we have planted churches dependent on foreign personnel and finances and patterned on foreign models of organization. We now know that for these churches to mature, they must become equal partners in mission. For this to happen, the churches must be organized in ways understood by the people.

Recently there has been a growing awareness that the ways churches are organized must also be adapted to the local social order. For example, leadership styles in the church must take into account the ways leaders operate in the society. In societies where decisions are based on social consensus, the church will stress harmony and accord. In democratic societies, voting is often used in the church to determine actions. If we introduce voting in societies where it is not found, confusion results. We must contextualize not only the gospel, but also our church polity.

Cultural Contextualization

Contextualization of the message must also take place on the cultural level. We must begin by learning to speak the language well so that we can communicate the gospel in the thought forms of the people we serve. If we do not, we risk talking past people by using categories that make no sense to them.

We must translate the Bible into local languages. Just as Christ remained fully God when he took human form, so the Scripture remains divine revelation even when it is written in different languages. As Lamin Sanneh points out (1993), no other act of the missionary empowers people and dignifies their culture more than Bible translation. It takes people seriously and says to them that God speaks their language.

Translation is no easy task. It is not replacing the words of one language with those of another. Languages give expression to the thought categories, beliefs, and worldviews of people. The translator must deal with the deeper meanings of languages or the message will be grossly distorted.

Contextualization must go further. Christians must find symbols and cultural forms they understand and appreciate to express their new faith. This involves adaptation of dress, architectural forms, worship forms, marriages, funeral rites, and songs. Songs, in fact, are one good measure of the extent to which people have made the gospel their own. Many sing foreign hymns translated into their language. For them the gospel is often something they have added onto their lives. Others, out of their living experiences with Christ, write songs from the core of their being.

The message of the gospel must be communicated in ways that people comprehend. Among the nonliterate, stories, rituals and dramas are effective means of communication. Among the literate, tracts, pamphlets, and other written forms can be used.

The thought categories and analogies used to communicate the gospel must also be understood by people (Nida and Reyburn 1981). Their understanding of gods, humans, sin, sacrifice, resurrection, salvation, and other key terms are often different from the meanings these have in Scripture. It is important to help the church leaders compare the meanings of these both in their culture and in Scripture so that they can help new Christians grow in their knowledge of the gospel.

People must learn to do theology. Much of their theological reflections will relate to the issues they face in life. We have seen that tribals face questions of ancestors, spirits, magic, and polygamy; peasants struggle with ethnic and class hostilities and social injustice; and urban people must deal with secularism, alienation, and self-centeredness. They all must learn that the gospel addresses their specific questions.

Finally, contextualization deals with the worldviews that shape peoples' beliefs and allegiances. It is easy to overlook this level of contextualization because worldviews are largely invisible, even to people themselves. If we communicate the gospel only on the level of explicit beliefs, in time the unconverted worldview will capture the meanings of the words and distort the message.

There is a tension underlying all efforts at contextualization. We proclaim a divine message, but it must be expressed in human languages and cultures. We are committed to a universal message, but we must minister to people in their local contexts. There are dangers in contextualization, but there are also great opportunities for the gospel to take flesh in the lives of human beings.

The Incarnate Christ

Finally, by "incarnational ministry" we mean that mission is first and foremost the work of God. The incarnation of the missionary, the message, and the church are meaningless if God is not present in the missionary endeavor. We must become incarnate because God himself is already incarnate among people before we arrive, preparing their hearts to hear God's Word, revealing that Word to them by the work of the Holy Spirit, and transforming them through the power of the cross.

Transformation

The goal of incarnational ministry is not that people understand the gospel. It is that they respond to God's invitation and are transformed by his power. They become new creatures through Christ and members of a new community, the church.

Transformation of Individuals

On one level, transformation is personal. In Christ, people become new creatures. As Paul points out, their lives should reflect the presence and power of the Holy Spirit, making them holy and Christ-like in character.

Transformation is both turning around and moving toward a new center (Hiebert 1994). Evangelism and Christian growth are parts of the same process. Evangelism calls people to turn from their idols and evil ways to Christ. At first there may be no dramatic change in their everyday lives but because they are in Christ, they are new creatures.

The motivations for conversion will differ greatly from person to person. Some come because they are convinced of the truth of the gospel, others because they experience love and fellowship in the church, and others because Christ has healed their spirits or bodies. Whatever their reason, they are now followers of Christ.

But transformation must go beyond turning around. It must lead to change in a person's whole life. People come with their sins and scars and we must begin with them where they are and gently lead them to maturity. But this means we must also define Christian maturity, for this describes our goals in faith and life.

Evangelizing and discipling. We need them both. The first without the second leads to weak, immature churches poorly grounded in faith. The second without the first leads to ingrown, pharisaical churches that die in their self-centeredness.

Transformation of Structures

On another level, transformation must be corporate. Christian conversion is not confined to the private, personal areas of peoples' lives. It transforms them, and through them the systems of which they are a part.

In this transformation, we use the text of divine revelation to judge human contexts. We are often tempted to judge other cultures and societies by comparing them with our own forms of Christian expression. This is cultural arrogance. We must rather evaluate them by the standards of the gospel and the kingdom of God. Where there is ill treatment of one group by another in the larger society, the church must be a voice calling for shalom (peace with both justice and love), protecting and caring for those in need.

Corporate transformation must begin in the church. It is the outpost of God's reign on earth. It must manifest the social order of the kingdom of God, which is based on love, reconciliation, servanthood, and submission to Christ.

The explicit beliefs and underlying worldview of the church must both be transformed to fit those in Scripture. If new converts learn Christian teaching, but continue to think in terms of the underlying categories and assumptions of their old worldview, the gospel will be subverted. In an animistic society, for example, Christian prayer is often seen as a new, stronger magic that enables people to command greater powers than they could with their old magic.

Both the social and cultural structures of the church must be transformed if it is to survive. A church that operates by biblical principles but that does not hold to an orthodox theology will lose its Christian moorings. It is living on the memories of the Christian faith of its forebearers. A church that has orthodox teachings but lives like the world denies the reality of the gospel. The vital continuity and expansion of Christianity require both a true gospel and a transformed church. The gospel gives life to the church, and the church proclaims the gospel. Either without the other soon dies.

Transformation of the Missionary

In missions, transformation takes place not only in the lives of the new converts, but also in the life of the missionary. If we go believing that we have much to teach but nothing to learn, we deny the divine nature of our task. We come to believe that it is we who convict and transform people through our efforts and forget that mission is God at work in human hearts and we are instruments of his work. We also believe that we are the priests and do not trust the work of the Holy Spirit in the lives of new believers.

As missionaries we have much to learn from the vital faith of new converts in other cultures. We come with our own cultural biases that distort our understanding of the gospel. As we read the Scriptures with our Christian sisters and brothers in other cultures, we see its truths through new eyes. We are in danger of seeing Christianity as ordinary and routine, or of professionalizing it. They remind us of the love and excitement of newfound faith. In incarnational ministry our lives are transformed as much as are those of the people we serve.

Notes

Chapter 1

1. One exception is the Nayar society of Kerala, South India. In the past, Nayar women had sexual relationships with Brahmin men from the highest caste, but could not marry them. The women formed households with their brothers, who helped them rear their children.

2. People do not have to like the leaders or agree with what they are doing to consider them legitimate. As long as people believe that these leaders should be in power, or at least are not willing to make the effort to depose them, the leaders will have enough legitimacy to rule. Not all Americans like the president of the U.S. or his policies, but they probably do consider him the legitimate leader of the U.S.

3. We are following the semiotics of Charles Peirce (*Philosophical Writings of Peirce*, 1955).

4. This model is based on a general theory of human systems developed at a seminar at Harvard University attended by leading sociologists, psychologists, and anthropologists. The proceedings were edited by Talcott Parsons and Edward Shils under the title, *A General Theory of Human Behavior* (Cambridge: Harvard University Press, 1952).

5. This point can be seen in the fact that people, when they disagree about what to do, often argue not about the proper course of action, but about the definition of the situation. For instance, Americans all agree that a child should not be allowed to "talk back." But if parents disagree, it will be over whether what Janie said was talking back or not! If the parents agree on the definition of the situation (i.e., it was talking back), the course of action will naturally follow—send Janie to her room.

6. The term *ethnic group* does not serve the purpose because it refers not only to tribes, but also to castes in societies such as India and to ethnic communities in urban settings. The term *primal* society is even more strongly associated with notions of early, primitive, and simple. The

real problem is not the word *tribe,* but the word *modern,* for this implies the superiority of contemporary societies over all other types of human organization.

Chapter 2

1. In one case, a couple working for a Christian development agency in the Kalahari Desert spent four years digging a well to provide the !Kung with water. As soon as the well was dug, the local wealthy ranchers appropriated it for their cattle. It took several more years of work with the Botswana court system for the couple to return the well to its original owners.

2. Modern bands practice a number of types of contraception, including herbal contraception, a long postpartum sex tabu, abortions, and infanticide.

Chapter 3

1. For an excellent analysis of sin as broken relationships in the Bible, and its use in witnessing to societies with a strong group orientation, see C. Norman Kraus, *God Our Savior* (Scottdale, Penn.: Herald, 1990).

Chapter 4

1. An exception is the Iau people of Irian Jaya, who forbid coming to a brother's aid in a dispute so as to avoid an escalation of the conflict. Those who do are punished.

2. A brief look into the history of that dispute demonstrates that some of the principles of tribalism are not absent from our society. The feud between the Hatfields and McCoys soon involved neighboring families, then caused friction between the states of Kentucky and West Virginia, and finally, in 1888, managed to divide the Supreme Court! See the *Encyclopaedia Britannica,* 15th ed., 1987, 5:746.

3. For an excellent description of the dynamics of witchcraft see Anthony J. Gittins, *Bread for the Journey* (Maryknoll, N.Y.: Orbis, 1993), chap. 7.

4. A good example is *The Nuer,* by E. E. Evans-Pritchard. Evans-Pritchard was sent by the British to study the Nuer, who are a pastoral group in the Sudan, in order to assist the government in quelling a political uprising.

5. See *Encyclopaedia Britannica,* 1987, 6:886.

6. For a full description of the effect of International Monetary Fund policies on the creation of poverty, see George (1990).

7. These cults, known as cargo cults, were so named because their prophets taught the return of ancestors or foreigners bearing enormous

wealth for the poor and powerless Melanesians. Members of the cults destroyed their own possessions, moved to the tops of mountains to await the arrival of the cargo planes, and even built runways for them.

8. Of course, especially during colonialism, missionaries also cooperated with unjust authorities, sometimes out of misguided views of what was best for local people. Their mistakes are reminders to us not to confuse God's views on what is valuable or just with the views of a human government.

Chapter 5

1. For an excellent discussion of roles and identification with tribal peoples see Jacob A. Loewen, *Culture and Human Values: Christian Intervention in Anthropological Perspective* (Pasadena: William Carey Library, 1975).

2. This becomes obvious if one listens carefully to most Sunday morning sermons and seminary classes. We like to discuss general principles and leave the application to the listener. Unfortunately, few listeners apply the sermon lessons concretely to their everyday lives.

Chapter 6

1. In India, for instance, Mahatma Gandhi, who understood these principles well, incorporated symbolic attempts to manufacture as part of his independence movement. He openly encouraged illegal textile weaving (a previously thriving Indian cottage industry that the British had crushed) and led a march to the sea where he refined salt, also an illegal act.

2. This description of Wallerstein's work is derived from Roseberry (1989).

3. This is one of the ironies of the market system: when demand falls, causing prices to fall, producers may increase their output to meet their own cash needs. The result is a further decline in price, due to the glut on the market. Eventually producers will be forced to take up another commodity, but the suffering, in human terms, involved in the switch may be intense.

4. The peasants' belief was that the rat-god had initially given them rice for their subsistence. Thus, they thought it important to allow the rats to take what they needed. With the older variety of rice, this practice had not amounted to much loss, but with the new variety, it was devastating to the crops. Still, killing the rats would have been tantamount to killing the initial source of all their food.

Chapter 8

1. It is, perhaps, necessary to remember that without the specialization made possible by the market, we, the authors, would not be sitting at computers writing this text, and you, the readers, might not be able to contemplate full-time missionary work. All of us would be in the fields during the day and would be restricted to engaging in other activities after hours.

2. Tony Campolo, a Christian speaker and writer, suggests that if people do not want to be regulated they should stop acting as if they need regulation.

References Cited

General Bibliography

Bakke, Raymond J. 1984. Evangelization of the world's cities. In *An Urban World: Churches Face the Future*, edited by Larry L. Rose and C. Kirk Hadaway, 75–93. Nashville: Broadman.

Barth, Fredrik. 1963. *The Role of the Entrepreneur in Social Change in Northern Norway.* Bergen: Scandinavian University Books.

Bellah, Robert N., and Phillip Hammond. 1981. *Varieties of Civil Religion.* New York: Harper and Row.

Bellah, Robert N. et al. 1985. *Habits of the Heart: Individualism and Commitment in American Life.* Berkeley: University of California Press.

Berger, Peter L., Brigitte Berger, and Hansfried Kellner. 1973. *The Homeless Mind: Modernization and Consciousness.* New York: Random House.

Bierstedt, Robert. 1970. *The Social Order.* 3d ed. New York: McGraw Hill.

Bonk, Jon. 1980. All things to all persons: The missionary as a racist-imperialist. *Missiology* 8: 285–306.

Buakasa, Tulu K. M. 1986. The African tradition of sharing. *Ecumenical Review* 38: 386–93.

Chaianov, A. V. 1931. The socio-economic nature of peasant farm economy. In *A Systematic Source Book in Rural Sociology,* edited by Pitirim A. Porokin, Carle C. Zimmerman, and Charles J. Galpin. Minneapolis: The University of Minnesota Press.

Christaller, Walter. 1966. *Central Places in Southern Germany.* London: Edward Arnold.

Codrington, Robert H. 1969. *The Melanesians: Studies in Their Anthropology and Folklore.* Oxford: Clarendon. Originally published in 1891.

381

Colson, Elizabeth. 1974. *Tradition and Contract: The Problem of Order.* Chicago: Aldine.

Conklin, Harold C. 1961. The study of shifting cultivation. *Current Anthropology* 2: 27–61.

Conn, Harvie M. 1987. *A Clarified Vision for Urban Mission.* Grand Rapids: Zondervan.

Cox, Harvey. 1965. *The Secular City: Secularization and Urbanization in Theological Perspective.* New York: Macmillan.

DuBose, Francis M. 1978. *How Churches Grow in an Urban World.* Nashville: Broadman.

Dye, T. Wayne. 1976. Toward a cultural definition of sin. *Missiology* 4:26–41.

Dyrness, William A. 1990. *Learning about Theology from the Third World.* Grand Rapids: Zondervan, Academie Books.

Ellul, Jacques. 1970. *The Meaning of the City.* Grand Rapids: Eerdmans.

Evans-Pritchard, E. E. 1937. *Witchcraft, Oracles and Magic among the Azande.* Oxford: Clarendon.

———. 1940. *The Nuer.* New York: Oxford University Press.

Ewert, D. Merrill, Peter Clark, and Paul Eberts. 1993. Worldview and sustainable community development. Paper presented at the annual conference of the Association of Evangelical Relief and Development Agencies, Lindale, Texas.

Filbeck, David. 1985. *Social Context and Proclamation: A Socio-Cognitive Study in Proclaiming the Gospel Cross-Culturally.* Pasadena: William Carey Library.

Fischer, Claude S. 1984. *The Urban Experience.* 2d ed. San Diego: Harcourt Brace Jovanovich.

Foster, George M. 1965. Peasant society and the image of the limited good. *American Anthropologist* 67: 293–315.

Friedl, John. 1981. *The Human Portrait.* Englewood Cliffs, N.J.: Prentice-Hall.

Geertz, Clifford. 1963. *Agricultural Involution: The Processes of Ecological Change in Indonesia.* Berkeley and Los Angeles: University of California Press.

___. 1973. *The Interpretation of Cultures.* New York: Basic Books.

___. 1979. Religion as a cultural system. In *Reader in Comparative Religion: An Anthropological Approach,* 4th ed., edited by W. A. Lessa and E. Z. Vogt, 78–89. New York: Harper and Row.

George, Susan. 1990. *A Fate Worse Than Debt: The World Financial Crisis and the Poor.* New York: Grove Weidenfeld.

Gittins, Anthony J. 1993. *Bread for the Journey.* Maryknoll, N.Y.: Orbis.

Goba, Boganjolo. 1974. Corporate personality: Ancient Israel and Africa. In *The Challenge of Black Theology,* edited by B. Moore. Ann Arbor: University Microfilm.

Greenway, Roger S. 1992. *Discipling the City: A Comprehensive Approach to Urban Mission.* Grand Rapids: Baker.

Grigg, Viv. 1992. *Cry of the Urban Poor.* Monrovia: MARC.

Guinness, Os. 1993. *Dining with the Devil: The Megachurch Movement Flirts with Modernity.* Grand Rapids: Baker.

Hannerz, Ulf. 1980. *Exploring the City: Inquires Toward an Urban Anthropology.* New York: Columbia University Press.

Hastey, Ervin E. 1984. Reaching the cities first: A biblical model of world evangelization. In *An Urban World: Churches Face the Future,* edited by Larry L. Rose and C. Kirk Hadaway, 147–65.

Hauerwas, Stanley, and William H. Willimon. 1989. *Resident Aliens: Life in the Christian Colony.* Nashville: Abingdon.

Headland, Thomas N., Kenneth Pike, and Marvin Harris, eds. 1990. *Emics and Etics: The Insider/Outsider Debate.* Newbury Park, Calif.: Sage.

d'Hertefelt, Marcel. 1965. The Rwanda of Rwanda. In *Peoples of Africa,* edited by James L. Gibbs, 407–40. New York: Holt, Rinehart and Winston.

Hiebert, Paul G. 1971. *Konduru: Structure and Integration in a South Indian Village.* Minneapolis: University of Minnesota Press.

———. 1994. *Anthropological Reflections on Missiological Issues.* Grand Rapids: Baker.

———. 1987. Critical contextualization. *International Bulletin* 11:104–12.

Hiebert, Paul G., and Young Hertig. 1993. Asian immigrants in American cities. *Urban Mission* 10: 15–24.

Hminga, Chhangte Lal. 1987. *The Life and Witness of the Churches in Mizoram.* Serkwan, Mizoram: Baptist Church of Mizoram.

Hobsbawm, E. J. 1959. *Primitive Rebels: Studies in Archaic Forms of Social Movement in the 19th and 20th Centuries.* Manchester: Manchester University Press.

Hoffer, Carol. 1974. Madam Yoko. In *Women, Culture and Society,* edited by Michelle Zimbalist Rosaldo and Louise Lamphere, 173–87. Palo Alto: Stanford University Press.

Hrangkhuma, F. 1989. *Mizoram Transformational Change: A Study of the Processes and Nature of Mizo Culture Change and Factors that Contributed to the Change.* Unpublished dissertation. Pasadena: Fuller Theological Seminary.

Keysser, Christian. 1980. *A People Reborn.* Alfred Allin and John Kuder, translators. Pasadena: William Carey Library. First published in 1929.

Kottack, Conrad. 1994. *Cultural Anthropology.* 6th ed. New York: McGraw Hill.

Kraft, Charles. 1979. *Christianity in Culture.* Maryknoll, N.Y.: Orbis.

Kraus, C. Norman. 1974. *The Community of the Spirit.* Grand Rapids: Eerdmans.

Lewis, Oscar. 1961. *The Children of Sanchez.* New York: Random House.

Lipton, Michael. 1988. Why poor people stay poor: Urban bias in world development. In *The Urbanization of the Third World,* edited by Josef Gugler, 40–51. Oxford: University Press.

Loewen, Jacob A. 1975. *Culture and Human Values: Christian Intervention in Anthropological Perspective.* Pasadena: William Carey Library.

————. 1989. Personal communication.

Lomnitz, Larissa. 1988. The social and economic organization of a Mexican shanty town. In *The Urbanization of the Third World,* edited by Josef Gugler, 328–37. Oxford: Oxford University Press.

Luria, A. R. 1976. *Cognitive Development: Its Cultural and Social Foundations.* Cambridge: Harvard University Press.

Malinowski, Bronislaw. 1954. *Magic, Science, and Religion and Other Essays.* New York: Doubleday. Originally published in 1925.

Maroney, Jimmy, Ronald Hill, and David Finnell. 1984. Urban ministry in Third World cities: Three examples. In *An Urban World: Churches Face the Future,* edited by Larry L. Rose and C. Kirk Hadaway, 117–45. Nashville: Broadman.

Marshall, Lorna. 1961. Sharing, talking and giving: Relief of social tensions among the !Kung Bushmen. *Africa* 31: 231–49.

Marty, Martin. 1991. Unpublished lecture given at the Evangelical Missiology meetings. Moody Bible Institute.

Mbiti, John. 1969. *African Religions and Philosophy.* New York: Praeger.

McConnell, C. Douglas. 1990. *Networks and Associations in Urban Mission: A Port Morseby Case Study.* Ph.D. dissertation. Pasadena: Fuller Theological Seminary.

Mead, Margaret. 1956. *New Lives for Old.* New York: Mentor.

Melbin, Murray. 1978. Night as frontier. *American Sociological Review* 43: 3–22.

Minturn, Leigh, and John T. Hitchcock. 1966. *The Rajputs of Khalapur, India.* Six Cultures series, vol. 3. New York: John Wiley and Sons.

Mullins, Mark. 1987. The life-cycle of ethnic churches in sociological perspective. *Japanese Journal of Religious Studies* 14: 321–34.

Neill, Stephen. 1961. *Christian Faith and Other Faiths.* London: Oxford.

Newbigin, Lesslie. 1989. *The Gospel in a Pluralist Society.* Grand Rapids: Eerdmans.

Nida, Eugene, and William Reyburn. 1981. *Meaning Across Culture.* Maryknoll, N.Y.: Orbis.

Ong, W. J. 1969. World as view and world as event. *American Anthropologist* 71:634–47.

Parsons, Talcott, and Edward Shils, eds. 1952. *Toward a General Theory of Action*. Cambridge: Harvard University Press.

Peirce, Charles S. 1955. *Philosophical Writings of Peirce*. Edited by Justus Buchler. New York: Dover.

Pfeiffer, John E. 1977. *The Emergence of Society*. New York: McGraw-Hill.

Polanyi, Karl. 1957. *The Great Transformation*. Boston: Beacon.

Postman, Neil. 1985. *Amusing Ourselves to Death: Public Discourse in the Age of Show Business*. New York: Viking.

Radin, Paul. 1957. *Primitive Man as Philosopher*. New York: Dover.

Reyburn, William D. 1978. Polygamy, economy, and Christianity in the East Camoroun. In *Readings in Missionary Anthropology II*, edited by William A. Smalley, 255–73. South Pasadena: William Carey Library.

Richardson, Don. 1978. *Peace Child*. Glendale, Calif.: Regal.

———. 1981. *Eternity in Their Hearts*. Ventura, Calif.: Regal.

Sahlins, Marshall D. 1968. *Tribesmen*. Englewood Cliffs, N.J.: Prentice-Hall.

Sanneh, Lamin. 1993. *Encountering the West. Christianity and the Global Cultural Process: The African Dimension*. Maryknoll, N.Y.: Orbis.

Sharp, Lauriston. 1952. Steel axes for stone age Australians. *Human Organization* 11:17–22.

Shenk, Wilbert. 1980. The changing role of the missionary: From "Civilization" to Contextualization. In *Missions, Evangelism and Church Growth*, edited by C. Norman Kraus, 33–59. Scottdale, Penn.: Herald.

Shorter, Aylward. 1988. *Toward a Theology of Inculturation*. Maryknoll, N.Y.: Orbis.

Smith, Donald K. 1992. *Creating Understanding: A Handbook for Christian Communication Across Cultural Landscapes*. Grand Rapids: Baker.

Taber, Charles R. 1978. The limits of indigenization in theology. *Missiology* 6: 53–79.

Taylor, John V. 1958. *The Growth of the Church in Buganda*. London: Greenwood.

Tippett, Alan R. 1971. *People Movements in Southern Polynesia*. Chicago: Moody.

Tournier, Paul. 1978. *The Violence Within*. New York: Harper and Row.

Turnbull, Colin, M. 1962. *The Lonely African*. New York: Simon and Schuster.

Turner, Harold. 1981. Religious movements in primal (or tribal) societies. *Mission Focus* 9: 45–55.

van Gennup, Arnold. 1960. *The Rites of Passage*. Chicago: University of Chicago Press.

Wallace, A. F. C. 1956. Revitalization movements. *American Anthropologist* 58:264–81.

Wallerstein, Immanuel. 1979. *The Capitalist World Economy.* New York: Cambridge University Press.

Warner, W. Lloyd, and Paul S. Lunt. 1941. *The Social Life of a Modern Community.* New Haven: Yale University Press.

———. 1960. *Social Class in America.* New York: Harper and Row.

Weiss, Michael J. 1988. *The Clustering of America.* New York: Harper and Row.

Wolf, Eric R. 1955. Types of Latin American peasantry. *American Anthropologist* 57:452–71.

Yinger, J. M. 1970. *The Scientific Study of Religion.* Toronto: Collier-Macmillan.

Bibliography on Band Societies

Balikci, Asen. 1970. *The Natsilik Eskimo.* Garden City, N.Y.: Natural History Press.

Briggs, Jean L. 1970. *Never in Anger: Portrait of an Eskimo Family.* Cambridge: Harvard University Press.

Cashdan, Elizabeth. 1989. Hunters and gatherers: Economic behavior in bands. In *Economic Anthropology,* edited by Stuart Plattner. Stanford: Stanford University Press.

Durkheim, E. 1915. *The Elementary Forms of the Religious Life.* London: George Allen and Unwin.

Dyson-Hudson, Rada, and Nevill Dyson-Hudson. 1980. Nomadic pastoralism. *Annual Review of Anthropology* 9: 15–61.

Galaty, John, ed. 1981. *The Future of Pastoral Peoples.* Ottawa: International Development Research Centre.

Grinker, Roy R. 1990. Images of denigration: Structuring inequality between foragers and farmers in the Ituri Forest. *American Ethnologist* 17 (February): 111–30.

Hart, C. W. M., Arnold Pilling, and Jane Goodale. 1988. *The Tiwi of North Australia.* New York: Holt, Rinehart and Winston.

Kroeber, Theodora. 1961. *Ishi in Two Worlds: A Biography of the Last Wild Indians in North America.* Los Angeles: University of California Press.

Lee, Richard B., and Irven DeVore. 1976. *Kalahiri hunter-gatherers: Studies of the !Kung San and Their Neighbors.* Cambridge: Harvard University Press.

Lee, Richard B. 1969. Eating Christmas in the Kalahari. *Natural History.* December.

Lewis, Henry T. 1989. Ecological and technological knowledge of fire: Aborigines versus park rangers in Northern Australia. *American Anthropologist* 81: 940–61.

Nietschmann, Bernard. 1994. Subsistence and market: When the turtle collapses. In *Conformity and Conflict,* edited by James P. Spradley and David W. McCurdy. New York: HarperCollins.

Ridington, Robin. 1988. Knowledge, power and the individual in subarctic hunting societies. *American Anthropologist* 90: 98–110.

Testart, Alain. 1988. Some major problems in the social anthropology of hunter-gatherers. *Current Anthropology* 29:1–15.

Thomas, Elizabeth M. 1959. *The Harmless People.* New York: Knopf.

Turnbull, Colin. 1972. *The Forest People: A Study of the Pygmies of the Congo.* New York: Simon and Schuster.

———. 1962. *The Mountain People.* New York: Simon and Schuster.

Bibliography on the Church in Band Societies

Buswell, James, III. 1985. A "people movement" among the Florida Seminoles. *International Journal of Frontier Missions* 2 (July): 267–82.

Ebert, Daniel J., III. 1963. Establishing indigenous churches among aboriginal people. *Practical Anthropology* 10: 34–38.

Engel, Frank G. 1970. Australia: Its aborigines and its mission boards. *International Review of Mission* 58: 286–303.

Merriweather, Alfred M. 1969. *Desert Doctor; Medicine and Evangelism in the Kalahari Desert.* London: Lutterworth.

Smalley, William A., ed. 1978. *Readings in Missionary Anthropology II.* South Pasadena: William Carey Library.

Woolington, Jean. 1985. Missionary attitudes to the baptism of Australian aborigines before 1850. *Journal of Religious History* 13: 253–83.

Bibliography on Tribal Societies

Achebe, Chinua. 1959. *Things Fall Apart.* New York: McDowell, Oblesky.

Barber, Karin. 1981. How man makes god in West Africa, Yoruba attitudes towards the Orisa. *The Journal of Modern Africa Studies* 51: 741.

Buakasa, Tulu K. M. 1986. The African tradition of sharing. *Ecumenical Review* 38: 386–93.

Champagne, Duane. 1989. *American Indian Societies: Strategies and Conditions for Political and Cultural Survival.* Cambridge, Mass.: Cultural Survival.

Evans-Pritchard, E. E. 1956. *Nuer Religion.* New York: Oxford University Press.

Forde, Darrell. 1954. *African Worlds.* Oxford: Oxford University Press.

George, Susan. 1990. *A Fate Worse Than Debt: The World Financial Crisis and the Poor.* New York: Grove Weidenfeld.

Gluckman, Max. 1944. The logic of African science and witchcraft. *Journal of the Rhodes-Livingston Institute* (June): 61–71.

Hoffer, Carol. 1974. Madam Yoko. In *Women, Culture and Society,* edited by Michelle Zimbalist Rosaldo and Louise Lamphere. Palo Alto: Stanford University Press.

Horton, Robin. 1967. African traditional thought and western science. *Africa* 37: 50–71, 155–87.

Idowu, E. B. 1973. *African Traditional Religion—A Definition.* London: SCM.

Johnson, Allen. 1989. Horticulturalists: Economic behavior in tribes. In *Economic Anthropology,* edited by Stuart Plattner, 49–77. Palo Alto: Stanford University Press.

Mbiti, John S. 1989. God, sin and salvation in African religion. *A.M.E. Zion Quarterly Review* 100: 2–8.

Metuh, Emefie Ikenga. 1981. *God and Man in African Religion.* London: Geoffrey Chapman.

Ray, Benjamin C. 1976. *African Religions: Symbol, Ritual and Community.* Englewood Cliffs, N.J.: Prentice-Hall.

Reed, Kenneth. 1980. *The High Valley.* New York: Columbia University Press.

Spindler, George, and Louise Spindler. 1977. *Culture Change and Modernization.* N.Y.: Holt, Rinehart and Winston.

Temples, Placide. 1953. *Bantu Philosophy.* Paris: Presence Africaine.

Thurnwald, Richard C. 1916. *Banaro Society: Social Organization and Kinship System in a Tribe in Interior New Guinea.* Lancaster, Penn.: American Anthropological Association.

Bibliography on the Church in Tribal Societies

Adeyemo, Tokunboh. 1979. *Salvation in African Tradition.* Nairobi: Evangel Publishing House.

Ahrens, Theodor. 1977. Concepts of power in a Melanesian and biblical perspective. *Missiology* 5: 141–73.

———. 1985. "The Flower Fair has thorns as well": Nativistic millennialism in Melanesia as a pastoral and missiological issue. *Missiology* 13: 61–80.

Barrett, David B. 1968. *Schism and Renewal in Africa: An Analysis of Six Thousand Contemporary Religious Movements.* Nairobi: Oxford University Press.

Bottignole, Silvana. 1981. Missionary activity as perceived by the Kikuyu of Kenya. *Missiology* 9:323–35.

Burnett, David. 1988. *Unearthly Powers.* Eastbourne, Great Britain: MARC.

Christiansen, Thomas G. 1978. Karnu: Witchdoctor or prophet. *Missiology* 6: 197–210.

Connor, John H. 1991. When culture leaves contextualized Christianity behind. *Missiology* 19: 21–29.

Dickson, Kwesi A., and Paul Ellingworth. 1969. *Biblical Revelation and African Beliefs.* London: Lutterworth.

Donovan, Vincent J. 1982. *Christianity Rediscovered.* Maryknoll, N.Y.: Orbis.

Downs, Frederick S. 1980. Christianity as a tribal response to change in Northeast India. *Missiology* 8: 407–16.

Ekechi, Felix K. The medical factor in Christian conversion in Africa: Observations from Southeastern Nigeria. *Missiology* 21: 289–309.

Elkins, Richard E. 1993. Blood sacrifice and the dynamics of supernatural power among the Manobo of Mindanao: Some missiological implications. *Missiology* 21: 321–31.

Fortosis, Steve. 1990. A model for understanding cross-cultural morality. *Missiology* 17: 163–76.

Fowler, J. Andrew. 1977. Towards wholeness in ministry among the Iban. *Missiology* 5: 275–84.

Gaskin, R. F. 1992. Conserving culture with biblical integrity. *African Journal of Evangelical Theology* 11: 105–28.

Gayman, Richard. 1987. *Doing African Theology.* Nairobi: Evangel Publishing House.

Gittins, Anthony J. 1993. *Bread for the Journey.* Maryknoll, N.Y.: Orbis.

Gration, John. 1984. Willowbank to Zaire: The doing of theology. *Missiology* 12: 297–306.

Hess, Mahlon M. 1957. Political systems and African church polity. *Practical Anthropology* 4: 170–84.

Hiebert, Paul G. 1982. The flaw of the excluded middle. *Missiology* 10: 35–47.

Holmes, Lowell D. 1980. Cults, cargo and Christianity: Samoan responses to western religion. *Missiology* 7: 471–87.

Hrangkhuma, F. 1992. How redemptive analogies can help churches grow. *Evangelical Missions Quarterly* 28: 182–87.

Imasogie, Osadolar. 1983. *Guidelines for Christian Theology in Africa.* Ghana: African Christian Press.

Jennings, George J. 1977. The American Indian ethos: A key for Christian missions? *Missiology* 5: 487–98.

————. 1983. A model for Christian missions to the American Indians.
Missiology 11: 55–74.

Kalu, Ogbu. 1990. Color and conversion: The white missionary factor in
the Christianization of Igboland, 1857–1967. *Missiology* 18: 61–74.

Kamuyu-wa-Kang'ethe. 1988. African response to Christianity: A case
study of the Agikuyu of Central Kenya. *Missiology* 16: 23–44.

Kemmerer, Cornelia A. 1990. Customs and Christian conversion among
the Akha highlanders of Burma and Thailand. *American Ethnologist*
17: 277–91.

Kirwen, Michael C. 1979. *African Widows.* Maryknoll, N.Y.: Orbis.

Loewen, Jacob A. 1986. Which god do missionaries preach? *Missiology*
14: 3–19.

Mullenix, Gordon R., and John Mpaayei. 1984. Matonyok: A case study
of the interaction of evangelism and community development among
the Keekonyoke Maasai of Kenya. *Missiology* 12: 327–37.

Mulumba, Mukundi. 1988. *Witchcraft among the Kasaian People: Challenge and Response.* Ph.D. dissertation. Pasadena: Fuller Theological
Seminary.

Nelson, Ron. 1983. Some crucial dimensions of ministry to Fulbe. *Missiology* 11: 201–18.

Niemeyer, Larry L. 1993. The unmet challenge of mission to the matrilineal peoples of Africa. *Evangelical Missions Quarterly* 29: 26–31.

Oosthuizen, Gerhardus C. 1990. Ecumenical burial societies in South
Africa: Mutual caring and support that transcends ecclesiastical and
religious differences. *Missiology* 18: 463–72.

Opoku, Kofi Asare. 1990. Communalism and community in the African
heritage. *International Review of Missions* 79: 487–92.

Reyburn, William D. 1959. Polygamy, economy and Christianity in Eastern Cameroon. *Practical Anthropology* 6: 1–19.

Rubingh, Eugene. 1974. The African shape of the gospel. *Impact*
(March): 3–5.

Shaw, R. Daniel. 1988. *Transculturation: The Cultural Factor in Translation and Other Communication Tasks.* Pasadena: William Carey
Library.

Shorter, Aylward. 1985. *Jesus and the Witchdoctor.* Maryknoll, N.Y.:
Orbis.

Starkloff, Carl F. 1985. Religious renewal in native North America: The
contemporary call to mission. *Missiology* 13:81–101.

Sterk, Vernon J. 1992. Evangelism with power: Divine healing in the
growth of the Tzotzil church. *Missiology* 20: 372–84.

Styne, Philip M. 1989. *Gods of Power.* Houston: Touch Publications.

Sundkler, Bengt. 1979. Towards a Christian theology in Africa. In *Readings in Dynamic Indigeneity*, edited by Charles Kraft and Tom Wisley, 493–515. Pasadena: William Carey Library.

Taylor, John V. 1977. *The Primal Vision: Christian Presence amid African Religions*. London: SCM.

Tienou, Tite. 1991. The invention of the "primitive" and stereotypes in mission. *Missiology* 19: 295–303.

Tippett, Alan R. 1977. Conversion as a dynamic process in Christian mission. *Missiology* 5: 203–21.

————. 1981. The evangelization of animists. In *Perspectives on the World Christian Movement*, edited by R. D. Winter, D-107–18. Pasadena: William Carey Library.

Trobisch, Walter. 1978. Pre-marital relations and Christian marriage in Africa. In *Readings in Missionary Anthropology II*, edited by William A. Smalley, 274–78. South Pasadena: William Carey Library.

Turnbull, Colin M. 1962. *The Lonely African*. New York: Simon and Schuster.

Urrutlia, Francisco Javier. 1981. Can polygamy be compatible with Christianity? *African Ecclesiastical Review* 23: 275–91.

Vicedom, G. F. 1961. *Church and People in New Guinea*. London: World Christian Books.

Wambutda, Daniel N. 1978. An African Christian looks at Christian missions in Africa. In *Readings in Missionary Anthropology II*, edited by William A. Smalley, 720–27. South Pasadena: William Carey Library.

Wilson, John D. 1991. What it takes to reach people in oral cultures. *Evangelical Missions Quarterly* 27: 154–58.

Bibliography on Peasant Societies

Bernstein, Henry. 1979. African peasantries: A theoretical framework. *Journal of Peasant Studies* 6: 421–44.

Cancian, Frank. 1989. Economic behavior in peasant communities. In *Economic Anthropology*, edited by Stuart Plattner, 127–70. Stanford: Stanford University Press.

Chayanov, A. V. 1966. *A. V. Chayanov on the Theory of Peasant Economy*, edited by Daniel Thorner, Basile Kerblay, and R. E. F. Smith. Homewood, Ill.: Richard D. Irwin for the American Economic Association.

Ewert, D. Merrill, Peter Clark, and Paul Eberts. 1993. World view and sustainable community development. Paper presented at the annual conference of the Association of Evangelical Relief and Development Agencies, Lindale, Texas.

Fei, Hsiao-Tung. 1939. *Peasant Life in China.* London: Kegan Paul, Trench, Trubner and Co.

Foster, George M. 1960. Interpersonal relations in peasant society. *Human Relations* 19: 1960–61.

Geertz, Clifford. 1960. *The religion of Java.* Glencoe: Free Press.

Harriss, John, ed. 1982. *Rural Development: Theories of Peasant Economy and Agrarian Change.* London: Hutchinson University Library.

Hiebert, Paul G. 1974. *Konduru: Structure and Integration in a South Indian Village.* Minneapolis: University of Minnesota Press.

Lewis, Oscar. 1956. *Peasant Society and Culture.* Chicago: University of Chicago Press.

Maloney, Clarence. 1988. *Behavior and Poverty in Bangladesh.* 2d ed. Dhaka, Bangladesh: University Press.

Mangin, William, ed. 1970. *Peasants in Cities.* Boston: Houghton Mifflin.

Marriott, McKim, ed. 1955. *Village India: Studies in the Little Community.* Chicago: University of Chicago Press.

Polanyi, Michael, and Harry Prosch. 1977. *Meaning.* Chicago: University of Chicago Press.

Redfield, Robert. 1947. The folk society. *American Journal of Sociology* 41: 293–308.

———. 1956. *Peasant Society and Culture.* Chicago: University of Chicago Press.

Reed-Denahy, Deborah, and Kathryn Anderson-Levitt. 1991. Backward countryside, troubled city: French teachers' images of rural and working-class families. *American Ethnologist* 18: 545–64.

Rogers, Everett M. 1969. *Modernization among Peasants: The Impact of Communication.* New York: Holt, Rinehart and Winston.

Roseberry, William. 1989. Peasants and the world. In *Economic Anthropology,* edited by Stuart Plattner, 108–26. Palo Alto: Stanford University Press.

Shanin, Theodor. 1987. *Peasants and Peasant Societies.* New York: Basil Blackwell.

Silverman, Sydel. 1979. The peasant concept in anthropology. *The Journal of Peasant Studies* 7: 49–69.

Smith, Carol. 1985. Anthropology and history look at peasants and capitalism. *Critique of Anthropology* 5: 87–94.

Wallerstein, Immanuel. 1974. *The Modern World-System.* New York: Academic Press.

———. 1979. *The Capitalist World Economy.* New York: Cambridge University Press.

Weatherford, Jack. 1994. Cocaine and the economic deterioration of Bolivia. In *Conformity and Conflict,* edited by James P. Spradley and David W. McCurdy. New York: HarperCollins.

Weyland, Petra. 1993. *Inside the Third World Village.* New York: Routledge.
Wolf, Eric R. 1966. *Peasants.* Englewood Cliffs, N.J.: Prentice-Hall.

Bibliography on the Church in Peasant Societies

Cadorette, Curt. 1987. Basic Christian Communities: Their social role and missiological promise. *Missiology* 15: 17–30.

Cook, William. 1983. Evangelical reflections on the church of the poor. *Missiology* 11: 47–53.

Franklin, Stephen T. 1983. A new Christian community and its surrounding culture in Northeast Thailand. *Missiology* 11: 75–94.

Henry, Rodney L. 1986. *Filipino Spirit World.* Manila: OMF.

Jenkins, Paul. 1980. Villagers as missionaries: Wurtemberg Pietism as a 19th century missionary movement. *Missiology* 7: 425–32.

Kelly, David C. 1984. Aymara ritual: The glimpse of an ethical system. *Missiology* 12: 103–9.

Klassen, Jacob. 1986. Training leaders for a church on the run. *Evangelical Missions Quarterly* 22: 54–59.

Luke, P. Y., and J. B. Carman. 1968. *Village Christians and Hindu Culture.* London: Lutterworth.

McClintock, Wayne. 1990. Demons and ghosts in Indian folklore. *Missiology* 18: 37–47.

Miller, Dave. 1988. 40 years in the Andes: An interview with Homer Firestone. *Evangelical Missions Quarterly* 24: 150–55.

Peck, Jane Cary. 1983. Evangelical reflections on the church of the poor. *Missiology* 11: 31–46.

Pike, Eunice V. 1980. The concept of limited good and the spread of the gospel. *Missiology* 8: 449–54.

Scotchmer, David. 1989. Symbols of salvation: A local Mayan Protestant theology. *Missiology* 17: 293–310.

Smith-Hefner, Nancy J. 1994. Conversion among the Khmer refugees. *Anthropological Quarterly* 67: 24–37.

Smutko, Gregory. 1992. Toward a new paradigm in spiritual formation; one example, the Mikito nation. *Missiology* 20: 55–68.

Thomas, Norman E. 1981. Evangelism and liberation theology. *Missiology* 9: 473–84.

Turner, Paul R. 1984. Religious conversion and folk Catholicism. *Missiology* 12: 11–121.

Webster, John C. B. 1978. Christianity in the Punjab. *Missiology* 6: 467–83.

Bibliography on Urban Societies

Appadurai, Arjun. 1991. Global ethnoscapes: Notes and queries for a transnational anthropology. In *Recapturing Anthropology: Working in the Present,* edited by R. G. Fox, 191–210. Santa Fe: School of American Research Advanced Seminar Series.

Auletta, Ken. 1983. *The Underclass.* New York: Vintage.

Cohen, Abner. 1969. *Custom and Politics in Urban Africa.* Los Angeles: University of California Press.

———. 1988. The politics of ethnicity in African towns. In *The Urbanization of the Third World,* edited by Josef Gugler, 328–37. Oxford: Oxford University Press.

Coquery-Vidrovitch, Catherine. 1991. The process of urbanization in Africa. *African Studies Review* 34: 1–98.

Dannhaeuser, Norbert. 1989. Marketing in developing urban areas. In *Economic Anthropology,* edited by Stuart Plattner, 222–52. Palo Alto: Stanford University Press.

Eames, Edwin, and Judith Goode. 1988. Coping with poverty: A cross-cultural view of the behavior of the poor. In *Urban Life,* edited by George Gmelch and Walter P. Zenner, 358–68. Prospect Heights, Ill.: Waveland.

Fox, Richard Wightman, and T. J. Jackson Lears, eds. 1983. *The Culture of Consumption.* New York: Pantheon.

Guigler, Josef, ed. 1988. *The Urbanization of the Third World.* Oxford: Oxford University Press.

Hall, Edward T. 1966. *The Hidden Dimension.* Garden City, N.Y.: Doubleday.

Jacobs, Jane. 1984. Cities and the wealth of nations. *The Atlantic Monthly,* March/April.

Lewis, Oscar. 1988. The culture of poverty. In *Urban Life,* edited by George Gmelch and Walter P. Zenner. Prospect Heights, Ill.: Waveland.

Schildkrout, Enid. 1990. Children's roles: Young traders of Northern Nigeria. In *Conformity and Conflict,* edited by James P. Spradley and David W. McCurdy. 7th ed. Glenview, Ill.: Scott, Foresman/Little, Brown and Co.

Shack, W. A. 1973. Urban ethnicity and the cultural process of urbanization in Ethiopia. In *Urban Anthropology,* edited by Aiden Southall. New York: Oxford University Press.

Bibliography on the Church in Urban Societies

Allen, Jere, and George Bullard. 1981. *Shaping a Future for the Church in the Changing Community.* Atlanta: SBC Home Mission Board.

Appleby, Jerry L. 1987. *The Urban Christian: Effective Ministry in Today's Urban World.* Downers Grove: InterVarsity.

———. 1990. *The Church Is a Stew: Developing Multicongregational Churches.* Kansas City: Beacon Hill.

Banks, Robert. 1993. The urban class and urban mission. *Urban Mission* 11: 6–21.

Bibby, Reginald. 1987. *Fragmented Gods.* Toronto: Irwin.

Claerbaut, David C. 1983. *Urban Ministry.* Grand Rapids: Zondervan.

Colson, Elizabeth. 1974. *Tradition and Contract: The Problem of Order.* Chicago: Aldine.

Conn, Harvie M. 1985. Lucan perspectives and the cities. *Missiology* 13: 409–28.

DuBose, Francis M. 1984a. Urban poverty as a world challenge. In *An Urban World: Churches Face the Future,* edited by Larry L. Rose and C. Kirk Hadaway, 51–74. Nashville: Broadman.

———. 1984b. Cities aren't all alike. *Urban Mission* 1, 3: 15–23.

Ellul, Jacques. 1964. *The Technological Society.* New York: Random House.

Fleming, Kenneth. 1986. The urban Zulu: Three cultures in conflict. *Evangelical Missions Quarterly* 22: 24–31.

Gilbert, Alan, and Joseph Gugler. 1982. *Cities, Poverty and Development.* London: Oxford University Press.

Greenway, Roger S. 1983. Don't be an urban missionary unless . . . *Evangelical Missions Quarterly* 19: 86–94.

———. 1992. *Discipling the City: A Comprehensive Approach to Urban Mission.* Grand Rapids: Baker.

Hunter, George G. 1992. *How to Reach Secular People.* Nashville: Abingdon.

Kyle, John E., ed. 1988. *Urban Mission: God's Concern for the City.* Downers Grove: InterVarsity.

Linthicum, Robert C. 1991. *City of God, City of Satan: A Biblical Theology of the Urban Church.* Grand Rapids: Zondervan.

Lott, Anastasia. 1988. Recovering the word of God today with and among the poor. *Missiology* 16: 321–30.

Niemeyer, Larry L. 1990. Church growth in Nairobi, Kenya. *Urban Mission* 8: 45–54.

Racine, Carl. 1981. Don't neglect Third World suburbia! *Missiology* 9: 171–80.

Salter, Owen. 1989. Seeing Christ in the slums. *Evangelical Missions Quarterly* 25: 6–15.

Shorter, Aylward, 1991. *The Church in the African City.* Maryknoll, N.Y.: Orbis.

Siebert, Rudolf J. 1985. Urbanization as a world trend; a challenge to the churches. *Missiology* 13: 429–43.

Smith, Henry N. 1989. Christianity and ancestor practices in Hong Kong: Toward a contextual strategy. *Missiology* 17: 27–38.

Tillapaugh, Frank R. 1982. *Unleashing the Church.* Ventura, Calif.: Regal.

Tournier, Paul. 1978. *The Violence Within.* New York: Harper and Row.

Winter, Bruce W. 1994. *Seek the Welfare of the City.* Grand Rapids: Eerdmans.

Index

397